Ocean of Trade

Ocean of Trade offers an innovative study of trade, production and consumption across the Indian Ocean between the years *c.* 1750 and 1850. Focusing on the Vāniyā merchants of Diu and Daman, Pedro Machado explores the region's entangled histories of exchange, including the African demand for large-scale textile production among weavers in Gujarat, the distribution of ivory to consumers in Western India, and the African slave trade from Mozambique that took captives to the French islands of the Mascarenes, Brazil and the Rio de la Plata, and the Arabian peninsula and India. In highlighting the critical role of particular South Asian merchant networks, the book reveals how local African and Indian consumer demand was central to the development of commerce across the Indian Ocean, giving rise to a wealth of regional and global exchange in a period commonly perceived to be increasingly dominated by European company and private capital. The book offers an important contribution to our understanding of the layered and entangled histories of Africa and South Asia within an oceanic and global context.

Pedro Machado is Assistant Professor in the Department of History at Indiana University, Bloomington.

Ocean of Trade

South Asian Merchants, Africa and the Indian Ocean, c. 1750–1850

Pedro Machado

CAMBRIDGE
UNIVERSITY PRESS

CAMBRIDGE
UNIVERSITY PRESS

University Printing House, Cambridge CB2 8BS, United Kingdom

Cambridge University Press is part of the University of Cambridge.

It furthers the University's mission by disseminating knowledge in the pursuit of education, learning and research at the highest international levels of excellence.

www.cambridge.org
Information on this title: www.cambridge.org/9781107070264

First published 2014

by Clays, St Ives plc

A catalogue record for this publication is available from the British Library

Library of Congress Cataloguing in Publication data
Machado, Pedro, 1970–
Ocean of trade : South Asian merchants, Africa and the Indian Ocean,
c. 1750–1850 / Pedro Machado.
    pages   cm
ISBN 978-1-107-07026-4 (hardback)
1. Merchants – South Asia – History – 18th century.   2. Merchants – South
Asia – History – 19th century.   3. Merchants – Indian Ocean – History.
4. Indian Ocean – Commerce – History – 18th century.   5. Indian
Ocean – Commerce – History – 19th century.   6. South Asia – Commerce –
History.   7. Africa – Commerce – History.   8. International trade –
History.   9. Production (Economic theory) – History.   10. Consumption
(Economics) – History.   I. Title.
HF3785.M325   2014
382.09182′4–dc23
                                                                    2014007200

ISBN 978-1-107-07026-4 Hardback

Contents

Figures

Maps

Tables

Acknowledgements

The process of writing this book has been a hugely rewarding one. It has involved the unfailing intellectual generosity of many colleagues and friends who provided countless opportunities to discuss my work and ideas. They have enriched these in ways that greatly exceeded my expectations. William Gervase Clarence-Smith was instrumental in shaping some of the early ideas on which this book is based, and I continue to benefit from his sharp intellect, wealth of knowledge about a host of topics and general good humour. From the first time we met in London several years ago, Richard B. Allen has been a steadfast interlocutor, critical reader and friend whose knowledge of Indian Ocean slavery is humbling and whose generosity of spirit I strive to emulate. That this book is being published with Cambridge University Press owes a great deal to the encouragement of Pier Larson, who read my work closely and commented extensively on its arguments and the ways in which it could be improved. His belief in the project's potential spurred me on at different times. Equally, conversations with Douglas E. Haynes and Prasannan Parthasarathi have also influenced my thinking and have sharpened my understanding of the histories of Indian textile production and merchant capital in the eighteenth and nineteenth centuries. Michael Pearson took an interest in my work at an early stage and offered sound advice regarding its development. His conceptualization and understanding of the worlds of the Indian Ocean have often stimulated my thinking.

As I was thinking about the conceptual framework for the book, Engseng Ho suggested that I consider seriously the formation, from the ground up, of the global structures in which I sought to locate my work. This helped me not to lose sight of the importance of seemingly "small" stories to the larger picture. Ned Alpers has always given freely of his time as well as insights, helping me refine my thoughts while deepening my understanding of Mozambique's African and Indian Ocean history through his scholarship. Gwyn Campbell has been an enthusiastic supporter of this project and its arguments, providing a keen ear and enquiring mind at different times. I have benefitted, further, from many stimulating conversations with

Lakshmi Subramanian in India, Canada and the United States, as we have shared our thoughts about India's oceanic history. Edmund Burke III gave me two unique opportunities to present my research to larger, non-specialist audiences by inviting me to participate in two stimulating NEH Summer Seminars for Teachers on "Production and Consumption in World History, 1450–1925" at the University of California, Santa Cruz in 2009 and 2011.

My editor, Michael Watson, has maintained an interest in the project from the beginning, and shepherded it along with an expert hand and great efficiency. This has been the case also with the entire production team. The final product was much improved by the insights and suggestions of CUP's anonymous readers.

I have received financial and practical support along the way from a number of institutions and their staff. Research and writing over the years were made possible by fellowships from the Gulbenkian Foundation, the Fundação Oriente and the Institute of Commonwealth Studies. At a crucial time, I benefitted enormously from my time as visiting scholar at the World History Centre of the University of Pittsburgh. I especially thank its director, Patrick Manning, for having provided a stimulating environment away from teaching to allow me to make significant progress on the writing of *Ocean of Trade*. Much of the research for this work was completed in Lisbon, London, Goa, Mumbai and Maputo, and I thank the staff at the many archives in which I conducted research: in Lisbon, at the Arquivo Histórico Ultramarino (particularly Fernando José de Almeida and Jorge Fernandes Nascimento), the Biblioteca Nacional de Lisboa, the Sociedade de Geografia de Lisboa, the Arquivo Nacional da Torre do Tombo and the Tribunal de Contas; in London, at the Oriental and India Office Collections of the British Library, the National Archives in Kew, the School of Oriental and African Studies, and Senate House Library; in Goa, at the Historical Archives of Goa, and the Xavier Centre of Historical Research; in Mumbai, at the Maharashtra State Archives; and in Maputo, at the Arquivo Histórico de Moçambique. It simply would have not been possible to write this book without their help, guidance and patience in responding to an eager researcher's incessant requests and questions.

Many of the ideas expressed on the following pages have benefitted greatly from the questions and comments of audiences in a number of venues, both near and far. These have included the Indian Ocean World Centre, McGill University; American Historical Association Annual Meeting (San Diego); Duke University; University of California, Irvine; University of California, Santa Cruz; Social Science History Association Annual Meeting (Miami FL); the Zanzibar Indian Ocean Research

Institute; Stanford University; Northwestern University; Association for Asian Studies Annual Meeting (Boston); Yale University; New York University; the Western Australian Maritime Museum; University of Pittsburgh; and the Gokhale Institute of Politics and Economics. I am thankful to everyone who participated at these various conferences, workshops and lectures.

For the countless opportunities to discuss shared interests, for their camaraderie, suggestions and intellectual energy that has sustained me throughout the process of producing this book, I am deeply grateful to Joseph Miller, Tirthankar Roy, Giorgio Riello, Scott Reese, Anne Bang, Jeremy Prestholdt, Matt Hopper, Thomas ('Dodie') McDow, Samira Sheikh, Rudy Bauss, James Brennan, Kerry Ward, Sarah Fee, Timothy Coates, Fahad Bishara, Richard Roberts, Pamila Gupta, Hideaki Suzuki, Johan Mathew, Chhaya Goswami, David Eltis, Thomas Vernet, Abdul Sheriff, Jelmer Vos, the late Jerry Bentley, George Souza, Roxani Margariti and Indrani Chatterjee. Venu Mehta shared her language teaching prowess and enthusiasm for all things Gujarati. These fellow travellers have made the journey that much more engaging and therefore immensely rewarding.

Since arriving at Indiana University, Bloomington, I count myself fortunate in having colleagues in the history department and elsewhere on campus who have shown me the true meaning of an engaged and collegial academic community. I have benefitted especially from the friendship, advice and support of Michael Dodson, Scott O'Bryan, Michael McGerr, Judith Allen, Eric Robinson, Peter Guardino, John Hanson, Alex Lichtenstein, Jason McGraw, Christina Snyder, Ellen Wu, Michelle Moyd, Claude Clegg, Nick Cullather, Mike Grossberg, Micol Seigel, Marissa Moorman, Carl Ipsen, Sarah Knott, Amrita Myers, Kon Dierks, John Nieto-Phillips, Maria Bucur, Wendy Gamber, Maria Grosz-Ngate, Lara Kriegel, Eric Sandweiss, Mark Roseman and Arlene Diaz.

Amy, Hans, Pei, Arthur, Michiko and Amar have made living in Bloomington a treat, plying my family and me with fine food and drinks.

My dispersed family in Cape Town, Lisbon, Porto and Sydney have been unsparing in their love and belief in me. I doubt that I will ever be able to repay the debts I owe my Mae, sister Fatinha and brother Rui and their families, my aunts Ló and Té, and my half-brother Victor, with Fati and Sergio. They will always fight my corner, no matter what. The Maglens and Ravens have become a second family, and I thank Leo, Fay and honour the memory of Jack and Leslie in embracing me as one of their own.

More than anyone, though, Krista ('special K') has been with me every step of the way, listening intently to my arguments about South Asian merchant networks with interest and reading many drafts of this work. A scholar in her own right, she is my touchstone and helps me navigate the vagaries of life with compassion, empathy and kindness. Our son, Mio, has been a joyous addition to our family, brightening every day with his humour, smile, laughter and infectious sense of fun. It is to them that I dedicate this book with all my love.

Note on currencies

As my text deals with a number of currencies, this note is for purposes of clarification.

Indo-Portuguese coinage was largely silver based. It can be understood in terms of a fictitious unit that was used as an imperial currency of account, the *real* (pl. *réis*). It was written 100 *réis* or $100, with the $ symbol marking the thousands. Thus, 100$000 is 100,000 *réis*, 900$000 is 900,000 *réis*. A figure written 10:000$000 is 10,000,000 *réis* and can be expressed as 10 *contos*. For reasons of clarity, I have chosen throughout to write "réis" after an amount (e.g. 10$000 *réis*).[1] Currencies in use in India that are mentioned in the text were thus convertible against the *real* at the following rates in the eighteenth and nineteenth centuries:

> *Xerafim* = 300 *réis*
> *Tanga* = 60 *réis*
> *Cruzado* = 400 *réis*

Reference in the text is occasionally made to the *Rupee* (Rs), the Indian unit of currency. While valuations of the *Rupee* varied throughout India, a tentative conversion rate is 1 Rs = 630 *réis*.

With regard to *piastres* and *patacas*, the Spanish silver dollars ($) that circulated in French and Portuguese territories, and that served as a basic trading currency in the western Indian Ocean from the late eighteenth century, I have calculated their value as follows[2]:

> $1 = 710 *réis*

---

[1] This information is based on Sanjay Subrahmanyam, *The Political Economy of Commerce: Southern India, 1500–1650* (Cambridge University Press, 1990); Joseph C. Miller, "Slave Prices in the Portuguese Southern Atlantic, 1600–1830", in Paul Lovejoy (ed.), *Africans in Bondage: Studies in Slavery and the Slave Trade* (Essays in Honour of Philip D. Curtin on the Occasion of the 25th *Anniversary of African Studies at the University of Wisconsin*) (Madison: University of Wisconsin Press, 1986), 43–77.

[2] I have arrived at this calculation from information provided in Rudy Bauss, "Textiles, Bullion and Other Trade of Goa: Commerce with Surat, other areas of India, Luso-Brazilian ports, Macau and Mozambique, 1816–1819", *IESHR*, 34, 3 (1997), 276; Richard B. Allen "Licentious and Unbridled Proceedings: The Illegal Slave Trade to Mauritius and the Seychelles during the Early Nineteenth Century", *Journal of African History* 42, 1 (2001), 102.

Abbreviations

AD	Alfandegas de Diu
ADm	Alfandegas de Damão
AHM	Arquivo Histórico de Moçambique, Maputo, Mozambique
AHU	Arquivo Histórico Ultramarino, Lisbon
ANTT	Arquivos Nacional da Torre do Tombo, Lisbon
APO	J. H. da Cunha Rivara (ed.), *Archivo Portuguêz Oriental*, 9 vols. (Nova Goa: Imprensa Nacional, 1857–77)
BN	Biblioteca Nacional de Lisboa
CD	Correspondencia de Diu
CDm	Correspondencia de Damão
CM	Correspondencia de Moçambique
Cx	Caixa (Box)
DAM	Francisco Santana (ed.), *Documentação Avulsa Moçambicana do Arquivo Histórico Ultramarino*, 3 vols. (Lisbon: Centro de Estudos Históricos Ultramarinos, 1964–74)
Doc.	Documento (Document)
FHGCM	Luis Fernando de Carvalho Dias, *Fontes para a Historia, Geografia e Comercio de Moçambique (sec. XVIII)* (Lisbon: Junta de Investigações do Ultramar, 1954)
HAG	Historical Archives of Goa, Panjim
IESHR	*The Indian Economic and Social History Review*
Moç.	Moçambique/Mozambique
MSA	Maharashtra State Archives, Bombay, India
OIOC	Oriental and India Office Collections, British Library, London
PD	A. B. de Bragança Pereira (ed.), *Os Portugueses em Diu* (Bastorá: Tipografia Rangel, 1938)
NA	National Archives, Kew, England
RMS	António Alberto de Andrade, *Relações de Moçambique Setecentista* (Lisbon: Agência Geral do Ultramar, 1955)

RSEA   George McCall Theal, *Records of South-Eastern Africa: Collected in Various Libraries and Archive Departments in Europe*, 9 vols. (Cape Town: Printed for the Government of the Cape Colony, 1898–1903)

Introduction

Laxmichand Motichand was enmeshed in a world on the move. As a prominent Vāniyā merchant from the island entrepôt of Diu located at the southern end of the Kathiawar peninsula of present-day Gujarat, he had over the course of the second half of the eighteenth century developed significant business interests in Mozambique in Southeastern Africa. Arriving as a young boy on Mozambique Island sometime in the early 1760s, Laxmichand began his commercial career as an apprentice in the family firm. He worked his way up the commercial hierarchy, learning Portuguese (a language of empire, trade and imperial administration) and likely a form of Emakhuwa (an African language utilized in commerce in northern Mozambique), as he became the firm's main partner in Mozambique by the 1780s. His standing as an "honourable" and "credit-worthy" merchant reflected both his and the firm's reputation within Mozambique and Diu that was to endure well into the nineteenth century.[1]

Along with other Vāniyā, who from early in the eighteenth century had begun to direct their trade to Southeast Africa, Laxmichand was heavily invested in the procurement and importation of Gujarati cotton textiles. These were essential as currency in the exchange economy of Mozambique and Laxmichand arranged for large volumes to be transported across the western Indian Ocean in long-distance Gujarati sailing vessels. Textiles arrived on Mozambique Island, the coastal entrepôt where Laxmichand owned property and maintained storehouses, where they served not only as exchange media for the purchase of ivory and slaves (the two main exports from Southeast Africa in the eighteenth century) but also as high-demand products among Africans throughout Mozambique. It was African consumer tastes that drove the variety of styles and qualities of

---

[1] This biographical sketch of Laxmichand Motichand draws on a diffuse range of information contained in a variety of documents in the AHU, Lisbon, Portugal; the AHM, Maputo, Mozambique; and the HAG in Panjim, India. Laxmichand, like other Vāniyā boys brought to Mozambique in the eighteenth century, "appl[ied] themselves in learning their [Yao or Makua] idiom..." AHU, Moç., Cx 47 Doc. 39, "Registo da carta...", n.d. [but c. 1784].

1

cloth that Laxmichand had to ensure were acquired in each trading season from weavers in Gujarat so that he would find buyers in coastal and interior markets.

That he was able to acquire the appropriate textiles in India owed much to the structure of the family firm. Laxmichand corresponded regularly with firm members in Diu, who used textile brokers to communicate details of the cloths "of a new fashion" that were in demand in Mozambique. Acquired first from African agents in his service, who in turn maintained relationships with long-distance traders and merchants in the interior of Mozambique, this vital information was transmitted along multiple chains of relation that connected Laxmichand and his agents to the interiors of Africa and India.

The centrality of Gujarati cotton textiles to the commercial economy of Mozambique – indeed to all economic exchange in the territory – placed Laxmichand, with access to networks of procurement and distribution on both sides of the Indian Ocean, in an influential and significant commercial position. Cloth financed credit as a vital component under-girding long-distance trade, allowing Laxmichand to extend loans widely to merchants along the coast and interior of Mozambique. For much of the eighteenth century, these loans financed the purchase of African ivory that because of its quality and durability was highly sought by Indian consumers in Kathiawar and elsewhere in Gujarat for use as marriage bangles and a variety of other products. Laxmichand ensured that the ships that had brought cloth from India to Mozambique returned across the Indian Ocean carrying thousands of tusks to Diu, where they were redistributed to regional markets such as Bhavnagar and Surat.

Increasingly from the middle of the century, the loans that Laxmichand was able to extend to merchants also financed African slave purchases as Mozambique developed from the 1750s into an important source of servile labour for the markets of the southwestern Indian Ocean and southern Atlantic. As with ivory purchases, the purchase of slaves required Gujarati cloth, and as one of the most prominent merchants in Mozambique, Laxmichand was among the Vāniyās who effectively underwrote the expansion of slaving through their dominance of the textile trade. In being able also to make *hundis* (bills of exchange) available to merchants, Laxmichand made possible the complex multilateral payments that were required in both the slave and the ivory trades. In particular, his wealth, commercial and financial prominence enabled Laxmichand to participate more directly in the slave trade by financing the acquisition of slaving vessels at Port Louis in Mauritius, the destination of a large number of African slaves as labour for the island's sugar plantations. This involvement entailed, further, entering into partnerships with Portuguese slavers, especially once the commerce in slaves began to intensify from the 1770s and 1780s.

Yet, despite deepening involvement, Laxmichand Motichand never redirected his business interests to the slave trade. His commercial focus, and that of the family firm from its earliest days in Mozambique, remained the ivory trade. The bulk of the textiles that were carried on his vessels – or that arrived on consignment in other Vāniyā ships – were destined for the purchases of ivory tusks that came principally from the Zambesi Valley in central Mozambique by the final quarter of the century and were shipped to Mozambique Island from Quelimane. Laxmichand adapted to the changing realities of the Mozambique (and regional Southeast African) economy by investing some capital in slaving and shipping modest cargoes of slaves to India, where military and domestic markets existed for African captives. As an importer of Gujarati textiles that were utilized to purchase slaves along the coast and interior of Mozambique, though, Laxmichand benefitted financially from the expanding trade by the payments he received for cloths in New World silver dollars from visiting merchants invested in the trade. Large cargoes of silver currency were brought to the coast of Mozambique beginning in the mid-eighteenth century and increased rapidly from the final quarter of the century as the slave trade expanded to include Brazilian merchants from Bahia and Rio de Janeiro, and slavers from Montevideo in the Río de la Plata. The exchangeability of cloth for silver made the purchase of slaves possible and therefore allowed an expansion of slave trading and brought the markets of the southern Atlantic and southwestern Indian Ocean into close relation with one another in a demonstration of the trans-oceanic linkages of the eighteenth-century trade. The silver coins that Laxmichand Motichand acquired as a result of selling cloth to slavers were shipped to India where they were used in payments to Gujarati bankers and to secure credit that was an indispensible component of long-distance trade.

This story of exchange, mobility, production and consumer demand are the subject of this book. Laxmichand Motichand's career is emblematic of the depth and extent of Vāniyā merchant networks in the western Indian Ocean and of their critical role in mediating its oceanic relationships. From late in the seventeenth century, and especially from the 1720s and 1730s, Gujarati Vāniyā merchants from Diu began redirecting business investments away from the Red Sea – where they had maintained a long-standing presence – and towards Southeast Africa. This included Vāniyā from Daman, a notable shipbuilding port on the west coast of India. By the middle of the century, these merchants had established a dominant position in the commercial and financial economy of Mozambique as their investments grew in African trade. Vāniyā control over the procurement, shipment and distribution of Gujarati cotton cloths was key in undergirding this dominance because of their central place in African exchange as both currency and commodity. High demand for Gujarati textiles derived from the many uses to which cloths were put, and from the myriad social and cultural meanings with which they were inscribed by African consumers. Without textiles, no merchant could trade successfully in Mozambique and its far interior that today forms part of Zimbabwe, Malawi and Zambia.

Trade expanded markedly from the 1730s with the growth of cloth imports amid greater Vāniyā involvement in the economy of Mozambique. Cloth was distributed along well-organized routes by long-distance traders and African agents who operated in a commercialized environment of widespread exchange. This expansion of African trade occurred within a broader Indian Ocean context of trans-oceanic exchange in which Laxmichand Motichand and other Vāniyā were key participants. In particular, consumer demand in Kathiawar, Kutch and more broadly throughout Gujarat for African ivory from Mozambique propelled Vāniyā interest and reflected the commercial resurgence of these regional Indian economies from the mid-eighteenth century.[2] A process of political consolidation among the principalities of Kathiawar, which is detailed in Chapter 1, helped to foster a stable economic environment where expanding networks of commodity production (especially textiles) forged links between agrarian India and newly expanding commercial markets in the wider Indian Ocean economy. Kathiawar thus emerged in the 1750s as a commercially vibrant region.[3] As a strategy for generating revenue through taxation, states supported and promoted trade. This occurred during a period of Mughal imperial decentralization when regional polities such as the Marathas consolidated their autonomy and power contra the imperial centre. The resulting political instability and insecurity that these reconfigurations caused on trade routes in Gujarat created a fluid environment in which commercial fortunes shifted from one port, city or region to another as merchants and artisans moved to less affected areas that were considered safer, such as the Kathiawar peninsula.[4]

---

[2] Throughout this book, I have used place names as they appear in the sources or that have accepted spellings in English, and have therefore not used contemporary designations – Kutch rather than Kachchh; Querimba Islands rather than Kerimba Islands, and so on.

[3] David Ludden, "World Economy and Village India", in Sugata Bose (ed.), *South Asia and World Capitalism* (Delhi: Oxford University Press, 1990), 159–77.

[4] Ghulam A. Nadri, "Exploring the Gulf of Kachh: Regional Economy and Trade in the Eighteenth Century", *Journal of the Economic and Social History of the Orient*, 51 (2008), 462; Lakshmi Subramanian, "The Political Economy of Textiles in Western India:

Although largely unexamined, Kathiawar's commercial vibrancy from the second half of the eighteenth century was bound up with the growth of trans-oceanic African trade which was driven both by high ivory consumption throughout the Kathiawar peninsula and by high Gujarati textile consumption in Mozambique. These intersecting consuming passions for the goods of Africa and India thus brought ivory hunters, African long-distance traders and agents into close relation with Gujarati weavers, cloth brokers and bankers. Though separated by thousands of miles of ocean, the choices and decisions made by these protagonists influenced one another and created an inter-regional oceanic embrace made possible by Vāniyā merchants who played a key integrative role for these economies of the western Indian Ocean.[5]

In emphasizing the importance of consumer demand in structuring relations across the ocean, *Ocean of Trade* urges a rethinking more broadly of the place of local markets in sustaining production between the economies of the ocean. Much scholarship has focused on the development of European demand and tastes for Asian goods and "luxuries" in the eighteenth century as central to the emergence of new social and cultural practices that informed changing ideas of fashion, dress, adornment and identification.[6] This scholarship has also recognized that the consuming habits of Europeans were an important element in the development of the global economy from the eighteenth century as rising demand for goods from South Asia, China and elsewhere stimulated commerce across different regions of the world.[7]

By contrast, far less attention has been given to the role of consumer demand as an economic, social and cultural activity among those assumed

Weavers, Merchants and the Transition to a Colonial Economy", in Giorgio Riello and Tirthankar Roy (eds.), *How India Clothed the World: The World of South Asian Textiles, 1500–1850* (Leiden and Boston: Brill, 2009), 253–80. That the Kathiawar peninsula experienced increased trade and was commercially vibrant when other areas of western India were adversely affected by the political realignments of the eighteenth century suggests that, rather than view India as possessing a single integrated economy, it might be more useful analytically to regard the subcontinent as possessing multiple "economies". See David Washbrook, "India in the Early Modern World Economy: Modes of Production, Reproduction and Exchange", *Journal of Global History*, 2, 1 (2007), 87.

[5] I draw here on an insight from Sven Beckert, "Reconstructing the Empire of Cotton: A Global Story", in Manisha Sinha and Penny Von Eschen (eds.), *Contested Democracy: Freedom, Race and Power in American History* (New York: Columbia University Press, 2007), 164–90.

[6] Useful summaries and overviews of this scholarship can be found in assorted essays in Frank Trentmann (ed.), *The Oxford Handbook of the History of Consumption* (Oxford University Press, 2012).

[7] See, for example, John Brewer and Roy Porter (eds.), *Consumption and the World of Goods* (London: Routledge, 1994); Maxine Berg, "In Pursuit of Luxury: Global History and British Consumer Goods in the Eighteenth Century", *Past and Present*, 182, 1 (2004), 85–113; *eadem, Luxury and Pleasure in Eighteenth-Century Britain* (Oxford University Press, 2005).

to be marginal actors in trade and exchange and in affecting larger economies of commerce and production. Indeed, the focus of much scholarship
on the material worlds of Africa and South Asia has continued to follow
a "production-dominated Marxian view", in which questions related to
patterns and processes of consumer demand and consumption have been
almost entirely overlooked.[8] This is explained, in the case of South Asia,
by, among other factors, the concerns of nationalist historians with the
impact of colonial rule and deep-seated Marxist traditions of scholarship
that favoured production as a framework.[9] The influence of Subaltern
Studies more recently has been limited to studying "subaltern" groups
and their political role in Indian history. For Africa, an exaggerated focus
on Africans as producers, whether as slave labourers or from the later
nineteenth century as members of an industrial proletariat, has overlooked their role as consumers whose tastes and preferences had repercussions beyond the continent.[10] Assumptions about the limitations that
colonial rule and rural poverty placed on the consuming behaviours of
Africans further explain this omission.

Taking consumer demand as a vantage point makes possible an appreciation of the influence of consumer tastes on commercial activity across
the Indian Ocean. African demand in Mozambique sustained large-scale
textile production among weavers in Gujarat who, as they developed
specialized knowledge about patterns and styles that were desired by
African consumers, became reliant on these African markets for their
livelihoods over the course of the eighteenth century.[11] In turn, high levels

---

[8] Arjun Appadurai, "Introduction: Commodities and the Politics of Value", in *idem*, *The Social Life of Things: Commodities in Cultural Perspective* (Cambridge University Press, 1985), 13.

[9] Douglas E. Haynes and Abigail McGowan, "Introduction", in Haynes, McGowan, Tirthankar Roy and Haruka Yanagisawa (eds.), *Towards a History of Consumption in South Asia* (New Delhi: Oxford University Press, 2010), 1–25. The introduction to this pioneering volume offers further discussion of the reasons why South Asian historical scholarship has often overlooked consumption as an analytical lens in the study of the past.

[10] There have been recent indications that this is beginning to change: Timothy Burke, *Lifebuoy Men, Lux Women: Commodification, Consumption & Cleanliness in Zimbabwe* (Durham and London: Duke University Press, 1996); Jeremy Prestholdt, "On the Global Repercussions of East African Consumerism", *American Historical Review*, 109, 3 (2004), 755–81; *idem*, *Domesticating the World: African Consumerism and the Genealogies of Globalization* (Berkeley: University of California Press, 2008); Dmitri van den Bersselaar, *The King of Drinks: Schnapps Gin from Modernity to Tradition* (Leiden and Boston: Brill, 2007); Pedro Machado, "Awash in a Sea of Cloth: Gujarat, Africa and the Western Indian Ocean", in Giorgio Riello and Prasannan Parthasarathi (eds.), *The Spinning World: A Global History of Cotton Textiles, 1200–1850* (Oxford University Press, 2009), 161–80.

[11] Scholarship on the Indian textile trade has almost entirely overlooked African markets in the Indian Ocean, focusing instead on Middle East or European markets, or on the

of demand in Kathiawar and Gujarat for Mozambique ivory influenced hunting patterns and trade routes in the African interior and coast. The local consumption of Africans and Indians was thus important to the development of inter-regional commercial activity.[12] *Ocean of Trade* contributes to an emerging appreciation that historically "under-considered populations" exerted leverage in shaping material relationships in fundamental ways.[13]

An overarching argument of this book is that Vāniyā merchants, with access to credit, shipping and maritime labour, were critical in mediating these linkages across regimes of consumption and production, and were therefore responsible for driving cross-oceanic exchange that stimulated the development of regional economies.[14] In operating at the interstices of producing and consuming markets in Africa and India, perhaps most crucially, Vāniyās were able to satisfy demand for ivory and cloth because their information of markets on both sides of the ocean was kept current and transmitted regularly across its waters. Merchants communicated market knowledge about the particular types of textiles that were in demand in any one season to brokers who, in turn, passed this information on to head weavers and ultimately weaving households producing cloth expressly for the Mozambique markets. This knowledge was particularly valuable because of seasonal changes in tastes among African consumers – a particular pattern and style of textile that was in demand in one season would no longer find buyers a few seasons later as preferences changed for new cloths.

Equally crucial for Vāniyā merchants, knowledge about ivory markets was gathered regularly and utilized to determine where supplies from Mozambique would be sent after their arrival in Diu or Daman. Although demand for ivory was widespread in the Kathiawar peninsula and more broadly in Gujarat, consumer markets shifted and could become concentrated in particular areas. Knowing where these were located was therefore invaluable in selling the many thousands of ivory tusks that arrived each year in increasing number from Mozambique from the 1740s and 1750s.

intra-Asian trade of European companies. A good discussion of this literature can be found in Om Prakash, *European Commercial Enterprise in Pre-colonial India* (Cambridge University Press, 1998).

[12] My thinking here has been influenced by Haynes and McGowan, "Introduction", 8–9.

[13] Prestholdt, "Global Repercussions".

[14] A similar argument, based around commodity chains, has been recently advanced for Latin America in Steven Topik, Carlos Marichal and Zephyr Frank (eds.), *From Silver to Cocaine: Latin American Commodity Chains and the Building of the World Economy, 1500–2000* (Durham and London: Duke University Press, 2006).

Vāniyā shipment of commodities and their commercial activity occurred across local and oceanic contexts. As noted earlier, Diu and Daman merchants were intertwined with the exchange dynamics of the Kathiawar peninsula and had been active in the ports of the southern Arabian peninsula and Red Sea for centuries. Their redirection of trade and financial resources to Southeastern Africa in the eighteenth century, the focus of this book, represented a continuation of their engagement with the economies of the Indian Ocean.

They operated also, however, within a particular European imperial context: Diu and Daman, and Mozambique, were part of the *Estado da Índia*, the imperial edifice that comprised Portuguese territories east of the Cape. Portuguese African and Indian possessions were administratively separated in the 1750s but their commercial and trading relationships were not adversely affected because their economies continued to be closely connected across the western Indian Ocean.[15] Moreover, in the second half of the eighteenth century, metropolitan interest in reviving the trade of Portugal's territories in the "East" resulted in state reforms that opened trade to private traders and merchants. This liberalization of commerce, together with Portuguese neutrality in the European wars of the period, revitalized trade in the imperial economies, a revival that in the western Indian Ocean was facilitated by the commercial and financial involvement of Vāniyā merchants.

Vāniyā merchants in Kathiawar and other groups such as Saraswat Brahmins of Goa were often dominant in the commercial and financial spheres of the *Estado da Índia*, in many cases underwriting state and private trade throughout the Indian Ocean. The Portuguese attempted on numerous occasions to displace Gujarati merchants from their positions of prominence in oceanic trade after they assumed imperial control of the important entrepôt of Diu in the sixteenth century because they were seen as draining the empire's economic patrimony.[16] Although these attempts included disrupting trading routes in displays of aggression during the early years of the Portuguese presence in India, Portuguese officials were unable ultimately to undermine the significance of Gujarati merchant capital to commerce in the Indian Ocean. Merchants from Diu and elsewhere in Kathiawar pursued commercial opportunities in

[15] Such lateral imperial connections, unmediated by a metropolitan centre, were important also during the British Raj period, for which, see Thomas R. Metcalf, *Imperial Connections: India in the Indian Ocean Arena, 1860–1920* (Berkeley, Los Angeles and London: University of California Press, 2007).

[16] This formulation is from Daviken Studnicki-Gizbert, *A Nation Upon the Ocean Sea: Portugal's Atlantic Diaspora and the Crisis of the Spanish Empire* (New York: Oxford University Press, 2007), 12.

the Persian Gulf and at Red Sea ports, and maintained links with Surat during its heyday in the seventeenth century as one of the western Indian Ocean's major ports. In the eighteenth century, as this book will show, some Gujarati merchant networks deepened their regional involvement in Mozambique as the result of developments – notably the commercial efflorescence of Kathiawar – that were not determined by the Portuguese state or private European interests.

While the extent of Indian commercial and financial dominance of the Portuguese imperial economy has been recognized to a certain extent, this scholarship has tended either to focus on the imperial capital of Goa (the centre on coastal western India of state and private Portuguese investment and trade) or has provided only brief, narrowly focused or generalized accounts of the involvement of South Asian capital in the maritime trade of Portuguese India.[17] There has been thus no detailed and systematic study of particular South Asian merchant networks who, while operating under the umbrella of the Portuguese imperial state and contributing to its fiscal income, were attached to broader Indian Ocean commercial currents. Vāniyā merchants in Diu and Daman ran their business concerns and pursued commercial and financial agendas that were not circumscribed by Portuguese state or private pressures as they weighed up and seized opportunities in the ocean's maritime sphere.

This is not to argue, however, that Gujarati merchants marginalized or were entirely indifferent towards the Portuguese state. Rather, they maintained a relationship of selective engagement with state offices and institutions that was made possible by their powerful economic position. Vāniyā merchants took advantage of the perquisites of imperial subjecthood when it appeared advantageous to do so but negotiated their relationship with Portuguese authorities in India and Mozambique from a position of considerable commercial and financial strength. The income of the imperial state in Diu and Daman was largely dependent on the

---

[17] See, for example, Michael Pearson, "Goa-based seaborne trade, 17th–18th centuries", in Teotonio de Souza (ed.), *Goa Through the Ages: An Economic History* (New Delhi: Concept Publishing Company, 1989), 146–75; *idem*, "Markets and Merchant Communities in the Indian Ocean: Locating the Portuguese", in Francisco Bethencourt and Diogo Ramada Curto (eds.), *Portuguese Oceanic Expansion, 1400–1800* (New York: Cambridge University Press, 2007), 88–108; Celsa Pinto, *Trade and Finance in Portuguese India: A Study of the Portuguese Country Trade, 1770–1840* (New Delhi: Concept Publishing Company, 1994); Rudy Bauss, "Indian and Chinese Control of the Portuguese Eastern Empire (1770–1850)", *Purabhilekh-Puratatva*, 10, 1 (1992), 1–19; Luis Frederico Dias Antunes, "A Actividade da Companhia de Comércio dos Banianes de Diu em Moçambique (1686–1777)", MA thesis, Universidade Nova de Lisboa, 1992; *idem*, "The Trade Activities of the Banyans in Mozambique: Private Indian Dynamics in the Panel of the Portuguese State Economy (1686–1777)", in K. S. Mathew (ed.), *Mariners, Merchants and Oceans: Studies in Maritime History* (New Delhi: Manohar, 1995), 301–31.

revenue generated by Vāniyā commerce, giving merchants considerable leverage in defining the terms of their relations with the Portuguese. As one well-informed Portuguese observer of the structure and nature of commercial relations noted about the Vāniyā role in sustaining commercial activity in Mozambique in the 1770s, "without these men, nothing can exist".[18]

As imperial subjects, Vāniyās had access to state protection and legal institutions such as the Office of the Judge where merchants could bring disputes for adjudication and present cases against errant officials. They did not abandon or forego recourse to customary practice as represented by the *mahajan* (guild-like organization) to settle differences among members of the merchant community – both of these are discussed in Chapter 1. In effect, a dual system of enforcing commercial, social and legal obligations operated in Diu and Daman, and whether merchants appealed to one or the other depended on perceived benefits. The *mahajan* and imperial courts operated as complementary mechanisms to regulate merchant and related commercial behaviour. This complementarity reflected, further, the adaptive capacity of Vāniyā merchants to certain aspects of the Portuguese imperial presence in the Indian Ocean. It suggests also that, instead of being dictated by an abstracted notion of imperial "policy" emanating from Goa or the metropole, the logics governing interaction between Vāniyās and the imperial state were often determined by local pressures and concerns.

This often resulted in little agreement between Portuguese imperial officials and between them and private metropolitan interests, which further allowed Gujarati merchants to exploit commercial opportunities in the western Indian Ocean. While local officials in Diu, for example, appreciated that the financial contribution of Vāniyās to the income of the treasury was critical for its solvency and therefore sought to foster a commercial and financial environment that was attractive to these merchants, high-ranking administrators in Mozambique and metropolitan merchants, wedded to the notion (no matter how unrealistic) that trade between the territories of the *Estado da Índia* should be the preserve of Portuguese merchants, were hostile and resentful of the prominent place occupied by Vāniyās in the imperial economy. Such tensions and paradoxes were not uncommon for South Asian and other merchant networks in the Indian Ocean because – though imperialists may have

---

[18] "Copia de Huma Informação dada pelo General Balthazar M.^EL. Per.^A do Lago", in Jeronimo Jose Nogueira de Andrade, "Descripção Do Estado em que ficavão os Negoçios do Anno de 1789...", *Arquivo das Colonias*, I (1917), 230. Its author, Balthazar Manoel Pereira do Lago, was Governor-General of Mozambique between 1765 and 1779.

derided them – they were often indispensable to the functioning and revenue of imperial economies.[19]

Vāniyā merchants were active in the waters of the western Indian Ocean also at a time of other expanding imperial interest in the region. In the early decades of the eighteenth century, the English East India Company began to broaden its commercial interests in western India, especially at Surat, as it sought increasingly to control textile procurement from the rich productive lands of Gujarat. Concerns over French imperial manoeu-vrings and aggression in the final quarter of the century – intensifying in the early nineteenth century with Napoleonic pretensions – prompted increased territorial conquest and spurred commitments to the region of the western Indian Ocean. The company extended its commercial and military operations into the Persian Gulf in the early nineteenth century and British naval patrols became active in attempting to suppress the trade in African slaves. This process of British imperial expansion along the west coast of India and in the western Indian Ocean was, however, fitful and constrained by the partial nature of the company's political authority. South Asian merchants continued to exercise control over commercial networks even as they competed or worked with company and private merchants. Some, like the Vāniyā merchants discussed in this book, had maintained commercial and oceanic trading interests that predated British colonial expansion in the second half of the eighteenth century, thus allowing them to exploit their market knowledge and networks to their advantage. Clearly, then, the encroachments of empire did not undermine older Indian Ocean trades.[20]

Another expansionist empire was entering the competitive maritime arena of the Indian Ocean in the eighteenth century. Under the leadership of the Busaidi dynasty from mid-century, Oman deepened its involve-ment in the western ocean by establishing itself at Zanzibar. Omani competition for control over the East African coast had been a feature of the seventeenth century when under an earlier dynasty, the Ya'rubi, they

---

[19] Claude Markovits, "Indian Merchant Networks and the British Empire", paper presented at XIV International Economic History Congress, Helsinki, 21–5 August 2006. See also *idem, The Global World of Indian Merchants, 1759–1947* (New York: Cambridge University Press, 2000); Rajat Kanta Ray, "Asian Capital in the Age of European Domination: The Rise of the Bazaar, 1800–1914", *Modern Asian Studies*, 29, 3 (1995), 449–554; Sugata Bose, *A Hundred Horizons: The Indian Ocean in the Age of Global Empire* (Cambridge, MA: Harvard University Press, 2006).

[20] Robert Travers, "Imperial Revolutions and Global Repercussions: South Asia and the World, c. 1750–1850", in David Armitage and Sanjay Subrahmanyam (eds.), *The Age of Revolutions in Global Context, c. 1760–1840* (Basingstoke: Palgrave Macmillan, 2010), 144–66.

attacked Portuguese settlements after expelling them from Muscat in 1650. They captured Mombasa at the end of 1698, effectively removing the Portuguese from the northern Swahili coast. The extension of control over the East African coast by the Busaidi, which in the nineteenth century would include re-establishing political control over Mombasa and moving the imperial capital from Muscat to Zanzibar, was financially and commercially driven by Kutchi merchant capital. Bhātiyā merchants primarily from Mandvi had in the late seventeenth century established trading and commercial ties with Muscat, and in the eighteenth century encouraged the Busaidis to expand into East Africa where their business interests had been growing. The state support and cooperation that Kutchi Bhātiyā received from Muscat's rulers allowed them to intensify their involvement in the southwestern Indian Ocean.[21] The implications of these developments for Vāniyā merchants of Diu and Daman was that, especially from the late eighteenth and early nineteenth centuries, they faced growing Bhātiyā competition in the trade and markets of Mozambique, particularly once Kutchi cloth began to penetrate its African interior.

The focus in this book on Vāniyā merchants, then, uncovers a history of human mobility and the circulation of goods and people in the eighteenth and nineteenth centuries that bears a distinctive Indian Ocean imprint. Such movements created the vital sinews of connection and shaped the ocean as an inter-regional arena of exchange.[22] An oceanic framework is useful not only because it challenges traditional approaches to the past that have focused on bounded spatial territories, usually the nation state, as their unit of analysis, but also because it allows us to go beyond the Cold War "Area Studies" maps that divided the world into discrete regions of study.[23] These frames have elided the multiple "connected histories" that

---

[21] M. Reda Bhacker, *Trade and Empire in Muscat and Zanzibar: Roots of British Domination* (New York: Routledge, 1992).

[22] Sugata Bose, "Space and Time on the Indian Ocean Rim", in Leila Tarazi Fawaz and C. A. Bayly (eds.), *Modernity and Culture: From the Mediterranean to the Indian Ocean* (New York: Columbia University Press, 2002), 365–88; *idem, Hundred Horizons.*

[23] Metcalf, *Imperial Connections*; Isabel Hofmeyr, "AHR Conversation: On Transnational History", *American Historical Review*, 111, 5 (2006), 1463. Oceanic frameworks, pioneered by Fernand Braudel over 50 years ago for the Mediterranean, are today much in vogue. For an introduction to this burgeoning field and reviews of recent work on the Mediterranean, Atlantic and Pacific Oceans (the Indian Ocean, surprisingly, was omitted), see the essays in "AHR Forum: Oceans of History", *American Historical Review*, 111, 3 (2006), 717–80. Overviews of the field of Indian Ocean history can be found in Markus P. Vink, "Indian Ocean Studies and the 'New Thalassology'", *Journal of Global History*, 2 (2007), 41–62; and Michael Pearson, "History of the Indian Ocean: A Review Essay", *Wasafiri*, 26, 2 (2011), 78–99.

often existed across territories and regions, as people, goods, ideas and religions travelled between and across them.[24]

However, the modalities of our story make it also a global history that is written from a regional perspective.[25] For Vāniyā merchants were enmeshed in a larger commercial world of goods and financial flows in the eighteenth century that they enabled and also from which they benefited. At the centre of this world, and a key component of the global economy of the eighteenth century, was African slave trading and the logics of labour demand for sugar and other products of plantation economies that were driven by rising European consumption. The contours of the slave trade and its place in the global economy have generally been seen by scholars to be defined by the Atlantic trade and its merchant capitalists. This has resulted in an overly narrow focus on one oceanic region and its history has been written as if it were somehow separate from the broader story of African slave trading.[26]

From the mid-eighteenth century in particular, this larger story belied the intellectual separation of the trade in African slaves into discrete spheres of activity: the Atlantic and Indian Oceans. As we will see in Chapter 5, Atlantic slave merchants, primarily from Brazil and to a certain extent the Río de la Plata region, began trading in growing numbers of slaves in Mozambique from the 1750s and 1760s for the plantations of the southern Atlantic. Attracted by lower slave costs and slave markets that especially in the first quarter of the nineteenth century were less closely patrolled by British anti-slaving squadrons, these Atlantic traders arrived on the African coast with large quantities of silver dollars that had originated in New World silver mines. Their ability to trade for slaves was due entirely to the capacity of Vāniyā merchants to accept these dollars as payment for Gujarati cloth, the indispensible commodity of exchange along the coast and interior of Mozambique. The exchangeability of silver

---

[24] Sanjay Subrahmanyam, "Connected Histories: Notes towards a Reconfiguration of Early Modern Eurasia", *Modern Asian Studies*, 31, 3 (1997), 735–62; and *Explorations in Connected History* (New Delhi: Oxford University Press, 2005).

[25] This is an approach I share with Tirthankar Roy, *India in the World Economy: From Antiquity to the Present* (New York: Cambridge University Press, 2012).

[26] A few "Atlanticists" have urged broadening the optic of the Atlantic Ocean in order to see it as part of larger oceanic histories. See Peter A. Coclanis, "Atlantic World or Atlantic/ World?" *The William and Mary Quarterly*, 63, 4 (2006), 725–42. This includes a recent volume on the British maritime empire that seeks to cast it as an "oceanic" empire across the Atlantic and Indian Oceans: H. V. Bowen, Elizabeth Mancke and John G. Reid (eds.), *Britain's Oceanic Empire: Atlantic and Indian Ocean Worlds, c. 1550–1850* (New York: Cambridge University Press, 2012). See also Richard B. Allen, "Satisfying the 'Want for Labouring People': European Slave Trading in the Indian Ocean, 1500–1850", *Journal of World History*, 21, 1 (2010), 45–73; *idem, European Slave Trading in the Indian Ocean, 1500–1850* (Athens, OH: Ohio University Press, forthcoming).

for cloth enabled Atlantic slavers to purchase slave cargoes in Mozambique, and provided Vāniyās with a source of liquidity that helped finance credit in India.[27] Together with intensified French demand for plantation labour in the Mascarenes, Atlantic slave trading pushed slave exports from Mozambique to new heights as the trade came to dominate its economy by the 1820s. While Vāniyā merchants became directly involved in the trade as slave merchants, it was as financiers and providers of credit in the form of cloth that they played the most critical roles in its growth. They were therefore integral to the slave trade's broader dimensions as a significant component of the global economy.

This book seeks, however, to do more than simply place the interconnected histories of Mozambique and India, mediated by Vāniyā merchants, on a larger canvas by locating them within the rapidly emerging global economy of the eighteenth and early nineteenth centuries; it suggests that the local and inter-regional circuits of production, commercialization, exchange and consumer demand addressed here were constitutive of this global economy and shaped its contours and parameters.[28] The larger histories of global exchange, in other words, need to be attentive to the multiple strands that underlie its structure.[29] By examining the commercial world of Vāniyā merchants, we can begin to provide historical depth in understanding how some of these strands functioned and were woven together.

This examination is structured around individual chapters that address selected themes, moving backwards and forwards in time within the temporal scope of the work, approximately 1750 to 1850. It begins in Chapter 1 by tracing the development of South Asian networks in the Indian Ocean, focusing on Vāniyā merchants and their activities in its western reaches. The chapter offers an account of their movement away from traditional markets in the southern Arabian Peninsula and Red Sea from the early eighteenth century and explains why Vāniyā redirected their business interests to Southeast Africa and specifically Mozambique. The chapter explores the mutually reinforcing circumstances and factors in India and Africa that propelled Vāniyā commerce from the 1750s, such

---

[27] Firearms would also become important slave exchange commodities in Mozambique from the 1830s but they would not displace cloth as vital to commercial exchange.

[28] For a similar argument for the Red Sea, see Jonathan Miran, "Space, Mobility and Translocal connections across the Red Sea since 1500", special issue, *Northeast African Studies*, 12, 1 (2012), ix–xxvi.

[29] As suggested also in C. A. Bayly in *The Birth of the Modern World, 1780–1914: Global Connections and Comparisons* (Malden, MA: Blackwell, 2004); and two volumes edited by A. G. Hopkins: *Globalization and World History* (New York: W. W. Norton, 2002); *Global History: Between the Universal and the Local* (New York: Palgrave Macmillan, 2006).

as the commercial vibrancy of Kathiawar and the existence of vast consumer markets for Mozambique ivory, and rising African demand for
Gujarati cloth. Their ability to extend credit and finance trade throughout
Mozambique by being able, critically, to supply cloth and offer bills of
exchange to Portuguese and other merchants gave them a central place
in its economy and exchange networks. At least as important was how
Vāniyā organized their business and managed the interplay between trust
and reputation in shaping relationships among merchants. Their relationships with the Portuguese imperial state were determined by their prominent commercial position in the exchange economies of Diu, Daman
and Mozambique, allowing them both to draw on the institutional resources of the state and to resist its demands.

Independently owned Vāniyā shipping capable of long-distance voyaging was critical to transporting voluminous cargoes of ivory and cloth
between western India and Mozambique. Chapter 2 argues that Vāniyā
shipping remained vital through a combination of sophisticated credit
mechanisms and arrangements, diversified labour recruitment, availability of rich natural resources, varied partnerships and the exploitation of
Portuguese imperial perquisites. Merchants built vessels capable of sailing
across the western Indian Ocean and of carrying large loads and sizeable
crews. The chapter challenges the still widely held view that South Asian
merchant shipping generally, and Gujarati shipping in particular, had
by the middle of the eighteenth century declined precipitously and was
confined largely to minor activity on the coast of western India. Vāniyā
merchants were successful in the Indian Ocean in part because of their
ownership of and access to sailing vessels that were equipped to sail great
distances with large quantities of cotton textiles, ivory and silver, along
with foodstuffs, African slaves, crews and passengers. This was particularly important in the eighteenth and nineteenth centuries in the context
of growing British and Omani imperial shipping and private European
activity in both South Asia and East Africa.

As already mentioned, Gujarati cloth was central to the "bundles of
relationships" that stretched from Kathiawar, Gujarat and western India
to coastal and interior Mozambique.[30] A central theme in Chapter 3 is
that Vāniyā networks enjoyed a comparative advantage over private
European merchants, the imperial state and Arab, Swahili and other
African merchants in the western Indian Ocean because of the tight control

---

[30] I borrow this evocative terminology from Tony Ballantyne, "Putting the Nation in its
Place?: World History and C. A. Bayly's *The Birth of the Modern World*", in Ann Curthoys
and Marilyn Lake (eds.), *Connected Worlds: History in Transnational Perspective* (Canberra:
ANU E-Press, 2005), 32.

they exercised over the procurement and importation of cotton textiles into Africa. These arrived on the Mozambique coast in vast quantities, in some years exceeding a million pieces. Of equal importance was regular Vāniyā access to centres of textile production in Gujarat to which information on textile styles and types that changed seasonally could be transmitted. In the eighteenth century, particular African markets in Mozambique became highly significant for Gujarati textile exports; these cloths were used as a primary measure of value for which ivory, slaves and silver were exchanged in areas that effectively constituted cloth currency zones of commercial contact. Crucially, however, this function was related to the particular social, cultural, political and symbolic meanings with which cloth was inscribed when it entered the markets of the African interior. Examining African consumer demand and tastes, and the production and procurement process in India which supplied these African markets, in the same analytic frame illuminates the particular desirability of Gujarati textiles as well as their place in the social, political, economic and cultural lives of Africans.[31] At the same time, it uncovers the impact of this demand on the productive capacity specifically of one of Gujarat's important eighteenth- and nineteenth-century weaving centres, Jambusar.

This large-scale procurement and shipment of cotton cloths across the ocean to Mozambique by Vāniyā merchants was concentrated on the African territory's ivory trade because of high levels of ivory consumption in a variety of markets in Kathiawar, Kutch and more broadly throughout Gujarat. Chapter 4 shows that, as resurgent local economies in Kathiawar especially created increased demand for ivory tusks that were fashioned into a variety of uses, from wedding bangles to knife handles used in warfare, Vāniyā imports into Diu and Daman could exceed a quarter of a million kilograms in some years in the late eighteenth century. Apart from acquiring ivory through long-distance traders in northern Mozambique, Vāniyās successfully exploited rich sources of supply in central and southern Mozambique when they expanded their business interests from Mozambique Island, the commercial and trading entrepôt where Vāniyā firms were based, from the final quarter of the eighteenth century.

The expansion of Vāniyā ivory trading occurred during a time of growing slave trading in Mozambique, as labour demand from the French Mascarene Islands for plantation agriculture stimulated the exports of large numbers of African slaves. Partly channelled through Madagascar and involving European, Swahili, Malagasy and other African merchants, this trade in human cargoes created a slaving nexus in the southwestern

---

[31] Like many others, I have been influenced by the seminal work of Sidney Mintz, *Sweetness and Power: The Place of Sugar in Modern History* (New York: Penguin Viking, 1985).

Indian Ocean that involved Vāniyā as financers and shippers of slaves both along the coast of Mozambique and to India where modest demand for African slaves existed among Kathiawar chieftancies. This nexus grew from early in the nineteenth century to include the southern Atlantic when merchants primarily from Brazil became heavily involved in Mozambique's burgeoning trade and shipped thousands of slaves to Bahia, Rio de Janeiro and Montevideo. The book's final chapter develops the argument that, because the slave extraction process was underpinned by consumer demand for Gujarati cotton cloth, Vāniyā merchants were key to slave commerce linking Mozambique to African slave trades in both the Indian and Atlantic Oceans. Crucially, that Vāniyās accepted New World silver dollars with which slavers arrived on the Mozambique coast as payment for cloth was decisive for the functioning of the slave trade in the eighteenth and nineteenth centuries.

By the 1830s and 1840s, however, Vāniyā merchants were struggling to compete in Mozambique and in the southwestern Indian Ocean. The conclusion explores the reasons behind their displacement and how they responded to it in the rapidly changing trading world of the mid-nineteenth century.

1   Merchants of the ocean

South Asian merchants such as Laxmichand Motichand had been active in the ports of the Indian Ocean for centuries, participating in long-distance trade whose routes criss-crossed the waterways of the ocean. Merchant networks involved groups that were drawn from different areas of the subcontinent, such as Chulias and Sindhis; however, it was merchants from Gujarat, both Hindu and Muslim, who for centuries had been perhaps most prominent in commercial exchanges throughout the Indian Ocean. Indeed, as a region marked by movement and connection to the oceanic space in which it was embedded, Gujarat is rightfully identified as "a land of the Indian Ocean as well as of India".[1] In early periods, close commercial ties between ports in Gujarat, Kathiawar and Kutch and the western Indian Ocean saw merchants visit and trade with ports in the Persian Gulf and Red Sea, as well as along the coast of the Horn of Africa.[2]

This has been the focus of most scholarship that has studied these merchants. However, from the late seventeenth and early eighteenth centuries, as this chapter will show, Gujarati merchants forced out of these traditional markets to varying degrees began to turn their attention increasingly towards Southeast African markets.

Their interest in African markets was not new to the early modern period, though, as South Asian merchants appear to have been present on Sokotra Island, located a short distance from the Northeast African coast, as early as the fourth century BCE. But over the following centuries

---

[1] David Ludden, "Presidential Address: Maps in the Mind and the Mobility of Asia", *The Journal of Asian Studies*, 62, 4 (2003), 1068. See also Ludden, "History Along the Coastal Zones of Southern Asia", paper presented at the South Asia Seminar, Columbia University, 18 October 1999.

[2] André Wink, *Al-Hind: The Making of the Indo-Islamic World. Volume I: Early Medieval India and the Expansion of Islam 7th–11th Centuries* (New Delhi: Oxford University Press, 1999), 65; Calvin H. Allen, "The Indian Merchant Community of Masqat", *Bulletin of the School of Oriental and African Studies*, 44, 1 (1981), 39–53; Richard Pankhurst, "The 'Banyan' or Indian Presence at Massawa, the Dahlak Islands and the Horn of Africa", *Journal of Ethiopian Studies*, 12 (1974), 185–212.

they were more frequently regular visitors to the Persian Gulf and destinations in the southern Arabian peninsula such as Aden, where Gujarati merchants had established firm trading ties by the ninth century CE.[3] Early in the twelfth century, Indian traders were active at Kish (at the entrance to the Persian Gulf), and by the fourteenth or fifteenth century significant numbers of merchants were trading in Muscat, an important entrepôt for South Asian trade. At the end of the sixteenth century, an Indian mercantile presence was reported in Massawa on the African coast of the southern Red Sea.[4] Gujarati merchants also broadened their networks across the eastern reaches of the ocean to Southeast Asia where early in the sixteenth century they traded with Malacca in competition with Tamil, Javanese and Chinese merchants. Aceh and the other North Sumatran ports, Kedah and Bantam, were regular destinations for Gujarati textiles and other exports such as wheat, iron and steel, while in return goods including pepper, cloves, ivory, gold and silver bullion and specie were shipped to India.[5]

By the seventeenth century, Gujarat and Gujarati merchant networks thus effectively operated as linchpins of trade in the Indian Ocean, and while their relative importance may have changed over time (in relation to Hadrami or Kutchi Bhātiyā merchants, for example), they played one of the most important integrative roles in its culture and economy as mediators of cross-regional contact and as facilitators of long-distance commerce.[6]

[3] Wink, *Al-Hind*, 65. Claude Markovits, *The Global World of Indian Merchants, 1750–1947: Traders of Sind from Bukhara to Panama* (Cambridge University Press, 2000), 10; Pankhurst, "'Banyan' or Indian Presence".

[4] Jonathan Miran, *Red Sea Citizens: Cosmopolitan Society and Cultural Change in Massawa* (Bloomington and Indianapolis: Indiana University Press, 2009), 137.

[5] Luís Filipe F. R. Thomaz, "Melaka and Its Merchant Communities at the Turn of the Sixteenth Century", in Denys Lombard and Jean Aubin (eds.), *Asian Merchants and Businessmen in the Indian Ocean and the China Sea* (New Delhi: Oxford University Press, 2000), 25–39; Sinnappah Arasaratnam, *Maritime India in the Seventeenth Century* (New Delhi: Oxford University Press, 1994), 54–89.

[6] Mark Horton, "Artisans, Communities, and Commodities: Medieval Exchanges between Northwestern India and East Africa", *Ars Orientalis*, 34 (2004), 67; Allen, "Indian Merchant Community"; Markovits, *Global World*, 11; M. N. Pearson, *Merchants and Rulers in Gujarat: The Response to the Portuguese in the Sixteenth Century* (Berkeley and Los Angeles: University of California Press, 1976); Sanjay Subrahmanyam, "Of Imârat and Tijârat: Asian Merchants and State Power in the Western Indian Ocean, 1400 to 1750", *Comparative Studies in Society and History*, 37, 4 (1995), 750–80; Sugata Bose, "Space and Time on the Indian Ocean Rim: Theory and History", in Leila Tarazi Fawaz and C. A. Bayly (eds.), *Modernity & Culture: From the Mediterranean to the Indian Ocean* (New York: Columbia University Press, 2002), 374; Philip D. Curtin, *Cross-Cultural Trade in World History* (New York: Cambridge University Press, 1984); Gareth Austin, *Industrial Growth in the Third World*, London School of Economics Working Paper, 44/98 (1998), 5.

Increasingly, however, Gujarati merchants concentrated their investments in the western Indian Ocean. Although Southeast Asian ports in the Melaka Straits and West Java remained of commercial interest to them until the last decade of the seventeenth century, from around mid-century they began to focus on Middle East markets as commercial opportunities expanded in Mocha and elsewhere under the encouragement of Qāsimī rule in Yemen. This was a period of marked growth for Gujarati trade, as Surat replaced Cambay as the pre-eminent Mughal maritime commercial centre and emerged as the pre-eminent port on the west coast of India. Other Gujarati ports such as Dabhol also featured significantly in the first half of the century in the long-distance oceanic trade of Gujarati merchant networks in the northwestern Indian Ocean.[7]

Hindu Vāniyā networks from Kathiawar, in particular, operated prominently in the region, and directed their trade primarily to Yemen and Hadramawt.[8] They were also active in the early eighteenth century in the southern Red Sea where Mocha and other ports such as Aden provided them with their principal markets.[9] Sources suggest that these Gujarati merchants overwhelmingly came from Diu, an island-entrepôt located a short distance from the southern coast of the Kathiawar peninsula that had been under Portuguese imperial administration from the mid-sixteenth century. Some were from Daman, another Portuguese territory to the south of Surat that served also as an important shipbuilding centre for Portuguese and Indian merchants alike in the eighteenth and nineteenth centuries (Map 1.1). In Mocha, Vāniyā worked as brokers, organized the banking sector and were prominently involved in the bulk trade with India.[10] As conduits of gold and silver from Europe, the eastern

---

[7] Further details are provided in Arasaratnam, *Maritime India*; and in the many works of Ashin Das Gupta collected in Uma Das Gupta (comp.), *The World of the Indian Ocean Merchant, 1500–1800* (New Delhi: Oxford University Press, 2001).

[8] Although the meaning of the term "Vāniyā" has proved somewhat difficult to define accurately, I have understood it to mean a caste-cum-occupational category. For a detailed discussion, see Lakshmi Subramanian, *Indigenous Capital and Imperial Expansion: Bombay, Surat and the West Coast* (New Delhi: Oxford University Press, 1996); *idem*, "The Eighteenth Century Social Order in Surat: A Reply and an Excursus on the Riots of 1788 and 1795", *Modern Asian Studies*, 25, 2 (1991), 323.

[9] Ashin Das Gupta, "Gujarati Merchants and the Red Sea Trade, 1700–1725", in Das Gupta, *World of the Indian Ocean Merchant*, 369–398.

[10] R. B. Serjeant, "The Hindu, Bāniyān Merchants and Traders", in Serjeant and R. Lewcock (eds.), *San'a: An Arabian Islamic City* (London: World of Islam Trust, 1983), 532–5; Das Gupta, "Gujarati Merchants"; Nancy Um, *The Merchant Houses of Mocha: Trade and Architecture in an Indian Ocean Port* (Seattle and London: University of Washington Press, 2009), 166, where the author notes an instance in 1720 of the arrival in Mocha of more than 300 Vāniyā from Diu.

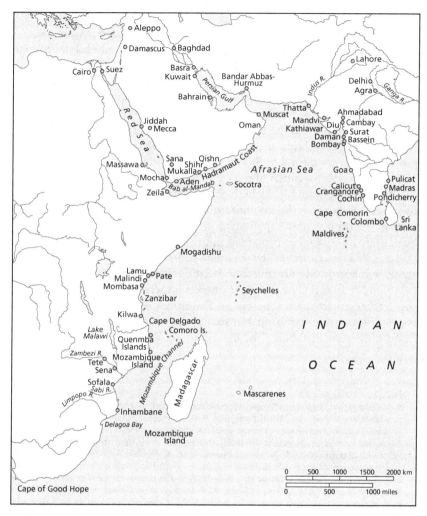

Map 1.1 Western Indian Ocean

Mediterranean and North Africa, Red Sea ports offered attractive financial and commercial opportunities for Indian merchants that outstripped those of the eastern reaches of the Indian Ocean.

Although often overlooked, the growth of regional Gujarati trade at this time also encompassed the northern and southern Swahili coasts of Africa as far down as Mozambique Island and possibly beyond into the

Mozambique Channel. Gujarati merchants had visited and traded with the coast prior to the seventeenth century, of course; for example, at the end of the fifteenth century, Indian merchants from Cambay were trading with Malindi, Mombasa, Kilwa and Pate in commercial exchanges that appear to have been firmly established by this time.[11] But despite this earlier presence, it would seem that regular and sustained Gujarati contact with Africa became a reality only from the seventeenth century and was mostly focused on the northern Swahili coast.[12] These merchants were, as in southern Arabia and the Red Sea, primarily Vāniyā from Diu.[13] Yet, it was the markets of Jidda and elsewhere in the Red Sea, and the trade of ports such as Mocha and al-Shihr in Hadramawt that remained central to Vāniyā networks for much of the century.[14]

This changed dramatically in the first quarter of the eighteenth century, however, particularly in the vibrant entrepôt of Mocha, as conditions became restrictive and exploitative in the 1720s. Legally, Vāniyās had been granted *dhimmī* or protected minority status (for which they paid a poll tax) as a "gracious act" by the imam in 1655–66 because normally this status was bestowed only on monotheistic communities in territories that came under Islamic law. While it offered imperial protection, the status involved restrictions on religious and sumptuary practice; some of these restrictions were overlooked but many were enforced strictly, resulting in an "inherent instability" in the status of Vāniyā merchants, traders

---

[11] Horton, "Artisans", 67.

[12] S. I. Gorerazvo Mudenge, "Afro-Indian Relations Before 1900: A Southeast Central African Perspective", in Shanti Sadiq Ali & R. R. Ramchandani (eds.), *India and the Western Indian Ocean States* (Bombay: Allied Publishing, 1981), 40; A. Rita-Ferreira, "Moçambique e os Naturais da Índia Portuguesa", in Luís de Albuquerque and Inácio Guerreiro (eds.), *II Seminário Internacional de História Indo-Portuguesa* (Lisbon: Instituto de Investigação Científica Tropical, 1985), 617; Edward A. Alpers, "Gujarat and the Trade of East Africa, c. 1500–1800", *The International Journal of African Historical Studies*, 9, 1 (1976), 22–44; Manuel Lobato, "Relações comerciais entre a India e a costa Africana nos séculos XVI e XVII: O papel do Guzerate no Comércio de Moçambique", *Mare Liberum*, 9 (1995), 157–73. For a useful recent overview, see M. N. Pearson, "Indians in East Africa: The Early Modern Period", in Rudrangshu Mukherjee and Lakshmi Subramanian (eds.), *Politics and Trade in the Indian Ocean World: Essays in Honour of Ashin Das Gupta* (New Delhi: Oxford University Press, 1998), 227–49.

[13] Pearson, "Indians". See also Pearson, "Banyas and Brahmins: Their Role in the Portuguese Indian Economy", in Pearson (ed.), *Coastal Western India: Studies from the Portuguese Records* (New Delhi: Concept Publishers, 1981), 93–115.

[14] It is possible that there was a bifurcation or segmentation of trade in the western Indian Ocean between Diu merchant networks concentrated on Arabia and the southern Red Sea and those focused on East Africa. Some may even have maintained interests in both commercial spheres. However, the sources are insufficiently detailed to provide a definitive answer.

and brokers. Moreover, in the late seventeenth century, the imam of
Mocha forcibly converted or ordered the massacre – together with
Jewish traders and merchants – of many Vāniyā. This was compounded
by their economic exploitation and heavy-handed treatment by certain
governors who demanded large cash "loans" from the Indian community
whenever the Royal Treasury was depleted. They often failed to repay
them. Additionally, Vāniyā were also subject to payment to the governor
of Mocha or the imam of entry and exit fees every time they arrived and
left the port-city, and there were even instances when merchants were
subjected to acts of violence to secure funds.[15]

We can get a sense of the damage of this treatment and its effects on
Vāniyā involvement in Mocha by considering the experiences of the leading family of "Virachand", who originated in Diu and whose members
served as important brokers and merchants in Yemen at the end of the
seventeenth century. When the father and founding member, Virachand,
died, the business was taken over by his son Pitambar in 1711. Perhaps
sensing that circumstances were worsening for Gujarati merchants and
businessmen in Mocha, Pitambar returned to Diu in 1716 to settle unspecified "family business" and never returned. His brother assumed responsibility for the family's financial and commercial concerns in Mocha but
around 1725 conditions for the family and other Vāniyā had worsened
to such an extent that, according to Ashin Das Gupta, they were being
"persecuted" by the authorities. As a consequence of this treatment, the
family, along with other Vāniyā merchants from Diu, decided to withdraw
most of their capital from Yemen and the southern Red Sea trade, and
sent back to Diu what money they could.[16]

The 1720s and early 1730s were thus decades of Vāniyā capital flight
away from southern Arabia and the Red Sea, though Vāniyā merchants
did not wholly abandon Mocha or the trade of ports such as al-Shihr.
Indeed, it was never possible or desirable for Qāsimī imams to expel all
Gujarati merchants from Yemen because of their need for poll tax
revenue and for the important financial and commercial roles such
merchants performed. Some governors even attempted to entice merchants back to Mocha.[17] Nonetheless, in spite of their efforts, it is clear
that Vāniyā investment and involvement in Yemen and the southern

---

[15] I base this paragraph on Um, *Merchant Houses*, 165–7.
[16] Das Gupta, "Gujarati Merchants". The example of the Virachand family is cited also in
Um, *Merchant Houses*, 165.
[17] When he returned for a second term as governor of Mocha in 1730, Faqīh Ahmad
Khazindār endeavoured to attract the Vāniyā back to the city who had suffered under
his predecessor's rule. See Um, *Merchant Houses*, 169.

Red Sea had declined markedly, if not entirely, by the beginning of the 1730s.

Looking west, heading south

There has been a tendency to interpret the withdrawal of Gujarati capital from Yemen and the southern Red Sea as signalling that "the role and position of the Gujaratis in the region [of the western Indian Ocean] declined considerably [at this time]", and would improve only under conditions of "commercial revival of the nineteenth century and increased British involvement in the region". It would be only then that Vāniyā merchants returned "solidly in a dominant position in the Red Sea and north-western Indian Ocean trade".[18] The withdrawal of Gujarati capital from Yemen and the Red Sea is thus equated with commercial deterioration exacerbated by growing British competition, while the later "return" of Vāniyā merchants to ports such as Massawa on the African coast of the Red Sea from the 1830s and 1840s is viewed as enabled by a European-led commercial revival in the region. While there is certainly truth to the claim that Vāniyā (and other South Asian) merchants took advantage of emerging new commercial opportunities created by European imperial states in the western Indian Ocean in the nineteenth century, this interpretation grossly overstates the extent of their regional "decline" in the eighteenth century and fails to consider the commercial opportunities that merchants actively identified and exploited in markets elsewhere in the ocean from mid-century, particularly, as this book shows, in Southeast Africa.[19]

Much of the Vāniyā capital that left the Red Sea region, according to David Hardiman, was transferred to Gujarat where it was "turned ... increasingly to internal enterprise" and a rising proportion used to finance the "ruling classes of the day".[20] This may have been the case but only partly so, for Vāniyā merchants did not retreat from the western Indian Ocean; instead, they redirected their commercial interests and redeployed

---

[18] Miran, *Red Sea Citizens*, 137–8.

[19] Richard Pankhurst, "Indian Trade with Ethiopia, the Gulf of Aden and the Horn of Africa in the Nineteenth and Early Twentieth Centuries", *Cahiers d'Études Africaines*, 55, 14, 3 (1974), 455–97. An important Indian community of merchants was noted at Mocha around 1810 but these merchants were probably Kutchi Bhātiyā. See Allen, "Indian Merchant Community".

[20] David Hardiman, "Penetration of Merchant Capital in Pre-colonial Gujarat", in Ghanshyam Shah (ed.), *Capitalist Development: Critical Essays* (Bombay: Popular Prakashan, 1990), 38.

considerable capital resources to the Mozambique coast. As previously noted, merchants from Diu, and to a certain degree Daman, had been active along the East African coast for much of the seventeenth century, and as their involvement in the northwestern Indian Ocean came increasingly under strain from the beginning of the eighteenth century, they redirected their focus to trade along the African coast of the Mozambique Channel from their base at Mozambique Island.

This island-entrepôt, the administrative centre of Portuguese East Africa, was located a short distance from the African mainland and was accessible to ocean-going ships and coastal vessels. It served as a commercial, financial and redistribution centre for oceanic imports, such as Gujarati cotton cloths, and African exports that included ivory and slaves.[21] In basing their African trade on Mozambique Island, Gujarati merchants were able to channel their investments into the East Central African interior and, eventually, into the Zambesi Valley of central Mozambique.

If Vāniyā merchants from Diu, as well as Daman, continued to call occasionally at ports such as Mocha and Jidda until the 1780s and 1790s, they complained regularly that their trade was unprofitable there as elsewhere in the region. This included Mukalla in Hadramawt and, importantly, Muscat where Vāniyā trade faced growing competition from merchant networks from Kutch in northwestern India that had become increasingly influential in the commerce of the Persian Gulf from mid-century.[22] Kutchi Bhātiyā, primarily from Mandvi, benefitted especially from the development of an aggressive Omani Busaidi state commercial policy from the mid-1780s that was aimed at achieving a monopoly over Arabian Gulf trade. These merchants facilitated and became integral to the expanding Omani commercial empire, supporting it financially and commercially by investing heavily in the cotton textile export trade, notably in East Africa where burgeoning state commercial and political interests in Zanzibar resulted in the ruler, Seyyid Saīd b. Sultān, transferring his residence there after 1830. The alignment of state and private merchant interests thus allowed Kutchi Bhātiyā

---

[21] For details see, for example, Alpers, "Gujarat and the Trade of East Africa"; and Luís Frederico Dias Antunes, "A Actividade da Companhia de Comércio dos Baneanes de Diu em Moçambique (1686–1777)", MA thesis, Universidade Nova de Lisboa, 1992.

[22] HAG, CD 996, D. Frederico Guilherme de Souza to Castelão, 8 August 1782; CD 999, da Cunha e Menezes to de Chermont, 28 March 1787; Coelho e França e da Costa to Governor, 11 October 1786; and CD 1001, "Mapa que trouxerão 2 embarcaçõens vindas do port de Macala...", 16 June 1789.

merchants to broaden their spheres of activity in the region of the western Indian Ocean.[23]

Taken together, the constraints that Vāniyā were facing in the Persian Gulf and Red Sea restricted their opportunities and caused these merchants to redeploy their capital and trade away from the northwestern Indian Ocean and focus their commercial interests instead in the African trade of the southwestern Indian Ocean. Indeed, from the 1740s and 1750s, Vāniyā voyages to Mozambique and Southeast Africa rapidly supplanted those to the Red Sea, Yemen and the Persian Gulf as Vāniyā merchants expanded their involvement in African markets and became increasingly entrenched in their commercial possibilities, particularly those connected to the ivory and slave trades in which Gujarati cotton textiles played a central role.[24]

This reorientation of Vāniyā business to Mozambique reflected broader developments from the middle of the eighteenth century that these merchants both benefitted from and helped to sustain. The Kathiawar peninsula, of which Diu formed a part and to which Daman was also closely connected, underwent a commercial efflorescence driven by robust consumer markets for the products of the Indian Ocean, and a highly productive cotton textile-manufacturing sector whose cloths were much sought-after among buyers in the western reaches of the ocean. Its mainland comprised a number of chieftaincies and principalities of varying size and political authority that, while formally under the control of the Mughals to which they paid annual tribute, were in reality under the administrative and organizational possession of local chiefs (*zamindars* or *rajas*). However, through a process which began early in the century, smaller chieftaincies were absorbed by larger expansionist neighbours amid war and raiding caused by the disintegration of the Mughal empire.

---

[23] Allen, "Indian Merchant Community", 41–5; and *idem*, "Sayyids, shets and sultans: politics and trade in Masqat under the Al Bu Said, 1785–1914", PhD diss., University of Washington, 1978; and Subramanian, *Indigenous Capital*, 271–86; M. Reda Bhacker, *Trade and Empire in Muscat and Zanzibar: Roots of British Domination* (New York: Routledge, 1992). In the Red Sea, Vāniyā merchants would also face competition in the 1830s and 1840s from Hadrami merchants who "extended their network in all of the ports" and in Jidda "eventually came to engross most of the port's trade". See Michael Tuchscherer, "Coffee in the Red Sea Area from the Sixteenth to the Nineteenth Century", in William Gervase Clarence-Smith and Steven Topik (eds.), *The Global Coffee Economy in Africa, Asia, and Latin America, 1500–1989* (Cambridge University Press, 2003), 58.

[24] HAG, CD 998, Sarmento to Guilherme de Souza, 15 September 1785; CD 1001, Belchior do Amaral de Menezes to Governor, 4 January 1789; CD 999, "Extracto da Carga de 4 navios vindos esta prezente monsão de 1786, 1 do porto de Macalla e 3 da capital de Moçambique", 9 October 1786; and CD 1001, Kunwarji Narsinh, Anandji Jivan, Mulji Raghunath et al. to Governor, 22 December 1788.

Kathiawar thus became characterized by a high degree of political central-
ization whereby three large states, Nawanagar in the west, Junagadh in the
south and Bhavnagar in the east, dominated the peninsula. Their rulers,
the latter in particular, sought to consolidate the economic foundations
of their states by following progressive commercial policies designed to
attract regional and overseas trade. Vāniyā merchants, as importers of
ivory cargoes that were in high demand in Bhavnagar as elsewhere in
Kathiawar, supplied these consumer markets annually with large-scale
cargoes from Mozambique. While they gained from state efforts in
Bhavnagar to expand the economy, Vāniyā capacity in organizing and
financing this trade, from establishing commercial relationships with
African suppliers to securing the procurement of textiles in India with
which to purchase their cargoes, was an essential component of the
commercial expansion of the wider region.[25]

A concomitant and no less important development enabling the reorientation of Vāniyā trade to Southeast Africa was the intensification in
cotton textile demand among African consumers from early in the eighteenth century. While consumption of Gujarati cloth predated the eighteenth century, from the 1730s and 1740s and especially from the middle
of the century demand for cotton manufactures in a variety of colours
and styles rose dramatically. This was connected for much of the century
until around the 1820s to the expansion of ivory trading in which Gujarati
textiles were required as currency for the purchase of tusks in interior
markets. The redirection of ivory trade routes early in the eighteenth
century by Yao long-distance traders away from northern ports to
Mozambique Island where Vāniyā merchants had based themselves,
and the expansion of ivory trading in central and southern Mozambique
from the third quarter of the century, brought large quantities of ivory
onto the export market that were purchased by Gujarati merchants with
increased textile imports.

At the same time, however, Mozambique experienced a marked rise in
slave trading from the 1750s with, at first, French slavers and from the end

---

[25] I have relied here in my discussion of developments in Kathiawar on Ghulam A. Nadri,
"Exploring the Gulf of Kachh: Regional Economy and Trade in the Eighteenth Century",
Journal of the Economic and Social History of the Orient, 51 (2008), 460–86; R. J. Barendse,
"On the Arabian Seas in the Eighteenth Century", paper presented at the Workshop
"Western India and the Indian Ocean", Heidelberg, 5 October 1999; *idem*, "Reflections
on the Arabian Seas in the Eighteenth Century", *Itinerario*, 25, 1 (2001), 25–49;
V. D. Divekar, "Western India", in Dharma Kumar (ed.), *The Cambridge Economic
History of India. Volume 2: c. 1757–1979* (Cambridge University Press, 1982), 332–52;
Harald Tambs-Lyche, *Power, Profit and Poetry: Traditional Society in Kathiawar, Western
India* (New Delhi: Manohar, 1997); *Gazetteer of the Bombay Presidency. Vol. 8: Kathiawar*
(Bombay: Government Central Press, 1884).

of the century Brazilian merchants seeking African plantation labour. For the French, slave demand originated in the establishment of sugar cultivation in the Mascarene Islands (Mauritius and Réunion), while Brazilian and Portuguese slaving interests stemmed from southern Atlantic slave markets in Bahia, Rio de Janeiro and the Río de la Plata in Spanish America. Slaves were also traded from Mozambique to labour in the Merina empire of highland Madagascar or transhipped by Swahili merchants to markets in the Arabian Peninsula and Persian Gulf. Additionally, slaves were also trafficked to the Cape colony where they were employed by the Dutch and English charter companies as well as their colonists. As with ivory purchases, slave purchases required the exchange in the African interior of Gujarati cotton textiles, and therefore ensured that Vāniyā merchants – as leading cloth importers – became entrenched as vital economic actors in the commercial economy of Mozambique as it grew under extensive slave trading from the 1790s and early 1800s.

There was, though, an additional factor connected to the slave trade that made Vāniyā participation in it central to its operation in both the Indian and the Atlantic oceans. The capacity of Vāniyā merchants to accept payment for cotton textiles with silver *piastres* and *patacas*, Spanish silver dollars, that French and Brazilian slavers began shipping in sizeable quantities to coastal Mozambique was critically important to the structural dynamics of this multi-nodal trans-oceanic trade. South American silver, acquired by Brazilian merchants in significant volumes through Luso-Spanish trading networks connected to the Río de la Plata in the third quarter of the eighteenth century, thus flowed into the western Indian Ocean to finance large-scale slave purchases. That Vāniyā merchants were able to sell cloths for specie was in turn related to the robust silver markets that existed in Kathiawar and Gujarat and which helped finance the credit relations merchants maintained with bankers for their long-distance trade in the Indian Ocean. Silver also allowed merchants to negotiate favourable terms on financial instruments such as *hundis* (bills of exchange) that were instrumental to the movement of capital within India and between the subcontinent and Africa. Thus, while demand for African slave labour in the southwestern Indian Ocean and southern Atlantic had spurred the growth of slaving in Mozambique, the involvement of Vāniyā merchants was instrumental to its functional dynamics.

These mutually dependent and reinforcing factors lie at the core of this book – rising African and Indian consumer demand for cloth and ivory as part of burgeoning commercial economies on both sides of the ocean, and the growth of slave trading financed by large-scale New World silver imports into the Indian Ocean. Together, they enabled the reorientation of Vāniyā interests away from the Arabian Peninsula and Red Sea and towards Southeast Africa.

Their redeployment of capital benefitted, further, from changes introduced within the Portuguese imperial state to the commercial tax structure of its Asian territories. Reform of imperial commerce was a feature of this period, beginning with the "pragmatic" mercantilism of the Portuguese metropolitan reformer, the Marquês de Pombal, in the 1750s.[26] Pombaline reforms aimed to "modernize" Portugal and its empire by stimulating imperial trade in an effort to generate greater income for the financially weak Crown through the taxation of trade. This included an administrative separation of the African territory of Mozambique from the *Estado da Índia* in 1752 and the opening of Asian commerce to private metropolitan merchants in 1765.

Additional changes in the early 1780s, however, acted as a catalyst for commercial revival in the empire. They marked a departure from Pombaline mercantilist reforms by introducing "freer" trade, which contributed significantly to stimulate "Portuguese" (this included Brazilian) trade with, and in, Asia until the 1830s and 1840s. They began in 1783 with legislation that lowered the export duty on goods from Goa to 3–4 per cent, and were followed in 1786 by the landmark *Plano de Comercio* that aimed to stimulate trade between Portuguese India and Mozambique through further reductions in import and export duties for Goa, Diu and Daman.[27] These carried advantages for Vāniyā merchants who stood to gain from the lowering of taxes on imports and exports of cotton textiles, ivory and slaves in Diu, Daman and Mozambique. At Diu and Daman, export duties were set at the low rate of 5 per cent, while imports

---

[26] For details of Pombaline reforms in regard to Mozambique, see Fritz Hoppe, *A África Oriental Portuguesa no Tempo do Marquês de Pomal (1750–1777)* (Lisbon: Agência-Geral do Ultramar, 1970), ch. VI; Alan K. Smith, "The Indian Ocean Zone", in David Birmingham and Phyllis M. Martin (eds.), *History of Central Africa, Vol. 1* (Essex: Longman, 1983), 231–3. See also Joseph C. Miller, *Way of Death: Merchant Capital and the Angolan Slave Trade, 1730–1830* (Madison: University of Wisconsin Press, 1988), ch. 16. Kenneth Maxwell provides a useful examination of Sebastião José de Carvalho e Melo, the Marquês de Pombal, in *Pombal: Paradox of the Enlightenment* (New York: Cambridge University Press, 1995).

[27] Celsa Pinto, *Trade and Finance in Portuguese India: A Study of the Portuguese Country Trade, 1770–1840* (New Delhi: Concept Publishing House, 1994), ch. 4; *idem, Situating Indo-Portuguese Trade History: A Commercial Resurgence, 1770–1830* (Tellicherry: Institute for Research in Social Sciences and Humanities, 2003); *idem,* "At the Dusk of the Second Empire: Goa-Brazil Commercial Links, 1770–1825", *Purabhilekh Puratatva,* VII, 1 (1990), 52; and Rudy Bauss, "A Legacy of British Free Trade Policies: The End of the Trade and Commerce between India and the Portuguese Empire, 1780–1830", *The Calcutta Historical Journal,* 6, 2 (1982), 81–115.

paid 3 per cent.[28] In Mozambique, fiscal reforms resulted in import duties being established at 10 per cent while exports were charged between 4 and 6 per cent.[29] Re-export duties from the island to "subordinate ports" (those, such as Quelimane and Inhambane, that were located south of Mozambique Island) were reduced from 40 to 30 per cent, and in 1793 were lowered again to 10 per cent.

The combined impact of these changes on Vāniyā trade became evident soon after the reforms were passed – whereas two to three Gujarati vessels had been arriving in Mozambique annually from mid-century, in 1789 three vessels from Diu and five from Daman sailed into Mozambique Island.[30] But fierce debate and protestations among private Portuguese merchants in Mozambique who were concerned about Vāniyā competition resulted in re-export duties from Mozambique Island to southern ports being raised once again to 30 per cent in 1801. This high tariff was, though, often circumvented through "illegal" shipping, while customs rates in Diu and Daman for trade to Mozambique remained unchanged.[31] This may have served to offset, at least in part, the high re-export duties charged at Mozambique Island, and may thus have played a role in sustaining Vāniyā involvement in Southeast Africa into the 1830s and 1840s, when Kutchi Bhātiyā competition in the cloth and ivory trades would serve as the catalyst for another reorientation of Vāniyā commerce, a return to Red Sea ports such as Massawa, albeit in a very different commercial environment.

Business organization

The capacity of Vāniyā merchants to redeploy their capital resources to the African markets of the southwestern Indian Ocean relied, to a significant degree, on the nature of their business organization. How merchants managed and channelled their investments into commercial enterprises and transactions, considerations that were particularly important for

---

[28] AHU, Moç., Cx 86 Doc. 22, Pedro Antonio José da Cunha to D. Rodrigo de Souza Coutinho, 9 October 1800.

[29] In 1803 exports to India were charged 4 per cent (AHU, Moç., Cx 107 Doc. 102, "Mappa do rendimento que houve...", n.d. [but 1804]), and in 1812 they were set at 6 per cent (Cx 140 Doc. 8, "Rendimento d'Alfandega...", 10 January 1812). Some officials regarded these fiscal changes as particularly favouring the Vāniyā. See AHU, Códice 1366, Luis Pinto de Souza to D. Diogo de Souza, 1796.

[30] HAG, Feitoria de Surrate 2603, Joze Ribeiro to Joze Gomes Loureiro, 1 December 1788; same to same, 2 March 1789.

[31] Alexandre Lobato, *História do Presídio de Lourenço Marques (1787–1799)*, 2 vols. (Lisbon: Tipografia Minerva, 1960), II, 310–13.

merchants involved in long-distance trade, were often determining factors in whether these would develop and be successful or not.

Vāniyā merchants structured their trade in the Indian Ocean around the basic organizational unit of the family firm whose members financed the circulation of goods and capital between India and Africa.[32] Family firms represented important means of capitalist enterprise in South Asia, as they did elsewhere in the early modern Indian Ocean. There is general agreement among scholars of merchant networks that the extended family was crucial for the expansion of trade in a variety of commercial environments and among a diverse body of trading groups.[33] Relying on kin as business allies has therefore been seen as a central component in the rise and growth of merchant networks. But the incorporation of non-kin into merchant networks was also necessary for a variety of reasons, not least of which was the need to expand what was a limited pool of organizational labour.

Although details of the kind that are available for Armenian, Sephardic and other merchant networks regarding family firms do not exist for Vāniyā merchants, it is nonetheless possible from the available evidence to present a picture (incomplete as it may be) of how Gujarati family firms organized their trade between India and the African shores of the south-western Indian Ocean.[34] Firms were structured hierarchically around senior members whose experience and especially their mercantile reputation were indispensable resources. Among their responsibilities, which they shared with others, was raising capital for the firm's commercial pursuits both in regional trade in India and in long-distance trade across the Indian Ocean. Heads of family firms did not travel to Africa but remained in Diu from where they oversaw business operations. Instead, senior kin members were sent overseas as partners, entrusted with the daily running of the firm's investments and trade. They travelled with junior kin members, often young or considerably younger men of the immediate extended family who had been introduced at an early age to the particularities of both the Indian and the African commercial environments. "Uncles", "nephews" and "cousins" were thus engaged in trade within Mozambique where they were afforded the freedom to organize the

---

[32] HAG, CDm 1065, Modi ... Rustomji (?) to Governor, 15 January 1816.

[33] Sebouh David Aslanian, *From the Indian Ocean to the Mediterranean: The Global Trade Networks of Armenian Merchants from New Julfa* (Berkeley: University of California Press, 2011), 144–5. See also Jack Goody, *The East in the West* (New York: Cambridge University Press, 1996), 138–62.

[34] See, for example, Aslanian, *From the Indian Ocean*; Francesca Trivellato, *The Familiarity of Strangers: The Sephardic Diaspora, Livorno, and Cross-Cultural Trade in the Early Modern Period* (New Haven: Yale University Press, 2009); Markovits, *Global World*.

trade in cloth and all commodity purchases, along with extending credit to African and European merchants and transferring profits to India.[35]

Junior members, the "travelling traders of Asia", made up the largest proportion of each firm's representatives in Mozambique, and it was they who were periodically the targets of complaints by both Portuguese authorities and private traders from the middle of the eighteenth century as their numbers and commercial importance grew in the African commercial sphere.[36] They circulated between Mozambique Island, the mainland directly opposite the island and ports along the southern coasts such as Quelimane. Junior members were also sent regularly upriver from Quelimane to Sena, a significant trading centre in the Zambesi Valley, where Vāniyā merchants established a presence in the 1770s to trade in cloth and ivory.

In many cases, kin members occupied the same position within a family firm's hierarchy. However, distinctions based on age, experience and reputation mostly determined one's place in this hierarchy. In the Punjia family, for example, Pitambar Punjia occupied the position of "partner" in Mozambique while his brother, Motichand Punjia, served as a "clerk". While we lack details about the precise nature of, and relationship between, these positions, it appears that Pitambar had his own financial investments in the firm, in contrast to Motichand who did not have funds invested or direct access to the operational capital of the firm.[37]

Kin members of family firms received some, if not considerable, training in early childhood in accounting and in the methods of the family business before leaving for Mozambique at a young age, where they were presented with an opportunity to develop their commercial skills and knowledge of the family business further.[38] The preparation of young boys for the responsibilities of a junior member was an important element of a firm's structure. Whether training was formalized, through specific institutions such as a trade school, is unclear. Certainly no evidence has surfaced for the kind of centralized training institution that existed in the

[35] HAG, CDm 1067, Karamchand Harchand to Manoel Joze Gomes Loureiro, March 1821; AHU, Moç., Cx 105 Doc. 36, Amarchand Jalal to Governor-General, ant. 7 March 1804; Cx 54 Doc. 16, Passport, Premchand Uddhavji, Terras Firmes, ant. 24 June 1782.

[36] AHU, Moç., Cx 32 Doc. 97-A, Anonymous to Governor-General, post 1779; Cx 36 Doc. 35, Joze Per.e Nobre, Duarte Aurelio de Menzes et al. to Governor-General, 14 July 1781.

[37] AHU, Moç., Cx 128 Doc. 20, Debts owed to Antonio Fernandes de Matteos by Pitambar Punjia and Motichand Punjia, n.d. [but 1809].

[38] This was a common practice among South Asian merchants. See, for example, Irfan Habib, "Merchant Communities in Precolonial India", in James Tracey (ed.), The Rise of Merchant Empires: Long-Distance Trade in the Early Modern World, 1350–1750 (Cambridge University Press, 1990), 383–4.

seventeenth and eighteenth centuries to instruct young Julfan Armenian merchants in the "arts of commerce". Merchants from Julfa, members of a wide-ranging merchant network encompassing the Mediterranean and parts of the Indian Ocean, appear to have received training in a special trade school that had been established in the compound of the All Saviour's Monastery in Julfa.[39] The Julfan case, though, appears to be unique among early modern merchant networks. What occurred with Vāniyā merchants, as it did more widely in South Asian networks, was that instruction in essential skills such as arithmetic and accounting was conducted informally by senior family members whose transfer of such knowledge among the young members of the family firm was part of a merchant's business education.[40]

Young boys thus travelled with family firms' representatives to Mozambique, where they occupied the most junior ranks. A population list from 1820, for example, enumerated the number of merchant houses on Mozambique Island and each one listed its members according to their "rank". The names of the "principal" or senior merchant(s), in all but two cases the oldest members of the merchant house, were followed by their "servants" or "attendants", members of the family firm, and ranged in age from 15 to 45.[41] Other evidence shows that as many as 20 per cent of Vāniyās in Mozambique were boys between the ages of 10 and 19.[42] Laxmichand Motichand, whose biographical sketch began our story in the introduction to this book, was a prominent Vāniyā merchant who (as we shall see in Chapter 5) invested heavily in the African slave trade of the late eighteenth and early nineteenth centuries. He provided credit to both African and European traders and merchants, having arrived in Mozambique in 1761 "with his family" as a young junior member of the family firm. By 1806, when he returned permanently to Diu for unspecified "family reasons", his reputation and that of the firm's was assured as the "most creditworthy and opulent in Mozambique".[43]

Vāniyā family firms were not, however, constituted exclusively of members of the immediate and extended family. Although the evidence is fragmentary, it appears that in addition to junior family members who

---

[39] Aslanian, *From the Indian Ocean*, 136–8.
[40] AHU, Moç., Cx 47 Doc. 39, "Registo da carta que a Camara escreveo...", n.d.
[41] ANTT, Ministerio do Reino, Maço 499, Cx. 622, "Mapa Geral dos Bananes...", 5 December 1820; Jeronimo José Nogueira de Andrade, "Descripção do Estado ... de Mossambique nos fins de Novembro de 1789...", *Arquivo das Colonias*, I (1917), 233.
[42] *DAM*, II, 114–15. Young adults aged between 20 and 29 constituted 42 per cent of the total, making the age group 10–29 responsible for 61 per cent of the Indians enumerated on Mozambique Island in 1830.
[43] AHU, Moç., Cx 96 Doc. 54, "Declaration of Lacamichande Motichande", n.d. [but 1803]; Códice 1374, "Segundo Protesto", n.d. [but 1807].

travelled regularly across the Indian Ocean, Vāniyā family firms also employed individuals from outside the family to work in the Africa trade.[44] The use of such agents was not unique to Vāniyās but was shared by such groups as the Chettiars and Khojas, as well as Sindhi merchants, where it took the form of the *shah-gumāshta* ("credit-agent") system.[45] Agents were, in all cases for which records exist, Vāniyā by caste and were based primarily in Diu for reasons related to monitoring trust among merchants, a theme taken up later in the chapter. How they became part of a family firm is unclear but it is likely, given the social and commercial value placed on reputation and hence trustworthiness, that they were recruited based on their or their family's "name". Knowledge of an individual's standing within the commercial milieu of Diu was shared informally among merchants through a verbal culture in which "talk and rumour" (and gambling among merchants on when ships might arrive from overseas) were apparently widespread on the island.[46] While this may have made obtaining reliable information about someone's commercial history challenging, requiring reliance on a trusted source, it did allow family firms to make well-founded decisions about the individuals with whom they wished to work. Having an unsound reputation would exclude someone from consideration.

Business relationships with agents appear to have been structured around partnerships. "The Banianes", noted an observer in the 1790s, "make agreements with their correspondents who leave Diu for Africa for extended periods and send back from there ivory and other riches of the land."[47] Whether these were finalized orally or in writing is unclear because no partnership documents appear to have survived in the archives. Details of their terms are therefore unavailable; however, fragmentary evidence suggests that Vāniyā merchants sent agents across the western Indian Ocean on contracts resembling the *shah-gumastha* partnership, whereby, according to Claude Markovits, "a capitalist partner, called *shah*, advanced the funds to one or several working partners called *gumasthas*, for a specific kind of business operation for a certain duration of time, and was remunerated by a share of the profits".[48]

---

[44] Whether any of these individuals may have had affine ties is impossible to tell from the available evidence.
[45] Rajat Kanta Ray, "Asian Capital in the Age of European Domination: The Rise of the Bazaar, 1800–1914", *Modern Asian Studies*, 29, 3 (1995), 536; Markovits, *Global World*, 157–66, 176–8.
[46] HAG, CD 1001, Belchior do Amaral de Menezes to Governor, 28 April 1788.
[47] HAG, CD 1003, Felix Joze ... da Gama to Governor, 7 January 1805.
[48] Markovits, *Global World*, 85. See also 157–76 for a detailed discussion of the system among Sindhi merchants.

While Markovits describes this system in relation to two merchant networks from Sind, the Shikarpuri and Hyderabadi networks, who maintained widespread business and commercial operations throughout a number of locales stretching from Latin America to East Asia in the nineteenth and first half of the twentieth centuries, variants existed in other South Asian merchant networks. Multanis, for example, staffed their branch offices with agents who were sent abroad under *shah-gumastha* partnership agreements, while in the case of Nattukottai Chettiars, "principals" (who remained in India) hired agents and "field staff" who ran the daily operations of their overseas business.[49] In this way, agents would travel great distances to specific locales where the family firm had business interests, where they would assume responsibility for its commercial operations. They made decisions and took actions to guide the business and to generate the profits in which they and the sedentary capitalists who had advanced them trade goods and money were invested. Profits were divided with the latter according to a pre-arranged share, usually around a third.[50]

Vāniyā partnership agreements appear mostly to have lasted from a few years up to several decades. Danji Natthu, for instance, returned to Diu in 1782 to conclude his partnership after having been in Mozambique for seven years. Another agent, however, spent 45 years working throughout the African territory before sailing back to India in 1806.[51] Being away from home for such long periods was not unusual in the early modern merchant world, as the evidence for Julfan *commenda* agents attests.[52] These extended periods allowed merchants to establish themselves and their reputations firmly and thereby create or continue, and in many cases expand, a firm's commercial interests in an area or region.

The agency system was also, according to Rajat Kanta Ray, "instrumental in the acquirement of skills, experience and connections which

---

[49] Markovits recognizes the existence of variants and makes reference to Nattukottai Chettiars, for which see the in-depth study by David West Rudner, *Caste and Capitalism in Colonial India: The Nattukottai Chettiars* (Berkeley: University of California Press, 1994). For Multanis, see Stephen Frederic Dale, *Indian Merchants and Eurasian Trade, 1600–1750* (Cambridge University Press, 1994); and Scott Camerson Levi, *The Indian Diaspora in Central Asia* (Boston: Brill, 2002); *idem*, "Multanis and Shikarpuris: Indian Diasporas in Historical Perspective", in Gijsbert Oonk (ed.), *Global Indian Diasporas: Exploring Trajectories of Migration and Theory* (Amsterdam University Press, 2008), 31–65.

[50] Aslanian, *From the Indian Ocean*, 222.

[51] AHU, Cx 39 Doc. 36, "Requerimento de Dangy Nattu e sobrinho", ant. 29 August 1782; Cx 90 Doc. 21, Izidro...(?) to Rodrigo de Souza Coutinho, 8 November 1801; Cx 96 Doc. 54, "Declaração de Lacamichande Motichande", n.d. [but 1803]; Códice 1374, "Segundo Protesto", n.d. [but *c.* 1806].

[52] Aslanian, *From the Indian Ocean*, 220–5. Among other South Asian groups such as the Multanis, contracts were of a shorter duration, with agents away from home for around three years.

would eventually enable the agents to set up independent firms of their own".[53] While there is no way of telling how often this may have happened among Vāniyā family firms in the eighteenth century, there is evidence to suggest that it was not uncommon. Purshottam Jivaji served in Mozambique as an agent for the family firm of Anandji Jivan and once he concluded his contract, used the knowledge and capital he had accumulated from trading in Mozambique to set up an independent business with two brothers, creating a new family firm in the late 1790s.[54] How agents concluded their involvement with a family firm before they were able to establish themselves independently is unclear but likely involved either an oral or written agreement acknowledging the termination of the partnership after all accounts – perhaps by presenting account books, as in the Julfan Armenian case – had been settled. Failing to do so would have placed an agent at great risk of damaging his reputation, trustworthiness and credit that were essential elements of mercantile life, and for establishing a new firm.

Vāniyā merchants did not, however, only establish and maintain business relationships with each other. By necessity, they had to engage African intermediaries in Mozambique who were instrumental in transporting Gujarati cotton textiles from the coast into interior markets and, in exchange, organize the purchase and delivery of goods such as ivory tusks for the Indian merchants at the coast. On Macuana, the mainland directly opposite Mozambique Island, Vāniyā merchants relied on African agents called *patamares*, who would travel from the coast to meet the large Yao trading caravans of the interior as well as regional Makua traders. Although its etymological origins are obscure, it appears that the term was a composite of words from one or more Indic languages and was often used to refer to a "messenger" or "courier" in southern and western India. A *"pattamar"* in the subcontinent was highly mobile but did more than simply transport trade goods – they played an important role in information gathering and sharing and were thus "figures central to the provision of intelligence and mediation in the mercantile and political spheres".[55] It is unclear when the term began to be used in the African context but it may have been appropriated by the Portuguese in India and re-applied on the other side of the Indian Ocean where it became part of a broader

---

[53] Ray, "Asian Capital", 536.
[54] HAG, CD 1003, Purshottam Jivaji to Tenente General, 23 August 1796.
[55] Gagan Sood, "The Informational Fabric of Eighteenth-Century India and the Middle East: Couriers, Intermediaries and Postal Communication", *Modern Asian Studies*, 43, 5 (2009), 1097. My discussion of *pattamar* relies entirely on Sood.

trans-oceanic imperial lexicon.[56] The term would, of course, have been familiar to Gujarati merchants who used it in their commercial correspondence with one another and with Portuguese authorities.[57] As already noted, African *patamares* were engaged by Vāniyā merchants to organize the sale and distribution of textile cargoes in the interior of northern Mozambique, in return for which they primarily purchased ivory tusks and brought these to the coast in large quantities. For these exchanges to take place successfully, *patamares* needed to make payments to chiefs whose land they traversed en route to meeting Yao caravans. They were therefore important intermediaries in the chains that connected Gujarati merchants to cloth consumers and to the products of the African interior.

The terms on which a *patamar* worked for Vāniyā are unavailable, as they appear to have been made orally through verbal agreements that were renegotiated upon the return of the African agent. This was probably standard practice for merchants, given that functional literacy was limited in the eighteenth century to a small minority in Mozambique.[58] Verbal agreements were premised on the reputation of the *patamares* that had been established through frequent interactions, and where loyal service was rewarded with the continued use of their services. These agents acted autonomously on behalf of Gujarati merchants with buyers and sellers in the African interior, and were therefore able to advance goods on credit to Yao merchants. They received payment for their service once they returned to the coast in a system that in certain respects may have been similar to the commission agency utilized in the early modern mercantile world by merchants such as the Sephardim and others. In commission agencies, defined mostly by short-term contracts, a "commission agent was normally rewarded with a percentage of value of the transactions that he conducted ... and seized the best available market opportunities".[59] In being entrusted with the trade goods of Gujarati merchants, often for extensive periods that lasted for a year or longer, *patamares* assumed responsibility for selling their cargoes at profitable rates for their mercantile sponsors upon whom they relied for credit but who, in turn, needed their participation because of the information they collected and the

---

[56] See, for instance, the discussion in Sebastião Dalgado, *Glossário Luso-Asiático*, 2 vols. (Coimbra: Imprensa da Universidade, 1919), I, 186.

[57] HAG, CM 1445, Vāniyā merchants to Castellão, 12 May 1787.

[58] This limitation was likely common throughout many of the lands of the western Indian Ocean, as it was in "Islamicate Eurasia" in the eighteenth century. See Gagan Sood, "'Correspondence is Equal to Half a Meeting': The Composition and Comprehension of Letters in Eighteenth-Century Islamic Eurasia", *Journal of the Economic and Social History of the Orient*, 50, 2–3 (2007), 175, fn. 5.

[59] Trivellato, *Familiarity of Strangers*, 153. Chapter 6 of this work provides an excellent discussion of commission agencies.

knowledge they accumulated about interior markets. This was invaluable in guiding Vāniyā business decisions, particularly with regard to quantities and styles of cloth cargoes that were indispensable to long-distance trade and which put Gujarati trade at an advantage over Portuguese competitors.

The focal location for the interaction and relationship between Vāniyā merchants and *patamares* were *palmares*, tracts of land on the mainland opposite Mozambique Island, on which Gujaratis maintained houses for warehousing and meeting purposes. As I discuss later in the chapter, Gujaratis had acquired them in many cases as a result of Portuguese merchants (in some cases officials) defaulting on loans they had secured from Vāniyās against the properties. Although some of the *palmares* were rented from the Portuguese, they were mostly owned by Gujarati merchants. Indeed, according to one claim about Mossuril (a much frequented settlement a short distance on the mainland north of Mozambique Island), "no building had escaped possession by the Vāniyā".[60] Although a list compiled in 1781 of owners of *palmares* suggests this may have been an exaggeration based more on perception than reality, Vāniyā ownership in Mossuril was indeed high and had been growing. In other parts of Macuana, they owned "most of the houses, goods, slaves, cattle, buildings and *palmares*".[61]

These properties served essentially as trading posts where cotton textiles and other goods were stored for distribution into the interior and where ivory was brought primarily before being taken to Mozambique Island for shipment across the western Indian Ocean to India. They were also sites where details of *patamar* agreements were finalized and where Gujarati merchants had sexual relations with African women, the male offspring of which were often raised to become *patamares*. While there are no details about how these relationships were formed or whether African children received specialized training to work specifically with Vāniyā, they were an additional source of commercial labour from which Gujarati merchants could draw in the eighteenth and nineteenth centuries.

When the scope of Gujarati commercial activity broadened in the 1760s and 1770s to the Zambesi Valley, as part of efforts to penetrate ivory markets more directly, Gujarati merchants relied on the services of other, equally important, African agents. Vāniyā established trading stores in Sena, a trading settlement on the Zambesi River that had been in existence

---

[60] AHU, Moç., Cx 36 Doc. 35, Joze Per.ᵉ Nobre, Duarte Aurelio de Menzes et al. to Governor-General, 14 July 1781.
[61] AHU, Moç., Cx 40 Doc. 10, Saldanha de Albuquerque to de Melo e Castro, 12 December 1782. Antonio Rita-Ferreira has suggested that a by-product of ownership of property on the coastal mainland for the Vāniyā was coconut palms, which provided "purified" food. See "Moçambique e os Naturais da Índia Portuguesa", 631.

since at least the fourteenth and fifteenth centuries (serving first coastal Muslim traders and later Afro-Portuguese as it became in the seventeenth century an important administrative and commercial centre, and a departure point for caravans bound for its northern and southern hinterlands), and engaged the services of professionalized African traders, the *vashambadzi*, drawn from the Chikunda of the Zambesi Valley. Sena served as a base from which to organize trade into the Manica and Barue regions of the interior, in particular to the trading fairs such as Masekesa that were "centres of commercial enterprise". While in the seventeenth century individual Portuguese residents had sent trading expeditions from Sena, this changed in the eighteenth as increasingly trade was conducted by the *vashambadzi* due to political vicissitudes that resulted in powerful Rozvi chiefs denying the Portuguese and others direct access to their country. In such a context, the *vashambadzi* emerged as the leading African agents for both Portuguese and Gujarati merchant firms. "[T]heir leaders", Malyn Newitt has argued, "were able to organize porters and negotiate their passage through the lands of different chiefs. They knew the best routes to the fairs and what goods the market required."[62] This included trading to Zumbo, a settlement and redistributive base far up the Zambesi River from Sena, that in the third quarter of the eighteenth century was an important centre of ivory supplies coming from the East-Central African interior. *Vashambadzi*, then, were lynchpins in African trade, leading caravans through lands where travel was often difficult because of the terrain or political circumstances, and where passing through a territory always required the payment of a gift to be permitted to do so. These African agents were organized, disciplined and assumed many of the physical risks of commercial life in eighteenth-century Zambesia.[63]

Because they were made orally, details of the agreements reached between Vāniyā merchants and *vashambadzi* are as elusive as they are for *patamares*. It is possible, nonetheless, to get a sense of the nature of the relationship from scattered and partial evidence. Agreements were made verbally about such practical matters as the volume of goods to be traded but, generally, *vashambadzi* were given a great deal of latitude to achieve the best possible trading outcomes during the many months that they were away in the African interior. Gujarati merchants could not control supply

---

[62] Malyn Newitt, *A History of Mozambique* (Bloomington: Indiana University Press, 1995), 199. The previous quote is from 198.

[63] Allen and Barbara Isaacman provide an excellent discussion of the *vashambadzi* in their recent history of the Chikunda from the middle of the eighteenth century to the first decades of Portuguese colonial rule in Mozambique in *Slavery and Beyond: The Making of Men and Chikunda Ethnic Identities in the Unstable World of South-Central Africa, 1750–1920* (Portsmouth, NH: Heinemann, 2004).

and prices and were therefore reliant, to a large degree, on the crucial information that the *vashambadzi* provided about market conditions to respond appropriately and effectively.[64]

Caravans led by *vashambadzi* from Sena in the lower Zambesi region could be attacked if there was disorder on the Sena *prazos* (leased Crown estates that formed the core of the Afro-Portuguese society of Zambesia) or in Barue, as often happened. Escaped slaves from the Sena *prazos* or dissident Barue headmen "building themselves strongholds in the broken escarpment country from which they could raid the trading caravans or plunder the villages of the prazos" were thus a permanent threat.[65] Trading to Zumbo was physically challenging and involved sailing by boat up the Zambesi River to Tete and porterage by land around the treacherous Cabora Bassa rapids; beyond the rapids, goods were once more transported by river past banks controlled by the *Monomotapa* who demanded payment from passing caravans. Additionally, caravans were attacked and robbed by starving populations whenever drought affected agricultural production, as occurred in the 1760s and again in the "great cycle of drought" that lasted from the mid-1790s until the 1830s. Under such fraught conditions, where the entire cargo of a *vashambadzi*'s caravan could be lost and effectively spell the end of their trading season, Vāniyā agreements were informal and established under generalized terms.[66]

An additional factor made this possible and highlighted a key difference from the relationship Gujarati merchants established with *patamares*: the *vashambadzi* were of slave status. However, they were not "enslaved" individuals in the sense that they could be sold or their movement circumscribed by a "master"; rather, social relationships were complex and slave status was, to a degree, malleable. It approximated that of a patron–client in which the former provided credit and trade goods that enabled the latter to function as a quasi-independent trader. The support and backing that Vāniyā (and Portuguese *senhores* of the *prazos*) provided *vashambadzi*, particularly during volatile periods, was an important source of both financial and – by the mid- to late eighteenth century – social and perhaps even political distinction in an environment in which being without a patron meant being vulnerable and therefore at risk. In the first few decades of the nineteenth century, increasingly this meant risk of enslavement as slave trading grew in the region for markets in the western Indian Ocean and also in the southern Atlantic.[67]

Although there were instances when *vashambadzi* did not repay the goods that they had been provided on credit or absconded with cloth

---

[64] *Ibid.*   [65] Newitt, *History of Mozambique*, 212.   [66] *Ibid.*, 213–16.
[67] Isaacman and Isaacman, *Slavery and Beyond.*

cargoes, the particular nature of the relationship and the economic incentives and benefits derived from continued cooperation (in particular access to Gujarati cotton textiles that were central to material exchange) mitigated against opportunistic and dishonest behaviour.[68] Precisely how Gujarati merchants first established relationships with *vashambadzi* is unavailable, but in serving their patrons, these African agents were guaranteed a regular supply of trade goods in a relationship defined more by mutuality than by subservience.

Gujarati merchants also established business relationships with European merchants, especially Portuguese, French and Brazilian slavers who began to ship captives from the Mozambique coast in increasing number from the middle of the eighteenth century. Vāniyā had entered into partnerships with Portuguese merchants before the growth of slave trading in the southwestern Indian Ocean, of course, primarily for the supply of Gujarati cotton textiles, and some worked as brokers for high officials; these relationships developed out of necessity for the Portuguese, whose reliance on Vāniyā as importers of cloths that were considered the "currency of the land" and as providers of crucial financial services (discussed below) was inescapable. These business relationships with Europeans continued once the slave trade developed from the 1750s and 1760s, and in some cases deepened as Gujarati merchants entered into partnerships with some prominent Portuguese slavers with interests in the Mascarenes, Cape colony and Brazilian trades.[69] Partnerships with Portuguese slavers were established for short periods and for specific voyages or purposes. For example, the prominent Vāniyā merchant Shobhachand Sowchand went into partnership with Joaquim do Rosario Monteiro in the early nineteenth century for voyages to the Cape colony where they sold slaves purchased on the Mozambique coast to Dutch and British buyers. Through Monteiro, whose mercantile connections seem to have stretched to Rio de Janeiro, the pair extended their involvement as partners in slaving to the southern Atlantic. Apart from providing financial capital for the voyages in the form of credit and textiles, Shobhachand purchased slaving vessels in Mauritius on which Monteiro sailed along

---

[68] Bruce Hall has noted that Muslim merchants used slaves in the nineteenth-century Sahara to conduct trade on their behalf as a commercial strategy aimed at reducing risk. See "How Slaves used Islam: The Letters of Enslaved Muslim Commercial Agents in the Nineteenth-Century Niger Bend and Central Sahara", *Journal of African History*, 52, 3 (2011), 279–97; and "Enslaved Paths of Circulation in the Sahara: Commercial Networks and Slave Agency between Ghadames (Libya) and Timbuktu (Mali) in the Nineteenth Century", in Chouki el Hamel and Paul Lovejoy (eds.), *Confluence of Cultures* (Princeton: Marcus Wiener, forthcoming).

[69] The details of these relationships are discussed in Chapter 5.

the Southeast African coast and from which the Portuguese merchant organized the actual shipment of slaves.

As with Vāniyā merchants' other trading relationships, it is unclear whether these kinds of partnerships were based on written agreements or formal contracts because none appear to have survived. Although documents detailing business relationships, such as letters of credit, bills of exchange and customs records with freighting manifests exist in the archival record, partnership agreements or contracts are conspicuously absent. It thus seems likely that, as with African agents, agreements about the terms of the partnership and its duration were verbal. As a Portuguese official suggests, merchants "meet in private at their houses and agree their business after much discussion".[70] While partnerships, such as that entered into between Shobhachand and Monteiro, were not unique, it was only the most highly capitalized Gujarati merchants who were able to establish such agreements because they entailed significant financial contributions possible for only a few of the wealthiest Vāniyā family firms.

There is also evidence that Gujarati merchants sold cloths to French slave merchants on contract and may have established partnerships with Brazilian merchants from the early nineteenth century; however, its limited nature makes it difficult to arrive at definitive conclusions about how the small number of these particular business relationships were formalized. It is reasonable to suggest, nonetheless, that as opportunities arose to enter directly into the slave trade through partnership agreements, Gujarati merchants with adequate financial means would have considered each possibility carefully in a context in which the slave trade was becoming dominant in the economy of East-Central Africa from the late eighteenth century.

Equally, this applied to the business arrangements that were developed with merchants and independent Swahili rulers of the northern Mozambique coast. Gujarati merchants had established commercial relationships in the 1760s and 1770s with "Arab" and Swahili merchants from Zanzibar, Kilwa, Pate and the Comoros who visited Ibo, one of larger islands of the Querimba archipelago located to the north of Mozambique Island, Quitangonha and Cabaceira Pequena (settlements on the mainland opposite Mozambique Island) to purchase cotton cloths seasonally for the coastal slave trade. When available, Vāniyā also purchased ivory from these merchants.[71] Elsewhere, Gujarati merchants traded regularly

---

[70] HAG, CM 1446, Mello e Castro to Cunha de Menezes, 7 August 1788.

[71] AHU, Cx 56 Doc. 40, Antonio...(?) to de Morães, 24 December 1788; Códice 1324 and 1329; AHU, Moç., Cx 57 Doc. 34, Antonio José Tigre to Governor, 18 April 1789; Cx 57 Doc. 31, Manoel Felipe de Menezes to Tigre, 3 April 1789; Anon, "Memorias da Costa d'Africa ... 1762", in RMS, 220.

along the stretch of coast immediately to the south of Mozambique Island, at Sancul and Sangage that were ruled as independent sheikhdoms with whom the Portuguese had maintained strained relations. Their proximity to Mozambique Island made sailing there relatively easy, and voyages took place well into the nineteenth century under encouragement, especially from the sheikhdom of Sangage. Despite competition between Sancul and Sangage, and the disruptions that this sometimes caused to Gujarati commerce, Vāniyā managed to trade successfully at the latter with Makua merchants, who were leading African traders, in the first quarter of the nineteenth century.[72]

The sustained mercantile activity with merchants in Ibo and at these Muslim settlements suggests that Gujarati merchants, at the very least, would have either entered into partnerships or reached trading agreements orally. Although trade was necessarily seasonal, Vāniyā were in regular contact with these areas and "carried news and information back and forth" to Mozambique Island.[73] Unusually, in Sangage, they established a political alliance with the ruling class and managed to exert considerable political influence over the sheikhdom as it sought economic expansion.[74] This influence, related to their mercantile capacity to supply cotton textiles that were vital for exchange along the coast and interior, may have negated the need for written agreements or contracts, as the incentives for the sheikh or Makua merchants to act dishonestly or behave deceitfully would have been low because the gains could not match those from honest cooperation.

In India, also, Vāniyā business organization required commercial arrangements with non-Vāniyā, the most important of which were established with cloth brokers (dalals). These individuals served as critical intermediaries in connecting cloth weavers in Jambusar, a cotton-producing and weaving centre in the interior of Gujarat that produced the overwhelming bulk of African textiles for the Mozambique trade, to Vāniyā merchants who through them were able to convey detailed information – likely through pattern books as I suggest in Chapter 3 – about textile styles and patterns most in demand among African consumers of the southwestern Indian Ocean. Brokers travelled to Diu and Daman annually to collect this information, deliver cargoes, settle outstanding debts for the advances they had made of textiles in a previous trading season or seasons and agree prices for the different types of textiles that were

---

[72] Nancy Jane Hafkin, "Trade, Society and Politics in Northern Mozambique, c. 1753–1913", PhD diss., Boston University, 1973.

[73] HAG, CM 1447, Antonio da Cruz e Almeida et al. to Jose Francisco Alves Barboza, 11 July 1818

[74] Hafkin, "Trade, Society and Politics".

sought by merchants in the following year. A broker, with whom a number of merchants could have agreements, conveyed textile orders to further intermediaries in Jambusar who in turn dealt directly with weavers. This protected weavers from direct contact with merchants and brokers, and thereby shielded them from possible harassment and exploitation in a practice that was common elsewhere in India.[75]

Brokers received cash advances, and in many cases ivory tusks, as payment from Vāniyā for cloth orders, though they were able also to provide textiles to merchants on credit in a system that seems to have rested entirely on verbal agreements.[76] Despite the possibility that weavers could refuse to honour their agreements with brokers (even after they had received cash advances to purchase raw materials such as yarn) and could therefore place both brokers and merchants in precarious positions, and despite the tensions that could arise between Gujarati merchants and *dalals* over the settlement of payments for cloths, this aspect of Vāniyā business organization operated effectively because it functioned as a mutually dependent system.

As much as merchants relied on weavers and brokers to supply them with African cloths, weavers depended on merchant capital for investment in their manufactures and for access to the ocean's export markets; in addition, they were protected from market fluctuations. Equally, brokers were reliant on the money and credit arrangements secured from Vāniyā, who also guaranteed purchase, for their textile procurement in the interior of Gujarat. Shared economic interests underlay these relationships and motivated cooperative behaviour among the different parties. The economic incentives offered by repeated interaction, then, outweighed any immediate benefits that may have been derived from cheating or dishonest conduct.[77]

"Not ideal men": trust, reputation and merchant competition

Central to the structure and maintenance of mercantile life, and an essential factor in long-distance trade, was trust. Commercial exchange

---

[75] This point is developed in Chapter 3.

[76] These may even have been preferred because, as noted earlier in the chapter, literacy was limited to relatively few individuals. Gagan Sood has argued that in eighteenth-century Surat and Bombay, these limitations prompted merchants to favour oral contracts over written ones. See "'Correspondence is Equal to Half a Meeting'". The ivory economy is discussed in ch. 4 of the book.

[77] I draw here on arguments in Sebastian Prange, "'Trust in God but Tie Your Camel First:' The Economic Organization of the Trans-Saharan Slave Trade Between the Fourteenth and Nineteenth Centuries", *Journal of Global History*, 1, 2 (2006), 219–39.

and agreements required confidence and shared expectations among merchants and agents that they would not be deceived or defrauded by the other party.[78] Being able to trust a fellow merchant with investment capital or trade goods was particularly important in contexts where contract uncertainty existed or enforcement through formal legal institutions was either non-existent or ineffective. In short, trust was fundamental in enabling business and commercial transactions to occur both between merchants, their brokers and intermediaries and between them and the bankers on whom they relied for the provision of finance.

Trust was intimately bound up with notions of reputability and creditworthiness that were integral to the functioning of merchant networks where a merchant's "name" – whether they could be regarded as "creditworthy" and therefore men of "public credit" or not – was determined by prior experience of the individual and evidence of past behaviour. It was thus a highly significant aspect of economic exchange for merchant networks generally. Among Chinese merchants in the Philippines, for instance, *xinyong* ("trustworthiness") was considered important for concluding commercial transactions successfully, while for Nattukottai Chettiar merchants from South India, active in Burma and Southeast Asia in the nineteenth century, *nanayam* (a reputation for trustworthiness) was essential to "attract deposits or reassure clients of honesty (or, at least predictability) and flexibility in the extension of credit". For eighteenth-century Armenian merchants, trust and reputation "were crucial factors in organizing long-distance trade".[79] Maintaining a good reputation and being regarded as trustworthy were indispensable assets without which it became difficult – and in certain instances even impossible – to sustain trade and business relationships. Once sullied, a merchant's reputation and thus credit would induce a loss of trust among his peers and thereby reduce his opportunities or, at worst, terminally damage long-term business prospects.

While scholars of merchant networks have recognized the centrality of trust to the functioning of markets and trade, they have often assumed it

---

[78] Aslanian, *From the Indian Ocean*, 166.

[79] *Ibid.*, 179. The quote about Nattukottai Chettiar merchants is from Rudner, *Caste and Capitalism*, 109. See also Rudner, "Banker's Trust and the Culture of Banking among the Nattukottai Chettiars of Colonial South India", *Modern Asian Studies*, 23, 3 (1989), 417–58. On Chinese merchants in the Philippines, see Wong Kwok-Chu, *The Chinese in the Philippine Economy 1898–1941* (Quezon City: Ateneo de Manila University Press, 1999), ch. 5; Rajat Kanta Ray, "Chinese Financiers and Chetti Bankers in Southern Waters: Asian Mobile Credit during the Anglo-Dutch Competition for the Trade of the Eastern Archipelago in the Nineteenth Century", *Itinerario*, 11, 1 (1987), 209–34. See also Michael Adas, "Immigrant Asians and the Economic Impact of European Imperialism: The Role of the South Indian Chettiars in British Burma", *Journal of Asian Studies*, 33, 3 (1974), 385–401.

to be a natural outcome of affective links, ties of family and of "closely knit communities" connected by religion, ethnicity or caste.[80] It is thus assumed that these ties among what are often conceptualized in romanticized terms as "communities of mercantile trust" remove the need for trust-building measures. In other words, trust is seen to exist as a "self-evident attribute of a merchant community".[81] Recently, however, scholars influenced by the New Institutional Economics have begun to explore trust as a rational calculation made by merchants in their commercial dealings and business transactions with fellow merchants. While contracting trade agreements with family, kin, caste or ethnic members may require less trust-building measures, it did not remove them entirely.

Rather, merchants involved in long-distance commercial arrangements made use of a number of measures and mechanisms to generate and regulate trust. The work of Avner Greif, in particular, has been influential in developing a reputation-based informal model of trust in which merchants are able to establish a linkage between past conduct and future utility through multilateral chains of information transmission.[82] His examination of a particular North African Jewish group (the so-called Maghribi traders) of the eleventh and twelfth centuries revealed that merchants operated as self-interested rational actors who were able effectively "to monitor the integrity of their overseas agents" through the circulation of letters containing information about an individual's actions and commercial behaviour. Merchant letters discouraged dishonesty because exposure meant sanctioning and marginalization, with the resultant serious damage to one's reputation.[83] In this context of information transmission, then, interest in maintaining an unblemished reputation provided merchants with an incentive to conduct themselves honestly, while at the same time it offered a means by which to establish an agent's trustworthiness based on the experience of other principles.[84] Greif was thus able to show that Maghribi traders, instead of relying on social

---

[80] Francesca Trivellato, "Sephardic Merchants in the Early Modern Atlantic and Beyond: Toward a Comparative Historical Approach to Business Cooperation", in Richard L. Kagan and Philip Morgan (eds.), *Atlantic Diasporas: Jews and Cryto-Jews in the Age of Mercantilism* (Baltimore: Johns Hopkins University Press, 2005), 102 quoted in Aslanian, *From the Indian Ocean*, 167.

[81] Trivellato, *Familiarity of Strangers*, 12.

[82] For example, "The Organization of Long-Distance Trade: Reputation and Coalitions in the Geniza Documents and Genoa during the Eleventh and Twelfth Centuries", *Journal of Economic History*, 51, 2 (1991), 459–62; *idem*, "Contract Enforceability and Economic Institutions in Early Trade: The Maghribi Traders' Coalition", *American Economic Review*, 83, 3 (1993), 525–48; *idem*, *Institutions and the Path to the Modern Economy: Lessons from Medieval Trade* (New York: Cambridge University Press, 2006).

[83] Francesca Trivellato, *Familiarity of Strangers*, 13.   [84] Prange, "Trust in God".

sanctions or ethics to manage their business relationships, used the economic institution of the reputation mechanism to manage and monitor trust among members of their "coalition".[85]

In identifying the role of reputation in regulating trust among medieval merchants and agents, Greif was thus able to demonstrate how informal institutions could play key roles in the organization and functioning of mercantile life. His insights have prompted debate among scholars about the role of institutions in long-distance trade and have generated interest among historians in how trust was actually generated and policed by merchant groups in the past. The recent work of Francesca Trivellato and Sebouh Aslanian is notable for its examination of these themes among the Sephardic diaspora of Livorno and Armenian merchant networks from New Julfa respectively in the seventeenth and eighteenth centuries. Importantly, while drawing extensively on Greif's contributions, Trivellato and Aslanian show that informal institutions, and either semi-formal or formal legal institutions could coexist in creating and monitoring trust among merchant networks.

For the Sephardim, a combination of legal mechanisms (contracts enforceable in tribunals) and "extralegal commitments" enabled by chains of information transmission conducted in the form of letter-writing generated economic incentives and social control. Additionally, expectations were standardized by shared norms of behaviour.[86] Among the early modern Julfan Armenian merchant network, merchants relied on an administrative and legal body known as the Assembly of Merchants to generate and maintain trust among coalition members. This body operated through formal and informal means as a centralized merchant juridical institution to establish trustworthiness and uniform business norms that enabled collective action and cooperation among merchants in Julfa and in Armenian merchant settlements in India and the Mediterranean. The Assembly of Merchants lacked written or codified rules or laws and met only as was required by circumstances, for instance when a petition or appeal was filed by a merchant detailing malfeasance or some form of opportunistic behaviour.[87]

---

[85] *Ibid.*; Avner Greif, "Reputation and Coalitions in Medieval Trade: Evidence on the Maghribi Traders", *Journal of Economic History*, 49, 4 (1989), 857–82. Trivellato provides an excellent summary of Greif's additional insights in *Familiarity of Strangers*, 13–15.

[86] Trivellato, *Familiarity of Strangers*.

[87] An excellent and detailed discussion of the relationship between *jumiat* courts (the so-called Portable Courts) and the Assembly of Merchants, as well as some of the ways in which merchants were compelled to be honest in their dealings with one another, can be found in Aslanian, *From the Indian Ocean*, ch. 7.

Similarly, among Vāniyā merchants, generating and maintaining trust was achieved through a combination of informal reputation-regulating mechanisms and the existence of a semi-formal institution, the Vāniyā *mahajan*. Details of the former are scarce but there is enough evidence to suggest that, as with the Sephardim and New Julfan merchants, the production and transmission of information through merchant letters spread knowledge about who was trustworthy and who was disreputable. Along with cargoes of ivory, cotton cloths and silver specie, Gujarati vessels carried letters back and forth between India and the African coast in which merchants corresponded with one another about commercial opportunities and conditions in Mozambique, and about Vāniyā whose "public credit" had been jeopardized as a result of opportunistic behaviour or close association with an individual of questionable reputation. This correspondence flowing regularly across the ocean, "containing merchant information", performed a regulatory function in spreading information about past behaviour and could thereby consolidate or undermine an individual's reputation.[88] It was critical for merchants to maintain their "public credit" among the commercial community because one's "name" determined expectations about behaviour and was therefore an invaluable intangible asset in business relationships.[89] A merchant's reputation would indeed precede him and informed those seeking to conduct business with him as to what they could "reasonably expect", as well as what sort of financial and commercial demands could be placed upon him for the successful completion of a transaction or business arrangement.[90] Those whose reputations had been impugned and who were, for example, regarded as credit risks or unreliable, would be marginalized and ran the risk of being unable to engage in future trading ventures.

For those with unblemished reputations, however, their creditworthiness and standing among their peers allowed them to operate widely in the Diu, Daman and Mozambique markets, and shielded them from suspicion when they suffered a setback. Kalyanji Tairsi, a Vāniyā merchant and shipowner of Diu, for example, lost a vessel in the voyage to Mozambique in the northeast monsoon of 1792. Although Kalyanji suffered a financial blow as a result of the shipwreck, as a merchant "who always conserved his credit and reputation", he was able to recover from the loss. Kalyanji had insured the ship and its cargo but his creditworthiness and reputation

---

[88] HAG, CD 1002, Diego de Mello … to Governor, 8 February 1791; CD 1003, Chatarbozo Curgy, Anandagi Givane et al. to Governor, November 1796.

[89] Janet Tai Landa, *Trust, Ethnicity and Identity: Beyond the New Institutional Economics of Ethnic Trading Networks, Contract Law, and Gift-Exchange* (Ann Arbor: University of Michigan Press, 1994), 126.

[90] Markovits, *Global World*, 260–1.

allowed him to secure further investment in order to maintain his trading interests in this African branch of his Indian Ocean commerce. Additionally, although the voyage had ended in "failure", because Kalyanji had been in no way responsible for the vessel's misfortune and as dishonesty was seen to have played no part in its loss (i.e. the cause had been the natural force of the monsoon winds), he remained beyond reproach.[91]

The centrality of creditworthiness and reputation in merchant life did not, however, preclude merchants in the eighteenth and nineteenth centuries from accusing one another of dishonesty or fraudulent behaviour that, in its potential to undermine trust in an individual, could threaten their standing in the community. The case of Kassam Manachand is illustrative. In Daman in 1820, Haribhai Kesar and Manachand Savai were partners in the trade of a vessel in the western Indian Ocean. With the death of Haribhai that year, however, Kassam Manachand, as a third partner with whom the deceased had maintained a business relationship, accused Manachand Savai in the Portuguese court of not being one of the dead man's partners. Kassam's motivation in taking this case before the Portuguese judge appears to have derived from a desire to free himself from any possible business obligations towards Manachand. In response, Manachand Savai (a merchant "who lives from his credit") denounced the accusation as wholly false and as severely damaging because "the confidence of other merchants in him was greatly diminished".[92]

Whether there was any truth to what Kassam alleged or not is unclear from the surviving evidence but the case suggests the ease with which a reputation could nonetheless be tarnished. Casting doubt on a merchant's actions, in this case that Manachand Savai either had been trading dishonestly as Haribhai Kesar's partner or was claiming a business relationship with the merchant that had not existed, was enough to make other merchants at least wary if not entirely suspicious of the individual. "Any violence [of an accusatory nature]", a Portuguese observer noted, "that is practised against any of the [Vāniyā] merchants can cause irreparable damage [to their reputation]."[93] In a commercial environment in which gossip and hearsay seem to have been as important as the circulation

---

[91] HAG, Registos Gerais da Feitoria de Diu 7970, "Carta Testemunhavel dos Papeis Malanangy Talcy", n.d. [but *c.* 1796]. David Hardiman also notes more broadly that if it was the result of circumstances beyond their control, merchant failure (whether of an entire business or single venture) did not undermine an individual's reputation or honour. See *Feeding the Baniya: Peasants and Usurers in Western India* (New Delhi: Oxford University Press, 1996), 75.

[92] HAG, CDm 1066, Complaint of Karamchand Harchand, Karamchand Amarchand et al. to Ouvidor, 25 December 1820.

[93] HAG, CD 1003, da Veiga Cabral to Governor, 2 December 1797.

of accurate information – there was always much "talk" among Gujarati merchants in Diu and Daman – accusations and counter-accusations levelled by merchants were perhaps to be expected.[94]

Indeed, evidence suggests that they were commonplace, at least by the eighteenth century. In Diu, an acrimonious commercial environment had formed by the final quarter of the century, amid internal divisions and competition among Vāniyā merchants. Complaints and cases began appearing regularly before the Portuguese judge, as merchants levelled charges against one another. They crystallized into two opposing factions: one headed by Mulji Raghunath and the other by Kunwarji Narsinh. While it is unclear when the animosities between these factions had begun to form, the shipwreck near the Gujarati coast of a vessel owned by Mulji on its return voyage to Diu from Mozambique in 1784 revealed deep-seated divisions among the merchants. These were expressed through vehement representations to the court by both sides.

They began when a number of merchants accused Mulji of ruining their "credit and honour" as the result of his "underhanded" tactics in dealing with the shipwrecked vessel's salvaged cargo.[95] Led by Kunwarji, the "principal merchant of Diu", they charged that Mulji had been able to recover all the goods that the ship was carrying from Africa but had failed to distribute these to their owners, the consigning merchants. He was thus accused of lying about the loss of these goods, and (together with his partners) had "taken advantage of the situation [to] take nearly the entire cargo of the vessel". This had, claimed Kunwarji, resulted in significant losses of more than 500,000 *xerafins* for the merchants invested in the vessel. They were "ruined" as a result of Mulji's fraudulent actions, a merchant who it was claimed stood to gain handsomely from the value of the trade goods and also from the insurance payments he would receive as compensation for the loss.[96]

Kunwarji Narsinh made a further claim in a separate declaration to the Portuguese judge that Mulji Raghunath had spread rumours about him having "cursed the vessel so that it would run aground". He was concerned that Mulji's "fraudulent" behaviour and "manifest theft … committed with treachery and deceit of all the goods that were [carried as] cargo aboard the vessel" would severely damage his commerce; moreover, because Mulji had "defamed and insulted" his name not

[94] HAG, CD 995, Conde de Ega to Mazanes, 9 November 1762.
[95] HAG, CD 998, "Representação da Ouvedoria Geral", 24 October 1784.
[96] HAG, CD 998, Kunwarji Narsinh, Khushal Devchand et al. to Ouvedoria Geral, 26 October 1784. This figure is derived from the amount which it was reported Mulji Raghunath and his partners alone received.

only in Diu but also in Mozambique by presenting "false papers about him to the Ouvedoria [*sic*] Geral [Judicial Court]" and had spread falsehoods about his commercial dealings on both sides of the western Indian Ocean, Kunwarji feared that his standing in the community had been irreparably damaged. Although probably tinged with hyperbolic language to sway the judge, Kunwarji even claimed that he had been caused such profound "fright and confusions" by these accusations that they had affected him physically and left him "bedridden from November [1783] to January [1784]".[97]

The response from Mulji Raghunath was swift and presented in equally emotive language. Communicating through his partners, Tairsi Amba(vi)das, Kanji Keshavji, Natthu Samji and Premchand Shobhachand, he claimed in turn that Kunwarji Narsinh was being "aggressive" and "disruptive" of their trade, resulting in "the complete ruin of our credit and mercantile reputation". They maintained also that Kunwarji had made unfounded complaints and representations to the Portuguese authorities that were adversely affecting their "honour".[98] Moreover, they stated that he and his partners, Anandji Jiv and Rupchand Vada, were conspiring in duplicitous behaviour against them. Apart from his alleged "aggressiveness", Kunwarji was characterized as a merchant seeking to enrich himself through the elimination of his competitors. The vitriolic tone of this response leaves little doubt about the animus that existed between the two factions.[99]

From the perspective of the Portuguese authorities in Diu, the schism was regarded as a threat to the commercial life of the island and, by extension, to its trans-oceanic African trade. Its possible consequences, a general rupture in trade, led the governor, Luis João de Souza Machado de Morães de Sarmento, to resign, his inability to resolves the differences between the merchants prompting his lament that "[W]ithout unity there cannot be commerce." Even though this may have been an exaggeration, it was no hollow statement, for the governor understood that such a deep-seated rift among merchants could jeopardize the vitality of Diu's African commerce, a branch of its Indian Ocean exchange that was vital to the Portuguese Indian state's fiscal revenues.[100]

The surviving details of this case make it difficult to determine which of the factions, merchants aligned with Kunwarji Narsinh or with Mulji

---

[97] HAG, CD 998, "Representação da Ouvedoria Geral", 24 October 1784.
[98] HAG, CD 998, Tairsi Amba(vi)das, Kanji Keshavji, Natthu Samji and Premchand Shobhachand to Judge, 28 February 1785.
[99] HAG, CD 1001, "Noticia do novo Governador...", n.d. [but 1789].
[100] HAG, CD 998, de Sarmento to Viceroy, 20 November 1785.

Raghunath, were responsible for the deceit and fraudulent behaviour of which they stood accused. While on the one hand there is a suggestion in the evidence that Mulji Raghunath had the support of the "majority of merchants who cultivate commerce", there is also an indication on the other that he and his partners – as creditors of a number of merchants – had pressured and intimidated them for their support against Kunwarji. Wherever the truth may lie, the possible ramifications of the situation caused the newly appointed Portuguese Governor of Diu to prioritize the reconciliation of the two factions when he began his tenure in 1789.[101] It is unclear how successful he was but at least Kunwarji and Mulji appear to have made no more formal complaints to the Portuguese judge. While this does not necessarily mean that they no longer competed for predominance in the trade of Diu and Mozambique, the disruption to exchange across the western Indian Ocean so feared by the administration did not materialise. Vāniyā appear to have reached some form of resolution because Gujarati vessels continued to carry sizeable cargoes of cotton textiles to the African coast and in return to ship large volumes of ivory and silver to the subcontinent after these years, as I discuss later in the book.

It is perhaps to be expected that merchants would seek to gain advantages over their competitors through whatever means were at their disposal – indeed, Ashin Das Gupta has shown, for example, that far from protecting their "common interests", Gujarati merchants in Mocha in the 1720s "saw one another as competitors rather than fellow merchants" and those "who were better treated saw no point in combining with the others who had the worst of everything".[102] Yet, the greater use of Portuguese courts and legislative institutions by Vāniyās is striking because of the existence in Diu and Daman of a semi-formal merchant institution that adjudicated disputes among its members, the Vāniyā *mahajan*. *Mahajans* had existed in Gujarat for at least eight centuries and played important organizational roles for merchants. Their precise nature has, however, been the cause of disagreement among scholars; for some, they were social organizations whose membership was restricted to narrow groups, while for others they were business organizations whose main purpose lay in securing the commercial interests of a body of traders.[103] Douglas E. Haynes has noted, though, that drawing a distinction between economic and cultural

---

[101] HAG, CD 998, de Sarmento to Viceroy, 20 November 1785; CD 998, Kunwarji Narsinh, Khushal Devchand et al. to Ouvedoria Geral, 26 October 1784.

[102] Das Gupta, "Gujarati Merchants and the Red Sea Trade, 1700–1725", in Blair B. King and M. N. Pearson (eds.), *The Age of Partnership: Europeans in Asia before Dominion* (Honolulu: University Press of Hawai'i, 1979), 138–9.

[103] Douglas E. Haynes, *Rhetoric and Ritual in Colonial India: The Shaping of a Public Culture in Surat City, 1852–1928* (Berkeley: University of California Press, 1991), 60–1.

institutions is flawed because it ignores "the extent to which commercial and social preoccupations interpenetrated and reinforced each other in the culture of high-caste Hindus and Jains". *Mahajan* leaders were concerned with managing the collective integrity of the group "by formulating, then enforcing, codes of behaviour . . . [and] promoting a more stable socio-commercial environment in which individual families could pursue greater security, profit and prestige".[104]

In Surat, the focus of Haynes' work, there appear to have been two types of *mahajans*: an occupational *mahajan* that encompassed all the traders engaged in the same commercial occupation; and a Samast Vanik or "Hindu" *Mahajan* which was a greater *mahajan* involving families who belonged to a wide range of occupational groups and was often referred to as a "city" or "city-wide" *mahajan*. Among their commercial functions and roles, occupational *mahajans* were responsible for controlling who could practice a certain trade, pressured merchants to uphold their business agreements and, importantly, provided arbitration in settling trade disputes between its members. Those who failed to comply with the *sheth*'s ("headman's") decision could be ostracized from the community and information of their transgression and unscrupulous behaviour shared among members. The Samast Vanik *Mahajan* similarly played a role in managing community issues (along with other responsibilities) but because it enjoyed broader authority than individual *mahajans*, it was able to resolve conflicts between members of different *mahajans*. Both *mahajans* thus provided "critical arenas in which authority was generated and perpetuated".[105]

In Diu and Daman, Vāniyā *mahajans* played an active role in the life of their members. Management of mercantile affairs and conflicts among Vāniyās were taken before the *mahajan* for resolution, and merchants deemed to have acted dishonestly faced the threat of marginalization by the community if they did not comply with its resolution. The *mahajan* was, however, susceptible to the influence of its leading members who, in many cases, were merchants of note with significant trans-oceanic investments. Velji Tairsi, for instance, was a wealthy merchant in Diu who was "heavily invested" in the Mozambique trade. Velji's status gave him an elevated position in the Vāniyā *mahajan* and seems to have allowed him to manipulate cases that were brought before it: "he makes grave threats and has arbitrary persuasions in his private councils called decisions of Mazanes [*Mahajan*]".[106] As a merchant of considerable means, he thus

---

[104] Both quotes come from *ibid.*, 61.
[105] *Ibid.* Useful also is Subramanian, *Indigenous Capital*, 122–4.
[106] HAG, CD 1009, Luis Manoel de Menezes to Provisional Government, 12 March 1826.

appears to have been able to exploit the *mahajan* to serve his own ends. This kind of opportunistic behaviour was not, however, uncommon among wealthy and influential merchants in Vāniyā *mahajans* elsewhere in India, as competition compelled merchants to act as "not ideal men".[107] For Velji Tairsi, this was further reflected in the close relationship he maintained with the Portuguese governor of Diu as a means to wield even greater influence across the island.[108]

That the Vāniyā *mahajan* was susceptible to manipulation by its prominent members may help explain why Gujarati merchants took complaints to the Portuguese juridical authorities in the eighteenth and nineteenth centuries. Even though merchants risked public exposure of their business dealings by doing so, and did not entirely abandon the *mahajan* for the court, merchants in both Diu and Daman increasingly brought complaints, petitions and cases before Portuguese judges from the 1750s and 1760s. This turn to the legal infrastructure of the imperial state may also have reflected a further weakness of the *mahajan* as an instrument for arbitration, resolution and generating trust among merchants: its inability to be exhaustive. While it functioned in principle as a semi-formal institution that could, through collective action, threaten to marginalize individual merchants who were found guilty of malfeasance, its authority and capacity to generate trust between merchants may have been more limited than is often assumed. Moreover, the "communal" or collective solidarity that was central to the functioning of the *mahajan* was likely insufficiently strong to prevent conflicts between parties from entering the public domain, and thus compromise business and the image of the Vāniyā community.[109] Vāniyā may have sought to appeal to Portuguese courts as an institutional complement to the *mahajan*, especially in cases where merchants were antagonistic to a particular ruling of the latter.[110]

---

[107] Das Gupta, "Gujarati Merchants and the Red Sea Trade", 134. For wealthy merchants exercising control over Vāniyā *mahajans* in Bombay, see Christine Dobbin, *Urban Leadership in Western India: Politics and Communities in Bombay City, 1840–1885* (Oxford University Press, 1972), 9.

[108] HAG, CD 1009, de Menezes to Provisional Government, 12 March 1826.

[109] This idea is inspired by Markovits, *Global World of Indian Merchants*, 259–60; C. A. Bayly, "Pre-Colonial Indian Merchants and Rationality", in Mushirul Hasan and Narayani Gupta (eds.), *India's Colonial Encounter: Essays in Memory of Eric Stokes* (New Delhi: Manohar, 1993), 3–24

[110] It is also possible that communal solidarity among the Vāniyā was weakening at a time when the political and economic landscape of South Asia was undergoing profound change. The increasing presence of the British in western India, coupled with the dangers of attack at sea from French and Maratha vessels, and the competition from other merchant groups in the western Indian Ocean such as the Kutchi Bhātiyā, may have contributed significantly to the creation of a commercial environment in Diu and Daman

Appeals to Portuguese judicial courts by Gujarati merchants reflected, further, an awareness of their rights of appeal as imperial subjects of the Crown.[111] Although Vāniyā regarded certain aspects of Portuguese rule to be intrusive and overbearing, such as increases in customs rates in Diu and Daman or attempts to restrict their movement in Mozambique, they were willing to accommodate the official Portuguese presence because it provided an additional, or auxiliary, authority to which they had access as imperial subjects and which suited their needs. Particularly from the mid-eighteenth century, merchants were often explicit in asserting their rights and expressing their loyalty as subjects of the Crown in correspondence with Portuguese authorities.[112] As such, they had full rights of appeal to the legal institutions of the state. This assertion of rights was related to changes in Portuguese official attitudes to the Indian inhabitants of its imperial territories. From the 1730s and 1740s, driven by "modernizing" tendencies that predated the reformist impulses of the Pombaline policies implemented after mid-century, there was a marked shift towards dissolving the distinction between "Indian" and "Portuguese" subjects with the explicit aim of creating a subjecthood defined by equality before the law.[113] Vāniyā appear to have taken advantage of this change to invoke rights as vassals of the state in their appeals, petitions and declarations to Portuguese authorities.[114]

The interest from Gujarati merchants in invoking their rights as imperial subjects was sustained by the capacity of the state to enforce its authority. Although it often faced difficulties in doing so, due largely to a shortage of manpower and inadequate financial resources, merchants could benefit from the intervention of the court and other state bodies. In 1797, "intrigue" within the Vāniyā merchant community was brought

in which solidarity between merchants of the same town was, paradoxically, weakened. In uncertain conditions, competition between merchants may have become heightened as economic interests were pitted against one another for a share of the ocean's markets.

[111] The use of colonial state legal structures was not unique to the Vāniyā, of course, as the examples, among others, of Chettiar merchants in the Straits (who "were not slow to avail themselves of the law") and Yokohama Sindhi merchants attest. However, in most cases, Asian merchants brought cases before colonial courts only once colonial law had become codified from the mid- to late nineteenth century. Ray, "Chinese Financiers", 224; Markovits, *Global World*, 259–60.

[112] See, for example, HAG, CD 1007, Mazanes to Provisional Government, 9 January 1822; CDm 1063, "Mazanes e negociantes…" to Viceroy, n.d. [but 1815].

[113] R. J. Barendse, "History, Law and Orientalism under Portuguese Colonialism in Eighteenth-Century India", *Itinerario*, 26, 1 (2002), 53.

[114] See, for example, AHU, Moç., Cx 14 Doc. 27, "Corpo dos Banianes", enclosed in Viceroy to Crown, n.d. [but 1758/1759]. It is worth noting that Gujarati merchants repeated a similar claim in Mozambique in the early twentieth century in response to an edict issued by the colonial state prohibiting them from trading. See Rochelle Pinto, "Race and Imperial Loss: Accounts of East Africa in Goa", *South African Historical Journal*, 57, 1 (2007), 91.

before the Portuguese authorities. Purshottam Jivaji made a declaration to the Diu judge that his deceased employer's widow had accused him of stealing from her. Purshottam had worked in Diu for the firm of Anandji Jivan whose business was centred on trade with Mozambique. Upon his employer's death, Purshottam began working for his unnamed widow who, together with a kin member, Natthu Samoji, were heirs to Anandji's holdings and property. When he was accused of stealing by her and Natthu Samoji, Purshottam left the employ of the family and moved away from Diu because they had threatened to kill him. In his absence, all his goods were "confiscated" by Anandji's heirs and the debts owed to Purshottam were "stolen" from him.

If his safety could be guaranteed, he assured the judge, he was eager to return to Diu to prove his innocence and to resume the business and trade he had established with three brothers in Mozambique. He worried that a prolonged absence would be damaging to their business. Purshottam thus sought a licence from the court (to be administered by the military office of the Lieutenant General) to allow him to return to Diu under state protection in order to clear his name. When it was granted, Purshottam was escorted by soldiers to the island from coastal Kathiawar where he had taken refuge. Although there are no details of the evidence he may have presented to the court as proof of his innocence, it was enough to convince the judge to issue an order instructing Anandji Jivan's heirs to cease their pursuit of him. It seems that the order was respected, for a few years later Purshottam was trading once again to Mozambique having been able to "recover his reputation [and] credit".[115]

Gujarati merchants could also draw on the penal capacity of the state, limited as it was. We return to consider Kassam Manachand, who – as discussed earlier – had accused Manachand Savai publicly of dishonest behaviour in claiming to be Haribhai Kesar's business partner. This accusation, while potentially damaging to the latter's reputation, appears to have been part of Kassam's modus operandi. This resulted in a large group of merchants issuing a formal complaint to the Portuguese governor regarding his "aggressive" and "intimidating behaviour" towards them. One of these merchants claimed Kassam had attempted to destroy his credibility by spreading "false" stories about his ability to repay loans. Kassam was accused, additionally, of being a "favourite" of Judge Vicente Salvador Rodrigues, and as such was seen to exert undue influence over

---

[115] The details of this case have been taken from HAG, CD 1003, Purshottam Jivaji to Tenente General, 23 August 1797; "Representação de Calanji Talco e Tacarsi Getha", 23 August 1797; CD 1004, "Banianes ao Governador", 23 October 1804.

the court's rulings, especially when it came to his competitors.[116] Merchants were perhaps justified in their concern for how operators such as Kassam could manipulate officials who were known to engage in commercial activities themselves.[117] The number of merchants making this complaint, and the evidence they were supposedly able to present, convinced the governor to jail Kassam sometime in 1820. But the judge, in a development highly suggestive of his corruption and close relationship with Kassam, secured the merchant's release on the grounds that "the prisoner should not suffer further personal damage without guilt".[118] While the intercession of Rodrigues may have freed Kassam from jail, it likely did nothing to repair the further damage that this public humiliation would have caused to his reputation generally among merchants. Kassam may have actually tacitly admitted his guilt by not responding to the accusations and was likely marginalized by Vāniyās because there is no further trace of him in the archival record.

In spite of its limited means and the corruption of some of its high-ranking officials, Vāniyā merchants were nonetheless able to benefit as imperial subjects from their relationship to the state. They, therefore, used both their own community regulatory institution – the *mahajan* – and the judicial institutions of the Portuguese imperial state to serve as mediators of internal struggles and competitive disputes.

Coordinating collective action

In taking cases before the court, Gujarati merchants could also coordinate collective action to protect their interests as a group when faced with Portuguese state malfeasance. We see this clearly when prominent merchants of Diu jointly accused the state's customs officer, Anastazio Aureliano Pinto, in 1810 of corruption and of "severe and unjust actions"; these were repeated in 1812 but supplemented with the claim that he was intentionally delaying the processing of ivory cargoes shipped from Mozambique. Goculdas Natthu, Jagjivan Khushal, Virchand Anandji and Sangaji Purshottam, principal merchants of leading family firms, recounted their experiences of long delays of several weeks for their shipments, with the result that Goculdas faced having to withdraw his ship

---

[116] HAG, CDm 1066, Vāniyā merchants to Governor, n.d. [but predating December 1820].

[117] HAG, CDm 1066, D. Lourenço de Noronha to Viceroy, 21 September 1820. South Asian merchants elsewhere were known also to manipulate officials to their own advantage. See, for example, Markovits, *Global World of Indian Merchants*, 262.

[118] HAG, CDm 1066, "Mandado" signed by Vicente Salvador Rodrigues, 19 December 1820.

as the *barco de viagem* for the following trading season. The perquisites afforded such a vessel in the trade with Mozambique (as I show in Chapter 2), such as being permitted to load its cargo before other vessels, gave merchants an advantage over their competitors and made the nomination of a vessel a highly sought-after privilege; relinquishing it was thus a dramatic step for a merchant to contemplate. As a result of Pinto's actions, which included threatening Goculdas with imprisonment in response to the merchants' case, the Vāniyā merchants sought his removal from office.[119]

Merchant opprobrium could at times be directed at the highest offices, including that of the judge himself. As *Capitão Mor dos Banianes* (a position created by the Portuguese for the "leading" Gujarati merchant whose role it was to mediate relations between Vāniyās and the imperial state), Sowchand Velji presented the governor of Diu with a formal petition in 1816 requesting the removal of the *Ouvidor*, Antonio João Lobo, from office. Referred to in the petition as a "thief", Lobo was accused of extorting money from and inflicting "false rulings and punishments" on members of the merchant community. His actions were proving disruptive to commercial life and, it was argued, the problem could be addressed only by ending his tenure as judge. The collective pressure from Vāniyā merchants, evidenced through the testimony of numerous aggrieved merchants, proved decisive in the case – Lobo was relieved of his duties in the same year by Governor Mauricio da Costa Campos.[120]

When acting collectively to protect their commercial and financial interests, Vāniyā merchants were often explicit in detailing how the Portuguese imperial state benefitted from their business interests. This is nowhere more evident than in a series of documents in which 17 leading merchants addressed a number of charges that had been levelled against them by the Portuguese authorities and *moradores* ("settlers") in Mozambique in 1781.[121] The latter accused Gujarati merchants of undermining "Portuguese" trade through "unfair" competition and sought to limit their involvement in the imperial economy by circumscribing their movement throughout the territory. While attempts to suppress Vāniyā commerce were not new – there were similar calls for action in

---

[119] HAG, CD 1005, Sowchand Velji, Chaturbhuj Kunwarji, Virchand Anandji et al. to Coronel Castelão Governador, 10 November 1810; Vāniyā merchants to Coronel Castellão Governador, n.d. [but probably 1812]. Other examples of complaints can be found in HAG, CD 996, 998, 1003–6; 1008.

[120] HAG, CD 1004, Mauricio da Costa Campos to Conde de Sarzedas, 30 May 1816.

[121] AHU, Moç., Cx 36 Doc. 35, "Resposta dos gentios ao Bando...", 28 June 1781; "Resposta dos mercadores gentios...", 14 July 1781; "Resposta dos mercadores banianes...", 3 August 1781; "Representação dos Banianes...", 4 August 1781.

the 1760s – opposition had intensified from the late 1770s amid deepening Vāniyā involvement in the commerce of Mozambique.[122]

Vāniyā responded to these charges with a sound appreciation of their importance to the commercial and financial viability of imperial trade, as much in Mozambique as in Diu and Daman. In a carefully worded response to the prohibition that authorities had imposed on their mobility and trade with the African interior in 1781, Vāniyā merchants stressed the effects of such action on the Royal Treasury: a drop in customs duties of more than 30 per cent. Should this have been insufficient to convince the governor and officials of their indispensability to the state, the merchants strengthened their case that "our commerce is the most useful to the Royal Treasury through the duties it generates" by noting that between 1770 and 1781 their trade had generated over 400 million *réis* in duties payments, an enormous sum. They added that, apart from the considerable risk associated with long-distance trade between India and Mozambique and the significant financial investment it entailed, they provided credit to merchants in the form of cotton textiles that was vital for the functioning of the African commercial economy.

These remarkably candid responses to what was considered an overbearing intervention by the state were intended to act as a bulwark against the threat of Vāniyā removal or curtailment of their business in Mozambique. Despite continued attempts in the 1780s to suppress Gujarati participation in the economy, the Portuguese were inevitably unsuccessful precisely because of the indispensability of Vāniyā merchant networks in the commercial spheres on both sides of the Indian Ocean, as well as their large contributions to state finances through customs payments that would remain a feature of their involvement in Southeast Africa. Vāniyā merchants, it is clear, were aware of their critical role and used it where necessary in ensuring the smooth running of their business ventures.

Agents of credit and finance

In drawing attention to their financial role as credit providers in Mozambique, Vāniyā merchants highlighted a key aspect underpinning the range of commercial relationships that Gujarati merchants were able to sustain. The availability and extension of credit was critical to the functioning of commerce and trade, and was therefore central to merchant life. Credit in Diu and Daman operated across all levels of commerce, from the procurement and provision of textiles in the interior of Gujarat to the

---

[122] Edward A. Alpers, *Ivory and Slaves in East Central Africa: Changing Pattern of International Trade to the Later Nineteenth Century* (London: Heinemann, 1975), 143–9.

purchase of trade goods such as ivory tusks in Mozambique. Brokers who acquired cloth for the export trade and African intermediaries and traders who brought ivory and slaves to the coast *all* operated through the provision of credit from Vāniyā merchants who, in turn, financed much of their business with credit from *sarrafs* ("bankers") in Surat. Although its position in western India as a premier trading and manufacturing centre was gradually undermined by the development of Bombay from the late eighteenth century, Surat remained a significant financial centre well into the nineteenth century.[123] A merchant's ability to raise credit depended on their good standing, reputation and therefore associated risk among bankers and their peers, and it was thus critically important for merchants to maintain their "creditworthiness" and be under no "suspicion" in the market place regarding their capacity to meet debt obligations.[124] Loss of credit could, at the very least, make raising capital difficult and at worst could result in such devastating consequences as the loss of one's business.[125]

Sarrafs in Diu lent money and managed credit arrangements both with Vāniyā merchants, Portuguese traders and officials and with local rulers in Kathiawar. Rates of credit varied according to an individual's reputation, and could be secured using collateral such as sailing vessels, ivory cargoes and even African slaves.[126] Portuguese merchants could secure

---

[123] W. G. Clarence-Smith, "Indian and Arab entrepreneurs in Eastern Africa (1800–1914)", in Hubert Bonin and Michel Cahen (eds.), *Négoce blanc en Afrique noire* (Paris: Société Française d'Histoire d'Outre-Mer, 2001), 342; Pamela Nightingale, *Trade and Empire in Western India 1784–1806* (Cambridge University Press, 1970), 171; Subramanian, *Indigenous Capital*, 142. Recently, Douglas E. Haynes has shown that, due to an "overall preoccupation" with the theme of Surat's decline from the early eighteenth century, scholars have overlooked that the city, its merchants and manufacturers "continued to maintain many of [their] linkages to the Indian Ocean mercantile world" into the middle of the twentieth century. See "Surat City, Its Decline and the Indian Ocean, 1730–1940", in *Port Towns of Gujarat* (Delhi: Primus, forthcoming).

[124] HAG, CD 996, D. Frederico Guilherme de Souza to Governor, 9 September 1779; AHU, Moç., Cx 96 Doc. 54, "Declaração de Lacamichande Motichande", n.d. [but 1803]; Códice 1374, "Segundo Protesto", n.d. [but *c*. 1806]. When two Gujarati vessels were lost in 1798 in the Mozambique trade, merchants with interests in the voyages found it difficult to raise credit with *sarrafs* in Surat because they were as a consequence regarded as being risky investments. See HAG, CDm, Harchand Hira, Jhaver Khushal et al. to Governor, 4 December 1798.

[125] C. A. Bayly encapsulates the potential risks associated with the loss of credit for merchants: "One of the features of merchant society before the middle of the nineteenth century was the devastating consequences of the loss of credit. A trader who could no longer buy and sell in the market might be reduced to penury more speedily even than a peasant who lost his land". *Rulers, Townsmen and Bazaars: North Indian Society in the Age of British Expansion 1770–1870*, First Indian edn (New Delhi: Oxford University Press, 1992), 380–1.

[126] HAG, CD 1006, Joaquim Mourão Garcez Palha to Viceroy, 27 April 1817.

credit at 6 per cent, and in the mid-1790s, *sarrafs* were willing to lend to regional rulers at rates of between 10 and 15 per cent that reflected the perceived risk of default on repayments. Rates for Vāniyā merchants were available from these bankers at or below 5 per cent.[127] Vāniyā also extended credit to one another at below-market rates, with senior members of family firms providing goods on credit at favourable rates to junior members who were thereby capitalized with commodities that were in demand in Mozambique, particularly cotton textiles.[128]

With their access to extensive credit resources, Vāniyā merchants were able to service the needs of both private and state commercial interests in Mozambique. Indeed, widespread indebtedness to Vāniyās was a feature of the eighteenth- and nineteenth-century Mozambique economy and confirmed their prominence as financiers and suppliers of credit for the African trade. Already by the middle of the eighteenth century, financial records showed the extent of public debt held by Gujarati merchants – between 1752 and 1757, for example, 73 per cent of state debt was in their hands, while in 1809 approximately 60 per cent of the credit made available to the Portuguese Royal Treasury was held by Vāniyās.[129] Debts to individual merchants could, however, vary enormously in scale. Mulji Raghunath was owed the considerable sum of 4:553$200 *réis* in 1756, and in the first decade of the nineteenth century just two merchants, Laxmichand Motichand and Shobhachand Sowchand, provided 27 per cent of the credit to the Royal Treasury. By contrast, Jetha Madhavi held debts for the small amount of 096$060 *réis*, and merchants such as Atmachand Vakhatchand, Amirchand Meghji and others were responsible for less than 1 per cent of credit provision to the state in Mozambique.[130]

Private trade depended also on Vāniyā credit, which Portuguese merchants could secure at rates of around 10 per cent.[131] While information on the rates that African agents may have been charged does not appear to exist, they were likely higher because of the increased risk of loss of

---

[127] HAG, CD 1008, Complaints against deceased debtors, 9 July 1821; CD 1002, Caetano de Souza Perreira to Governor, 2 October 1795. The reality of the risks of lending to regional rulers was demonstrated in 1795 when Diu *sarrafs*, for unspecified reasons, lost the large sum of 80,000 *xerafins* to the "Parva Saucar" and the *Diwan* of Sutrapura.

[128] HAG, AD 4952–4969; ADm 4836–4852. This was a practice widely utilized by South Asian merchant family firms throughout the subcontinent and elsewhere in the western Indian Ocean. See, for example, Dale, *Indian Merchants*; Levi, *Indian Diaspora in Central Asia*; Clarence-Smith, "Indian and Arab Entrepreneurs".

[129] AHU, Moç., Cx 14 Doc. 20, "Copia da Rellação das Dividas...", 5 June 1758; Cx 129 Doc. 115, "Relação dos credores da Fazenda Real", 14 November 1809.

[130] AHU, Moç., Cx 14 Doc. 20, "Copia da Rellação das Dividas..."; Cx 129 Doc. 115, "Relação dos credores da Fazenda Real".

[131] AHU, Cx 46 Doc. 31, de Saldanha de Albuquerque to Crown, 12 August 1783; BA, 54-XIII-3 (3), Francisco Alves Barbosa, "Analyse Estatistica", 30 December 1821.

trade goods in the Mozambique interior. How high these may have been is suggested by evidence from elsewhere along the East African coast: in Pangani in the 1880s, Indian merchants charged annual rates of 15–25 per cent on advances made to caravan leaders for goods carried on routes that were regarded as being high risk; and in the 1890s in Merca on the Somali coast, Gujarati merchants lent to Arab merchants at 10 per cent and to local Somali at 20 per cent, while the rate for inland traders, unreliable suppliers of gum from the interior, could be as much as 200 per cent. Given that the risks associated with inland commerce in Mozambique were comparable at the end of the eighteenth century, we can reasonably assume that Vāniyā lenders would have charged in the region of 15–30 per cent.[132]

Vāniyā also offered loans to private Portuguese merchants and officials with commercial interests in Mozambique. These were secured through bills of credit signed by the lending merchant and debtor, and in many cases were contracted for extended periods of time. In 1782, for example, 11 individuals owed Jetha Mulji a combined total of nearly 10:000$000 *réis*, an extremely large total debt. One of the debtors, Joaquim de Almeida, had been extended credit by Jetha in 1773 and was due to maintain his debt beyond 1782. In certain cases, debts were maintained for several decades.[133] They also involved high-ranking officials: towards the end of the eighteenth century, Governor Pedro de Saldanha was indebted to two creditors, Mulji Raghunath to whom he owed the considerable sum of 12:000$000 *réis*, and Natthu Vissaram as a result of his large-scale involvement in coastal shipping and trading.[134] Additionally, Gujarati merchants often acted as guarantors for varying sums of money for Portuguese merchants and provided the state with significant capital to finance projects and pay its officials in Mozambique. Of the 33:000$000 *réis* provided to the Royal Treasury in the form of trade goods and foodstuffs by the "most able merchants" of Mozambique in 1797, Vāniyās contributed just under two-thirds.[135]

---

[132] Jonathan Glassman, *Feasts and Riot: Revelry, Rebellion, and Popular Consciousness on the Swahili Coast, 1856–1888* (Portsmouth, NH: Heinemann, 1995), 72–3; G. Cattelani, *L'avvenire coloniale d'Italia nel Benadir* (Naples: F. Giannini e Figli, 1897), 97.

[133] AHU, Moç., Cx 57 Doc. 69, "Devedores de Getta Mulji", n.d. [but 1782]; HAG, CM 1447, Joze Francisco de Paula Cavalcante de Albuquerque to Conde de Rio Pardo, 28 July 1818.

[134] AHU, Moç., Cx 67 Doc. 102, Aranha e …(?) and Benjamy Ferrão to Juiz ordinaria, 8 July 1794; Cx 57 Doc. 12 Antonio Manoel de Mello e Castro to Senado da Camara, 22 February 1789.

[135] Among the Vāniyā, the contributions from Jiv Sangaji and Laxmichand Motichand to the state exceeded what even wealthy slave traders such as João da Silva Guedes were able to provide. AHU, Moç., Cx 77 Doc. 69, "Catalogo das Pessoas…", 22 April 1797. Numerous examples exist of Vāniyā merchants serving as guarantors for Portuguese merchants, officials and the Catholic clergy on Mozambique Island – see, for example,

The dominance of Gujarati capital in the financial sector of Mozambique reflected the extent to which credit offered by Vāniyās was central to economic life. In a context in which "formal" banking institutions did not exist, Gujarati private capital and credit resources were indispensable in facilitating exchange in the territory and, thereby, in connecting it to the broader commercial cross-currents of the western Indian Ocean and Atlantic. But for the Portuguese, this was overshadowed by a view that the state and traders had become dependent on Gujarati credit and loans. As a result, they were "ruining Portuguese trade", and Vāniyās were characterized as "birds of prey", "rapacious" and "usurious".[136] Yet, despite attempts to curtail Vāniyā involvement in the commercial economy of Mozambique by restricting movement away from Mozambique Island or to expel them from the colony altogether – an approach adopted in the 1770s and 1780s – it was inescapable that in making capital available for state and private trade, Vāniyās were indispensable to the structure and functioning of trade.

The centrality of Vāniyā finance to the Mozambique trade was a reality that, if only reluctantly, the Portuguese were forced to accept: "They [Vāniyā merchants] are the ones who animate commerce because the Portuguese [merchants] cannot match their financial capacity as they are few in number and have limited means to effect much [economic] impact." Thus, despite the "great sums" that they were owed by the Portuguese state and private merchants, Gujarati merchants were responsible for "sustaining" and "maintaining" the commerce of Mozambique by what they "gave on credit".[137] Because of the nature of the structure of trade in Mozambique, in which exchange with the interior was conducted through African agents who could be away from the coast with cargoes of Gujarati textiles for two or more years and often faced the threat of theft of their goods, the capacity of Vāniyās to provide long-term credit to both Portuguese and African traders was essential.[138]

AHU, Moç., Cx 66 Doc. 45, Joaquim Joze de Mello e Castro to D. Diogo de Souza, 5 January 1794 for Karva (?) Mulji acting as guarantor for Fr. Vitoriano de São Jose in 1780; and Cx 67 Doc. 49, "Certificação...", 21 May 1794 for an unnamed Vāniyā merchant acting as guarantor of Jose da Costa Pereira for the sum of 1:500$000 réis. Further examples can be found in AHM, Fundo do Século XIX, Códice 11–1716.

[136] AHU, Moç., Cx 36 Doc. 35, Joze Per.ᵉ Nobre, Duarte Aurelio de Menzes et al. to Governor-General, 14 July 1781; Cx 39 Doc. 49, "Pela copia do Bando...", 28 November 1782; Cx 40 Doc. 10, Saldanha de Albuquerque to de Melo e Castro, 12 December 1782.

[137] AHU, Moç., Cx 34 Doc. 40, Jose Vasconcellos de Almeida to Crown, 20 August 1780; Cx 33 Doc. 52, Antonio Manuel de Mello de Castro to Crown, 17 July 1780.

[138] AHU, Cx 28 Doc. 88, Officio from Pereira do Lago, 20 August 1768; Cx 39 Doc. 49, "Pela copia do Bando...", 28 November 1782. Vāniyā held "very old" debts, including for large sums (400,000 cruzados) that Yao traders had owed them "for many months" in the 1760s.

Their extensive provision of credit throughout much of the coast and interior of northern and central Mozambique meant Vāniyā merchants travelled regularly from their base at Mozambique Island to recover debts throughout coastal northern Mozambique. As a creditor of "most" of the Swahili and Makua chiefs of Macuana in 1789, Natthu Vissaram was often away settling debts and managing his financial interests. This was done partly on a *palmar* where Natthu owned a house. He travelled also to "loges" (trading stores) in Quelimane, Sena and elsewhere in the Zambesi Valley. Increasingly, Gujarati merchants established these stores from the middle of the eighteenth century as they expanded their commerce from its base at Mozambique Island and focus on Macuana and northern Mozambique. Like *palmares*, they operated both as sites where credit arrangements with African agents were finalized and debts settled, and as redistributive centres for trade goods.[139]

A key difference, however, was that Vāniyā acquired *palmares* as the result of Portuguese merchants defaulting on loans. Although few details survive, it appears that Portuguese merchants were able to secure loans by mortgaging land and property. This gave the creditor financial control over the property and allowed him to foreclose if the debtor failed to meet their debt obligations.[140] As noted earlier, this resulted in a number of properties on the mainland opposite Mozambique Island, in Mossuril and elsewhere in Macuana, coming into the possession of Gujarati merchants from the 1750s as the commercial economy expanded around textile, ivory and slave trading. The proportion of land owned by Vāniyās in relation to that owned by the Portuguese thus began gradually to grow in coastal northern Mozambique. This was augmented by Gujarati property and land purchases – for example, Vāniyā bought *machambas* and *palmares* on Mossuril, Lumbo and other places on the northern Mozambique coast in 1804 and 1815.[141] On Mozambique Island, where they also rented properties from the Portuguese state and church, a small number of wealthier merchants owned properties in an area of concentrated Vāniyā residence in the east of the island-capital, the so-called "Rua direita dos Banianes". This included residences and warehouses where goods were collected and stored for redistribution and export.

---

[139] AHU, Moç., Cx 57 Doc. 12, Antonio Manoel de Mello e Castro to Senado da Camara, 22 February 1789; Cx 101 Doc. 4, Passport for Atmachand Mavji, ant. 7 August 1803; Doc. 31, Passport for Tarachand Gopal, ant. 20 August 1803; Cx 98 Doc. 67, Passport for Bhimji Manji, ant. 29 March 1803.

[140] AHU, Moç., Cx 34 Doc. 38, Vicente Caetano Maria Vasconcellos to Governor, 1780.

[141] AHU, Moç., Cx 105 Doc. 33, "Representaçã de Pitambar Pungia", ant. 2 January 1804; AHM, Fundo do Século XIX, Códice 11–4486.

The properties were also places where Vāniyā conducted business with Portuguese merchants and officials.[142]

Yet despite acquiring land either through debt default or purchase, Gujarati merchants did not pursue large-scale property or land ownership at this time. This was due likely to a reluctance to tie up capital in immovable assets, given that Vāniyā business interests were concentrated overwhelmingly in commercial and financial capital.[143] Just like Indian merchants in Zanzibar and Pemba on the Swahili coast to whom Omani Arabs would mortgage large numbers of clove plantations to raise capital in the 1870s, Vāniyā avoided assuming ownership of property when a debtor defaulted and may similarly have rewritten debts to avoid foreclosing on properties. In so doing, the creditor was able to collect as much of the interest as the debtor could afford, while the latter – even if they had relinquished financial control over it – did not lose their property.[144] Similar arrangements in Mozambique may therefore account for an absence of evidence of extensive land transfers to Vāniyā merchants in the eighteenth and nineteenth centuries.

The critical role of Vāniyā merchants in providing credit for trade in Mozambique was matched by their equally important and related financial involvement in transferring capital between Africa and India – and also within India – through bills of exchange known as *hundis*. These financial instruments circulated primarily on Mozambique Island but could also be found in the Zambesi Valley and southern Mozambique. *Hundis* had long been a feature of India's banking system and may have been "the oldest surviving form of credit instrument" in the subcontinent. They were the most important means by which Indian merchant firms transferred capital, particularly large sums, from one individual or firm to another. They consisted of a written order, usually unconditional, "made by one person on another for the payment, on demand or after a specified

---

[142] Alexandre Lobato, *Ilha de Moçambique: Panorama Estético* (Lisbon: Agência Geral do Ultramar, 1966); AHU, Moç., Cx 65 Doc. 17, "Rellacao dos Baniances que tem suas casas nesta capital...", 19 September 1793; AHM, Fundo do Século XIX, Códice 11–4486. Some merchants, such as Jetha Nana and his son, Bhavanidas Jetha, owned multiple properties on Mozambique Island and on the mainland opposite the island. *DAM*, II, 114–15.

[143] I should note that, generally, Indian merchants and traders in South Asia were reluctant to own property in the eighteenth century; apart from a similar concern about tying up capital in land, merchants were wary of entering into "demeaning social relationships" that land management would entail, and did not want agrarian resources to affect their creditworthy status as merchants. See Bayly, *Rulers, Townsmen and Bazaars*, 384; Bayly, "Pre-colonial Indian Merchants", 7.

[144] Frederick Cooper, *Plantation Slavery on the East Coast of Africa* (New Haven: Yale University Press, 1977), 141–5.

time, of a certain sum of money to a person named therein".[145] *Hundis* were handled primarily by *sarrafs*, who used them to finance commerce; they charged discounts on the bills to cover interest, the cost of insurance and the transmission of money. Because they were fully saleable, a merchant with cash on hand could invest in *hundis* by discounting them. The acceptance of *hundis* in the market rested on the reputation of the *sarrafs* who issued them. *Hundis* could also be used for cash advances and were thus a significant instrument for extending credit to merchants. Sales of *hundis* had become so widespread in Gujarat by the eighteenth century that commercial payments were usually made in these bills and seldom in cash. They were thus used principally if not exclusively in all cotton purchases by Indian and European merchants alike, and were even integral to financing British military efforts in western India.[146] The reach of the *hundi* network stretched from Surat in Gujarat to Murshidabad in Bengal, and few if any transactions were conducted in India without them because they offered merchants a more secure medium for transferring or remitting funds and specie from one location to another.

This included locations scattered throughout the western Indian Ocean, allowing merchant family firms in India to move capital safely and effectively between network centres and agents in the Red Sea, Persian Gulf and East Africa. We thus find that among Vāniyā merchants in Mozambique *hundis* were used extensively in financial transactions and were key instruments for the transfer of money to and from India. Large sums were often involved – in the mid-1780s, for instance, merchants were using *hundis* to remit 300,000–400,000 *cruzados* annually to Diu.[147] Wealthy merchants could hold several bills at any one time, as demonstrated by Laxmichand Motichand whose *hundis* in Mozambique in 1807 were valued at the extraordinary amount of 200:065$440 *réis*. They were held for Gujarati and Portuguese merchants who sought to transfer capital funds within

---

[145] L. C. Jain, *Indigenous Banking in India* (London: Macmillan and Co. Limited, 1929), 70, 71.

[146] Irfan Habib, "Usury in Medieval India", *Comparative Studies in Society and History*, 4 (1964), 402; *idem*, "The System of Bills of Exchange (Hundis) in the Mughal Empire", *Proceedings of the Indian History Congress* (Delhi, 1973), 290–303; *idem*, "Merchant communities in Precolonial India"; Lakshmi Subramanian, "'Banias and the British': The Role of Indigenous Credit in the Process of Imperial Expansion in Western India in the Second Half of the Eighteenth Century", *Modern Asian Studies*, 21, 3 (1987), 503. Further details on the English East India Company's use of *hundis* to finance a military presence in India can be found in Subramanian, *Indigenous Capital and Imperial Expansion*, and in Michelguglielmo Torri, "Trapped Inside the Colonial Order: The Hindu Bankers of Surat and their Business World during the Second Half of the Eighteenth Century", *Modern Asian Studies*, 25, 2 (1991), 49–79.

[147] AHU, Moç., Cx 47 Doc. 39, "Registo da carta que a Camara escreveo...", n.d. [but 1784].

Mozambique and also to India. His financial role as banker complemented Laxmichand's extensive commercial interests in the ivory and slave trades (as later chapters will reveal), and was commonly practised among prominent Vāniyā in Mozambique.[148]

Once they reached India, *hundis* could be cashed by *sarrafs* in Diu for discounted rates of 2–3 per cent but in times of money shortages these could be as high as 20 per cent. The credit and money market there was closely connected to Surat, allowing Diu *hundis* to be saleable against Surat *hundis* at discounts of 10–12.5 per cent.[149] As the financial capital of western India and the "nodal point of the credit exchange system",[150] Surat offered merchants access to a broader and deeper base of financial capital and credit, and enabled the rapid movement of money between locales in Kathiawar, Gujarat and western India. It also both allowed for the existence of a multilateral payment structure for imported trade goods that were widely distributed, and enabled raising capital for shipbuilding in Daman.[151] The integration especially of Diu into the Surat financial and banking nexus, as demonstrated by the negotiability of its *hundis* for Surat *hundis*, was a critical element in a financial structure that undergirded its (and Daman's) commercial involvement in the Southeast African trade of Mozambique.

Conclusion

If the growth and consolidation of Vāniyā interests in Mozambique from the early to mid-eighteenth century owed much to their capacity to raise credit and finance the circulation of capital between India and Africa, their turn away from Red Sea markets in the 1720s and 1730s to Southeast Africa was both caused and made possible by interdependent factors. Vāniyā dominance of textile procurement in India and cloth distribution in Mozambique (fully explored in Chapter 3) formed the material basis for this shift, closely connected as it was to ivory and slave trading – and by extension New World silver that the latter generated – in the eighteenth and nineteenth centuries. Vāniyā trade reflected the robust consumer

---

[148] AHU, Códice 1374, "Segundo Protesto", n.d. [but 1807]. In 1814, Laxmichand, along with another wealthy and prominent merchant (Shobhachand Sowchand), received monetary deposits in Mozambique from several private Portuguese traders ostensibly as payment for earlier transfers of unspecified capital funds to India. See AHU, Moç., Cx 147 Doc. 77, "Depositos...", 17 July 1814.

[149] HAG, CD 998, de Noyers to de Souza, 26 July 1784; CD 999, Kunwarji Narsinh, Mulji Raghunath et al. to Governor, 23 December 1786.

[150] Subramanian, "Banias and the British", 478.

[151] HAG, CD 996, Dom Pedro da Camara to Castelão of Diu, 24 November 1774.

markets of Kathiawar and Southeast Africa and at the same time was a key component in their development as part of burgeoning commercial economies on both sides of the Indian Ocean.

The nature of their business organization, however, provided the foundational structure on which they developed and consolidated their trade. Family firms were key units around which merchants based their commerce, where partnership agreements with agents who travelled abroad from India as well as with African agents in Mozambique were key to its successful operation. Equally important, was generating and regulating trust in business relations, either through the semi-formal Vāniyā organization, the *mahajan*, or the Portuguese colonial institution of the court. The latter, it has been suggested, may increasingly have supplanted the former in the second half of the eighteenth century as merchants sought to draw on the judicial authority of the colonial state as subjects of the Portuguese Crown. Although enforcement was limited due to financial constraints, merchants nonetheless brought cases against one another in the office of the Portuguese judge that could threaten to undermine or enhance the reputation, and hence trust, of an individual, while at the same time it legitimated the very existence of that office. Nonetheless, the merchant competition that prompted court cases dissolved in the face of threats to the broader merchant community.

Vāniyā merchants understood how vital their financial and commercial contributions were to the Mozambique economy and income of the Portuguese state, and used this to their advantage by coming together to communicate this to the latter in compelling language. The central place of Vāniyā merchants in propelling, and undergirding, the trade and economy of Mozambique, Diu and Daman by the middle of the eighteenth century was simply undeniable and also facilitated and was connected to Portuguese imperial trading interests.

Their success in trans-oceanic trade was related, moreover, to control and ownership of shipping vessels large enough to transport their bulk cargoes between India and Africa, and it is to this topic that we now turn.

2 Crossings

The Indian Ocean lives of Vāniyā merchants were intimately bound up with oceanic crossings between India and Africa. They made these voyages in well-constructed ocean-going vessels that enabled regular patterns of aquatic circulation in the eighteenth and nineteenth centuries. Their ships were well equipped and manned for the long and at times arduous voyages between Kathiawar and Gujarat and the Mozambique coast. Oceanic crossings in the western Indian Ocean were a well-established part of Gujarati commerce by at least the fifteenth and sixteenth centuries, with merchants from Surat making annual voyages to Mocha and other ports in southern Arabia in the seventeenth century. Voyages to Africa, however, became a regular occurrence only from the eighteenth century as Vāniyā networks from Kathiawar expanded into the regional markets of the southwestern Indian Ocean.[1] In most years from the middle of the century, at least three (and at times up to five) vessels were outfitted annually from Diu and Daman for voyages across the ocean, carrying large cargoes and sizeable crews. This was a greater number of ships than sailed from Goa to Mozambique and was on a par, and in some years even exceeded, the number of Lisbon vessels that arrived at the Portuguese Indian capital.[2] Moreover, when many merchants and traders on the west coast of India were increasingly being compelled to accept English carriage services from the 1740s and 1750s as the latter assumed greater control over the freight trade of the western Indian

---

[1] Edward A. Alpers, "Gujarat and the Trade of East Africa, c. 1500–1800", *The International Journal of African Historical Studies*, IX, 1 (1976), 22–44.

[2] For instance, in 1780, only two vessels arrived in Goa from Lisbon. See Celsa Pinto, *Trade and Finance in Portuguese India: A Study of the Portuguese Country Trade, 1770–1840* (New Delhi: Concept Publishing Company, 1994), appendix 4, 270. There was an exceptional year, 1785, when nine Lisbon vessels arrived at Goa.

Ocean, Vāniyā ownership and access to independent shipping contributed decisively to their competitiveness in oceanic trade.[3]

While some of the wealthy and prominent merchants were at the same time shipowners, in most cases Vāniyā merchants either leased vessels or, as was most common, freighted their cargoes on vessels owned by the shipowners of Diu or Daman who themselves would often have a stake in the voyages across the ocean. Portuguese merchants depended on Indian merchants and shipowners for the transportation of their own Indian trade goods to and from Mozambique. In most cases, this was arranged in partnership with either the owner of the vessel or done on consignment with a Vāniyā sending goods in either direction.

Given this lively and sustained maritime exchange, reflecting the continued presence and importance of Gujarati merchant shipping in the regional waters of the western Indian Ocean, it is surprising that a misperception has nonetheless persisted that this shipping had declined precipitously by the middle of the eighteenth century. In contrast to the impressive existence in the seventeenth century of Indian merchant princes such as Mulla Abd al-Ghafur, who at the height of his wealth owned around 20 ships that sailed from Surat to various Indian Ocean ports, Gujarati shipping is generally regarded as having become moribund by mid-century. The combination of a decline in the great Islamic empires of the Safavids, Ottomans and especially Mughals in the eighteenth century and the increase of private British shipping over the course of the century, it is argued, had fundamentally disruptive and destructive effects generally on South Asian Indian Ocean trade, and as a consequence specifically on Gujarati shipping: "[T]he man who had virtually disappeared was the Gujarati shipowner and the vessel which was little to be seen was the medium ship of around two hundred ton carrying capacity." While, in this view, Indian shippers "were still active" in the eighteenth century, "they had been relegated to the smaller vessels and the trade of the roadsteads" to such an extent that "by the turn of the nineteenth century ... the Indian ship had sailed into oblivion".[4] Apart from overstating the disruptive

---

[3] On the process whereby merchants in Surat and Bombay were increasingly challenged in the western Indian Ocean's carrying trade, see Lakshmi Subramanian, *Indigenous Capital and Imperial Expansion: Bombay, Surat and the West Coast* (Delhi: Oxford University Press, 1996).

[4] Ashin Das Gupta, "India and the Indian Ocean in the Eighteenth Century", in Das Gupta and M. N. Pearson (eds.), *India and the Indian Ocean 1500–1800*, paperback edn (New Delhi: Oxford University Press, 1999), 134, 143; *idem, Indian Merchants and the Decline of Surat c. 1700–1750*, reprint (New Delhi: Manohar, 1994); *idem*, "Trade and Politics in 18th-century India", in D. S. Richards (ed.), *Islam and the Trade of Asia* (Philadelphia: University of Pennsylvania Press, 1970), 181–214; *idem*, "Indian Merchants and the Trade in the Indian Ocean, c. 1500–1750", in Tapan Raychaudhuri and Irfan Habib (eds.), *The Cambridge Economic History of India. Vol. I: c. 1200–c. 1750* (Cambridge University Press,

affects of the "decline" of these Eurasian empires, a controversial notion
bound up with European justifications for conquest, this view has exaggerated the diminution of Gujarati shipping in the ocean. It has largely
overlooked the continued and indeed expanded presence of medium-
sized ocean-going ships in the western Indian Ocean well into the nineteenth century. Gujarati shipping to Mozambique and coastal Southeast
Africa represented an especially vibrant – but by no means exceptional –
segment of this shipping.[5]

That this shipping was Hindu, as represented by Vāniyā merchants
from Diu and Daman, challenges a further misconception about the
Indian Ocean – namely, that it was an Islamic historical space overwhelmingly dominated by Muslim shipping and groups. While "Muslim" shipping certainly was important in the western Indian Ocean in the
eighteenth and nineteenth centuries – from the final quarter of the eighteenth century Omani Arab shipping in particular underwent a resurgence
that was largely the result of the rise of Muscat as a powerful maritime
state[6] – it would be a gross misrepresentation to characterize the ocean as
purely an Islamic or "Arab lake".[7] Seafaring Gujarati Vāniyā merchants,
as well as other "Hindu" groups, owned and operated their own vessels in
these waters, and occupied niche positions throughout the region to an
extent that belies one-dimensional and reductionist perspectives of the
ocean as Muslim and as defined by Islamic merchant networks and their
shipping. Medium-sized shipping of the type that was operated by Vāniyā
merchants in the trade between Kathiawar and Mozambique displayed
great adaptability, resilience and vitality in the commercial worlds of the
ocean.[8]

1982), 407–33. A collection of Das Gupta's articles can be found in Uma Das Gupta
(comp.), *The World of the Indian Ocean Merchant 1500–1800: Collected Essays of Ashin Das
Gupta* (New Delhi: Oxford University Press, 2001). The notion of general Islamic decline
and its affect on maritime trade has recently been questioned by [M]ichael [N] Pearson,
The Indian Ocean (New York: Routledge, 2003), 117–18.

[5] Examples of other segments that drew Gujarati shipping in the second half of the eight-
eenth century were Muscat in Oman (Kachchhi Bhātiyā merchants), and from the 1830s
Massawa in the Red Sea. See M. Reda Bhacker, *Trade and Empire in Muscat and Zanzibar:
Roots of British Domination* (New York: Routledge, 1992); and Jonathan Miran, *Red Sea
Citizens: Cosmopolitan Society and Cultural Change in Massawa* (Bloomington: Indiana
University Press, 2009).

[6] Subramanian, *Indigenous Capital*, 271–86. See also N. Benjamin, "Arab Merchants of
Bombay and Surat (c. 1800–1840)", *IESHR*, 13, 1 (1976), 85–95.

[7] Subramanian, *Indigenous Capital*, 273. This view echoes older scholarship – for example,
C. S. Nicholls, writing about the nineteenth-century Swahili coast, argued that "generally
[Indians were] sending their goods to India on Arab vessels or boats manned by Arabs".
The Swahili Coast: Politics, Diplomacy and Trade on the East African Littoral, 1798–1856
(London: George Allen & Unwin, 1971), 348.

[8] As with other "indigenous" shipping in the western Indian Ocean, such as the dhow
economy of East Africa, Gujarati shipping did not disappear with the increased penetration

What this chapter seeks to do, then, is examine Vāniyā shipping from Diu and Daman to show how its financial and organizational structures, from the availability of maritime insurance services and speculative capital to access to local experienced sailing crews in India and Africa, shipyards and shipyard labour in India, enabled it not only to "survive" during a period of transition and flux but also to expand into the African waters of the southwestern Indian Ocean. Moreover, it suggests that the existence of this shipping both underpinned and reflected the vibrancy of Kathiawar and its communities of Vāniyā merchants.

Ships and their crews

The most common type of Vāniyā vessel used in trans-oceanic trade was the *pala*. Possibly a corrupted European rendering of a vernacular term, it may have been a derivation of *pāl*, the Marathi-Konkani name for a type of vessel used throughout coastal western India for trade.[9] Another possibility is that *palas* had once been war ships of two or three masts with a capacity to carry up to 40 guns, and had been transformed into merchant vessels in ways similar to some Maratha *pāls* and *gurābs*.[10]

Given their widespread use by Vāniyās in the western Indian Ocean, however, it is most likely that *pala* was a corruption of *pahala*,[11] a type of *kotia* used along the northwest coast of India throughout the eighteenth and nineteenth centuries. According to one source, *kotias* approximated closely "in general appearance, construction and rig ... the smaller of the Arab *baghla*[12] type, being a two-masted decked vessel with a high poop,

---

of steam ships in the late nineteenth century and the consolidation of British imperial rule. See Erik Gilbert, *Dhows and the Colonial Economy of Zanzibar, 1860–1970* (Oxford: James Currey, 2004).

[9] Sebastião Dalgado, *Glossario Luso-Asiatico*, 2 vols. (Coimbra: Imprensa da Universidade, 1919–21), II, 141. The definition provided by Fritz Hoppe, which probably drew on Dalgado, refers to this type of vessel in vague terms as a "ship of war and oriental merchant ship". See *A África Oriental Portuguesa no tempo do Marquês de Pombal 1750–1777* (Lisbon: Agência-Geral do Ultramar, 1970), 474, fn 143.

[10] D. Jose Maria de Almeida and Araujo Corréa de Lacerda, *Diccionario Encyclopedia ou Novo Diccionario da Lingua Portuguesa para uso dos Portugueses e Brazileiros, Correcto e augmentado, n'esta nova edição*, 5th edn (Lisbon: Imprensa Nacional, 1879), II, 490; H. Leitão and J. Vicente Lopes, *Dicionario da Linguagem de Marinha antiga e actual*, 2nd edn (Lisbon: Centro de Estudos Historicos Ultramarinos da Junta de Investigacoes Cientificas do Ultramar, 1974), 299; Jean Deloche, *Transport and Communications in India Prior to Steam Locomotion. Volume II: Water Transport* (New Delhi: Oxford University Press, 1994), 193.

[11] Clifford W. Hawkins, *The Dhow: An Illustrated History of the Dhow and Its World* (Lymington: Nautical Publishing, 1977).

[12] This was a large vessel of between about 80 and 300 tons, used extensively off the Arabian peninsula for the transport of cargo. J. G. Lorimer, *Gazetteer of the Persian Gulf, Omān and Central Arabia*, 2 vols. (Calcutta: Superintendent Government Printing, 1908–15), II, appendix Z, 3.

[and] a raked transom counter".[13] The dimensions of "fine" *kotias* could be "from 40 to 80 ft in length between the perpendiculars or 70–100 ft overall".[14] They were two or three-masted, lateen-rigged[15] vessels with covered decks, and had an average carrying capacity of 100–200 tons.[16] *Kotias* sailed extensively throughout the Indian Ocean, and were particularly widely used in voyages to the Persian Gulf and the East African coast.[17]

Although detailed descriptions of Gujarati *palas* appear not to exist, scattered documentation confirms that they were *pahalas* of two masts,[18] and could carry loads between about 80 tons and 250 tons.[19] Although in some cases sources indicate that they may have been larger three-masted vessels, these appear to have been exceptions.[20] The tonnage of these medium-sized vessels was at the higher end of much indigenous shipping in the second half of the eighteenth century, and compared favourably even with the growing imperial Omani shipping fleet of the early nineteenth century.[21] Cargo lists showing that *palas* carried large and heavy cargoes confirm their size. Besides a sizeable ivory cargo of almost 40,000 kg, the *Nossa Senhora dos Remedios*, a *pala* owned by Jhaver Khushal, transported gold, silver coins, iron and *madeira* wine on its return voyage to Diu in 1800. The vessel also carried crew and passengers, slaves and their provisions, and food and cooking utensils.[22] *Palas* were capable of carrying between 50 and 125 people and could transport up to

---

[13] James Hornell, "The Sailing Craft of Western India", *Mariner's Mirror*, 32 (1946), 197.

[14] *Ibid.*, 198.

[15] This denoted a rig with a triangular (or lateen) sail that was bent to a yard and hoisted to the head of a low mast. See L. Dimmock, "The Lateen Rig", *Mariner's Mirror*, 32 (1946), 35–41. Despite its wide usage, Michael Pearson has argued that the term "lateen" is actually a misnomer because it derives from the Crusades. See *Indian Ocean*, 67.

[16] A. H. J. Prins, "The Persian Gulf Dhows: Two Variants in Maritime Enterprise", *Persica*, 2 (1966), 2.

[17] Hornell, "Sailing Craft", 198.

[18] See, for example, ANTT, Minstério do Reino, Maço 499, "Relação das Embarcaçoens de Gavia que actualmente pertencem aos Negociantes de Mossambique...", 21 August 1801; and HAG, CDm 1067, D. Lourenço de Noronha to Viceroy, 5 November 1820.

[19] See, for example, Gonçalo de Magalhães Teixeira Pinto, *Memorias sobre as Possesoes Portuguezas na Azia, escriptas no Anno de 1823 (e agora publicadas com breves notas e additamentos de Joaquim Heliodoro da Cunha Rivara* (Lisbon: Imprensa Nacional, 1859), 27–8. See also HAG, CDm 1067, D. Lourenço de Noronha to Viceroy, 24 October 1820.

[20] HAG, CDm 1061, Caetano Souza Pereira to Governor, 4 November 1802.

[21] Between 1790 and 1802–3, Muscat built up a fleet of 50 ships, with the Sultan owning several of these "with a tonnage capacity of 200 tons each". See Subramanian, *Indigenous Capital*, 279. With the support of the Imperial Treasury, this fleet would grow large so that by the 1830s there were up to 14 vessels of 1,000–2,000 tonnes burden.

[22] HAG, CDm 1061, "Mappa da Carga que trouxe de Mocambique a pala de viagem...", 26 September 1800.

6,000 tusks of ivory.[23] The largest *palas* exceeded even these volumes and could transport up to 170 individuals.[24] Clearly, these were large ocean-going vessels that could sustain long-distance maritime trade.

Palas also possessed the capacity to carry artillery, and in some cases did so, particularly when there was a high risk of attack at sea.[25] In the early 1780s, fearing an attack from "pirates" along the Mozambique coast – likely French privateers – a group of Vāniyā merchants contributed to the cost of outfitting two *palas* with cannon.[26] Generally, however, Vāniyās (and other South Asian merchants) were reluctant to sacrifice cargo-carrying capacity to accommodate artillery that, apart from adding considerable weight to a vessel, occupied valuable deck space.[27] A vessel that had to carry a lot of additional weight faced the prospect of a slow crossing with possible costly delays. *Palas* were noted for their speed and manoeuvrability, and were regarded as ideal for the crossings between India and Mozambique.[28] A Portuguese official even commented enthusiastically about how better suited they were than Portuguese vessels for negotiating the difficult passage through the Comoro Islands and Madagascar.[29]

While *palas* were the most widely owned and used vessels in the trade between India and Mozambique, Vāniyā merchants owned and made use of other vessels in the coastal trade of the Kathiawar peninsula. *Machwas*, for instance, were used along the west coast of India in "minor" coastal traffic and for fishing.[30] They were especially useful for sailing up rivers

---

[23] HAG, CDm 1056, João Homen da Costa to Governor, n.d. [but *c.* 1784]; HAG, CDm 1060, "Rellação do Marfim e mais generos . . .", 25 October 1793. The estimate for the number of people carried by larger *palas* has been calculated from lists contained in HAG. See, for example, CD 1008, "Mapa da Tripulação e Carga da Palla . . .", 28 October 1824; *ibid.*, "Mapa da Tripulação da Palla N. Senhora do Socorro. . .", 13 November 1825; and CDm 1061, "Mapa da Tripulação e Carga da Palla Nossa Senhora da Penha de França", 29 September 1804.

[24] HAG, CDm 1067, "Mapa da tripulação e carga da Palla d'viagem Azia Feliz. . .", 24 October 1820.

[25] For a pala carrying artillery, see for example, AHU, Códice 1324, Passport for Narsinh Haridas to return to Diu, 16 July 1762. Detailed evidence does not exist of the artillery carried onboard but see HAG, CDm 1061, Francisco Antonio da Veiga Cabral to Governor, 3 November 1800, for the need to carry some guns for the crossing between western India and Mozambique.

[26] HAG, CD 996, Premoji Siva and Hirchand Manilal to Castellan of Diu, 28 April 1783.

[27] Ashin Das Gupta, "The Early 17th Century Crisis in the Western Indian Ocean and the Rise of Gujarati Shipping in the Early 18th Century", in B. Arunachalam (ed.), *Essays in Maritime Studies* (Mumbai: Maritime History Society, 1998), 55–65.

[28] HAG, CD 1009, Francisco de Mello da Gama e Araujo to Viceroy, 8 September 1827; HAG, Feitoria de Surrate 2603, Joze Gomes to Ribeiro, Hubens & Co., 16 June 1788.

[29] HAG, Feitoria de Surrate 2603, Ribeiro, Hubens & Co., 28 November 1788.

[30] Hornell, "The Sailing Craft", 202.

that *palas* were too large to navigate, and could also carry guns.[31] Riverine sailing was also done by small *kotias*, whose speed and manoeuvrability enabled the efficient transportation of goods.[32] Vāniyā merchants engaged larger vessels along the coast called *batils* that had a carrying capacity of between 40 and 100 tons, and ordinarily were two-masted, lateen-rigged vessels.[33] In some cases, wealthier Vāniyās owned European-designed *galeras* and *curvetas*. In Mozambique, besides making use of *palas* and *batils* for coastal navigation, Vāniyā merchants also used a range of small coastal craft such as *sumacas, galvetas* and *curvetas*. These likely included locally built *pangaios*, or "dhows", and *almadias*. Short trips along the northern coast of Mozambique were made in small local craft capable of carrying light loads.

Navigation in all of these vessels was the responsibility of skilled and highly experienced sailors. As in the sixteenth- and seventeenth-century Indian Ocean world, Indian vessels in the eighteenth and nineteenth centuries were made up of a rigid command structure and clearly defined onboard positions.[34] The nature of these positions within the hierarchy of the vessel, however, may have changed in these later centuries. Overall command of a vessel was the responsibility of a senior figure, the *nakhudha*, who determined the course of a voyage. Although in earlier periods the *nakhudha* very often referred to the captain of the ship or its owner, by the seventeenth century greater diversity in ship-owning resulted in the position being increasingly fixed as the individual to whom the owner entrusted his vessel and trade goods. Equally importantly, the *nakhudha* exercised authority over the crew and passengers. He possessed no skill in maritime navigation but his singular role marked him as one of the most central figures on board a vessel. If merchants were not accompanying their cargo, it was the *nakhudha* who was responsible for its disposal or transfer.[35] Navigation was the responsibility of a *sarhang*, who was in technical control of the vessel. He was assisted by the *mu'allim* or

---

[31] HAG, CDm 1056, João Homen da Costa to D. Frederico Guilherme de Souza, 19 October 1783.

[32] HAG, CDm 1061, Candido Joze Mourão Garcez Palha to Governor, 20 October 1802.

[33] Larger *batils* sometimes carried a third small mast. Hornell, "The Sailing Craft", 206. See also Casimiro de Sequeira Nazareth, "Barcos Nativos da India", *O Oriente Portugues*, vol. IX (1912), 230.

[34] Ashin Das Gupta, "The Maritime Merchant and Indian History", in Uma Das Gupta (comp.), *World of the Indian Ocean Merchant*, 23–6; Sinnappah Arasaratnam, *Maritime India in the Seventeenth Century* (Delhi: Oxford University Press, 1994), 262.

[35] Nancy Um, *The Merchant Houses of Mocha: Trade & Architecture in an Indian Ocean Port* (Seattle: University of Washington Press, 2009), 92; Arasaratnam, *Maritime India*, 262. For the early role of *nakhodas*, see Ranabir Chakravarti, "Nakhudas and Nauvittakas:

pilot, who was responsible, critically, for navigating the vessel along its route. In turn, the *tandel* was in charge of the crew, the largest group onboard a vessel.

In the eighteenth century, this structure may have undergone some change and the terminology may have become more fluid in its designation of the individuals who ran a ship. According to Ashin Das Gupta, "the merchant or the official as *nakhuda* tended to disappear and the *sarhang*, the *muʿallim* or the *tandel* appeared more and more as *nakhudas* on the Indian Ocean".[36] Available crew lists for Vāniyā *palas* show that positions such as *sarhang* and *tandel* were common.[37] These changes were caused, in Das Gupta's view, by the "decline" of larger Indian merchant ships and the "rise" of British shipping in the nineteenth century. While the growing presence of British vessels throughout the ocean from the mid- to late eighteenth century began to challenge South Asian and other indigenous shipping by displacing vessels from certain routes and challenging their carrying capacity, it is important not to exaggerate the picture or generalize from partial evidence. British shipping never managed to remove or entirely marginalize South Asian maritime traffic from the ocean nor did it necessarily send Indian merchant vessels into "decline". When we disaggregate the picture by looking at specific routes and the trade of particular groups such as the Vāniyā in the southwest Indian Ocean, it is clear that some South Asian shipping managed not only to "survive" in the face of British challenges but its dynamic nature enabled it to thrive well into the nineteenth century. The persistence of the position of *nakhudha* on Vāniyā vessels in the eighteenth and nineteenth centuries attested to this dynamism, even while new positions such as *mukaddam* – responsible for assisting the *sarhang* on voyages – began to make their appearance.

Given the inherent dangers of sailing to the coast of Mozambique, the *muʿallim* played an indispensible role on board a vessel. They were drawn almost exclusively from among the seafaring Muslim populations of either Diu or Daman. Responsible for guiding a vessel beyond the bar of the harbour and into the open sea for the duration of its passage, pilots were men who had gained an intimate knowledge of coastlines and harbours from entire lives spent at sea, and who could benefit from the

Ship-owning Merchants in the West Coast of India (c. AD 1000–1500)", *Journal of the Economic and Social History of the Orient: Special Issue in Honour of Ashin Das Gupta*, 43, 1 (2000), 34–64.

[36] Das Gupta, "The Maritime Merchant", 27.

[37] See, for example, AHU, Moç, Cx 93 Doc. 44, Passport & Crew List of Brig, Santo Antonio Deligente, owned by Jiv Sangaji and Velji Tairsi, 18 May 1802; Cx 97 Doc. 25, Crew List of Brig, Boa Caetana, 12 January 1803; Cx 131 Doc. 94, Crew List of Palla, Nossa Senhora dos Remedios e Estrela do Mar, 7 March 1810.

kinds of navigational manuals that are described later in the chapter. Although one *muʿallim* was usually enough to guide a vessel safely out of harbours, it was not uncommon for *palas* to sail with up to three pilots, each of whom possessed specialized knowledge of the different parts of the coasts along which vessels had to navigate in sailing to Mozambique.[38] The most sought-after pilots were those who had an intimate understanding of the coasts of both western India and Southeast Africa but merchants usually had to engage the services of local pilots on both coasts for the safe passage of vessels from their anchorages. The particularly difficult entry into Mozambique Island made this an unquestionable necessity.[39]

Pilots did on occasion misjudge conditions, resulting in vessels running aground. Although this did not necessarily mean the loss of an entire cargo, it could adversely affect merchants with a stake in the voyage because they would be forced to wait for the ship to be repaired before they could sail again. It is thus not surprising that *muʿallim* error elicited strong responses from merchants – in 1821, Amarchand Dharamchand accused the pilot Salmanji Valji of gross negligence in miscalculating the depth of the bar inside Diu harbour, which caused his vessel to run aground and suffer structural damage.[40] Serious errors in judgement could prove costly and cause delays at best, and at worst result in irreparable damage or even the loss of a ship. At times, pilots who had been bribed by rival merchants to guide a vessel into trouble did this intentionally.[41]

Equally important to the success of Gujarati voyages across the ocean was engaging the service of crews who were experienced in sailing the particular routes taken by Vāniyā vessels. Their number was rarely made up exclusively from a single group, with the majority of crews recruited from among Hindu and Muslim sailors. They did, though, have one thing in common: long histories of sailing to coastal Mozambique. Both free and enslaved Africans also laboured as crew members on voyages along the Mozambique coast and across the ocean to India.[42] Sailors for voyages

---

[38] HAG, CD 1000, "Mappa da tripulação e carga da galera N. Senhora do Socorro Estrela do Mar do proprietario Saguldas Nattu...", 19 October 1823; HAG, CD 1008, "Mappa da tripulação e carga da pala ...", Diu, 28 October 1824; AHM, Fundo do Século XIX, Governo Geral, 8–21, Passport for Palinha Anna Feliz, 10 May 1839; *ibid.*, 8–227, "Rol d'equipagem", 23 May 1839; "Relação da matricula", 5 September 1839; "Relação da Matricula", 5 September 1839; "Matricula da equipagem", 2 December 1839.

[39] See appendix No. II, "Directions for entering Mosambique Harbour, extracted from Captain Thomas Weatherhead's Journal", in Henry Salt, *A Voyage to Abyssinia ... in the Years 1809 and 1810* (London: F. C. and J. Rivington, 1814), xxviii.

[40] HAG, CDm 1067, Lourenco de Noronha to Viceroy, 14 February 1821.

[41] HAG, CD 1006, Joaquim Mourão Garcez Palha to Viceroy, 2 April 1818.

[42] Africans were widely used as dhow crews along the coast, becoming a ubiquitous presence in the nineteenth century when – along with Indian workers – "seedies" also began to

were engaged in Diu mostly from the fishing settlement of Gogola,[43] and from the nearby coastal town of Ghogha that had a long history as a maritime labour recruitment centre going back to the 1650s.[44] Muslim sailors tended to be drawn from Daman, while Hindu sailors came overwhelmingly from Diu.[45]

Along the Mozambique coast, Vāniyā-owned or -financed vessels carried crews comprising slave and non-slave sailors. African seamen were recruited all along the Mozambican coast, with a number of Makua from the mainland directly opposite Mozambique Island, known as Macuana, sailing on coastal voyages as far south as Delagoa Bay; African sailors from Sofala, Quelimane and Inhambane were also among crews of Vāniyā-owned vessels. Some of these men who were slaves worked – as in the nineteenth century – as personal dependents of the owner of the vessel and may have been trained to labour specifically on vessels.[46] Thus, in 1802, Virchand Mulji's *pala* sailed from Mozambique Island to India with a crew of 22 individuals, among whom were eight African slave sailors "of his house".[47] It is unclear how African slave sailors were recruited but they do not appear to have been coerced into service as they were in the Atlantic.[48]

However, most of the crews on Gujarati vessels seem to have been freedmen recruited on the coast as skilled maritime labour with substantial knowledge of the Mozambique coast, for which they received a wage or compensation in the form of trade goods that they could sell at their destination. Freedmen worked alongside "lascars" (South Asian sailors) but never outnumbered sailors from the subcontinent and in many cases represented only a small percentage of the crew on trans-oceanic voyages. They made up the majority of the crew on voyages along the

labour increasingly on British vessels. See Janet J. Ewald, "Crossers of the Sea: Slaves, Freedmen and Other Migrants in the Northwestern Indian Ocean, c. 1750–1914", *American Historical Review* 105, 1 (2000), 69–91.

[43] Teixeira Pinto, *Memorias Sobre as Possessoes Portuguezes*, 27–8.

[44] R. J. Barendse, *The Arabian Seas, 1640–1700* (Research School, CNWS, Leiden University, 1998), 37. For the castes of sailors at Ghogha, see *Gazetteer of the Bombay Presidency, Vol. 8: Kathiawar* (Bombay: Government Central Press, 1884), 153.

[45] See, for example, HAG, CDm 1067, Lourenço de Noronha to Viceroy, 29 March 1821; HAG, CD 1000, "Mappa da tripulação e carga da galera N. Senhora do Socorro Estrela do Mar do proprietario Saguldas Nattu...", 19 October 1823; HAG, CD 1008, "Mappa da tripulação e carga da pala de viagem Nossa Senhora do Mar Flor de Dio do proprietario Natu Saugi", 28 October 1824; HAG, CDm 1067, "Mapa da tripulação e carga da pala d'viagem Azia Feliz...", 24 October 1820.

[46] Frederick Cooper, *Plantation Slavery on the East Coast of Africa* (New Haven: Yale University Press, 1977), 32–3.

[47] HAG, CD 1003, Cargo list and accompanying letter, 28 May 1802.

[48] The reference here is to the south Atlantic. See Mariana P. Candido, "Different Slave Journeys: Enslaved African Seamen on Board of Portuguese Ships, c. 1760–1820s", *Slavery and Abolition*, 31, 3 (2010), 397.

Mozambique coast, however, where their experience made them an invaluable source of maritime labour.

African sailors were part of a seafaring class that existed on and around Mozambique Island, and that laboured within a broader regional context of maritime work carried out by seamen all along the East African coast and across the Mozambique Channel in Madagascar.[49] In serving on African, Arab and South Asian vessels in the late eighteenth and throughout the nineteenth centuries, these men were members of communities of maritime labour circulation that helped maintain commercial exchange in the western Indian Ocean. Vāniyās could recruit Makua or Swahili sailors seasonally for coastal trade and to serve as crew on long-distance voyages to the subcontinent. African sailors may also have been indispensable on board Indian vessels in acting as linguistic intermediaries between the cargoes of enslaved individuals (found aboard every Vāniyā vessel sailing to India in the eighteenth and nineteenth centuries) and the ship's *nakhuda* and other South Asian crew who – unlike some Vāniyā merchants – may not have spoken local African languages such as Emakhuwa.[50]

In addition to their South Asian and African sailors, Gujarati *pala* crews were part of broader oceanic and itinerant circuits of maritime labour that not only circulated in the western Indian Ocean but also had connections to the Atlantic. When the vessel owned by Dharamdhor Ramji arrived at Mozambique Island in 1809, its pilot departed for Madagascar a few days later and was replaced by a Dane who had arrived at Mozambique Island from Rio de Janeiro.[51] Although details on how these seafaring individuals were recruited are not available, it is clear that they constituted a highly mobile labour force that was hired seasonally to work on Vāniyā (and other) vessels throughout the western Indian Ocean, and whose skills were indispensable to the success of long-distance trade.

Ship construction

Palas were built in western India, and from the middle of the eighteenth century many were constructed for Vāniyā merchants at Daman. With access to teak forests and with the availability of skilled Indian

---

[49] Samuel Sanchez, "Navigation et gens de mer dans le canal du Mozambique: Les boutres dans l'activité maritime de Nosy Be et de l'Ouest de Madagascar au XIXe siècle", in Didier Nativel and Faranirina V. Rajaonah (eds.), *Madagascast et l'Afrique: Entre indentité et appartenances historiques* (Paris: Karthala, 2003), 124–5.

[50] This idea is suggested for the Atlantic by Candido, "Slave Journeys".

[51] AHU, Moç, Cx 128 Doc. 19, Passport for Curveta owned by Dharamdor Ramji, ant. 8 August 1809.

shipwrights, Daman became an attractive shipbuilding centre in western India not only for Indian merchants but also for their Portuguese and English counterparts. While Vāniyā may have had vessels constructed in other regional shipbuilding centres such as Mandvi, Bhavnagar or Bombay (where Parsi shipbuilders were becoming prominent from the final quarter of the eighteenth century), or purchased ships from Arab owners at ports in the Arabian peninsula, Vāniyā merchants overwhelmingly built their own *palas* for their western Indian Ocean commerce at Daman, which they found to have "good conditions" for their shipping needs.[52] These vessels were constructed through partnerships among Vāniyā merchants and between them and Portuguese and English merchants.[53]

Despite its extensive shipbuilding activity, however, the place of Daman as a significant shipbuilding port in western India has been overlooked, largely as the result of the establishment of Bombay's famous shipyards in the nineteenth century. The history of the development of Bombay as an important regional shipping and commercial centre within the British Raj from the 1850s and 1860s has thus overshadowed Daman and marginalized its importance.[54] With its proximity to teak forests, historically the most important timber for ship construction in India and in other parts of the western Indian Ocean, and the availability of skilled labour, Daman was ideally suited to develop as a shipbuilding centre for Indian and Portuguese merchants.

Yet it was only once the Portuguese had acquired "Dadra" and "Pragana" (*pargana*, local district) Nagar Haveli, east of Daman, in the late eighteenth century as part of their settlement with the Marathas (the outcome of a Luso-Maratha agreement to end hostilities between Maratha forces and Portuguese state territories in the eighteenth century) that Daman was able fully to develop a flourishing industry of some importance on the west coast of India.[55] Crucially, the territory of Nagar Haveli, covering a

---

[52] HAG, CD 999, D. João Joze de Mello to Castellão, 19 November 1770. See also HAG, CD 995–1012 and CDm 1056–1068.

[53] See, for example, HAG, CDm 1063, João Vicente Roiz to Lourenço Varella d'Almeida, 25 April 1808 for a partnership between a Vāniyā and English merchant; and AHU, Moç, Cx 31 Doc. 42, Amarchand Madhavji to Governor, n.d. [but *c.* 1774] for a Vāniyā–Portuguese merchant partnership.

[54] There is one notable exception, the work of Ernestina Carreira: "L'Empire et ses Vaisseaux: La Construction Navale dans l'Ocean Indien Occidental aux XVIIIᵉ et XIXᵉ Siècles", in Carreira and Idelette Muzart-Fonseca dos Santos (eds.), *Éclats d'empire, du Brésil à Macao* (Paris: Maisonneuve et Larose, 2003), 127–71; *idem*, "From Decline to Prosperity: Shipbuilding in Daman, 18th–19th Centuries", in Lotika Varadarajan (ed.), *Indo-Portuguese Encounters: Journeys in Science, Technology and Culture* (New Delhi: Aryan Books International, 2006), 593–629.

[55] Carreira, "L'empire"; *idem*, "From Decline to Prosperity"; M. N. Pearson, *The Portuguese in India* (New York: Cambridge University Press, 1987), 152; [W.] G[ervase] Clarence-Smith,

sizeable area of approximately 300 km^2 and comprising 72 villages, was rich in teak forests as well as sheesham wood, an Indian rosewood used also in shipbuilding and in the outfitting of vessels.[56] Its significant teak reserves, in particular, were of great value to Daman and guaranteed its shipbuilders access to the best hardwoods for ship construction.

The emergence of Daman's shipbuilding industry also owed a great deal to the presence of skilled master shipbuilders and to the availability of maritime labour. Portuguese interest in Indian shipbuilding developed soon after their arrival in western India in the sixteenth century and reflected an admiration for the skill of local shipwrights and the sophistication of Indian design. It was not long before Indian shipbuilders were being commissioned to construct ships according to European specifications at shipyards in Goa. Found in abundance along the Malabar coast, teak was generally considered to be the best quality wood for ship construction because of its exceptional durability and lighter weight. Its natural attributes made teak popular and it became used throughout the Indian Ocean for the construction of vessels engaged in both coastal and long-distance voyaging.[57]

Daman received a further boost to its shipbuilding industry in 1776 with the passing of a Royal decree that made Crown vessels exempt from the burden of taxation on ship construction.[58] It was enacted in the context of the reform spirit that was increasingly finding its voice in Lisbon at this time, and which would culminate in the ambitious project of the 1780s (discussed in Chapter 1) aimed at improving the "moribund" state of the economy of Portuguese India by increasing its trade with Mozambique and East Africa.[59] By promoting the construction of "Portuguese" vessels in Daman by imperial subjects, the authorities hoped to increase the number of merchant vessels trading in the western Indian Ocean and thus bolster the revenues of the beleaguered Royal Treasury with the greater customs revenues that, it was hoped, this

The Third Portuguese Empire 1825–1975: A Study in Economic Imperialism (Manchester University Press, 1985), 45; Carlos Xavier, "A Cidade e o Porto de Damão nos séculos XVIII e XIX", *Studia*, 46 (1987), 299.

[56] Carreira, "From Decline to Prosperity", 608. Access to the teak forests of Nagar Haveli was at times disrupted by the Marathas in the 1790s and into the nineteenth century, caused in part by Anglo-Maratha tensions. See HAG, CDm 1061, Candido Joze Mourão Garcez Palha to Viceroy, 16 February 1804.

[57] Xavier Mariona Martins, "Portuguese Shipping and Shipbuilding in Goa, 1510–1780", PhD diss., Goa University, 1994; K. N. Chaudhuri, *Trade and Civilization in the Indian Ocean: An Economic History from the Rise of Islam to 1750* (Cambridge University Press, 1985), 140, 148.

[58] HAG, CDm 1060, Antonio Leite d'Souza to Sebastião Joze Ferreira Barroco, 14 December 1790.

[59] Further details of how these reforms affected broader Portuguese imperial shipbuilding efforts can be found in Carreira, "From Decline to Prosperity".

would engender. Instead of purchasing vessels at ports such as Bombay, merchants were encouraged to build them in Daman.[60] Together with private Portuguese merchants who were enticed from Surat to Daman to construct vessels, Vāniyā merchants took advantage of this opportunity and from the 1780s prominent merchants such as Jhaver Khushal were having ships built at Daman.[61] Although Surat may have provided competition to Daman as a shipbuilding port, its industry was stagnant by the mid-1780s and only a small number of ships seem to have been completed at its yards.[62]

By ending taxation on shipbuilding, the Portuguese removed one of the primary obstacles that had previously prevented the development of this industry in Daman. However, this alone proved insufficient in attracting merchants to the shipyards. What enticed them to Daman was a combination of the availability of skilled and experienced shipwrights, and cheap labour.[63] An official was thus able to boast that building any type of ship at Daman was cheaper than purchasing one "which ordinarily always has defects" either there or in Bombay.[64] Allowing for the possibility that this was an exaggerated claim, the increased level of activity at the port is a clear indication that, at least in part, this was true. Indeed, vessels constructed in Daman were regularly sold at auction in Bombay, though not, it seems, necessarily always at a profit.[65] Some of these were ordered by Portuguese merchants who were resident in Bombay and had ties with China related, especially in the early nineteenth century, to the Malwa opium trade that expanded through Daman in response to restrictions that the East India Company was imposing elsewhere on opiate exports from the subcontinent.[66]

---

[60] See, for example, HAG, CDm 1063, Principe to Francisco Antonio da Vieiga Cabral and Joze Caetano Pacheco Tavares, 8 March 1799. See also Carreira, "From Decline to Prosperity".

[61] HAG, CDm 1057, João Gomes da Costa to Viceroy, 17 May 1786; CDm 1061, Jhaver Khushal, Harchand Hirchand et al. to Governor, 4 December 1798. See also Anne Bulley, *The Bombay Country Ships 1790–1833* (Richmond: Curzon Press, 2000), 37.

[62] HAG, Feitoria de Surrate 2603, Joze Gomes Loureiro to Loureiro, Hubens & Co., 6 February 1788.

[63] HAG, CDm 1065, Castro e Almeida to Viceroy, 5 November 1818.

[64] HAG, Copiador Indiano da Feitoria de Surrate 2533, Carlos Joze Pereira, Surat, 13 November 1787. A further claim was that having ships built at Daman was more "convenient" than having them built elsewhere. See HAG Feitoria de Surrate 2603, Joze Gomes Ribeiro to Ribeiro, Hubens & Co., 21 May 1787.

[65] See Feitoria de Surrate 2603, Joze Gomes Loureiro, Bombay, 19 May 1789, for the case of a 700 tonne ship that could fetch only a price equal to that for which it had been constructed.

[66] On the Malwa opium trade to Macau and China from the 1810s, see, for example, Clarence-Smith, *Third Portuguese Empire*, 25–9; Pinto, *Trade and Finance*, ch. 5; A. F. Moniz, *Noticias e Documentos para a Historia de Damão – Antiga provincia do Norte*,

Daman was not, however, the only port where Vāniyā merchants involved in the commercial circuits of Indian Ocean Africa could purchase or build ships. For centuries, boat building and repair work had been carried out at various places along the East African coast, such as Mogadishu and Kilwa. The most important centres in the sixteenth and seventeenth centuries were located on the southern coast at Mozambique Island and the Comoros.[67] They were close to timber supplies and possessed the labour required to carry out skilled work. In the eighteenth century, shipbuilding was taking place at other coastal sites such as Quelimane but it was occasional and vessels were smaller than *palas*. A *curveta* was completed in Quelimane in 1801,[68] while in 1817 in the Querimba Islands a *brig de guerra* was constructed by "Africans of the *moradores*, some Muslims and Makua".[69] Vāniyā merchants also purchased vessels in the region, most notably at Port Louis in the Ile de France once the southwest Indian Ocean slave trade gained in importance from the late eighteenth century. Port Louis offered a ship-buying market where Vāniyā and other merchants purchased vessels not only for the regional slave trades that connected Mozambique to Madagascar and the Mascarenes but also for the slave trade to Portuguese and Spanish ports in the southern Atlantic, as I show in Chapter 5.[70]

These shipbuilding possibilities notwithstanding, however, Gujarati merchants had many of their long-distance vessels built at Daman. Their interest in its shipyards withstood erratic teak supplies in the early nineteenth century, and the temporary takeover of Portuguese India by British forces seeking to protect the Portuguese state after the outbreak of war with France.[71] The latter may also have been responsible for

---

4 vols. (Bastorá: Tipografia Rangel, 1904–23), II, 174; "Comercio de Opio em Damão no Governo do Prefeito Bernardo Peresda [*sic*] Silva (1833)", in *idem, Noticias e Documentos*, IV, 81.

[67] [M]alyn [D.] [D.] Newitt, *A History of Mozambique* (Bloomington: Indiana University Press, 1995), 6–7. Sofala was also used but not extensively. See Newitt, *Portuguese Settlement on the Zambesi: Exploration, Land Tenure and Colonial Rule in East Africa* (New York: Africana Publishing Company, 1973), 32.

[68] AHU, Moç, Cx 89 Doc. 10, Passport for Curveta, Felix Costa, 25 September 1801.

[69] AHU, Moç, Cx 153 Doc. 24, João Rebello de Albuquerque to Governor, 22 April 1817.

[70] AHU, Códice 1365, Passport for Shobhachand Sowchand to send his partner to Ile de France to purchase vessel of 2–3 masts and between 500–600 tonnes, 10 November 1806; Passport for Shobhachand Sowchand to send his partner Manoel Jose Gomes to Ile de France to purchase vessel, 12 June 1807; Passport for Ile de France, 4 May 1798 and Passport for Ile de France to purchase the *Carlota Africana*, 10 June 1803.

[71] Ernestina Carreira, "Moçambique, Goa e Macau durante as Guerras Napoleonicas 1801–1810", in Luis F. F. Reis Thomaz and Artur Teodoro de Matos (eds.), *As Rellações entre a Índia Portuguesa, a Asia do Sueste e o Extremo Oriente: Actas do VI Seminario Internacional de Historia Indo-Portuguesa* (Macau/Lisbon: Comissão Nacional

the slowdown in the construction of vessels at Surat and Bombay.[72] The end of hostilities brought a renewed increase in shipbuilding activity at Daman, which once again assumed its position as a prominent shipbuilding centre in western India. Between 1814 and 1816 alone, ten vessels were built in its yards. A contemporary noted that between 1800 and 1820, 30 "large" vessels were finished in Daman, among them "a number" of ships for Vāniyās with African commercial interests. Others included frigates for the Portuguese imperial navy in the Atlantic. In the years from 1820 to the early 1840s, construction increased dramatically with the completion and launch of 149 vessels. These ranged from *machwas* built to "escort" vessels out to sea, to a 600 tonne frigate and gunships to resist Sakalava raids in the waters off Northeast Mozambique.[73]

The impressive accomplishments at Daman drew the attention of English contemporaries who wrote enthusiastically about its shipbuilding capacity, noting that apart from Bombay "most vessels required for the foreign trade ... [are] built at ... Daman". They commented favourably on the geographical position of Daman as the "best place" to lay-up small vessels during the monsoon, and in some cases English merchants even showed a preference for Daman over Bombay.[74] Some private traders purchased vessels from Vāniyā merchants in Daman.[75] Its shipbuilding yards were also preferred by others, in particular Arab merchants, confirming Daman's position in western India and the western Indian Ocean as a serious challenger to Bombay.[76]

But this level of "foreign" interest in Daman's shipyards paradoxically became a cause of concern for Portuguese high officials. The viceroy in particular sought to restrict English and other non-Portuguese construction in Daman in the belief that it undermined that of Crown subjects. This view was not shared by the governor of Daman, however, who argued that for much of the latter half of the eighteenth century Portuguese merchants had successfully managed to have vessels built there, in addition to English and

para as Comemorações dos Descobrimentos Portugueses, 1993). The British feared that the militarily weak Portuguese would be unable to repel a French attack. See also Pearson, *Portuguese in India*, 146–7.

[72] HAG, CDm 1061, Candido Joze Mourão Garcez Palha to Viceroy, 8 May 1804.

[73] Teixeira Pinto, *Memorias Sobre as Possessões Portuguezas*, 38–40; HAG, CDm 1056, "Carta Testemunhavel aos Mercadores Christoes, Gentios e Mouros...", n.d. [but *c.* 1784]; CDm 1065, D. Joze Mª de Castro e Almeida to Viceroy, 13 August 1817; *ibid.*, Joze Francisco de Paulla Cavalcanti de Albuquerque to D. Joze Maria de Castro e Almeida, 3 September 1818; Carreira, "From Decline to Prosperity".

[74] William Milburn, *Oriental Commerce, Containing a Geographical Description of the Principal Places in the East Indies, China...*, 2 vols. (London: Black, Parry & Co., 1813), I, 158, 168; Bulley, *Bombay Country Ships*, 35.

[75] See, for example, the sale to an English merchant of a vessel by Raghunath Samji in HAG, CDm 1063, Manoel da Lima Roiz to Governor, 25 April 1808.

[76] HAG, CDm 1065, Jose Maria de Castro e Almeida to Viceroy, 11 February 1817.

other merchants. Yet, despite presenting his case formally to the viceroy in a series of letters, it was disregarded in the firmly held belief that "foreign" construction at Daman was displacing that of Crown subjects.[77] The reason for the viceroy's intransigence lay in growing concerns over supplies of teakwood, which resurfaced in 1817 when it was discovered that teak was not only collected in the forests of Nagar Haveli but also in different parcels of Maratha and other lands not under Portuguese administration.[78] Portuguese royal builders were consequently sent to assess the condition of both the public and the private forests in the same year, and reported that the forests of the *pargana* Nagar Haveli had to be preserved as the only source of supply of teak for the Daman shipbuilding industry.[79] Despite this recommendation, and appreciating that the revenues generated from shipbuilding at Daman were too valuable for the Portuguese state to lose, the viceroy made the decision to allow foreigners to have vessels built in Daman once they had acquired passes in Goa.[80]

A notable attraction of Daman for any merchant was that, unlike Bombay, it specialized predominantly in medium to large vessels capable of withstanding arduous long-distance voyages in the western Indian Ocean. Bombay shipyards were increasingly catering to the growing China trade in raw cotton that required extremely large vessels capable of transporting bulky cargoes.[81] It was precisely because it did not specialize in the construction of such sizeable vessels that Daman was able to retain its position in the face of competition from Bombay. The number of large vessels constructed at Daman is unclear from the sources but there is evidence suggesting that no more than five or six vessels on the scale of those in Bombay were completed there in the nineteenth century.[82] On the few occasions when large ships were constructed at Daman, the prices they fetched in Bombay were not favourable and clearly demonstrated how the market for these vessels was dependent on a continually buoyant cotton market in China. In other words, prices and demand for large vessels fluctuated with oscillations in the price of cotton in China.[83]

---

[77] HAG, CD 1006, Manoel Duarte Leitão to Viceroy, 9 September 1818.
[78] HAG, CDm 1065, Jose Maria de Castro e Almeida to Viceroy, 11 February 1817 and same to same, 8 April 1817.
[79] HAG, CDm 1065, Jose Maria de Castro e Almeida to Viceroy, 10 February 1817.
[80] HAG, CDm 1065, Viceroy to Jose Maria de Castro e Almeida, n.d. [but 1817].
[81] Pamela Nightingale has shown that Parsis were already influential in the shipbuilding industry by the late eighteenth century. See *Trade and Empire in Western India 1784–1806* (Cambridge University Press, 1970), 22.
[82] See, for example, HAG, CDm 1065, Jose Maria de Castro e Almeida to Viceroy, 26 October 1817.
[83] HAG, Feitoria de Surrate 2603, Joze Gomes Loureiro to Ribeiro, Hubens & Co., Bombay, 21 May 1789.

But while the Daman shipbuilding industry continued to attract Vāniyā merchants throughout the nineteenth century, it entered a final phase of decline in the 1840s. Access to the teak forests of Nagar Haveli had proved increasingly difficult in the nineteenth century because the territory between it and Daman had come under the control of the East India Company, which despite agreeing conventions between 1819 and 1844 with the Portuguese imperial state for free movement, did not always honour these agreements.[84] The bigger problem, however, was that the large-scale and intense exploitation of the land and teak forests of Nagar Haveli, unmatched by reforestation efforts, had resulted in a scarcity of teakwood that raised shipbuilding expenses in Daman, compelling merchants to look to other ports to meet their shipping needs.[85] Daman's decline should not be overstated, though, for in the late nineteenth century it was reported that around 10 per cent of the vessels moored at Bhavnagar had been constructed in Daman's shipyards, a figure that represented the third highest number of vessels at the port.[86] Even though it may not have regained its earlier vitality, shipwrights continued to build vessels in Daman, likely with teak imports from territories in British India.

For Vāniyā merchants, access to the skilled and affordable quality of the Daman shipbuilding industry in the eighteenth and first few decades of the nineteenth centuries had served as a significant contributing factor to the continuation of independent Vāniyā mercantile activities across the Indian Ocean.

Sailing the ocean

Like all shipping in the western Indian Ocean, Vāniyā merchant shipping was regulated by the monsoon winds that acted as the ocean's primary unifying force. From the Arabic *mawsim*, or "season", the monsoons were critical to economic, religious and cultural exchange across the ocean. Vāniyā merchants had experience of the force of the monsoons and of the unforgiving schedule they imposed on participants in oceanic trade. Knowledge of how to harness the winds and currents of the Indian Ocean was therefore key to the organization of successful maritime commerce

---

[84] Carreira, "From Decline to Prosperity", 623.

[85] Carlos José Caldeira, *Apontamentos d'uma viagem de Lisboa a China e da China a Lisboa*, 2 vols. (Lisbon: J. P. M. Lavado, 1852–3), II, 55–6. According to Ernestina Carreira, the deforestation of the teak forests of Nagar Haveli was almost complete when 1,350 "big trees" were to be cut down in 1839, leaving only 400 standing. See "From Decline to Prosperity", 621, 623.

[86] *Gazetteer of the Bombay Presidency: Vol. 8*, 227.

between India's west coast, the Persian Gulf, the Red Sea and East and Southeast Africa. Although for centuries sailors had known of the power and rhythm of the winds, it was only once Arab geographers began to formalize their knowledge into navigational guides from the ninth and tenth centuries that could be disseminated among sailors and seafaring communities, that long-distance sailing became a less arbitrary experience.[87]

Sailing remained, nonetheless, an arduous undertaking whose schedules were determined by the monsoon system (Map 2.1). Beginning in November, the northeast monsoon built up, during which time ships from Arabia and India could leave the coast to reach African destinations as far south as Kilwa in a period of 30 to 40 days. Strong tropical storms in the eastern Arabian Sea in the months of October and November meant that the best times for vessels to sail from western India was in December when the monsoon had moved as far south as Zanzibar; vessels could then make the crossing in the considerably shorter period of 20 to 25 days.[88] To the south of Zanzibar, especially below Cape Delgado, navigation was further complicated by the change in "constancy" of the monsoon winds as they met the southeasterly winds that blew towards Mozambique. This produced variable winds and unstable weather "prone to tropical cyclones" in the Mozambique Channel, and thus made voyages south of Cape Delgado extremely arduous and dangerous. Only the most experienced captains and pilots were capable of navigating these successfully.[89]

The reversal in the wind(s) in April (the northeast monsoon having begun to break up in the south by March) signalled the start of the southwest monsoon, which was when vessels left the Southeast African coast for their return voyage(s) north to the Arabian Sea. However, between mid-May and mid-August there was an interruption when winds became "much too strong" for any sailing to take place.[90] The choice for captains, then, was between making the homeward voyage either in the "build-up" of the southwest monsoon in April, or possibly at its "tail-end" in late

---

[87] It is widely recognized that by the time that Ibn Majid wrote his treatise on navigational theory and practice in the late fifteenth century, seamanship in the western Indian Ocean had become fully professionalized. See G. R. Tibbets, *Arab Navigation in the Indian Ocean before the Coming of the Portuguese* (London: Royal Asiatic Society of Great Britain and Ireland, 1971).

[88] Abdul Sheriff, *Slaves, Spices & Ivory in Zanzibar: Integration of an East African Commercial Empire into the World Economy, 1770–1873* (London: James Currey, 1987), 8–10; M[ichael] N. Pearson, *Port Cities and Intruders: The Swahili Coast, India, and Portugal in the Early Modern Era* (Baltimore: Johns Hopkins University Press, 1998), 51–4.

[89] Sheriff, *Slaves, Spices & Ivory*, 8–12.

[90] Bashir Datoo, "Misconceptions about the Use of Monsoons by Dhows in East African Waters", *East African Geographical Review*, 8 (1970), 5; Sheriff, *Slaves, Spice & Ivory*, 10.

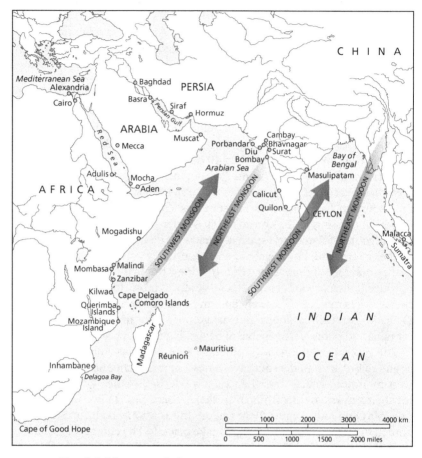

Map 2.1 Monsoon winds

August or September.[91] Failure to sail at these times increased the risk of conditions being too treacherous for departure or raised the possibility of shipwreck if a vessel was able to set sail. Merchants were generally reluctant for their vessels to winter on the African coast unless they required repairs or had outstanding accounts that needed to be settled urgently on the coast. The preference was to leave in the build-up of the southwest monsoon in April, and this strategy became particularly

[91] *Ibid.*, 3.

necessary if vessels needed first to proceed to coastal destinations south of Zanzibar such as Mozambique Island.[92]

There appears to have been another option for the return to India if vessels missed these departure dates but managed to set sail before the onset of the contrary northeast monsoon. In a letter to a colleague in 1792, a Portuguese official discussed the existence of a much longer and therefore more costly route to India that entailed sailing around Madagascar. But the added time at sea and the resultant financial implications, coupled with the threat of attack from Sakalava vessels of northern Madagascar at the end of the eighteenth century, made this route unpopular and it was little used at the time.[93]

Of equal importance to the winds in the monsoon system, and therefore of serious consideration for merchants, were sea currents. The East African coastal current is seasonal and by April, after it had struck the coast near Cape Delgado, it bifurcated into a powerful north-flowing current that, while ideal for sailing north, made departures from Mozambique hazardous.[94] Vessels could sail across the Mozambique Channel to make use of the northward flowing current up the west coast of Madagascar and via the Comoro Islands. For vessels wishing to sail directly to India from ports to the south of Mozambique Island, and vice versa, the currents were an even greater consideration. A vessel departing too late from a port such as Inhambane, for instance, would have little choice but to winter on the coast.[95] By the same token, if the same vessel intended to make a direct voyage to one of the ports south of Mozambique Island but had departed late from India, its crew ran the risk of being unable to navigate the vessel much beyond the island, thus restricting their African endeavours for that season.

As was common throughout the western Indian Ocean, Vāniyā seafarers followed a particular maritime calendar when planning sailing schedules – the solar Naroj calender. Derived from the Iranian New Year (Nayruz), it was divided into 365 sequentially numbered days (months were not used) that corresponded roughly to a solar year. It was further divided into segments of 100 days and, because it did not take into

[92] Sheriff, *Slaves, Spices & Ivory*, 8–12.
[93] HAG, CM 1446, Francisco de Cunha de Menezes to Antonio Manoel de Melo e Castro, 15 January 1792.
[94] Sheriff, *Slaves, Spices & Ivory*, 8–12; Mark Horton, however, provides a different account by arguing that the East African coastal current turns east into the Indian Ocean near Lamu, which is where vessels from the Middle East would end their voyage so as to avoid the current. See "Early Muslim Trading Settlements on the East African Coast: New Evidence from Shanga", *Antiquities Journal*, 67 (1987), 292, quoted and discussed in Pearson, *Port Cities*, 53–4.
[95] Datoo, "Misconceptions", 5–6.

account leap years, required adjustments periodically to correspond to the appropriate sailing season.[96] The Naroj calender served also as a standard method for seafarers to mark the passing of time in crossings of the Indian Ocean. Nava (New) Naroj, the first day of the year, was celebrated in August and represented both "the symbolic end of the monsoon and the ritualized commencement of a new sailing season". It served another important function in marking the beginning of a new accounting year and was thus indispensable in establishing dates for the settlement of debts throughout the annual trading season.[97]

While the Naroj calendar established a system of accounting for time, Gujarati navigation in the ocean in the eighteenth century appears to have relied on detailed maps and written sailing directions. Along with reports from Diu of "maps being used by sailors", the discovery recently of an early eighteenth-century Gujarati *rahmani* (pilot's manual) or *mālam-nī-pothī* (captain's book) offers compelling evidence which challenges the view that pre-colonial South Asian sailors utilized land – and sea–marks – exclusively to guide them around the waters of the Indian Ocean.[98] Written in both Gujarati and Arabic, the navigational manual contains, among other information, sailing directions for navigating a vessel to the ports of Surat and Jidda and – perhaps most significantly – a list of roughly 90 Indian Ocean ports and their stellar altitudes (Figure 2.1). Apart from including Gujarati ports such as Bharuch, Diu and Ghogha, other Indian ports (e.g. Calicut and Cochin in South India) and southern Arabian ports, the manual also listed ports along the East African coast. As noted by Samira Sheikh, these wide-ranging destinations may have denoted separate itineraries and reflected detailed navigational knowledge of some of the most important eighteenth-century western Indian Ocean ports.

Besides navigational information, the manual included a detailed map of the Gulf of Cambay drawn with grid lines and, exceptionally, featured a Cartesian depiction of the coast in contrast to "contemporary South Asian maps that favoured a more notational rendering supplemented by indicators of sailing time" (Maps 2.2 and 2.3).[99] Use of this particular graphic depiction of space, commonly used by contemporary European cartographers, is

[96] Abdul Sheriff, *Dhow Cultures of the Indian Ocean: Cosmopolitanism, Commerce and Islam* (London: Hurst, 2010), 120; Um, *Merchant Houses of Mocha*, 33.

[97] Edward Simpson, *Muslim Society and the Western Indian Ocean: The Seafarers of Kachchh* (New York: Routledge, 2006), 112–13; Um, *Merchant Houses*.

[98] HAG, CD 1014, Vitorino José Mendes Gouveia e Sousa to Viceroy, 19 June 1821; Samira Sheikh, "A Gujarati Map and Pilot Book of the Indian Ocean, c. 1750", *Imago Mundi* 61, 1 (2009), 67–83.

[99] Sheikh, "Gujarati Map", 73.

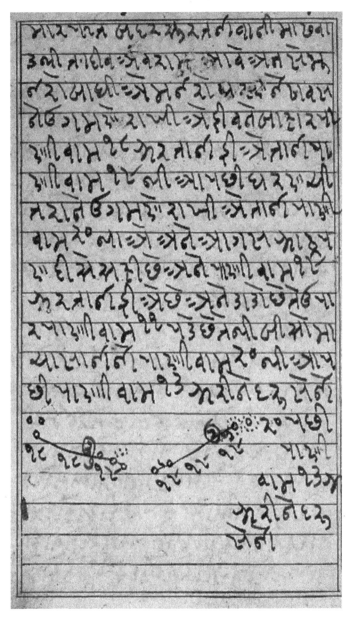

Figure 2.1 Instructions for sailing to Surat from eighteenth-century pilot's manual. Courtesy of Samira Sheikh, and with thanks to St John's College, Oxford

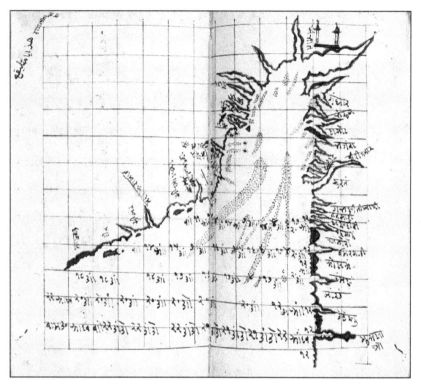

Map 2.2 Gujarati map of Gulf of Cambay. Courtesy of Samira Sheikh, and with thanks to St John's College, Oxford

likely explained as the result of contact between Gujarati merchants and seafarers and Portuguese, Dutch and British seamen, and their selective appropriation of sailing technologies, a practice rooted in the nautical traditions of the western Indian Ocean which were shared among Indian, Arab, European and possibly even Chinese seamen. While the eighteenth-century Gujarati map thus made use of a grid structure and particular depiction of the coastline of western India, at the same time it provided measurement information on depth soundings in *vams* (a unit of distance measured according to an onboard watch of three hours) and listed altitudes of the Pole Star at each port in a manner consistent with local maritime practice. By appropriating selective elements from a European seafaring tradition, Gujarati sailors and mapmakers were able to render maps that both reflected a sustained and vibrant engagement with the cosmopolitan maritime environment of the western Indian

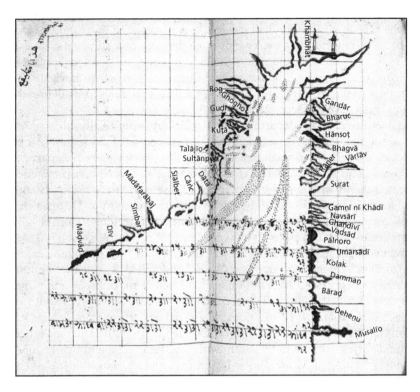

Map 2.3 Gulf of Cambay (in English transcription). Courtesy of Samira Sheikh, and with thanks to St. John's College, Oxford

Ocean and satisfied "a need for accurate and updated information".[100] Most significantly, the existence of this manual and map indicates that Gujarati merchant vessels were able to sail between India and Africa with detailed nautical and cartographic information that could be shared among, and updated by, seafarers. This reduced the risk involved in trans-oceanic trading, mitigating loss and delay, and helping safeguard profitability.

Ideal departure dates for Vāṇiyā vessels sailing to Mozambique from Kathiawar, if they wished to reduce the possibility of either being blown off course or of being shipwrecked during crossings that could be completed

[100] I base these arguments on Sheikh, "Gujarati Map", 77. For an interesting discussion, in the later colonial context of the British empire, of hybridized cadastral survey map-making practices involving British and Indian knowledge, see Kapil Raj, *Relocating Modern Science: Circulation and the Construction of Knowledge in South Asia and Europe, 1650–1900* (Basingstoke: Palgrave Macmillan, 2007), especially ch. 2.

in about 30 days, were November–December once the unsettled weather of the receding monsoon had passed.[101] Adherence to these months was especially important if a merchant vessel planned to sail directly to one of the southerly coastal destinations in Mozambique, such as Quelimane or Inhambane. It became increasingly difficult for a vessel to navigate the currents in the Mozambique Channel the longer it delayed its departure from India beyond December.[102]

Given these strict departure dates, it is surprising to find that, overwhelmingly, Vāniyā vessels left the Indian coast for Southeast Africa considerably later, in most cases either in January or early February.[103] This is likely explained by two related factors. The first was the preference for merchants sailing to Mozambique to voyage to Mozambique Island, an entrepôt for trade along the entire coast as far south as Delagoa Bay and throughout the Mozambique Channel, before embarking on any voyages to southern ports. No evidence exists of Vāniyā vessels making direct voyages from India to southern destinations such as Quelimane or Inhambane, suggesting that merchant ships sailed across the western Indian Ocean first to Mozambique Island before making any additional voyages down the coast. The second factor was that voyages south of this African island were still possible – if riskier – even when vessels left India as late as January. This meant that merchants could still reach their intended destinations in the south without having to spend two or three months waiting at Mozambique Island for currents, winds or inclement weather conditions to improve before making the onward journey.[104]

In addition, the challenges that at times beset the preparations for vessels to sail across the ocean – such as securing export cargoes in time for outward voyages – resulted in a number of merchants experiencing difficulties in readying ships for departure even by the end of January. Those who failed to sail before the end of the month risked disastrous outcomes. One of many, the case of Kanchand Manachand reveals the possible dangers of a delayed departure. Having been unable to prepare his vessel to sail in the northeast monsoon of 1784 before 2 February, Kanchand Manachand was forced to drop anchor at Zanzibar after strong

[101] HAG, CD 1001, Diogo de Mello de Payo to Governor, 20 October 1790; Simpson, *Muslim Society*.
[102] HAG, CDm 1065, D. Joze Mª de Castro e Almeida to Viceroy, Daman, 26 October 1817; HAG, Feitoria de Surrate 2603, Joze Gomes Loureiro to Ribeiro, Hubens & Co., Bombay, 28 November 1788.
[103] HAG, AD 4952–4969 and ADm 4836–4852. These departure times are confirmed in other sources. See, for example, HAG, CD 1001, Belchior do Amaral de Menezes to Governor, 16 June 1789; CDm 1067, D. Lourenço de Noronha to Viceroy, 1 February 1821.
[104] HAG, CDm 1061, Candido Joze Mourão Garcez Palha to Governor, 4 November 1802.

winds had made the voyage south of Cape Delgado impossible. As a result, the vessel arrived late at Mozambique Island and thus incurred a costly delay to the sale of its cargo.[105] Late departures from India also added the risk that a vessel would not reach its intended destination at all. For instance, when a *pala* sailed from Diu in the second week of February, 1830, it was forced off course after 47 days and had to make anchor at Anjouan in the Comoro Islands to take on water and provisions; after a six-day recovery period, the crew and vessel departed for Mozambique Island but they encountered a storm in the Mozambique Channel after two days that made it impossible to reach the island. They were left with little choice but to redirect the *pala* to Zanzibar where, presumably, they either waited for the storm to pass before completing their journey or, given that they would have reached Mozambique Island only sometime in late March or early April, tried to sell as much of their cargo as would have been possible in the Zanzibar market.[106]

The risk of shipwreck also increased proportionally to the length of delays in departures from India beyond the end of January, as experienced by Vakhatchand Harchand, who appears to have been unaware of the extent of the danger to his vessels when he set sail for Mozambique extremely late on 12 February. His vessel did not make it far, sinking a day later to the west of Daman "for reasons of strong winds" and causing merchants invested in the cargo to suffer significant losses.[107] For some merchants, such setbacks left them with little choice but to mortgage their property to creditors to maintain their solvency and creditworthiness.[108]

These and other losses as the result of delayed departures began to concern Portuguese authorities. It was first voiced in correspondence with the viceroy from the governor of Diu, Antonio Baptista da Cunha, who expressed his dismay at the magnitude of these losses. He estimated that between the early 1780s and mid-1790s, Vāniyā ships had lost cargoes worth in excess of three million *xerafins* as a result of shipwrecks because of late departures from India.[109] The effects of these losses, Baptista da Cunha suggested, were thus not only damaging to the merchants involved but also had serious implications for the revenue of the Portuguese imperial state. Such a large sum both provided a stark indication of the level

[105] HAG, CDm 1056, João Homen da Costa to Viceroy, 12 June 1784.
[106] *DAM*, II, 812.
[107] HAG, CDm 1067, D. Lourenço de Noronha to Viceroy, 14 February 1821.
[108] HAG, Registos Gerais da Feitoria de Diu 7970, Registered statement of Kalanji Talsi to Judge of Diu, 10 November 1798.
[109] HAG, CD 1002, Antonio Baptista da Cunha to Francisco Antonio da Veiga Cabral, 19 December 1795.

of Vāniyā investment in trade from Diu and underlined the dangers of oceanic crossings in the western Indian Ocean. Delays in the arrival of cloths in Diu for the Mozambique markets from the interior of Gujarat were thought to be the primary cause for the late departures of vessels.[110] Coordinating the supply of cloths through Indian agents from far in the interior of Gujarat with appropriate sailing times was never easy, and remained a challenge that – despite their vast experience in maritime commerce – Vāniyās at times found difficult to overcome.

Portuguese disquiet over the timing of Gujarati departures – and in particular the threat which the loss of vessels posed to valuable state income from customs revenues – appeared regularly in correspondence between officials in Diu and Daman, and between them and the authorities in Goa. It reflected a rising level of concern attached to the significance of Vāniyā merchant shipping that ultimately found its fullest expression in the publication of a Royal decree by the Diu authorities in 1809 ordering annual African ivory imports to reach Jambusar, where the majority of textiles for Mozambique were procured, no later than 15 November so that cloth cargoes from there would be ready for export in the following monsoon by the beginning of January.[111] This elicited a response from a number of Vāniyā merchants: they pointed out that the difficulty in coordinating the supply and delivery of cloths from Jambusar with prescribed shipping departure times meant that they were unable (and unwilling) to comply with the dictates of the decree.[112]

The matter did not end there. Undeterred, the Portuguese authorities pressed for further measures in 1817 to curb what they deemed "reckless" and "irresponsible" behaviour by prohibiting vessels from sailing after January 31.[113] Angered once again by the overly interventionist stance of the Portuguese imperial government, Vāniyā merchants opposed these measures vehemently on the grounds that it represented undue intervention in their Indian Ocean trade. Vāniyā merchant shippers were themselves equally if not more concerned about how late departures could jeopardize their shipping but sought above all to be free from attempts to restrict their movement. This desire was expressed in bold language reflecting Vāniyā confidence in the importance of their contributions to what was the financial lifeblood of Diu and Daman: customs payments

[110] HAG, CDm 1060, Sebastião Ferreira Santos to Viceroy, 11 March 1793.
[111] HAG, Registos Gerais da Feitoria de Diu 7971, Bando, 11 December 1809; Moncões do Reino 162A, Viceroy to Crown, 24 April 1800.
[112] HAG, CD 1005, Sowchand Velji, Chaturbhuj Kunwarji, Virchand Anandji et al. to Judge of Diu, n.d. [but c. 1811].
[113] HAG, CDm 1065, Castro e Almeida to Viceroy, Daman, 26 October 1817.

generated by their Indian Ocean trade.[114] Like attempts to impose a
sea route to Mocha, Portuguese measures that were unpopular were
ultimately doomed to fail because Gujarati merchant opposition to them
could not be suppressed. The Portuguese were in a precarious position
due to their financial dependence on Vāniyā commercial activity in
the Indian Ocean, giving Vāniyās the upper hand in the imperial relationship. Officials were thus left with little choice but to encourage adherence
to the spirit, if not the letter, of their "restrictions" of 1809 and 1817.
Such were the limitations of an enfeebled imperial state in the eighteenth
century, and the importance of Vāniyā merchants within imperial
oceanic commerce.

While Vāniyā could consequently afford to be brazen in their responses
to the Portuguese, they could not be dismissive of the natural restrictions placed upon their Indian Ocean crossings by the monsoon system.
The trading season on Mozambique Island began in March and ended
in late August or early September. Although there may have been some
room for manoeuvre in the westward crossing from India, it was important especially for merchants planning on sailing to southern destinations such as Quelimane to adhere as closely as possible to these
dates. Southerly voyages were usually undertaken in March, April and
November, returning to Mozambique Island in July, August and late
September or early October.[115] The passage to Quelimane (the most
frequently visited port south of Mozambique Island from the late
eighteenth century), though of relatively short duration, brought with
it considerable risk. Besides winds and currents in the Mozambique
Channel, coral reefs dotted the coast all the way to Delagoa Bay. They
were not continuous, though, and the gaps in them could allow vessels
to sail inside the reefs if they kept close to the coast.[116] Still, they were
a hazard and vessels had to be cautious when sailing through the
Mozambique Channel, as was starkly demonstrated in 1834 with the loss
due to strong winds and currents of two merchant vessels in Quelimane.[117]

For longer voyages south of Quelimane to Inhambane and Delagoa
Bay, merchants needed also to be mindful of appropriate sailing
times. Vessels sailed for Delagoa Bay generally between the months of
October–November and January–February. For the return, in order to

---

[114] HAG, CD 1001, Petition from Kunwarji Narsinh, Anandji Jivan et al., 22 December
1817.
[115] Virginia Rau, "Aspectos étnicos-culturais da ilha de Moçambique em 1822", *Studia*, 11
(1963), 145, 147.
[116] Pearson, *Port Cities*, 53–4.
[117] The conditions "tore" the vessls apart. HAG, CD 1010, Francisco de Mello da Gama
Araujo to D. Manoel de Portugal e Castro, 7 November 1834.

take advantage of favourable northerly currents, the best time for their departures was between May and the middle of June. Any departure after 15 June risked shipwreck.[118] With only two exceptions, a list of 22 voyages to Delagoa Bay compiled between 1787 and 1799 shows that merchant vessels kept diligently to this schedule.[119] For those voyaging to Inhambane, a strict departure schedule was also important, especially if they intended to sail onto Delagoa Bay as was often the case. A vessel arriving at Inhambane in December would have afforded its crew relatively little time to offload cargo and/or conduct trade in the town, before sailing onto Delagoa Bay and returning to Inhambane, and then calling at Quelimane enroute to Mozambique Island where it had started its coastal journey. One such vessel, the *São Luis Restaurador*, arrived at Inhambane on 14 December 1816 but remained at the port for a number of months until April. It did not reach Delagoa Bay until 9 July, and as a result found it impossible to sail back up the coast because of "contrary winds". It would have had to wait until August before it sailed to Inhambane, and eventually Mozambique Island.[120] Clearly, vessels intending to sail from Mozambique Island to Quelimane, Inhambane and/or Delagoa Bay in a single lengthy voyage had to plan carefully and avoid, as best they could, late departures from each of these destinations.

Observing correct sailing times reduced the risk of shipwreck, but unseasonable weather could also surprise merchant vessels. The Vāniyā-owned *galera* the *Nossa Senhora do Rozario*, in making its return to Diu, left Mozambique Island on 6 September 1803 but ran into serious trouble north of the Comoro Islands. A combination of poor navigation and treacherous weather blew the vessel way off course; it sank somewhere near the Kilwa coast, with 35 men losing their lives and a cargo worth the considerable sum of 400,000 *cruzados*.[121] A similar fate befell the *pala* the *Ana Joaquina* when it sailed from Mozambique Island on 10 January in the same year. At approximately seven in the evening it "lost its way 36 leagues from the capital" and sank, presumably due to strong winds. Of the 40 people onboard, only 22 survived, and the entire cargo valued at 160,000 *cruzados* was lost.[122] These were grim reminders of the death and loss that accompanied maritime navigation in the Indian Ocean.

---

[118] AHU, Códice 1347, Antonio Manoel de Mello e Castro to Joaquim Giraldes Roza, 7 November 1791.

[119] Alexandre Lobato, *História do Presídio de Lourenço Marques (1787–1799)*, 2 vols. (Lisbon: Tipografia Minerva, 1960), II, 409–10.

[120] AHU, Moç, Cx 154 Doc. 55, Luis Correa Monteiro de Matto to Governor, 20 August 1817.

[121] AHU, Códice 1370, Izidro d'Almeida Souza e Sa to Governor, 14 November 1803.

[122] AHU, Códice 1370, Izidro d'Almeida Souza e Sa to Governor, 27 March 1803.

A trading season was not necessarily ruined whenever a vessel was forced to seek refuge from poor weather on its way to the Mozambique coast. With luck, the enforced break in the journey lasted only a few days. If the vessel sailed into the start of a storm, however, those on board faced lengthier interruptions with the possibility of returning to India empty-handed. Premchand Sowchand was forced into this situation when his vessel was violently blown off course by strong winds in 1785 not long after departing from Diu. Preferring not to endanger his crew and cargo any further by weathering the storm at sea or by choosing to return to India, Premchand decided to put in at Muscat where he was able to sell all of his cargo, returning to Diu with approximately 4,000 *patacas*. Premchand was relatively fortunate in having been able to reverse a potentially disastrous situation for himself and others invested in the voyage, and though the gains for that season may have been less than what they had hoped for in Mozambique, this had clearly been the most expedient decision in the circumstances.[123] Premchand avoided significant financial losses for all perhaps due to greater business acumen, connections or luck (or a combination of all three) but this was not always possible. Reflecting the uncertainties of maritime trade in the eighteenth-century western Indian Ocean, when another vessel encountered the same winds in 1787, it suffered losses of more than 40 per cent when it made a forced stopover at Muscat.[124]

When a vessel ran aground or sank, it was still possible to recover some or all of its cargo if it had been within sight of shore. Specialized divers were available on the Kathiawar coast to offer their services to seafarers eager to salvage whatever was possible from such misfortune. This could include a sizeable proportion of a ship's cargo. In 1808, a group of divers recovered a number of the *patacas* from a *pala* owned by Velji Darci that had run into trouble off Brancavara. While there is little evidence about how these individuals were contracted or engaged, how and what they were paid, and whether this was a full-time occupation, they were clearly an indispensable labour force on whom merchants relied for salvage work. Divers and salvage workers may have been members of communities that offered other services such as towing damaged vessels that had run aground back to shore.[125] The availability of salvage services,

---

[123] HAG, CD 998, Luis Joze de Souza Machado de Moraes Sarmento to Guilherme de Souza, 15 September 1785.
[124] HAG, CD 1001, Petition from Kunwarji Narsinh, Anandji Jivan et al, 22 December 1788.
[125] HAG, CD 1004, Joze Leite da Cruz to Conde de Sarzedas, 8 January 1808; Joze Leite da Cruz to Governor of Diu, 18 January 1808; CDm 1067, Harichand Ira to de Souza Pimental, 28 April 1821.

as noted by Roxani Margariti, were already in the premodern era a common feature of seafaring in the western Indian Ocean. In the early twelfth century, Aden shippers were able to rely on expert divers and others with considerable experience and expertise to salvage cargoes from shipwrecks, in some cases recovering enough property to allow relatives of a man who had drowned as the result of the loss of a vessel to present legal claims for financial compensation.[126] Vāniyā merchants in eighteenth-century Diu and Daman, as elsewhere along the coast, could equally benefit from maritime services that afforded some at least the possibility of reducing their losses at sea.

Sailing in the Indian Ocean involved maintaining a delicate equilibrium between meeting the demands of trading seasons in both India and Africa – involving most importantly securing cloth cargoes from producers in the subcontinent and ensuring their delivery to consumers thousands of miles away – and adhering to the rhythms of the ocean's winds and currents. It was challenging to maintain this balance and for those who could or did not, the results were often disappointing at best and disastrous at worst. Merchant success thus not only required effective communication and the establishment of networks of trust but also depended on the natural systems and ravages of the ocean and those who understood it.

Costs of oceanic trade

In addition to the challenges of sailing across the ocean, Vāniyās faced a number of financial costs associated with their trade. Some of the most important were related to freight charges, insurance premiums and maritime loans. Given that the majority of Vāniyā were not shipowners, the only option available to them was to freight their cargoes on vessels owned by others that were making the seasonal trans-oceanic crossings. This included owners of vessels with no direct trading interests in Mozambique and who were therefore "little interested in loading vessels on their account, [being instead] satisfied with the profits [they earn] from freighting".[127] Charges of around 8 per cent per voyage from India were generally the norm, though in some cases they could be as high as 20 per cent. Once they reached Mozambique, there were additional charges attached to the transport of goods from Mozambique Island to coastal ports. These were set at 7 per cent of the value of the goods, while charges

---

[126] Roxani Eleni Margariti, *Aden & Indian Ocean Trade: 150 Years in the Life of a Medieval Arabian Port* (Chapel Hill: University of North Carolina Press, 2007), 169–73.

[127] HAG, CD 999, Natthu Samji to Governor, n.d. [but 1787].

on the return voyage to the island-capital were marginally lower at 5 per cent.[128] Once the vessel(s) on which the goods had been transported both in India and in Mozambique safely reached its destination, the charges were settled by the interested parties.[129]

The dangers associated with shipping in the Indian Ocean – from the vagaries of the monsoon winds and weather patterns to the threat of attack from vessels on the open seas – placed a premium on maritime insurance and its attendant businesses. Over the second half of the eighteenth century, these seem to have undergone a huge expansion in Kathiawar in a context of intensified piracy and resistance to the encroachments of the British imperial state, which I discuss later in the chapter.[130] In general, insurance of cargoes and ships against loss was a critical element in affecting the capacity of Vāniyā merchants to prepare goods for coastal and trans-oceanic commerce. The potential dangers of an oceanic crossing made insuring a vessel's cargo of the utmost importance. Insurers undertook to indemnify total or partial loss caused by maritime perils, in consideration of a certain amount called a "premium". Insurance policies were drawn up in the form of *Jakmi hundis* that enjoyed wide currency.[131] The charge for insuring goods and ships depended upon the perceived risks involved on a particular route and on the nature of the goods that were being transported. Insurance rates, varying also according to the size of a vessel, were usually set at between 7 and 10 per cent of the value of the cargo, with merchants often also insuring their goods individually.[132]

In a number of cases of voyages to Mozambique, merchants assumed responsibility for the goods that were being carried by the vessel. Such goods were loaded onto vessels "under the responsibility and risk [of the merchant]". This suggests that it was the sole responsibility of the merchants who had freighted goods to seek coverage from individual insurers independently of the arrangements made by the shipowner

---

[128] AHU, Moç., Cx 86 Doc. 22, Pedro Antonio Jose da Cunha to D. Rodrigo de Souza Coutinho, 9 October 1800. Numerous examples of payments of freight charges to Vāniyā vessels in Mozambique can be found in AHM, Fundo do Século XIX, Códice 11–4783.

[129] HAG, Registos Gerais da Feitoria de Dio 7970, "Registo do requerimento dos mercadores carregadores do navio do Senhorio Anandagy Givane que fez viagem para Moçambique no anno de 1797", n.d.

[130] Lakshmi Subramanian, "The Politics of Restitution: Shipwrecks, Insurance and Piracy in the Western Indian Ocean", paper presented at *The Story of the Voyage Colloquium*, University of the Witwatersrand, Johannesburg, 2–3 October 2008.

[131] Pinto, *Trade and Finance*, 67.

[132] HAG, CD 1006, João Vicente Lencoza to Viceroy, 29 November 1819. Pinto has posited that insurance rates were in some cases as high as 35 per cent but I have found no evidence of this. See *Trade and Finance*, 68.

for the insurance of the vessel and of his own goods.[133] A shipowner and freighting merchants could also secure maritime insurance collectively for the value of the vessel's entire cargo. In 1792, as part of the arrangements for the insurance of the goods being carried by a *pala* to Mozambique, insurers underwrote the risk for the entirety of the goods onboard. When the ship was shipwrecked on its return to Diu in the same year, they agreed to pay compensation for 93 per cent of the value of the lost goods.[134]

Wary of the risks involved in maritime voyages, insurers reserved the right to refuse insurance for a vessel if the voyage was considered too dangerous, or if a ship was due to leave Diu or Daman very late in the season, thus increasing significantly the possibility that it would not reach its destination on time for the trading season or at all. Insurers for Anandji Jivan, Jagjivandas Mulgi, Natthu Samji (?), Chaturbhuj Kunwarji, Jaichand Jivan, Kalyanchand Hemachand (?), Rupchand Vada (?), Karva Kanadas and Tairsi Madhavji refused outright to insure the cargoes they had freighted on a vessel sailing across the western Indian Ocean to Mozambique in the monsoon of 1795:

the merchants of this city have made the effort throughout this country to insure their goods which are to be shipped to the town and capital of Moçambique [*sic*] but it is impossible to find anyone who will insure the risk of this vessel because the insurers have repeatedly lost with the vessel of Dio [*sic*].[135]

Unwilling to risk losing more money because of the real or perceived risks attached to this route, or perhaps as a result of repeated late departures from India, the insurers left the merchants to freight their goods on a newly built vessel in Daman that was to sail the following year. The merchants presumably were able to identify other insurers who would have been willing to insure their cargoes on the new vessel.

When Vāṇiyā merchants encountered problems or difficulties with insurers, they turned at times to the institutional apparatus of the Portuguese state. They maintained an ambivalent attitude towards the Portuguese authorities, and were quick to challenge decisions that they found constraining or prejudicial to their trade and commerce in the Indian Ocean. As I have shown in the first chapter of this book, they nonetheless sought the protection or intervention of state bodies in matters of business, and these included settling insurance claims. On its voyage to the Mozambique coast in 1793, the *pala* owned by Chaturbhuj

---

[133] Numerous examples exist in HAG, AD 4952–4969; and ADm 4836–4852.

[134] Merchants of Diu to Joze Agostinho da Silva e Menezes, n.d., in T[eotonio] [R.] de Souza, "Marine Insurance and Indo-Portuguese Trade History: An Aid to Maritime Historiography", *IESHR*, 14, 3 (1977), 381–2.

[135] HAG, CD 1002, Anandji Jivan, Jagjivandas Mulji et al to Governor, 28 November 1795.

Kunwarji sank near the Querimba Islands, "causing the ruin of all [consigning] merchants".[136] Having faced difficulties in getting insurers to settle the resulting claims, these Vāniyā merchants submitted several letters to a range of Portuguese officials in Diu urging them to pressure insurers to settle claims promptly. But as the owner of the vessel, Chaturbhuj Kunwarji took it upon himself to approach the *Castellão*, a high-ranking official in Diu, to ask that he compel the insurers to settle the claims as quickly as possible. The matter was urgent, he argued, because the payments from the claims would enable the merchants to finance the purchase of future African cargoes of Gujarati cloths from Jambusar. Despite these entreaties, the *Castellão* appears to have been unsuccessful in compelling the insurers to pay the merchants promptly; more than eight months later Chaturbhuj Kunwarji continued to complain that the majority of the claims remained unpaid.[137]

Because of the considerable costs associated with insuring cargoes for oceanic crossings, merchants at times were tempted to underinsure them despite the considerable risks involved in adopting such a strategy. The advantages would have outweighed the disadvantages if the vessel made a safe return, turning an ill-considered practice into a worthwhile gamble. It was an entirely different matter, however, if the vessel and its cargo were lost at sea, and those invested in the voyage faced the resultant financial blow to their business, which could be devastating. Kalyanji Tairsi suffered "the shame" of losing his vessel on the way to Mozambique in 1792. Likely motivated by a desire to save money on insuring in full an extremely valuable cargo worth 110,000 *xerafins*, Kalyanji Tairisi had insured it for only 27,500 *xerafins*, or a mere 25 per cent of its value. To add to his misfortune, some of the *sarrafs* (bankers) who had underwritten this insurance had gone bankrupt not long after the vessel's departure from India and he was left with an even greater proportion of the loss than might otherwise have been the case. The blow from such a reckless – if perhaps understandable – decision would have been difficult to overcome and would likely have crippled Kalyanji Tairsi's ability to trade again in the western Indian Ocean.[138]

The fraught nature of much maritime commerce, and the attendant risks attached to any single sea voyage, made it imperative that merchants spread their risk by consigning cargoes on a number of different vessels. Anandji Jivan explained the advantages of this practice for the merchants

---

[136] HAG, CD 1002, Chaturbhuj Kunwarji to Castellão, 7 November 1793.

[137] HAG, CD 1002, Chaturbhuj Kunwarji to Castellão, 24 August 1794.

[138] HAG, Registos Gerais da Feitoria de Diu 7970, "Carta Testemunhavel dos Papeis Malanangy Talcy", n.d. [but *c.* 1796].

of Diu in letters he wrote to the governor in 1785. He was responding
to the information he had received that Vāniyā should send only one
vessel to Mozambique in the northeast monsoon of that year. Adopting
a more cautious approach to the one which Kalyanji Tairsi would adopt
a few years later, Anandji Jivan stressed that sending a single voyage
placed merchants at a significant disadvantage because of the risk the
vessel faced of being lost at sea, or of being blown off course and having
to drop anchor somewhere in the western ocean en route to Mozambique.
He argued, rather, that merchants should be allowed to "divide their
risks across the vessels, so that should one of these be forced to put in
at a port [on the way to Mozambique], and the other [vessels] continue
their voyage the merchants would suffer less damages".[139] This risk-
minimizing strategy was common among merchants in the Indian Ocean
and helped protect them from the uncertainties and vagaries of oceanic
trade.

Closely associated with insurance were maritime loans, which represented another important element in the trading life of Vāniyā merchants
with interests in the Indian Ocean. Diu merchant correspondence refers
to loans for the purchase of ship's cargoes but provides relatively few
details of their particulars. There is mention of individuals lending
money to merchants for the singular purpose of arranging the purchase
and transport of a cargo of cloth across the ocean.[140] Despite the paucity
of information, these loans were likely a form of respondentia that in
the second half of the eighteenth century grew along with the insurance
business. These loans were in widespread use in Surat, Bombay and
elsewhere on the littoral of western India, and were financial instruments
by which investors lent money to merchants for the purchase of cargoes.
Although no equivalent vernacular term appears to exist in western India,
a form of speculative investment in a vessel's cargo called "avog" has been
identified for the seventeenth century that seems to correspond closely
to the nature of respondentia loans.[141] Recent work has identified these
maritime loans as firmly established along coastal western India by the
middle of the eighteenth century. They could be underwritten by a
number of interested parties and were repaid once the ship had carried
the cargo safely to its intended and stipulated destination. Merchants

---

[139] HAG, CD 998, Anandji Jivan to Governor, 12 March 1785.
[140] See, for example, HAG CD 1002, Rupachand Virji and Premchand Kunwarji to
Governor, 26 September 1792.
[141] Lakshmi Subramanian, "Merchants in Transit: Risk-Sharing Strategies in the Indian
Ocean", in H. P. Ray and Edward A. Alpers (eds.), *Cross Currents and Community
Networks: The History of the Indian Ocean* World (New Delhi: Oxford University Press,
2007), 283 fn 3.

paid premiums on the principal that were decided according to the perceived risk of the voyage, a factor around which there was also a robust betting and futures market in Diu and Daman.[142] Loans appear to have been possible for a single merchant's cargo (no matter how large) or could be arranged for the entire cargo of a vessel. Along with the insurance business of which they formed an integral part, these maritime loans were indispensable to the financial edifice of merchant trade in western India and throughout the western Indian Ocean.

Piracy and privateering

Other dangers made insuring vessels essential for merchants. Most notable was the threat of attack by "pirates" and privateers whose actions, in many instances, were state supported and sanctioned. In the second half of the eighteenth century, Vāniyā merchants from Diu and Daman began to express concern over pirate activity along the Kathiawar littoral and the Konkan coast. Some of the earliest concerns were related to the pirates of Sootrapara who had "infested" the waterways of the coast of Kathiawar in the 1760s and were attacking Vāniyā merchant shipping. A few years later, there were reports of merchant vessels being attacked and ransomed by the Sidis of Jaffrabad.[143] In the 1780s and 1790s, the Kolis of Rajapur and pirates from Novabunder were active in the coastal shipping channels around Daman and between Daman, Surat and Bombay, making voyages dangerous and threatening long-distance sailing in the western Indian Ocean.[144] The losses from these attacks and related shipwrecks were estimated at three million *xerafins* between 1781 and 1793.[145]

---

[142] HAG, CD 995, D. João Joze de Mello to Castellan of Diu, 5 August 1768; CD 997, de Macedo e Couto to Joze Fereira Pestana, 4 December 1845; Subramanian, "Merchants in Transit" and "Imperial Negotiations: The Dynamics of British-Indian social networks in early colonial Bombay", unpublished paper.

[143] HAG, CD 995, João Baptista Vas Pereira to D. João de Mello, 14 November 1766; D. João Joze de Mello to Castellan of Diu, 17 November 1770.

[144] HAG, CD1002, Luiz Caetano de Calvoz (?) Coelho e França to Governor, 22 October 1791. It was claimed in one report from 1788 that this coast was "always infested with pirates". HAG, Copiador Indiano da Feitoria de Surrate 2533, Jacinto Domingues to Luis Vieira de Abreu, 8 June 1788.

[145] HAG, CD 1002, Antonio Baptista da Cunha to Francisco Antonio da Veiga Cabral, 19 December 1795. Whether these may have included attacks by Qasimi vessels, active in the Persian Gulf waters of eastern Arabia and in shipping lanes reaching the Makran coast, for whom both local and British shipping (especially in the nineteenth century) were targets, is unclear from the evidence. That I have found no instances of Vāniyā merchants complaining about these attacks – even when they sailed to Muscat which fell within the orbit of Qasimi activity – suggests at least that their shipping was unaffected. The shift in focus by Vāniyās away from the northern Arabian Sea to the African coast of

Other pirates with connections to Mandvi preyed on shipping between Kutch and Porbandar in the first decade of the nineteenth century.[146] Merchants also had to contend with Maratha maritime predation by naval fleets that resulted in the loss of valuable cargoes of ivory and silver currency from the southwestern Indian Ocean slave trade.[147] Despite the settlement reached by the Portuguese with the Marathas in 1783, their fleets remained a threat until at least the late 1810s when they were finally defeated by the encroaching British naval forces.[148]

Piracy had presented a challenge for maritime groups in the Indian Ocean from at least the time of the *Periplus of the Erythraen Sea*, the first-century CE commercial and mariner's guide, and perhaps even earlier.[149] Although often dismissed simply as "maritime marauding" by European officials whose views were informed by conventional models of state sovereignty and legitimacy, piracy involved a complex matrix of relationships that defined who became a pirate.[150] While it may be useful to think of piracy as constitutive of violent maritime predation, the question of who was or was not a pirate, however, is notoriously difficult to answer, given the fluidity of the category and particularly the "ambiguity that permeated the understanding of piracy" in the western Indian Ocean in the second half of the eighteenth century.[151] According to Lakshmi Subramanian, European policies were important in formalizing the category

the southwestern Indian Ocean may also have insulated them from Qasimi attacks. For more on the Qawasim, see Rheda Bhacker, *Trade and Empire*, 31–52; and J. E. Peterson, "Britain and the Gulf: At the Periphery of Empire", in Lawrence G. Potter, *The Persian Gulf in History* (New York: Palgrave Macmillan, 2009), 277–93 for British policy towards their "pirate" activity. Useful also is the recent short overview in Edward A. Alpers, "On Becoming a British Lake: Piracy, Slaving, and British Imperialism in the Indian Ocean during the First Half of the Nineteenth Century", in Robert Harms, Bernard K. Freamon and David W. Blight (eds.), *Indian Ocean Slavery in the Age of Abolition* (New Haven and London: Yale University Press, 2013), 45–58.

[146]   HAG, CD 1006, Joaquim Mourão Garcez Palha to Viceroy, 13 November 1817.

[147]   See, for example, the case of a Maratha ship that captured a *pala* on its return to Daman from Mozambique in 1789 in HAG, Feitoria de Surrate 2603, João Nogueira Porto to Joze Gomes Loureiro, 11 December 1789.

[148]   Only then was it considered safe to sail off the waters of Daman. HAG, CDm 1065, João Vicente Lencoza to Manoel Joze Gomes Loureiro, 1 March 1816. For details of the Luso-Maratha settlement, see *APO*, 22–31; Ernestina Carreira, "India", in Valentim Alexandre and Jill Dias (eds.), *O Império Africano 1825–1890* (Lisbon: Editorial Estampa, 1998), 659–717. The details of earlier relations are in Alexandre Lobato, *Relações Luso-Maratas, 1658–1737* (Lisbon: Centro de Estudos Históricos Ultramarinos, 1965).

[149]   Margariti, *Aden & Indian Ocean Trade*, 164.

[150]   For a useful discussion of how European ideas of state-centred notions of sovereignty and legitimacy at sea have influenced the study of piracy in the Indian Ocean – ignoring local practices and understandings of maritime violence – see Sebastian R. Prange, "A Trade of No Dishonor: Piracy, Commerce, and Community in the Western Indian Ocean, Twelfth to Sixteenth Century", *American Historical Review*, 116, 5 (2011), 1269–93.

[151]   Subramanian, "Politics of Restitution".

of the "pirate". Beginning in the sixteenth century with Portuguese attempts to impose monopoly control over the carrying trade in the Indian Ocean through the *cartaz* (maritime permit) system and claims to exclusive jurisdiction over the seas, European officials and lawmakers targeted groups and individuals who defied their singular understandings of maritime sovereignty.[152] Clandestine or "unlawful" activity was regarded as a challenge to the authority and jurisdiction of the imperial state, and therefore seen as legitimately punishable. At best, it was to be eliminated and at the very least marginalized by coastal patrols and by the policing of the high seas with well-armed naval vessels. The institution and mechanism of the *cartaz* endured into the seventeenth and eighteenth centuries, influencing Europeans and South Asians alike by engendering the notion of maritime sovereignty as "a new political conception that defined the right to the seas and to the vessels that plied over them".[153]

In the eighteenth century, particularly in a context of rising British commercial and political interest in coastal western India, piracy became an abiding concern for imperial and company officials increasingly bound by notions of "free and fair trade", the rule of law and private property. This was connected to a commitment to influence, if not dominate, coastal politics and shipping, which the company aimed to achieve from around the middle of the century both by enforcing the use of the English *cartaz* and by deploying a rhetoric that drew on earlier constructions of piracy and was aimed at subverting coastal political rivals.

The response from local groups and coastal potentates was to seek an "alternative indigenous coastal dispensation" underpinned by a "politics of displacement forcing marginalised groups along the littoral to contest the European offensive".[154] The rise of groups in coastal western India such as the Angrias along the Konkan coast, the Desais of Savantwadi and the Malvans of Sindhudrug embodied the growth in opposition to the efforts by the British to control maritime movement and trade, and signalled an increase in the militarization of coastal politics and society. The Angrias, for example, used well-armed vessels to attack ships that did not carry *dastak* (shipping licences) and often ransomed their crews.[155]

---

[152] Enforcing tribute by having vessels call at certain ports to pay tax to rulers was not particular to the Portuguese; indigenous precedents had existed in the Red Sea and South India, for which see Prange "Trade of No Dishonor".

[153] Lakshmi Subramanian, "Of Pirates and Potentates: Maritime Jurisdiction and the Construction of Piracy in the Indian Ocean", in Devleena Ghosh and Stephen Muecke (eds.), *Cultures of Trade: Indian Ocean Exchanges* (Newcastle, UK: Cambridge Scholars Publishing, 2007), 26.

[154] Subramanian, "Pirates and Potentates", 26.

[155] Ghulam Nadri, *Eighteenth-Century Gujarat: The Dynamics of its Political Economy, 1750–1800* (Leiden: Brill, 2008), 20–1; Subramanian, "Politics of Restitution".

At the same time, piracy and mercantile activities became increasingly entangled as coastal potentates and seafaring communities maintained complex symbiotic relationships that brought political and commercial advantage to both, and allowed them to challenge the authority of the Bombay Marine.[156] That they were able to do so successfully reflected the difficulties the British faced in translating growing political and military influence in western India into regional economic hegemony.

Similar tripartite relationships between pirates, merchants and local leaders had emerged by the late eighteenth century along the Kathiawar littoral and elsewhere in coastal Gujarat, making local sailing and venturing out to the high seas a hazardous undertaking for merchants with commercial and financial interests in the western Indian Ocean. The local political structure in coastal Kathiawar was made up of a number of chieftains and polities that existed loosely under Maratha and Rajput rule. This allowed them a degree of autonomy to pursue independent political and economic objectives. Coastal rulers competed with one another to dominate commercial circuits in a fluid political situation where control over ports and areas could change rapidly.[157] In many cases, they maintained relationships with seafaring groups upon whom they relied to enforce control over stretches of the coast, and to whom they promised protection. For instance, the Nawab of Junagadh and the Rajas of Porbandar and Sootrapara had associations with groups who attacked shipping along the west coast of India that did not carry their licences, and who returned to ports under their control with the plundered goods.[158] Mandvi, especially, had emerged by the end of the century as a regional centre for the sale of these trade goods. Rulers benefited politically and financially from these actions while local merchants with ties to these ports, likely participants in the markets that developed for the disposal of these goods, gained commercially from this trade.[159]

---

[156] Subramanian, "Politics of Restitution", 12. The alignment of interests between these groups is described as "organically connected with the political economy of coastal society confronting the hegemonic policies of the Bombay Marine and the East India Company" (13). We should note that collusion between pirates, merchants and rulers for mutual benefit had been a feature also of coastal politics and trade in earlier periods, as evidenced along the sixteenth-century coast of Malabar. See Prange, "Trade of No Dishonor".

[157] Nadri, *Eighteenth-Century Gujarat*, 45.

[158] Subramanian, "Politics of Restitution". In one case involving Vāniyā merchants from Daman, goods stolen from their shipwrecked vessel were sold in Bhavnagar. HAG, CDm 1056, Testimony presented by Vāniyā merchants to Governor of Daman, March–May 1784.

[159] I have derived my arguments here from Subramanian, "Politics of Restitution", 9–10 and Subramanian, *Medieval Seafarers of India* (New Delhi: Roli Books, 2005), 101–27.

The political and commercial entanglements behind maritime predation on the Kathiawar peninsula thus made it a particularly effective
strategy to achieve the various aims of the parties involved. For many
merchants, however, the situation was fraught with the danger of attack
and loss of vessels and trade goods. Vāniyā merchants from Diu,
concerned about the perilous nature of sailing along the coast and out
to the high seas in the late eighteenth century, regularly expressed their
concerns to the Portuguese authorities, primarily about the financial costs
of losing vessels and cargoes.[160] They did so to seek protection from the
small naval fleet maintained by the Portuguese imperial authorities on
the west coast of India. It is worth noting that the issue of European
protection of Indian shipping was at the time an ambiguous proposition
for South Asian merchants, particularly when it came to the East India
Company and the Bombay Marine. While accepting an English licence
and hence English naval protection was not without advantage, it was
restrictive in the sense that it demanded future loyalty to the growing
regional commercial interests of the company. These interests were
enforced through coercive means that at times disrupted local trade and
alienated merchants.

By contrast, however, the Portuguese imperial state was largely dependent for its financial existence on the commercial pursuits of South Asian
merchants, particularly in Diu and Daman, and could therefore ill-afford
to alienate them. As I discussed in the opening chapter of this book, the
imperial state and local merchants maintained a relationship in which
Vāniyā merchants could pursue commercial interests with little restraint
from Portuguese officials or the administration because of their considerable commercial and financial contributions to the state's revenues.
Gujarati merchants approached the state for protection of their investments and, aware of their financial importance, expected the Portuguese
authorities to accede to their requests for armed naval assistance.
Portuguese officials had acknowledged how critical Vāniyā trade and
business was to the state throughout the eighteenth century, a recognition
that meant that whenever possible they commissioned warships to escort
Vāniyā vessels out to the high seas beyond the dangers of coastal pirates.[161]
As one of its privileges, ships granted the status of *barcos de viagem* – which
I discuss below – were guaranteed this protection until they were some
distance beyond the coast. Portuguese authorities at Diu also financed
the construction of *machwas*, and in 1770 the viceroy in Goa sent four of

---

[160] See, for example, HAG, CD, 1004, Velji Darci to Governor, 8 January 1808.
[161] HAG, CD 1005, Jorge Frederico Lecos[e] (?), Manoel Inais (?) Remora (?) & João
Bernardo de Oliveira to Governor, 20 March 1810.

these vessels to the island to escort its shipping to the high seas.[162] In 1784, a *palla* and two *machwas* commissioned by the state undertook maritime reconnaissance 36 hours prior to the voyage of two Vāniyā ships sailing to Mozambique to ascertain that the first part of their journey would be unhindered by attacks from roaming armed seafarers.[163]

But Portuguese fleets were often beset by problems, such as chronic shortages of appropriate ships and crews. Authorities were therefore forced at times to augment their naval fleet with Gujarati *palas* or had to resort to encouraging Vāniyā merchants to finance the construction of their own armed vessels.[164] For others, it was possible to seek English assistance but, as already mentioned, merchants were reluctant to pursue this option.[165] When writing to the governor of Diu in 1789 to complain about the lack of reliable naval protection from the Portuguese, a group of merchants expressed disdain for the English presence along the west coast of India. They regarded it as disruptive to commercial networks and as a threat to their regional trade.[166] Consequently, despite problems and their limited fleet, Vāniyā merchants continued to rely on the Portuguese authorities for protection into the nineteenth century.

In the southwestern Indian Ocean, the question of maritime protection was just as compelling. Vāniyā merchants faced an equally dangerous scenario along the African coast and in the Mozambique Channel, one that in the late eighteenth century caused insurance claims and costs to rise. The threat came from increased French privateer activity in the waters surrounding Portuguese territories as a result of the declaration of war on Portugal by France. Corsairs caused untold problems for all shipping along much of the Mozambique Channel.[167] An indication of this threat is clear from the 200 vessels that privateers, licensed by

---

[162] HAG, CD 995, D. João Joze de Mello to Castellan of Diu, 17 November 1770. See also João Baptista Vas Pereira and D. João Joze de Mello to Castellan of Diu, 12 November 1766.

[163] HAG, CD 998, Diogo Sagnes Miles de Noyers to Governor of Diu, 15 March 1784.

[164] HAG, CD 995, D. João Joze de Mello to Castellan of Diu, 17 November 1770; HAG, CD 1006, Joaquim Mourão Garcez Palha to Viceroy, 13 November 1817. *Palas* were modified to carry weaponry on board.

[165] HAG, CDm 1060, Antonio Leite d'Souza to Sebastião Jose Ferreira Barroco, 14 December 1790; Feitoria de Surrate 2603, Joze Ribeiro to Ribeiro Hubens & Co., 17 July 1788. The Portuguese vessel the *Princeza de Portugal* had to join an English flotilla north from Bombay that was sailing to Daman in 1788 because of the absence of adequate Portuguese naval assistance. See HAG, Feitoria de Surrate 2603, Joze Gomes Loureiro to Ribeiro Hubens & Co, 28 November 1788.

[166] HAG, CD 1000, Natu Savaji, Mulji Raghunath, Kurji Narsi, Kalanchand Anaidas and Talsi Ambaidas to Governor, 4 January 1789.

[167] For details of the French threat and Portuguese diplomatic efforts in India at this time, see Carreira, "Moçambique, Goa e Macau", 217–34.

French authorities on the Ile de France (Mauritius), captured between 1793 and 1802.[168] The possibility of attack from French corsairs led the Portuguese authorities in India in the late 1790s to encourage all merchant vessels sailing to Mozambique to do so with a full complement of arms onboard.[169] Merchants were reluctant, however, to devote valuable onboard space to heavy and cumbersome cannon and gunpowder. Their reluctance made them vulnerable to attack by the well-armed French vessels, as happened to the established merchants Chaturbhuj Kunwarji and Premchand Rupchand in 1807. In the southwest monsoon of that year, two of their (unarmed) vessels were fired upon and captured by French ships soon after they had sailed from the African coast. With the outbreak of hostilities in 1807, Vāniyās feared an escalation in random French naval attacks, and as a result threatened to suspend their voyages to Mozambique until the Portuguese could ensure adequate protection for their merchant vessels.[170] Able to provide only limited naval protection because of its small, impoverished and undermanned fleet, Portuguese authorities resorted to echoing earlier warnings that Vāniyā merchants should undertake the African crossing only on adequately armed vessels. The French threat was diminished greatly in the Mozambique Channel, however, by their defeat by British forces in 1810 and loss of the Ile de France, after which approaches to – and sailing along – the East African coast became a safer undertaking.

There was, however, one further threat to Vāniyā shipping along the African coast. Beginning in 1790 and continuing on a regular basis for the next three decades, well-armed raiders from Madagascar attacked island communities in the Mozambique Channel and Swahili villages on the African mainland.[171] The raiders were drawn from within the Sakalava empire whose leaders, by using violence or the threat of violence and a politics of incorporation and allegiance among various groups, had managed to expand their control over the west coast and northwest

---

[168] Pearson, *Indian Ocean*, 197.

[169] HAG, CD 1003, Francisco Antonio da Veiga Cabral to Caetano de Souza Pereira, 24 November 1800; CDm 1061, Francisco Antonio da Veiga Cabral to Governor, 4 October 1800.

[170] HAG, Registos Gerais da Feitoria de Dio 7971, Joze Leite d'Souza et al to Real Fazenda, 31 October 1808; *ibid.*, Joze Leite d'Souza to Real Fazenda, 15 January 1809.

[171] I have drawn my information and arguments about these raids from Edward A. Alpers, "Madagascar and Mozambique in the nineteenth century: The Era of the Sakalava raids (1800–1820)", *Omaly sy Anio*, 5–6 (1977), 37–53; Alpers, *Ivory and Slaves in East Central Africa: Changing Pattern of International Trade to the Later Nineteenth Century* (London: Heinemann, 1975), 182–183; and especially Jane Hooper, "An Empire in the Indian Ocean: The Sakalava Empire of Madagascar", PhD diss., Emory University, 2010.

of Madagascar in the seventeenth and eighteenth centuries. Apart from controlling vital food supplies of rice and cattle for the southwestern Indian Ocean, the Sakalava were closely connected to the growing slave trade in the Mozambique Channel from the mid-eighteenth century, with ports under their control serving as shipment centres of slave exports that were carried by European, Arab and other regional merchants to markets throughout the western Indian Ocean.[172]

Madagascar was thus a notable commercial hub with strong ties to the mainland and islands of the southwestern Indian Ocean. Its political connections with the Comoro Islands, with which Malagasy had maintained commercial, religious and political relationships for at least two centuries, appear likely to have precipitated the raids in the final decade of the eighteenth century. They began with Anjouan in 1792 and were followed by attacks on Mayotte in 1797 and Grand Comore between 1808 and 1814. Well-organized and coordinated raids also took place on coastal communities in Kilwa and elsewhere along the Swahili coast, including Mozambique. These raids were disruptive to local shipping and coastal routes. In 1800, coastal communities near Mozambique Island were robbed and their slaves stolen in attacks that were probably related to the earlier attacks. Malagasy fleets continued to threaten communities in northern coastal Mozambique for the following two decades, including the Swahili settlement of Sancul (located a short distance from Mozambique Island) and the Querimba Islands with whom Vāniyās maintained commercial relationships. Although in the end there were no large-scale attacks on the Mozambique coast, for reasons related to Portuguese resistance and to the targeted nature of the attacks that largely precluded indiscriminate violence, the presence of Malagasy vessels capable of carrying up to 60 men in the waters of the Mozambique Channel until around 1820 concerned both Vāniyā and Portuguese merchants with commercial interests in the southwestern Indian Ocean and in trans-oceanic long-distance trade. A few Vāniyā merchants wrote to the governor of Mozambique asking for maritime patrols but these appeals were never satisfied. Despite their fears, there were no recorded Malagasy attacks on Vāniyā shipping in the Mozambique Channel but merchants nonetheless continued to worry into the early 1820s, a few years after the last attacks had taken place on the Southeast African coast, about the overall effects of the raids on trans-channel trading.[173]

---

[172] Hooper, "Empire in the Indian Ocean".
[173] HAG, CD 1008, Francisco de Mello da Gama Araujo to D. Manoel da Camara, 22 September 1824.

Preferential shipping

If Vāniyā merchants faced unavoidable costs and unwarranted dangers in their Indian Ocean crossings, they benefitted from a system of preferential shipping devised by the Portuguese in the eighteenth century. It operated as a commercial mechanism for maritime trade across the ocean: in every trading season, a merchant vessel from Diu and Daman was nominated as a *barco de viagem* by the Portuguese authorities, received a military convoy and enjoyed a number of other protections for its voyage to Mozambique. The motivation for the Portuguese in devising this system was that it served as an inducement to trade between Gujarati merchants and their counterparts in Mozambique, and helped generate much-needed income for the Portuguese state from customs revenue. It also allowed for the possibility of some control over the routes and timing of merchant voyages.

The *barco de viagem* was officially nominated by the governors of Diu and Daman and carried privileges of considerable advantage for any merchant or merchants with a stake in the Mozambique trade: the vessel was permitted to load its cargo at the dock before any of the other vessels; it was given an escort by an armed Portuguese naval fleet (when possible); and generally was provided with all the assistance needed to ensure a successful voyage. Any vessel owned by a Crown subject could, in theory, be nominated for the *barco de viagem* provided that it met with the approval of the Portuguese authorities. Because vessels owned by Vāniyā merchants from Diu, and to a lesser extent from Daman, were dominant in the sea route linking western India and Mozambique, they were regularly nominated as *barcos de viagem*. Portuguese vessels were nominated but this was rare.[174]

Additional vessels were permitted to sail to Mozambique with the *barco de viagem* if there were enough export cargoes to warrant it, and/or if interested merchants managed successfully to petition their respective governors and Portuguese officials. This happened in 1789 when three Vāniyā vessels sailed with the *barco de viagem* in the northeast monsoon from Diu to Mozambique.[175] Given the advantages which a nomination carried, it is not surprising that competition between merchants for the status of *barco de viagem* was fierce. A particularly bitter rivalry developed between Hira(chand?) Raicane (?) and Jhaver Khushal in Daman in the 1780s over the nominations for the 1786 season. The governor,

---

[174] See, for example, HAG, CDm 1061, Caetano de Souza Pereira to Governor of Daman, 27 June 1800.
[175] HAG, Feitoria de Surrate 2603, Joze Gomes Loureiro to Joze Ribeiro, 2 March 1789.

D. Christovão Pereira de Castro, seems to have understood that to antagonize either merchant would have been unwise and decided instead to mollify Hirachand and Jhaver by nominating both of their vessels as *barcos de viagem*. This was a common strategy when the authorities faced situations that were potentially disruptive to Vāniyā shipping.[176] Vessels deemed to be in state of disrepair or too old for the successful completion of the voyage could be rejected by the Portuguese authorities but this seems to have occurred relatively infrequently.[177]

In view of the perquisites granted to nominees of the Mozambique voyage, there were instances of Portuguese officials colluding with Indian merchants in the selection process. Wealthy merchants and shippers such as Sowchand Premji, owner of three vessels, recognized that official favour removed or at the very least lessened competition, and thus would guarantee him an upper hand over fellow merchants in the trade to Mozambique. It was an advantage he was willing to cultivate by maintaining personal relationships with local Portuguese authorities.[178] Officials stood to gain either through a share of this trade or by receiving a cash bribe for their complicity. It was difficult to detect official malfeasance, however, unless aggrieved merchants were vocal in their complaints against the individual concerned. Even then, there were no guarantees that the issue would be addressed by the state, concerned as it was to protect trade and the customs income it generated, the cornerstone of its fiscal base.[179]

The fiscal realities facing the state meant that the maritime route to Mozambique remained, for the most part, free from any interference by the Portuguese. There was a notable exception, however, in the second half of the eighteenth century when officials began increasingly to demand that those vessels chosen as the *barco de viagem* sail to Mocha enroute to Africa. As discussed in Chapter 1, Vāniyā merchants had been drawn to Mocha in Qāsimī Yemen in the second half of the seventeenth century and became central to the port city's economic and financial infrastructure. Merchants from Diu in particular were prominently represented among the city's merchant classes; they provided banking and credit facilities, worked as brokers for European merchants and, according to Nancy Um, "played a commanding role in ordering the

---

[176] HAG, CDm 1057, D. Christovão Pereira de Castro to Viceroy, 12 February 1786.

[177] See, for example, HAG, CD 1003, D. Rodrigo da Costa e Noronha to Governor of Diu, 30 October 1798.

[178] HAG, CD 1001, Francisco da Cunha e Menezes to Diogo de Mello de Sampaio, 7 October 1790.

[179] HAG, CD 998, Premchand Sowchand, Kanji Keshavji, Tairsi Ambaidas, Natthu Samji to Governor of Diu, 28 February 1785.

city's international bulk trade".[180] Through the use of the Mocha dollar, the dominant currency in wholesale accounting, Gujarati Vāniyā were also instrumental in structuring a widely used system of financial reckoning. But the combination of regular harassment by authorities and the political upheavals within Yemeni leadership that undermined commercial activity had by the mid- to late eighteenth century greatly reduced Diu Vāniyā activity in Mocha. The merchants thus began increasingly to shift their capital and business interests away from the southern Red Sea to coastal Southeast Africa from the 1740s and 1750s, as Mocha's prominence and importance in the western Indian Ocean and in global trade began to wane.

Yet, despite their overwhelming reorientation to Mozambique, Portuguese officials insisted in the early 1770s that any Vāniyā merchant whose vessel(s) had been nominated as a *barco de viagem* sail to Mocha before making its way to Mozambique Island. Vāniyā merchants responded with little enthusiasm because they reported that they had managed only poor returns on their investments there and were deterred by the relatively high customs charges.[181] Nonetheless, although left with little choice, the authorities were forced to revise their position: Vāniyā would continue to call at Mocha but were "required" to do so only in alternate years. As an incentive, and reflecting their insistence, the Portuguese proposed to nominate as *barco de viagem* any Vāniyā ship that had sailed to Mocha in the previous year, regardless of whether it had done so as a nominated vessel or not.[182] What seems to have interested Portuguese officials in Mocha was the silver and gold markets that were linked to the export of coffee to the Red Sea, Persian Gulf and western Indian Ocean.[183] The disinterest expressed by Vāniyā merchants in Mocha suggests, though, that these currency markets were not sufficiently valuable or available to them at this time to warrant making a stop there.[184] Lacking detailed knowledge of local conditions except for what they could learn from Vāniyā merchants themselves, the Portuguese probably had not appreciated the extent to which Mocha's commercial and financial marketplace had declined for these Gujarati merchants

---

[180] Um, *Merchant Houses*, 167.
[181] BN, Codice 8841, Petition from Vāniyā merchants to Governor of Diu, 21 December 1773.
[182] HAG, CD 998, D. João de Mello to Castellão of Diu, 17 November 1772.
[183] HAG, CD 998, Diogo Sagnes Miles de Noyers to Antonio Leite de Souza, 14 April 1784.
[184] HAG, CD 998, D. Frederico Guilherme de Souza to Luiz Joze de Souza, 30 April 1785.

by the final quarter of the eighteenth century as the Red Sea had been eclipsed by the possibilities of the African coast.[185]

The repeated calls by the Portuguese authorities that Vāniyā vessels call at Mocha eventually elicited a formal response from seven leading merchants in 1784 who wrote a series of letters expressing their disenchantment to the governor of Diu. They argued that they should be allowed to chart their own course to Mozambique and be free from Portuguese interference in their commercial affairs. Besides prolonging the length of their voyage, Vāniyās stated that the Mocha stop greatly increased the possibility of missing the monsoon winds to Mozambique should they be detained in the Red Sea. Furthermore, their commercial gains appear to have been greatly reduced and they were therefore disinclined to invest significantly in the Yemen route. In the face of such explicit expressions of discontent, Portuguese officials succumbed to Vāniyā pressure and from 1785 allowed vessels to choose their own routes and itineraries, thereby demonstrating once again their dependence on Vāniyā trade for generating income for the state's treasury. The moribund state of Mocha's Indian Ocean commerce was reflected in the late 1780s and 1790s by infrequent Vāniyā visits and by the end of the century Gujarati voyages to the port had all but ceased.[186]

In Mozambique, where vessels were also nominated as *barcos de viagem* for coastal voyages, Vāniyā merchants managed regularly to get theirs nominated in this privileged category.[187] The wealthy and prominent merchant Shobhachand Sowchand was successful in getting his *pala* the *Nossa Senhora da Penha de França* nominated in 1810 for a voyage to Quelimane, as he had managed to do for other destinations

---

[185] Um, *Merchant Houses*; Richard Pankhurst, "The 'Banyan' or Indian Presence at Massawa, the Dahlak Islands and the Horn of Africa", *Journal of Ethiopian Studies* 12, 1 (1974), 188–9. According to Lakshmi Subramanian, Mocha was a source of bullion imports into Surat through the end of the eighteenth century, carried by English East India Company vessels as "treasure consignment". Mocha silver allowed the company to raise loans from the city's *shroffs*, and also allowed the city's Banias, operating as brokers-cum-bankers, and as contract merchants, "continued participation . . . albeit on a modest scale, in the declining traffic of Surat with the ports of West Asia". See *Indigenous Capital*, 141–2. Any loss of silver from Mocha for Diu and Daman Vāniyā as a result of their redirection of trade away from the Red Sea and to Mozambique was more than compensated in the second half of the century by the significant silver imports they secured from the latter, connected to the expanding African slave trade. I develop this topic in the book's final chapter.

[186] HAG, CD 998, Requerimento of Mulji Raghunath, Premchand Sowchand, Tairsi Ambaidas et al. to Castellão of Diu, 23 September 1785; Luiz Joze de Souza Machado de Moraes Sarmento to Viceroy, 7 December 1785.

[187] Manuel Joaquim Mendes de Vasconcellos e Cirne, *Memoria sobre a Provincia de Moçambique* (ed. José Capela) (Maputo: Arquivo Histórico de Moçambique, 1990), 69–70.

along the Mozambique coast.[188] But in striking contrast to the situation in India, officials attempted to put an end to this practice because of their dissatisfaction with the dominance and success of Vāniyā vessels. There were annually two nominations for *barcos de viagem* in Mozambique "for all the ports of the province".[189] As happened with vessels nominated in India for voyages to Mozambique, these had exclusive rights to the export trade of the port(s) to which they sailed. These included no other vessel being permitted to load an export cargo such as ivory until the *barco de viagem* had taken on its full complement of export goods. There was an obligation that the nominated vessel(s) carry Crown cargoes for Portuguese factories at reduced freight charges but the authorities made no attempt to pressure merchants to drop anchor at any particular ports along the Mozambique coast.[190] The great length of the Mozambique coast and the limited number of Portuguese naval vessels required to enforce these prescriptions likely meant that there were merchant vessels that failed to respect the privileges of the nominated *barco(s) de viagem*.

Competition to secure the nomination of *barco de viagem* in Mozambique was as fierce as it was for the nomination for voyages between the subcontinent and Africa. The advantages that could be gained by having a vessel chosen caused Vāniyā merchants at times to resort to underhanded and duplicitous tactics. This is well illustrated by a case in 1819. The Portuguese merchant Atanasio Joze Rodrigues chartered the brig *São Luis Restaurador* to transport a variety of trade goods to Inhambane. In the same year, Shobhachand Sowchand was himself readying a vessel for Inhambane, and because he sought to minimize competition on the route, he tried to get his vessel nominated as a *barco de viagem*. Shobhachand approached the governor of Mozambique with the proposition that he would be willing to transport the state's trade goods free of charge if he were awarded the nomination. This would have placed the *São Luis Restaurador* at a severe disadvantage because it would have been made to wait until Shobhachand's vessel had loaded its cargo and was ready to sail to Inhambane. The offer proved too enticing for the governor, who two days after being approached by Shobhachand announced the selection of his vessel as the *barco de viagem* for Inhambane.

Feeling much aggrieved because the departure of his sailing ship would as a result be delayed, Joze Rodrigues wrote an indignant letter to the

---

[188] AHU, Moç., Cx 132 Doc. 85, Nomination of Vessel Nossa Senhora da Penha de França, 17 May 1810.
[189] Vasconcellos e Cirne, *Memorias*, 69–70.   [190] *Ibid.*, 70.

governor complaining bitterly about what he regarded as Shobhachand's deceitful behaviour. In unabashed self-serving language, he demanded that the privilege of *barco de viagem* be rescinded and that his own brig be offered the privilege instead. Joze Rodrigues offered to carry government goods free of charge not only to Inhambane but also to Sofala as a tactic to sway the governor.[191] The exact sequence of events that this challenge might have set in motion is unknown but in November 1819 another of Shobhachand's vessels sailed to Inhambane, possibly as the *barco de viagem*.[192] Joze Rodrigues may also have been allowed to sail his ship under the same privileges some time during the year because there appear to have been no further complaints from him. This episode underscores the importance that merchants attached to these particular nominations and the lengths to which they were willing to go to secure it as a distinct commercial advantage in the trade of the western Indian Ocean. It reflected also the tensions that at times underlay relationships between Gujarati and Portuguese merchants on the one hand, and between them and the imperial state on the other. However, while a nomination as a *barco de viagem* brought with it certain responsibilities, the privileges associated with preferential shipping made these kinds of battles and the intrigue often associated with them worthwhile for Vāniyās.

Conclusion

What each of the intricacies of shipbuilding, crew, navigation and schedule shows is an active maritime engagement with the western Indian Ocean which facilitated the mercantile successes enjoyed by Vāniyās. Those with African interests had access to the critical financial services of insurance and maritime loans that, together with being able to draw on skilled maritime labour and a well-developed shipbuilding infrastructure, enabled them to expand their African trade in the second half of the eighteenth century. The view that, in contrast to the seventeenth century, medium-sized Gujarati vessels were in decline by the 1750s has overlooked the presence of merchants from Diu and Daman in the ocean's waterways. On the contrary, the maritime currents of smaller ports such as these sustained extremely active seafaring and contributed to the robust commercialized regional economies that especially

[191] AHU, Moç., Cx 165 Doc. 53, "Copia do Requerimento d'Atanasio Joze Rodrigues", n.d. [but 1819].
[192] This point and the preceding paragraph are drawn from AHU; Codicé 1376, Passport for Vessel S. João Baptista, 15 May 1819.

characterized Kathiawar from the 1750s and 1760s. They allow for a broader understanding of the South Asian merchant experience during a period assumed to represent a dramatic shrinking of Gujarati shipping, and sees in them a commercial vibrancy of merchants operating beyond centralized imperial ports such as Bombay and rather, appearing elsewhere on the coast.

3   Threads that bind

At the centre of Vāniyās' circuits of exchange, which connected South Asia to Mozambique and Southeast Africa, were textiles. For centuries, the Indian subcontinent had produced and supplied textiles of varying quality and size to markets that stretched beyond the Indian Ocean, from northwestern Europe and West Africa, to the eastern Mediterranean, Southeast Asia and the Americas. This global flow of textiles was sustained by high productivity and low prices, and in turn fuelled by widespread cultures of consumption.[1] Within the region of the western Indian Ocean, a stream of textiles linked South Asia to the African coast, islands and interior, bringing African consumers into relation with South Asian producers in intimate and complex material histories of oceanic connection. Through their access to long-distance shipping, credit facilities, agents and brokers on both sides of the ocean, Vāniyās played critical roles in enabling and mediating this intra-regional engagement.

Gujarati merchants enjoyed a comparative advantage over European merchants and states, as well as over Swahili merchants and traders from southern Arabia, because of the tightly controlled hold they exercised over the importation into Indian Ocean Africa of cotton textiles produced in western India. These textiles were in great demand as exchange commodities in the African trade of the interior and were regarded as the "currency that is accepted in ports".[2] Gujarati textiles had a critical function in African material exchange and relations because of their use as primary measures of value for which ivory, slaves and other commodities were exchanged across the Indian Ocean in areas that effectively constituted cloth currency zones.[3]

---

[1] Prasannan Parthasarathi, "Global Trade and Textile Workers, 1650–2000", unpublished paper presented at "Globalization and Trade Conference", International Institute of Social History, November 2004.
[2] AHU, Moç., Cx 46 Doc. 31, de Albuquerque to Crown, 12 August 1783.
[3] I borrow this terminology from Richard Roberts, "Guinée Cloth: Linked Transformations within France's Empire in the Nineteenth Century", *Cahiers d'Etudes africaines*, 32, 4 (1992), 597–627.

However, most importantly, this function was the result of the particular social, cultural, political and symbolic meanings which cloth attained through complex processes of domestication. In its journey from a weaver's loom in India to the hands of a local ruler, trader or patron-client in Africa, a piece of cloth underwent a transformation as it became inscribed with meanings that reflected local articulations of fashion, taste and political authority. Central to the question of African consumption and the broader processes it affected across the Indian Ocean, this chapter argues that demand was shaped by the local particularities of African consumer tastes and, as such, dictated the varieties of textiles that entered the Mozambique markets.[4] Thus, far from being marginalized, African consumers were able to negotiate the terms of the trade and their engagement in the relations of exchange in which they formed an integral part. In order to remain competitive, Vāniyā merchants needed to supply this market with textiles that were in demand or in fashion. They thus had to ensure that information on the types of cotton textiles that were sought in each trading season was always kept up to date. In identifying the influence of African consumer taste, this chapter contributes to the growing appreciation that Africans, historically "under-considered populations" in narratives of regional and global interconnectivity, exerted leverage in defining material relationships through processes shaped by "direct reciprocities", a view that is challenging conceptions of seemingly marginal actors as ineffective in influencing larger frameworks of economic exchange.[5]

Equally important, African demand had an influence beyond the continent as it stimulated production in a specific locale in Gujarat, Jambusar, where the bulk of the western Indian textiles for the African markets were manufactured.

The capacity of Vāniyās to supply the African market relied on regular access to this centre of textile production in western India to which information on textile types was transmitted annually. Far from exercising control over the supply and production of textiles for the African markets, however, Indian merchant procurement of these supplies was secured through middlemen with whom they agreed oral contracts on an annual basis. Merchants thus had to negotiate contracts regularly with brokers who were ultimately responsible for acquiring textiles from weavers and

---

[4] A similar point has been recently argued by Carolyn Keyes Adenaike for West Africa. See Carolyn Keyes, "West African Textiles, 1500–1800", in Maureen Fennell Mazzaoui (ed.), *Textiles* (Aldershot: Varorium, 1998), 251–61.

[5] Jeremy Prestholdt, "On the Global Repercussions of East African Consumerism", *American Historical Review*, 109, 3 (2004), 755–81; *idem, Domesticating the World* (Berkeley: University of California Press, 2008).

for providing the merchants with their export cargoes. The trade in Indian textiles thus depended on the dynamics of the interrelation between both the consumer demand and the production and procurement across the ocean as binding modalities that connected seemingly distant communities through intimate material ties. In order to trade successfully, Gujarati merchants needed to balance the intricacies of these through networks of information and agents in both spheres of their operations in the Indian Ocean. It was their ability to connect both ends of this trans-oceanic commercial nexus which gave them the advantage over competitors.

By attending to the particularities and dynamics of these connections and connectors, this chapter underscores the need to place African consumption and the production and procurement process in India which supplied the African market within the same analytic frame. Treating them separately provides only a partial view of historical processes that bound people together through the mediating agency of Vāniyā merchants in the entangled worlds of the western Indian Ocean.

India, cloth and the Indian Ocean

For centuries, cotton and silk textiles produced in India were used in commercial exchanges throughout the Indian Ocean and beyond. Among the greatest strengths of the Indian textile industry was its specialization in serving distinct networks of long-distance trade, its adaptability and its capacity for product differentiation. These resulted in the creation of extensive regional markets that made the Indian textile sector unique among Asian manufacturing industries.[6] The main production areas which specialized in the manufacture of cotton textiles for export were located in Gujarat, the Coromandel coast, Bengal, the Punjab and Sind.[7] Cloths woven in the latter regions were mainly destined for the markets of Afghanistan, eastern Persia, Central Asia, Muscat and Basra. Outlets for the manufactures of Coromandel and Bengal were exported primarily to Southeast Asia, with some trade also taking place to the Red Sea and Persian Gulf. Gujarati textiles were traded extensively to Southeast Asian

---

[6] Tirthankar Roy, "Introduction", in Roy (ed.), *Cloth and Commerce: Textiles in Colonial India* (New Delhi: Sage, 1996), 11–32; K. N. Chaudhuri, *The Trading World of Asia and the English East India Company 1660–1760* (Cambridge University Press, 1978), 205; R. J. Barendse, "Reflections on the Arabian Seas in the Eighteenth Century", *Itinerario*, 25, 1 (2001), 25–49; M. N. Pearson, *Port Cities and Intruders: The Swahili Coast, India, and Portugal in the Early Modern Era* (Baltimore: Johns Hopkins University Press, 1998).

[7] K. N. Chaudhuri, "The Structure of Indian Textile Industry in the Seventeenth and Eighteenth Centuries", in Roy, *Cloth and Commerce*, 40–1. See also Tapan Raychaudhuri and Irfan Habib (eds.), *The Cambridge Economic History of India: Vol. I. 1200–1750* (Cambridge University Press, 1982), 270.

markets, but it was to the western Indian Ocean that the bulk of its cotton textiles were sent, particularly to the markets of the Red Sea and Persian Gulf, and to East Africa.[8]

Cotton in Gujarat was grown and processed in the rich black soils of the river valleys, and weavers in the main manufacturing centres of Ahmedabad, Pattan, Baroda, Broach and Surat produced cotton textiles of many different qualities and in an impressive range of styles and colours for both internal and foreign markets.[9] The technical advantages enjoyed by Indian handicraft production (such as the development of multiple shafts and peddles which allowed weavers to maximize productive capacity), coupled with the availability of relatively inexpensive dyes such as indigo, which was grown in Sarkhej near Ahmedabad, and skilled labour engaged in all the stages of textile production from cotton growing to the spinning of thread, printing and weaving, resulted in an extremely efficient and highly competitive industry with which no other region could compete in terms of price or quality until the development of machine-production in Europe from the latter half of the eighteenth and early nineteenth centuries.[10]

When the Portuguese arrived on the East African coast in the late fifteenth century, they soon established how far participation in coastal trade relied on Gujarati textiles. While gold extracted from Shona mines and exported north through Sofala was used as currency along the coast, these textiles served a critical and widespread function as currency in a largely non-monetized world. But cloth was not used solely for its exchange value: it also had "use value" and was "a means of bestowing moral and social qualities, of marking both high and low status".[11] The

---

[8] Chaudhuri, "Structure of Indian Textile Industry", 41. Chaudhuri notes that while it is difficult to arrive at precise estimates of the number of textile exports sent by Gujarat, the Coromandel coast and Bengal to the Red Sea and Persian Gulf, the "descriptive material available indicates that the volume of textiles carried to these areas from western India was very large". See also Raychaudhuri and Habib, *Cambridge Economic History of India: Vol. I.*

[9] M. N. Pearson, *Merchants and Rulers in Gujarat: The Response to the Portuguese in the Sixteenth Century* (Berkeley: University of California Press, 1976); *idem, Port Cities*, p. 101; Raychaudhuri and Habib, *Cambridge Economic History of India: Vol. I*, 269; K. N. Chaudhuri, "European Trade with India", Raychaudhuri and Habib, *Cambridge Economic History of India, Vol. I*, 382–407.

[10] Chaudhuri, "Structure of Indian Textile Industry", 127–30; *idem, Trading World of Asia*, 274; Om Prakash, "Bullion for Goods: International Trade and the Economy of Early Eighteenth Century Bengal", *IESHR*, 13, 2 (1976), 159–87 and *idem, European Commercial Enterprise in Pre-Colonial India* (Cambridge University Press, 1998), 22; Lotika Varadarajan, "Syncretic Symbolism and Textiles: Indo-Thai Expressions", in Om Prakash and Denys Lombard (eds.), *Commerce and Culture in the Bay of Bengal 1500–1800* (New Delhi: Manohar 1999), 361–82; Pearson, *Merchants*, 97–8.

[11] Mark Horton and John Middleton, *The Swahili: The Social Landscape of a Mercantile Society* (Oxford, UK, Malden, MA: Blackwell, 2000), 111–12.

conspicuous consumption of textiles was as important as their political use in rituals of exchange which fostered and underpinned ties between people. Cloth givers could, for instance, ensure that receivers were committed "to loyalty and obligations in future",[12] and rulers legitimized the power of successors or regional chiefs in investiture ceremonies by using selectively chosen imported textiles. Africans thus used imported and local textiles in ways which were socially, politically, economically and symbolically sophisticated, and whose complexity we are only now beginning to appreciate.

This should not obscure the widespread African textile production that existed on the coast, islands and interior of East Africa. There was a vibrant weaving industry before the sixteenth century which served local demand, and textile production took place in many East African towns between Mogadishu in the north and Sofala in the south.[13] Cotton was grown at Kilwa, and artisans in Sofala, Angoche and the Querimba archipelago were known to weave cotton textiles which were used in local and long-distance trade.[14] In Mozambique, local hand-woven cotton cloth was worn by women in the Delagoa Bay area.[15] It is within this broader context of local textile production that we need to place Indian imports and see them as supplementing local supplies in this early period.[16] Still, there can be little doubt that Indian textiles were regarded as integral to the East African textile trade which stretched from the northern coast down to the Zambesi Valley where they were consumed in their original state (i.e. the design was not altered in any way) by consumers who could afford the foreign imports.[17] From the coast, they were then sent directly into the interior.

Although East Africa and Mozambique were not the largest export markets for Gujarati textiles in this period, the greatest number going to

---

[12] Annette B. Weiner and Jane Schneider, "Introduction", in Annette B. Weiner and Jane Schneider (eds.), *Cloth and Human Experience* (Washington & London: Smithsonian Institution Press, 1989), 3; Richard Roberts, *Two Worlds of Cotton* (Stanford University Press, 1996).

[13] H. A. R. Gibb, *The Travels of Ibn Battūta, A.D. 1325–1354*, 2 vols. (Cambridge University Press, 1958–62), II, 374.

[14] Pearson, *Port Cities*, 122; Jeremy Prestholdt, "As Artistry Permits and Custom May Ordain: The Social Fabric of Material Consumption in the Swahili World, Circa 1450–1600", *Program of African Studies Working Papers No. 3* (Evanston, IL: Program of African Studies, Northwestern University, 1998), 26; A. Rita-Ferreira, *African Kingdoms and Alien Settlements in Central Mozambique (c. 15th-17th Cent.)* (Coimbra, Portugal: Departamento de Antropologia, Universidade de Coimbra, 1999), 116–19.

[15] Patricia Davison and Patrick Harries, "Cotton Weaving in South-East Africa: Its History and Technology", in Dale Idiens and K. G. Ponting (eds.), *Textiles of Africa* (Bath: Pasold Research Fund, 1980), 175–92.

[16] Pearson, *Port Cities*, 124–5.   [17] Prestholdt, "As Artistry Permits".

the Middle East, the way this trade operated provides an illuminating example of the particular desirability of Indian textiles, and the ability of Vāniyā merchants and their producers to maintain supply. The acknowledgement that at least until the first quarter of the nineteenth century, if not later, indigenous merchants controlled the majority of textile exports from India – and that consumer tastes in Indian Ocean markets were important for Indian labour and its productive capacity – is one which will gain greater acceptance as historians come to appreciate more fully the true place of respective mercantile interests in the subcontinent's textile trade.

Contours of African consumption

The dominance of Gujarati textiles in the import trades of Mozambique continued into the eighteenth century as particularly the latter area became commercially important for the Portuguese possessions of western India after the Portuguese had suffered significant territorial losses to the Dutch in the Indian Ocean.[18] For the Vāniyā merchants of Diu and Daman, this provided an opportunity to expand their textile exports to a region where demand for Indian manufactures had grown once supplies through the northern East African coast no longer fed African markets. It also enabled Gujaratis to secure their control over the carrying trade in these manufactures. Although in previous centuries Indian textiles had been overwhelmingly procured by Gujarati merchants, they were sent for the most part to East Africa and Mozambique on Portuguese (Crown) vessels due to imperial regulations aimed at monopolizing cross-oceanic trade.

From the eighteenth century, however, this changed markedly. In the context of a shift in state policy away from mercantilist underpinnings to one that increasingly favoured a free trade regime from the middle of the century in an effort to generate higher fiscal income, as examined in Chapter 1, Vāniyā merchants assumed complete control over the direct shipment of textiles to Africa, and thus were able to command a powerful presence in its economy in an openly competitive environment.

With this shift to free trade, the evidence relating to textile exports to Mozambique improved considerably, as Portuguese State efforts to quantify this trade demanded more detailed records. These record the volumes of cloths that arrived at Mozambique Island and elsewhere on the

---

[18] M. N. Pearson, "Indians in East Africa: The Early Modern Period", in Rudrangshu Mukherjee and Lakshmi Subramanian (eds.), *Politics and Trade in the Indian Ocean World* (New Delhi: Oxford University Press, 1998), 242.

coast in *corjas*, which were bundles of 20 *peças* or "pieces" of textiles. Because of the range and varying styles of Gujarati textiles that circulated in Mozambique, and their different exchange values, these "pieces" were sorted and arranged into *bares* of 400 *panos* ("cloths") of different types, each measuring approximately 3.5 metres long and 0.6 metres wide.[19] The textile pieces brought to Mozambique by Vāniyā merchants that are here discussed, then, actually represented a higher number of trade cloths which were distributed ultimately throughout the African interior. It was these trade cloths that were the "currency of the land" against which ivory, slaves and other goods were exchanged.[20]

The textile trade was extremely large in the eighteenth century. Imports of textiles under State contract into Sena in the Zambesi Valley alone, to which the greatest number of textiles were sent, amounted to 120,000–160,000 pieces per year. Imports to the rest of the territory were estimated at 200 *bares* or *c.* 80,000 pieces. However, it has been suggested that in a year such as 1753, when "the introduction of free trade goods in the Rivers of Sena (Zambesi Valley) in relation to Crown goods was considerably higher", the numbers of textiles that entered Mozambique from India reached half a million pieces.[21] With this opening of trade to Crown subjects, the import of Gujarati textiles may have risen to between 800,000 and 1,000,000 pieces annually.[22] Although probably an overestimate, an increase in the number of textiles brought to the coast is discernible from around this time. It is more likely that annual imports of Indian textiles stood at 300,000–500,000 pieces from the middle of the century, a remarkable volume that represented close to two million metres of cloth. To put this trade into perspective, Bombay exports of locally made Indian cloth to Zanzibar in the 1870s, at a time when the trade was beginning to increase markedly as the island consolidated its position as the most important commercial centre on the East

---

[19] Fritz Hoppe, *A África Oriental Portuguesa no Tempo do Marquês de Pombal (1750–1777)* (Lisbon: Agência-Geral do Ultramar, 1970), 219; José Fialho Feliciano and Victor Hugo Nicolau (eds.), *Memórias de Sofala* (Lisbon: Comissão Nacional para as Comemorações dos Descobrimentos Portugueses, 1998), 35; Alexandre Lobato, *Evolução Administrativa e Economica de Moçambique 1752–1763* (Lisbon: Agência Geral do Ultramar, 1957), 258.

[20] Each cloth type, as established by the Portuguese authorities in Mozambique as part of efforts to regulate exchange, had a particular conversion rate from *peças*/pieces into *panos*/cloths that were then taken into the African territory. The complexity of these official conversion rates is explained in Alexandre Lobato, *História do Presidio de Lourenço Marques (1787–1799)*, 2 vols. (Lisbon: Tipografia Minerva, 1960), II, 375–80.

[21] Lobato, *Evolução Administrativa*, 258. This is drawn from "Oficio de 20 de Novembro de 1753…" published in *Memoria e Documentos acerca dos Direitos de Portugal aos Territorios de Machona e Nyassa* (Lisbon: Imprensa Nacional, 1890), 166–7.

[22] Hoppe, *África Oriental Portuguesa*, 219.

African coast, reached 2.8 million yards annually.[23] The scale of Vāniyā trade, clearly, was impressive.

The supply of Mozambique cloths depended overwhelmingly on Vāniyā merchants from Diu – either active in Gujarat or on Mozambique Island (which served as an entrepôt through which textiles entered the African interior) – to such an extent that a Portuguese official was led to comment that "when these [Indians] fail [in their textile imports] will be when there is no longer any cotton in the world".[24] Thus, whenever Gujarati vessels failed to arrive on the African coast in a trading season due to problems of supply, finance or the monsoon, private Portuguese merchants and officials alike complained bitterly of the resultant shortages for interior African markets.

In the late eighteenth century, the Portuguese Crown and office of the Viceroy introduced reforms to the customs regime of Portuguese Asia in measures that further reflected the imperial aspirations of the Portuguese State to establish liberalized commercial conditions in the Portuguese Asian empire in the late eighteenth century and thus stimulate trade and consequently increase revenue, a development discussed in Chapter 1. The lowering of import and exports tariffs in Diu, Daman and elsewhere provided an impetus for a significant commercial resurgence in the Portuguese empire of the Indian Ocean, and helped to maintain the high number of textiles traded by Gujarati merchants to Africa. An average of a little over 381,000 pieces of cloth were exported from Diu in the late 1780s, confirming its predominance as the primary textile supplier for Africa.[25] Exports from Daman, a secondary port through which Jambusar textiles were shipped to Africa, are difficult to ascertain before the nineteenth century and appear to have been irregular, as indicated by the failure of its merchants to supply the market at Mozambique in the late 1770s and early 1780s. Nonetheless, shipping lists from the end of the century suggest that they were likely to have been up to 200,000 pieces a year.[26] African textile exports from Goa, the

---

[23] Prestholdt, *Domesticating the World*, 80.

[24] AHU, Moç., Cx 29 Doc. 56, Pereira do Lago to Crown, 12 August 1769.

[25] This confirms estimates that placed the trade of textiles through Diu at around 360,000–400,000 pieces per year to the end of the century. Vāniyā merchants also made this clear in a statement to the Portuguese governor in 1788 – HAG, CD 1003, Indian merchants to Governor, 25 April 1788. Extant textile export lists show that between 1780 and 1784 a total of approximately 1,800,000 pieces of assorted textiles were sent to Africa, most of which were supplied through Diu. These figures have been calculated from tables contained in HAG, CD 999, "Mappa Geral … 1780, 1781, 1782, e 1784", n.d. See also CD 1003, Indian merchants to Governor, 25 April 1788; and Lobato, *Evolução Administrativa*.

[26] HAG, CDm 1057, da Costa, Caetano Coutinho, Javer Khushal et al to Governor, ant. 21 April 1784. On shipping lists see, for example, AHU, Moç., Cx 69 Doc. 95, "Carga…",

Portuguese Indian capital, were by contrast small and were likely Gujarati re-exports organized through the Portuguese factory of Surat, which also supplied the southern Atlantic markets of West Central Africa through Portuguese and Brazilian networks centred on Bahia in Brazil.[27]

The large numbers of Gujarati cotton textiles that began entering African markets in the final quarter of the eighteenth century became of growing concern to the Portuguese authorities, who sought to achieve full regulatory control over the trade throughout the territory. Besides attempting to control textile imports from India, the Portuguese also sought to exert control over their distribution with a view to determining price and thus to curbing inflationary pressures that they deemed to have been caused by unrestricted textile importation. The latter had already become a matter of grave concern in the 1760s, leading the Governor-General Pereira do Lago to complain bitterly about the "damage" being done to trade by the "free introduction of cloths into the interior". His logic was that if it were possible to prohibit merchants from sending textiles into the interior, then African traders would be forced to bring their goods to towns and fairs under Portuguese administration where exchange could be better regulated, and Crown profits more securely obtained.[28]

Portuguese officials began to focus their attention increasingly – particularly from the 1770s – on Gujarati merchant networks as the importers of the vast bulk of textiles that arrived in Mozambique. Concern was largely directed at maintaining exchange price levels as stable as possible between imported Gujarati cotton cloths and ivory, the premier export commodity.[29] Officials argued that the circulation of large numbers of textiles in Macuana, to which Gujarati merchants sent African agents to trade with long-distance Yao and Makua merchants, had caused inflationary pressures in exchange transactions and that, far from benefitting State and private Portuguese merchants, was advantageous only to Vāniyā merchants. It was claimed, for instance, that by 1772 the exchange value of ivory had increased fivefold on

March 1794; Cx 73 Doc. 34, "Carga...", 11 March 1796. For problems in securing African cloth supplies, see HAG, CDm 1057, João Gomes da Costa, Francisco Caetano Coutinho, Javer Khushal, Hira (?) Raicarane (?) et al. to Governor, ant. 21 April 1784.

[27] Rudy Bauss, "A Legacy of British Free Trade Policies: The End of the Trade and Commerce between India and the Portuguese Empire, 1780–1830", *The Calcutta Historical Journal*, 66, 2 (1982), 81–115; and Bauss, "Textiles, Bullion and Other Trades of Goa: Commerce with Surat, Other areas of India, Luso-Brazilian ports, Macau and Mozambique, 1816–1819", *IESHR*, 34, 3 (1997), 275–87.

[28] AHU, Moç., Cx 25 Doc. 91, de Mello to Juiz Ordinario, 4 December 1765.

[29] This relationship was expressed in the *bar de fato*, a standardized measure of weight. The *bar* was approximately equal to 248 kg on Mozambique Island and to 294 kg in the Zambesi Valley.

Macuana while the value of the *bar* of cloths on Mozambique Island and in the Zambesi Valley had fallen precipitously.[30] And in Inhambane, a southern port emerging as a prominent slave shipment centre, officials argued that textile imports had "flooded" the market.[31]

In response, leading Gujarati merchants drafted two detailed letters to the governor-general in July and August 1781. Punjia Velji, Laxmichand Motichand, Jalal Ganesh and others argued that, had the Royal Treasury been able to purchase all of their imports, they would not have needed to distribute their cloths into the African interior. Further, they stressed that there were simply not enough private Portuguese merchants on Mozambique Island to purchase their annual cargoes. As a result of the inadequacies of state and private capital, Vāniyā merchants maintained that trading their cloths into the widespread markets of Mozambique through African agents was their only option. While their language was self-serving, it reflected an understanding of the realities of eighteenth-century African trade and of the inability of the Portuguese state to regulate commercial exchange within its imperial territories.[32] Textiles were traded on such a large scale that it was simply impossible to impose fixed exchange equivalencies. As Shobhachand Sowchand, Jiv Sancarji and several leading merchants made clear to the governor-general, "cloths are to be found in the hands of many individuals who ... try to exchange them speedily to settle debts with their creditors".[33] Despite their attempts to control the entry of piecegoods into Africa, and also the free movement of Vāniyās and their African agents in the African interior, the Portuguese were unable ultimately to control exchange rates beyond Mozambique Island.[34]

[30] AHU, Moç., Cx 30 Doc. 68, "Oficio de Pereira do Lago", 10 August 1772, which states that whereas "previously" Africans had sold ivory for two cloths, they sold it for ten cloths in 1772.; Cx 46 Doc. 31, Pedro de Saldanha de Albuquerque to Crown, 12 August 1783; Códice 1366, Luis Pinto de Souza to D. Diogo de Souza, 7 October 1796; Edward A. Alpers, *Ivory and Slaves in East Central Africa: Changing Pattern of International Trade to the Later Nineteenth Century* (London: Heinemann, 1975), 174.

[31] AHU, Moç., Cx 42 Doc. 44, Jose Ferreira Nobre to Governor-General, 7 June 1783.

[32] AHU, Moç., Cx 36 Doc. 35, Reply of Vāniyā to Governor-General, 7 July 1781; Punjia Velji, Laxmichand Motichand, Jalal Ganesh et al. to Governor-General, 3 August 1781; Representação of Vāniyā, 4 August 1781.

[33] AHU, Moç., Cx 75 Doc. 61, Shobhachand Sowchand, Jiv Sancarji, Antonio da Cruz e Almeida, Joze Henrique da Cruz Freitas et al. to Juiz Ordinario, 11 October 1796

[34] AHU, Moç., Cx 86 Doc. 29, da Cunha to Souza Coutinho, 9 October 1800. For further details, including accusations that Gujaratis were importing "falsified" cloths (textiles that did not conform to official size and quality specifications), see Pedro Machado, "Gujarati Indian Merchant Networks in Mozambique, 1777-c. 1830", Ph.D diss., University of London, 2005.

Consumer demand for Gujarati cloths was high throughout Mozambique, and the market was able to absorb large imports especially in the final quarter of the eighteenth century. Textile demand alone from the Portuguese factories of Quelimane, Sena and Tete in the early 1780s stood on average at 80,000–100,000 pieces a year, or 200,000 if we include private Portuguese trade.[35] Despite occasional and ill-informed protestations that the African market was small,[36] officials in Mozambique agreed (mostly reluctantly) over the extent to which Gujarati textiles were needed for purposes ranging from acquiring cloths for *sagoates*,[37] to payment of garrisons whose soldiers could not trade for even the most basic provisions without cloth.[38]

Indeed, the officials in Africa openly admitted that Gujarati textiles were the "currency" of the region. The Portuguese complaints about markets being "flooded" with cotton cloths, then, highlighted a poor understanding of consumer demand, or frustration at how distribution networks had been disturbed, rather than simple oversupply.[39] Their complaints reveal a concern about price stability caused by the difficulties faced by both official and private traders in an open market. They were unable to compete with Gujarati merchants without the imposition of monopoly trading practices or measures to restrict Indian trade, such as prohibiting the contact of merchants with – and movement in – the African interior, a practice that intensified in the 1780s amid the growth of Vāniyā trade (see Chapter 1), and that revealed intra-imperial differences in approaches to the place of South Asian capital in territories under Portuguese suzerainty in the western Indian Ocean. Gujarati merchants were aware that they were the commercial lifeblood of these territories and provided an invaluable contribution to Portuguese royal income

---

[35] AHU, Códice 1345, "Portaria...", 13 May 1782; AHU, Moç., Cx 36 Doc. 3, "Mappa...", n.d. [but 1781]. For cloths ordered by the factories of Sena, Inhambane and Lourenço Marques in 1786, see Cx 52 Doc. 93, "Fato...", 30 October 1786.

[36] See, for example, AHU, Moç., Cx 75 Doc. 61, de Souza to Tenente General, 22 October 1796.

[37] These were tribute payments made to African rulers in order to be allowed to trade in or through a particular area. See, for example, AHU, Moç., Cx 33 Doc. 27, Tenente General to Governor-General, 8 March 1780; Cx 38 Doc. 59, Melo e Castro to Tenente General, 6 June 1782.

[38] It was estimated in 1778 that "for the annual payment of the garrisons of the entire territory" it was necessary to spend 100,000 *cruzados* "for the purchase of cloths from Asia on account of the Royal Treasury". See Montaury, "Moçambique, Ilhas Querimbas...c. 1788", in *RMS*, 346.

[39] AHU, Moç., Cx 38 Doc. 14, "Memoria...", 24 January 1782; Cx 55 Doc. 35, Mello e Castro to Governor-General, 27 September 1787; Cx 30 Doc. 68, "Oficio...", 10 August 1772; Cx 42 Doc. 44, Ferreira Nobre to Governor-General, 7 June 1783.

through customs payments, and consequently any attempts to control or undermine their trade were likely to fail.

Furthermore, Vāniyā merchants possessed a well-developed understanding of the nuances of demand in the African textile market. This was gained on Mozambique Island and in Macuana primarily through sustained contact with *patamares*, African trading agents and traders, and in Sena at the entrance to the Zambesi Valley from *vashambadzi* (sing. *mushambadzi*), the Chikunda caravan leaders of slave status who were responsible for organizing trade caravans into the interior from the late 1770s after Vāniyās had established a presence there. As knowledgeable agents relaying important information about market demand to Gujarati merchants, the *patamares* and *vashambadzi* were central figures in the chains of relation linking intraregional exchange and local cloth consumers. Similar to caravan leaders in the later nineteenth-century East African interior,[40] they maintained direct contact with consumers and thus developed in-depth knowledge of the contingencies of local demand. The information that the *patamares* and *vashambadzi* collected in the interior and the knowledge that they accumulated, including an understanding of the complexities of changing exchange equivalencies, was critical not only to the success of their own trade but also to that of Vāniyā merchants who sought, therefore, to maintain direct contact with African agents to ensure that the makeup of their textile piecegood imports corresponded to demand in a particular season and/or region.[41] The Gujarati merchants appear to have understood well how indispensable this contact was for them:

[Indian merchants] compete ... *to give cabayas that are in fashion*, toucas ... ordering them especially from Diu with new designs that are communicated to their partners in the monsoons, from which we can see that the Africans, seeing these painted *cloths of a new fashion*, every year hurry to the [Indian merchants] and not to any Christian [merchants], and when one [Christian] by chance does appear he leaves disappointed and will certainly not return on another occasion.

In regard to the painted cloths *of new manufacture* that it is said ... are brought from the north [Gujarat] in order that they can attract to themselves all the goods brought by the Yao; it is well known that *the cloths after the fashion*

[40] Jonathan Glassman, *Feasts and Riot* (Portsmouth, NH: Heinemann, 1995); Stephen J. Rockel, *Carriers of Culture: Labor on the Road in Nineteenth-Century East Africa* (Portsmouth, NH: Heinemann, 2006); Prestholdt, "Global Repercussions"; *idem*, *Domesticating the World*.

[41] AHU, Moç., Cx 36 Doc. 35, Pereira Nobre, de Menezes, et al. to Senado da Camara, 14 July 1781.

or of new invention are brought [to Mozambique Island] by the [Vāniyā] merchants.[42]

The Portuguese suggested that Vāniyās were unfairly "creating" demand through the introduction of "new cloths" but while this may contain some truth, it was also an admission of being unable to compete with either the distribution networks which the Indians had in place or the knowledge they possessed of the market. The latter was especially indispensable because consumer tastes were not uniform throughout the territory in which Gujarati textiles were distributed. For example, at the Manica fair of Masekesa (located southwest of Sena on the Zambesi River), it was noted with some surprise how cloths which were in demand a few years earlier no longer found a market in the mid-1790s:

previously the best cloths were *capotins* and *ardians*, which generated a great deal of profit because they were not discounted and were cheaper, and now at this fair nothing is sold other than *zuartes* and some *dotins*, which are good quality cloths, that is, the *mossambazes* [*mushambadzi*] do not want to take any other quality cloth ... the *zuartes* and *dotins*, besides being the most expensive cloths, are only of this particular quality ...any other quality of cloth serves for [the acquisition of] provisions only.[43]

Merchants thus had to be attentive to the fluctuations in demand and to how these fluctuations informed choices about which cloths would be accepted or rejected by consumers. Towards the end of the eighteenth century, a European official lamented that two Gujarati cloths, *capotins* and *ardians*, had been rejected at Lourenço Marques. "The Africans", he wrote, "do not accept them for the purchase of provisions because they had been of inferior quality than were normally traded."[44] The challenges and complexities of supplying African markets was illustrated, further, in 1793, in the Delagoa Bay area, where

an abundance of cloths caused the Africans to not want half *ardians* in exchange for provisions which are needed by the army, and [*ardians*] only serve for the ivory trade in the Rivers [Zambesi Valley] ... it is damaging that the esteem for the other cloths has been lost ... *capotins* and *longuins* were also not exchanged in great abundance for payments ... and some are taken only as gifts by rulers.[45]

---

[42] These quotes are from AHU, Códice 1345, "Resposta...", 2 July 1781; and Moç., Cx 36 Doc. 35, Punji Velji, Laxmichand Motichand, Narsinh Ranchor et al. to Juiz Ordinario, 3 August 1781, respectively. The emphasis is mine.

[43] AHU, Moç., Cx 69 Doc. 22, de Almeida to Governor-General, 26 October 1794.

[44] AHU, Moç., Cx 31 Doc. 7, Luis Correa Monteiro de Mattos to dos Santos, 15 June 1794.

[45] AHU, Moç., Cx 64 Doc. 19, de Mattos to Governor-General, 12 May 1793.

Clearly, it was critical for merchants to be aware of fluctuations in consumer tastes, and failure to supply the appropriate cloths of the correct quality could have damaging or disastrous consequences. If buyers rejected unwanted textiles, merchants would be left with cargoes that would be difficult or impossible to sell, thereby ruining the season's trade.[46]

Reflecting a lack of understanding of how demand changed among African consumers, and exposing stereotypical perceptions of Africans as willing to accept any article of foreign production, the Portuguese labelled their tastes as "fickle" and subject to random change.[47] This kind of perception was common among other Europeans in different parts of Africa, but Africans did not blindly accept any commodity that was on offer. Vāniyā merchants unfailingly understood very early on that commercial success depended in large part on being attuned to the changing regional differences of textile demand in Mozambique. Because they did not venture into interior markets, critical information was provided to them, as noted in the book's earlier pages, by the *patamares* and *vashambadzi*, with whom Vāniyās maintained contact on a regular basis. The Portuguese attempted to undermine this system by restricting Vāniyā movement from Mozambique Island but were unsuccessful because of the pressures which the Indians exerted on the authorities whenever such policies were pursued, including threats to suspend textile imports.[48]

A growing realization that consumer demand and tastes – at least as much as if not more than production – played a critical role in determining commercial transactions between foreign merchants and African consumers has recently prompted historians to consider the precise extent to which these influenced precolonial African economic exchange. For example, Joseph Miller has shown how African demand for Indian textiles shaped Portuguese and Brazilian trade between the 1770s and the first quarter of the nineteenth century, noting that "imports are likely to prove more momentous for Africa's history than its better publicized exports, since what Africa received from abroad enabled people there to consolidate old, or to develop new, production techniques and productive relations". This scholarship has alerted historians to the important role played by consumer tastes in shaping African precolonial commercial

---

[46] AHU, Moç., Cx 31 Doc. 7, de Mattos to dos Santos, 15 June 1794.
[47] AHU, Moç., Cx 40 Doc. 9, Coelho to da Fonseca, 21 October 1782.
[48] AHU, Moç., Cx 38 Doc. 59, Vicente Caetano da Maia e Vasconcellos to Martinho de Melo e Castro, 18 August 1781.

exchanges.[49] Yet, despite the importance of this work and the shift of focus it proposes, it has not adequately traced out the repercussions of African demand on the structures of material exchange and/or production. Rather, as we will see here in the case of Gujarati cotton cloths in Mozambique, Africans influenced the broader parameters of the processes in which they were embedded as integral actors. By placing African demand in Mozambique in the eighteenth and early nineteenth centuries within a broader Indian Ocean context, the role of Africans in its emergent global economy of the late eighteenth and early nineteenth centuries becomes quite clear.[50]

Of many hues

The complexities of African consumer tastes are perhaps best understood through the vast array of textiles which were imported from Diu (and to a lesser extent Daman), and which recall the range of textiles that Richard Burton noted and described in Zanzibar in the 1850s.[51] While a comparable list does not exist for Mozambique, it is possible from the lists of cloths located in the sources to identify some of them reasonably accurately.[52] These, however, represent only a small proportion of the textiles which were supplied by Vāniyā merchants to African markets. A number of the cloths appear to have been traded across

---

[49] Joseph C. Miller, "Imports at Luanda, Angola 1785–1823", in G. Liesegang, H. Pasch, and A. Jones (eds.), *Figuring African Trade: Proceedings of the Symposium on the Quantification and Structure of the Import and Export and Long Distance Trade in Africa, 1800–1913* (Berlin: D. Reimer Verlag, 1986), 164. This line of enquiry was further developed in *Way of Death* (Madison: University of Wisconsin Press, 1988). See also the important early work of David Richardson, "West African Consumption Patterns and their Influence on the Eighteenth-Century English Slave Trade", in A. Gemery and J. Hogendorn (eds.), *The Uncommon Market: Essays in the Economic History of the Atlantic Slave Trade* (New York: Atlantic Press, 1979), 303–30; and more recently G. Metcalf, "A Microcosm of Why Africans Sold Slaves: Akan Consumption Patterns in the 1770s", *Journal of African History*, 28, 3 (1987), 377–94. Carolyn Keyes Adenaike established the understanding that "African consumers' tastes dictated the market" where the latter were "discriminating buyers whose tastes strongly influenced not only the marketing but also the production of cloth". See "West African Textiles", 251–61.

[50] This is a perspective I share with Prestholdt, "Global Repercussions"; and *idem*, *Domesticating the World*.

[51] Richard Burton, *The Lake Regions of Central Africa*, 2 vols. (London: Longman, Green, Longman and Roberts, 1860), II, appendix I, "Commerce, Imports and Exports", 387–419.

[52] This has been a difficult undertaking because of the large variety of cloth names that appear in the sources. I located lists of cloths in the AHU, Caixas de Moçambique and Códices, and in the HAG, CD and CDm, and AD and ADm series. Alexandre Lobato, *História do Presídio de Lourenço Marques (1787–1799)*, 2 vols. (Lisbon: Tipografia Minerva, 1960), II, 328–29 also provides a list of a number of these cloths but does not attempt to describe them or trace their distribution.

large areas of coastal and interior Mozambique, such as *capotins* (blue and white chequered or striped cloths); *canequins* (coarse indigo-dyed blue or black calicoes); and the highly valued *samateres* (narrow white cotton cloths) and *zuartes* (indigo-dyed cloths), the best of which one contemporary author noted came from Jambusar.[53]

Local contingencies in consumer tastes were influenced, in part as I have been suggesting, by the way cloth was used.[54] In Manica in the Zambesi Valley, for example, *zuartes* and *dotins* (strong, coarse cotton cloths) were in great demand.[55] Other textiles sent to the Masekesa trading fair included *samateres*, *savagagins* and "primarily the *Dotins* ... that are accepted in all the lands of Manica". Cured *savagagins* were worn by the royalty and nobility, while *samateres* were used for sacrificial ceremonies "performed in order to appease the *Vadzimu* [an ancestral spirit]" and to denote mourning.[56] It is clear, however, that from the 1780s, *zuartes* had increasingly become the most sought-after cloths when *vashambadzi* pointedly refused to accept any other textiles.[57] In the Rozvi empire, Gujarati textiles were sent by the emperor as part of the regalia at the investiture of new provincial chiefs. Cloths were also given as presents to the *mhondoro*, the Mutapa spirit medium, while rulers who regularly brought tribute to the Zimbabwe were rewarded with cloth.[58] Rulers in the Lunda kingdom of South-Central Africa attached great prestige in the late eighteenth century to acquiring Indian imports as they sought to adorn themselves with cloths that "showed the influence of [their] involvement in world trade".[59]

On the southern coast, *canequims*, *samateres*, *capotins*, *ardians* and *cutonias* (a striped cloth of mixed silk and cotton weave) were regularly traded in Sofala where, in a development similar to that in Manica, *zuartes*

[53] A. C. P. Gamitto, *King Kazembe and the Marave, Cheva, Bisa, Bemba, Lunda, and Other Peoples of Southern Africa, Being the Diary of the Portuguese Expedition to That Potentate in the Years 1831 and 1832*, 2 vols. (Lisbon: Junta de Investigações do Ultramar, 1960), II, appendix I, B, "Table showing the types of cotton cloth...", 198.

[54] This was noted years ago in John Irwin and Paul R. Schwartz, *Studies in Indo-European Textile History* (Ahmedabad: Calico Museum, 1966).

[55] H. H. K. Bhila, *Trade and Politics in a Shona Kingdom: The Manyika and Their Portuguese and African Neighbours, 1575–1902* (Harlow: Longman, 1982), 131.

[56] Manoel Galvão da Silva, "Diario...", 14 November 1788, in *FHGCM*, 328; Bhila, *Trade*, 131.

[57] AHU, Moç., Cx 69 Doc. 22, de Almeida to Governor-General, 26 October 1794.

[58] S. I. Mudenge, *A Political History of Munhumutapa* (Harare: Zimbabwe Publishing Co., 1986), 185.

[59] Ian Cunnison, "Kazembe and the Portuguese, 1798–1832", *Journal of African History*, 2/1 (1961), 65.

were most in demand.[60] *Doutins* and *capotins* were actively traded also as cloths worn exclusively by the elites as markers of distinction and connection to a global trading world. In Delagoa Bay in the far south, economic expansion by the end of the eighteenth century also provided a fillip for the demand for various Gujarati textiles.[61] *Capotins, ardians, zuartes, doutins* and *longuins* were among the established imports that were used as bridewealth and accumulated by rulers as part of the payments that merchants were required to make to be allowed to trade in their lands.

How did the large-scale importation of Gujarati cloths by Vāniyā merchants affect local African textile production? Did these Indian manufactures displace African manufacturing? It is difficult to provide conclusive answers to these questions. As noted earlier, within the broader East African region, a vibrant weaving industry had existed serving local demand in a number of towns along the coast until at least the sixteenth century. Despite this established industry, however, it is clear that by around the middle of the seventeenth century weaving had declined considerably throughout the region and while it would not disappear entirely, it would not regain its vitality. In certain areas African production did thrive, perhaps most notably in southern Somalia where around a thousand weaving households in Mogadishu produced considerable numbers of cottons for regional markets in the 1840s.[62] In Madagascar also, with its long history of cotton cultivation and textile production for internal and regional consumption, in the mid-eighteenth century slave traders on the northwestern coast were able to purchase textiles for the growing trade in human cargoes; and on the central plateau, cotton weaving remained a significant occupation into the first half of the nineteenth century.[63]

---

[60] João Julião da Silva, "Memoria...", in Feliciano and Nicolau, *Memórias de Sofala*, 144–5. The editors of this collection of documents suggest that da Silva was writing after 1838 and had therefore constructed his narrative retrospectively.

[61] Malyn Newitt, *A History of Mozambique* (Bloomington: Indiana University Press, 1995), 159. See also: Benigna de Jesus Lurdina Mateus Lisboa Zimba, "Overseas Trade, Regional Politics, and Gender Roles: Southern Mozambique, ca. 1720 to ca. 1830", PhD diss., University of Michigan, 1999, 328; Alan Smith, "The Struggle for Control of Southern Mozambique, 1720–1835", PhD diss., University of California, 1970, 164; "Plano e relação da Bahia ...", in Caetano Montez, *Descobrimento e Fundação de Lourenço Marques, 1500–1800* (Lourenço Marques: Minerva Central Editora, 1948), 172.

[62] Edward A. Alpers, "Futa Benaadir; Continuity and Change in the Traditional Cotton Textile Industry of Southern Somalia, c. 1840–1980", in A. Forest and C. Coquery-Vidrovitch (eds.), *Entreprises et entrepreneurs en Afrique, XIXe et XXe siècles* (Paris: L'Harmattan, 1983), I, 77–98.

[63] Pier Larson, *History and Memory in the Age of Enslavement* (Portsmouth, NH: Heinemann, 2000)

In Mozambique, local textiles continued to be manufactured and traded in the eighteenth and nineteenth centuries in at least two locales. Most well known are cloths called *machiras*, thick unwoven white cotton cloths of the Zambesi and Shire region, about which S. I. Mudenge has argued that "throughout the history of their relations with coastal traders until the twentieth century, the Shona never replaced their indigenous products for imported ones. The animal skins and the roughly woven *machira* cloth both saw the dawn of the twentieth century."[64] *Machiras* were traded extensively on *prazos*, inheritable Portuguese Crown estates in the Zambesi Valley that were leased to Portuguese settlers, where they were made into blankets, hammocks, cloaks and belts; they were popular among the Nsenga Chewa, southern Lunda and Karanga-related peoples. They were also traded at Masekesa and throughout the Shire Valley.[65] Although there can be little doubt that Indian cloths were more prestigious, *machiras* remained well into the twentieth century a staple commodity thanks to their durability and range of uses. Additionally, locally grown cotton was woven in Sofala where the production of cloths called *gondos* continued well into the nineteenth century; they were traded in the Zambesi Valley where they were used for making sails.[66]

Yet, the persistence of African production in these contexts cannot mask the reality that local textile manufacturing throughout Mozambique and East Africa was much reduced by the end of the eighteenth century, even if it did not disappear altogether. Whether rising imports of Indian textiles caused this change is difficult to establish definitively. W. G. Clarence-Smith, for example, has argued that far from undermining local production, imports of Indian textiles may actually have stimulated these industries, with weavers in some cases adopting strategies such as unravelling imports and incorporating the threads into textiles that had been produced locally.[67] There is perhaps more compelling evidence, however, suggesting that Indian imports

[64] Mudenge, *Political History*, 187.

[65] Davison and Harries, "Cotton Weaving in South-East Africa", 181–91; Allen F. Isaacman, *Mozambique. The Africanization of a European Institution* (Madison: University of Wisconsin Press, 1972), 66, 73; Newitt, *History*, 214; Alpers, *Ivory and Slaves*, 86.

[66] da Silva, "Memoria", 99; Gerhard Liesegang (ed.), *"Resposta das Questoens sobre os Cafres" ou Noticias Etnográficas sobre Sofala do Fim do Século XVIII* (Lisbon: Junta de Investigações do Ultramar/Centro de Estudos de Antropologia Cultural, 1966), 23. Cotton and bark cloth production between the Limpopo and Rovuma rivers survived into the twentieth century, for which see Liesegang, "A First Look at the Import and Export Trade of Mozambique, 1800–1914", in Liesegang et al., *Figuring African Trade*, 452–523.

[67] W. G. Clarence-Smith, "The Expansion of Cotton Textile Production in the Western Indian Ocean, c1500–c1850", in Stefan Halikowski-Smith (ed.), *Reinterpreting Indian Ocean Worlds: Essays in Honour of Prof. K. N. Chaudhuri* (Newcastle: Cambridge

weakened – if did not destroy – domestic manufacture. Even in Madagascar, which had had perhaps the most diverse textile industry in Eastern Africa, the growing popularity of Gujarati cloth imports from the 1780s, and especially after 1800 "when it gained momentum", cut into markets for local cloths.[68] Indeed, elsewhere, the regional dominance of Indian textiles was captured in the popular poem "*Hindi ndiko kwenyi nguo*" (India is where clothes are made) by the famed *mashairi* poet Muyaka bin Haji in Mombasa sometime in the first half of the nineteenth century.[69] If Indian manufactures perhaps did not "fatally undermine" African production, they consolidated or established new consumer markets that in the eighteenth and nineteenth centuries were supplied by competing South Asian merchant networks from Kathiawar and later also Kutch.

What is clear is that the trade in African textiles was not incompatible with the import of Gujarati textiles: they complemented one another because they did not necessarily compete for the same markets. Ultimately, local contingencies such as the uses to which cloths were put, how they were integrated into local systems of consumption and the meanings with which they were inscribed determined whether local textile production was or was not undermined by imports. Indian cloths were invested with a variety of meanings by local consumers, from gaining prestige value as visible reminders of a person's place in society, to their social uses in initiation and investiture ceremonies. Cloths were also offered as gifts to rulers to allow merchants to conduct trade in their lands, were accumulated as a reflection of a ruler's wealth and were used to pay troops.[70] At the same time, and equally importantly, Gujarati textiles served as exchange media against which ivory tusks and human beings could be purchased in much of Mozambique.

Networks of procurement and production: Gujarat

The importance of African consumer tastes in affecting Gujarati textile exports from western India is clear. Success in the textile trade depended

---

Scholars Publishing, 2011); Clarence-Smith, "The Cotton Textile Industry of Sub-Saharan Eastern Africa in the Longue Durée", Unpublished paper presented at the conference "Understanding African Poverty over the *Longue Durée*", Accra, Ghana, July 15–17, 2010. As a result, Clarence-Smith concludes that "South Asian textiles failed to de-industrialize eastern Africa in early modern times."

[68] Larson, *History and Memory*, 127–129.

[69] Mohamed H. Abdulaziz, *Muyaka: 19th Century Swahili Popular Poetry* (Nairobi: Kenya Literature Bureau, 1979), 166–8. I thank Elizabeth McMahon for bringing this poem to my attention.

[70] See, for example, BA, 54-XIII-3 (3), Barbosa, "Analyse Estatistica", 30 December 1821, for cloths being sent to Zambesia as payment for troops.

on a well-developed understanding of which types of cloths were in demand in the African interior, and providing these accordingly. Of equal importance to the success of this trade was the regular and efficient procurement of textiles in the interior of Gujarat. Without a regular supply of appropriate textiles for the African trade, Vāniyās would have been unable to satisfy consumer demand, and consequently would have been severely restricted in their trade with the African interior. As a small and infertile island, Diu was a poor and unproductive area that had to rely for its textile supplies on mainland western Gujarat.[71] Its position at the southern tip of the Kathiawar peninsula, close to Gujarati production centres, however, meant Diu was potentially well placed to take advantage of this vast hinterland for its textile supplies. Effectively, it functioned as an entrepôt through which flows of goods from Africa and India intersected and were redirected.

The study of the importation of Indian textiles into Africa has paid little or no attention to issues of supply and production in South Asia.[72] This has generated an incomplete appreciation of the extent to which Indian weavers and people beyond South Asia were intimately connected in trans-oceanic material relationships mediated by Vāniyā merchant networks. A more rounded account needs to incorporate South Asia into the discussion and thus highlight the connections that – through histories of merchant circulation – bound Africa and the Indian subcontinent.

Textile manufacturing in India differed across the producing regions. In Bengal and the Coromandel, for example, the textile industry was found in both town and country.[73] By contrast, in the Punjab and Gujarat, weavers were located in urban centres or close to the main cities. Cities such as Surat served as a market for small weaving towns that were located a short distance away. Other major textile centres of Gujarat were all urban (Map 3.1). There were certain advantages for producers in being located in or near an urban centre, not least of which was the concentration of large populations with regular consumption needs.

---

[71] M. N. Pearson, "Brokers in Western Indian Port Cities", *Modern Asian Studies*, 22, 3 (1988), 467.

[72] There are notable exceptions here: Roberts, "Guinée Cloth"; Pearson, *Port Cities*; Prestholdt, "East African Consumerism"; *idem, Domesticating the World*.

[73] There is evidence from Dutch records for the northern Coromandel suggesting, however, that weavers were entirely dispersed in "industrial villages" scattered throughout coastal districts. Om Prakash, *European Commercial Enterprise in Pre-colonial India* (Cambridge University Press, 1998), 163–4; Joseph J. Brennig, "Textile Producers and Production in Late Seventeenth Century Coromandel", in Sanjay Subrahmanyam (ed.), *Merchants, Markets and the State in Early Modern India* (Delhi: Oxford University Press, 1990), 66–89.

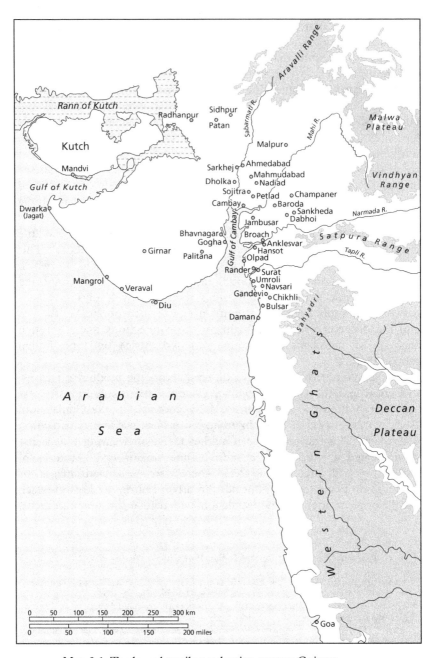

Map 3.1 Trade and textile production centres Gujarat

Other no less important considerations were proximity to sources of raw cotton, skilled, semi-skilled and unskilled labour, and a supply of good-quality water essential for dying.[74]

There is much evidence to show that Indian weavers were able to adjust their production effectively to respond to changing consumer tastes in the vastly different Indian Ocean markets. Export production was therefore characterized by a high degree of specialization based on product differentiation as well as market orientation.[75] Thus, weavers in Bengal produced textiles for Middle Eastern markets, while those in the Coromandel supplied the Southeast Asian markets. The capacity of weavers to adjust their production to conform to the tastes of purchasers in distant markets is perhaps nowhere more clearly seen than in the case of Gujarat, where weavers "had *fully* adopted their manufacturing techniques and the fabrics to suit the needs of . . . buyers".[76]

Production for African markets was equally specialized.[77] What is striking, however, is that in the eighteenth and nineteenth centuries production was not dispersed across Gujarat but was concentrated almost exclusively in a single locale. Jambusar was a weaving and cotton- and indigo-producing centre located southeast of Cambay, across the Mahi River and approximately 80 miles southwest of Baroda in the "great Cotton district" of western India.[78] It was situated in one of the most fertile regions in India consisting of extremely rich soil watered by the Mahi, Narmada and Tapti Rivers. It had been a collecting point for goods produced in the surrounding areas in the seventeenth century, and owed its importance "to the fact that [it] lay along the trade routes and hence catered to the need of passing

---

[74] Chaudhuri, "Structure", 39, 44.   [75] *Ibid.*, 40–1.

[76] *Ibid*, 42. The emphasis is mine.

[77] Cloth production, of course, entailed more than the manufacturing process, starting in the cotton marts where raw cotton was first cleaned and followed by spinning, dyeing and "pasting" before the thread was ready for the weaver's loom. This involved several sets of artisan families. While these different stages were important in the production of a piece of cloth, I focus here on weavers and the procurement process because of the limitations of the sources. For discussion of the manufacturing process in India, see, for instance, Hameeda Hossain, *The Company Weavers of Bengal: The East India Company and the Organization of Textile Production in Bengal, 1750–1813* (New Delhi: Oxford University Press, 1988); Prasannan Parthasarathi, *The Transition to a Colonial Economy: Weavers, Merchants and Kings in South India, 1720–1800* (New York: Cambridge University Press, 2001); Lakshmi Subramanian, "The Political Economy of Textiles in Western India", in Giorgio Riello and Tirthankar Roy (eds.), *How India Clothed the World: The World of South Asian Textiles, 1500–1850* (Leiden: Brill, 2009), 253–80.

[78] John Briggs, *The Cities of Gujarashtra: Their Topography and History Illustrated, in the Journal of a Recent Tour, with Accompanying Documents* (Bombay: Times, 1849), 148.

caravans". It served also as a prominent indigo-producing town in the region.[79]

Weavers in Jambusar manufactured textiles exclusively for African consumers, and did so according to the particular specifications that Vāniyā merchants provided annually to them through middlemen. As a producer of large volumes of textiles for the African markets, Jambusar's existence as a prosperous weaving and manufacturing centre depended to a large extent on the demands of African consumer tastes.[80] Over the course of the eighteenth century (if not earlier), weavers in Jambusar and African consumers were brought together in a relational trans-oceanic material dynamic defined by the particularities of taste and fashion.

The eighteenth century was one of prosperity for Jambusar for two related reasons. The first concerned commercial policies adopted by the Marathas who controlled the area. Maratha potentates appear to have been aware of the value of production and commerce for the prosperity of their regimes, and were therefore eager to provide or maintain favourable conditions to this end. This is one of the reasons why trade grew over the period from the 1740s to the 1820s.[81] The second reason contributing to the prosperity of Jambusar was the decline of production in Cambay. Within a context of growing Anglo-Maratha rivalry, the Marathas had declared freedom of trade both in Cambay and in its *parganas* (local districts) in the 1740s but the latter benefited from this measure much more than Cambay, which was at the time suffering unstable political and social conditions. Indeed, production in the *qasbas* (markets) of Cambay declined considerably in the following years and, along with it, the revenue of the Nawab.

By contrast, cotton production and trade in the *parganas* increased significantly as artisans and workers left the *qasbas* and city of Cambay for nearby towns. One of the towns to which artisans migrated and which saw a growth in its production was Jambusar, which "began to prosper not only as a wholesale mart but also as a trading center that took away much

---

[79] Surendra Gopal, *Commerce and Crafts in Gujarat, 16th and 17th Centuries: A Study in the Impact of European Expansion on Precapitalist Economy* (New Delhi: People's Publishing House, 1975), 151, 197.

[80] This confirms K. N. Chaudhuri's position that "one of the best indicators of a region's industrial ties to a particular market area is the degree to which producers [are able to] adjust their products to consumer tastes". See Chaudhuri, "Structure", 42.

[81] Sumit Guha, "Potentates, Traders and Peasants: Western India, c. 1700–1870", in Burton Stein and Sanjay Subrahmanyam (eds.), *Institutions and Economic Change in South Asia* (Oxford University Press, 1996), 71–84.

of Cambay's resources".[82] The migration of weavers away from cities that Maratha rule had destroyed in the early eighteenth century, such as "beleaguered" Ahmedabad, may also have benefited Jambusar.[83] Production remained buoyant into the nineteenth century, and "a great trade was carried on from Jambusar in cotton piece-goods with Bombay and other places".[84] What has been mostly overlooked, however, in the prosperity and vibrancy of the town, has been the importance of African consumer demand on the growth of the productive capacity of its weaver households.

Vāniyā merchants acquired textiles manufactured in Jambusar for the African markets through a system of advances that rested on oral agreements between contracting merchants and their brokers on the number and types of textiles required for the trading season. Merchants likely used pattern books to transmit information to brokers about cloth styles and patterns that were in demand among African consumers. Surviving Gujarati pattern books from the late nineteenth century for the markets of Southeast Asia suggest that this was a common practice among merchants (Figure 3.1).[85] Prices for the different types and qualities of textiles were also agreed with the broker. Brokers (who could work for a number of merchants) took the merchants' orders to Jambusar and presented the details to further intermediaries who dealt directly with the weavers. Brokers did not just work as intermediaries, but were known to purchase textiles from weavers themselves to sell to merchants.[86] A broker might have dealt directly with weavers in Jambusar but there is evidence to suggest that most commonly he did not. This is in keeping with commercial practices in other parts of India where brokers tended not to deal with producers but with their representatives, such as headweavers in the South Indian case, where Sinnappah Arasaratnam has pointed to the complex social structure of weaving villages that prevented direct contact

---

[82] Aniruddha Ray, "Malet Collection on Cambay (Gujarat) at the End of the 18th Century", in Ernestine Carreira (ed.), *Sources européennes sur le Gujarat* (Paris: Société d'Histoire de l'Orient and L'Harmattan, 1998), 22.

[83] Chaudhuri, *Trading World*, 310.

[84] William Milburn, *Oriental Commerce; Containing a Geographical Description of the Principal Places in the East Indies, China, and Japan, with Their Produce, Manufactures, and Trade*, 2 vols. (London: Black, Parry & Co., 1813), I, 156. See also *Gazetteer of the Bombay Presidency. Vol. 2: Gujarat: Surat and Broach* (Bombay: Government Central Press, 1877), 563–5.

[85] Prasannan Parthasarathi, *Why Europe Grew Rich and Asia Did Not: Global Economic Divergence, 1600–1850* (New York: Cambridge University Press, 2011), 33.

[86] HAG, CDm 1068, "Representação...", 30 May 1821. This was a widespread practice which is confirmed in evidence for southeastern India. See Sinnappah Arasaratnam, "Weavers, Merchants and Company: The Handloom Industry in Southeastern India, 1750–1790", *IESHR*, 17, 3 (1980), 267.

Figure 3.1 (a) and (b) Gujarati Pattern book with specific design for Thai textile market, early twentieth century. Image courtesy of John Guy, Metropolitan Museum of Art

Figure 3.1 (cont.)

between weavers and brokers, and thereby offered weavers some protection from capital.[87]

The broker also arranged for the finishing of the textiles that was generally not the responsibility of the weaver. In a few cases this may have been done in Diu and Daman, where by the second decade of the nineteenth century there were "painters" and "printers".[88] As found throughout India, advances to weavers in Jambusar were made in cash and the money was used to purchase necessary raw materials such as yarn. Weavers could refuse to honour their agreements with brokers, in many cases returning the advance if a higher offer was made. There are examples where weavers failed to return advances and placed brokers and merchants in awkward positions, without much chance for redress.[89]

This procurement system worked well for the merchants, the brokers and the weavers who produced the textiles for the export market. Gujarati merchants, removed from production centres, were supplied with the types and quantities of textiles needed for their trade on a regular basis. Weavers were provided with the capital for their work, given access to export markets and were protected from market fluctuations. The brokers benefited from the money and credit arrangements that were made with merchants for their purchases.[90]

However, relationships between merchants and brokers were not always without conflict. The experiences of Panachand Jalalchand are illustrative.[91] For over 25 years, Panachand Jalalchand had been a broker supplying Vāniyā merchants in Daman with textile cargoes for the African markets of Mozambique. He supplied these on an annual basis through loans which were settled approximately a year after they were issued by him. These annual travels from Jambusar to Daman served also to "settle accounts". When he arrived in Daman in early 1821 to deliver goods and settle his debts, however, he was ordered by the Portuguese governor to leave the territory promptly because of an alleged fraud he had committed against two merchants. According to the accusation, Panachand had dishonestly recorded the amount of debt owed by Karamchand and Milabo (?) Amarchand, merchants with

---

[87] Arasaratnam, "Weavers"; Parthasarathi, *Transition to a Colonial Economy*, 86.

[88] HAG, AD 4955; MR 193A, "Mappa...", 14 Oct 1814; MR 169C, "Mappa...", 31 Dec 1818.

[89] Arasaratnam, "Weavers".

[90] Chaudhuri, *Trading World*, 254–62; Parthasarathi, *Transition to a Colonial Economy*, 22–3; Arasaratnam, "Weavers".

[91] I base my discussion of Panachand in the following several paragraphs on HAG, CDm 1067, Testimony of Panachand Jalalchand, 30 May 1821; "Rellação...", n.d. [but 1821]; Governor of Daman to Viceroy, June 1821; CDm 1063, Panachand Jalalchand to Viceroy, 13 June 1821.

investments in the Africa trade. As a broker, Panachand was in a strong position in relation to the brothers Amarchand because they relied on his good character and reputation to procure piecegoods for them at "honest" prices. They trusted him to record their debts correctly from year to year and, when necessary, to carry debts over into the following year if they were unable to settle accounts when they took delivery of an order.

As a man of "public credit", Panachand Jalalchand was an important broker to whom approximately 30 merchants in 1821 owed in excess of Rs 60,000 for the supply of African trade textiles. His expulsion from Daman shortly after his arrival reveals another aspect of the merchant–broker relationship. The risk merchants took in becoming indebted to brokers was calculated against projected future gains from ivory imports. Therefore, if a merchant who owed a broker money for textiles did not enjoy a good trading season, he would be unable to settle his debt with the broker. Karamchand and Milabo Amarchand appear to have fallen into debt with Panachand, and as a result had approached the governor of Daman with allegations of dishonesty against the broker – claiming he had "invented" debts – in the likely hope that the imperial state would intercede on their behalf.

In response to these public and therefore damaging charges, Panachand maintained that he had always been honest in his dealings with the merchants of Daman. He complained bitterly of never having been expelled from a territory for seeking to settle debts, and that he could not leave Daman without being paid by the merchants with whom he had agreed contracts. We should not forget that Panachand was himself indebted to the suppliers of textiles, and failure to collect payment in Daman would have left him in an extremely precarious position, harming his creditworthiness and hence reputation in Jambusar. He accused the governor of collaborating with the accusing merchants and of accepting a bribe to expel him from Daman.

These accusations reveal that the broker was probably a widely and intensely disliked figure among merchants, despite the critical role he occupied in the procurement of textiles for the export trade. While merchants relied on brokers for their supplies, it seems a certain merchant animosity underlay their relationship because of the merchants' indebtedness to such brokers. The language of the testimonies of eight merchants against Panachand Jalalchand exposes an unmistakable level of hostility: he is described as a "thief with a knavish character", who profited from "usurious practices both in the purchase of textiles and in the sale of ivory". Faced with allegations and counter-allegations, and a lack of details about any resolution, it is difficult to know which account was the more accurate. Certainly, Panachand could not have maintained dealings with Daman for over 20 years if he had not been a broker in good standing with Vāniyā merchants and his own creditors in Jambusar. This is not to say, however, that Panachand was necessarily without blame in his business practices. Some of what the merchants of Daman said about him may well have been true but it may not have been any worse than occurred elsewhere in western India at this time. The veracity of the merchants' case is considerably weakened by the fact that two of the merchants who had been supposedly wronged by Panachand fled Daman shortly after his arrival, presumably because they lacked the funds to settle their debts with him. Wherever the truth may lie, the case highlights the tensions which defined the relationship between merchants and brokers.

Although it is uncertain when Vāniyā merchants first established procurement from Jambusar, it seems that by the 1730s most of its artisans were already producing textiles specifically for the Mozambique markets.[92] By the mid- to late eighteenth century, they concentrated their procurement there to the almost complete exclusion of other weaving centres in Gujarat, with between 85 and 95 per cent of all textiles exported to Africa on Indian vessels having been manufactured in Jambusar.[93] This likely represented a high proportion of Jambusar's productive capacity and thus provided work for many of the town's spinners and weavers. The extremely large investment of Rs 400,000 in 1800 by Vāniyā merchants in Diu for the purchase of Jambusar textiles expressly for Mozambique consumers is an indication of the scale of this investment and of the financial resources that these Gujarati merchants could mobilize. Indeed, such was the scale of Gujarati merchant capital investment that it worried brokers working for the East India Company, who complained vociferously that it was proving an impediment to

---

[92] Aniruddha Ray, "Cambay and its Hinterland: Early Eighteenth Century", in Indu Banga (ed.), *Ports and Their Hinterlands in India (1700–1950)* (New Delhi: Manohar Publications, 1992), 140–1. It was noted in 1732 that, apart from Mocha and Jidda, most of the artisans in Jambusar "were working for goods to be exported to Mozambique".

[93] This has been calculated from HAG, AD 4952–4968 and CD 995–1012; CDm 1055–1068. Edward A. Alpers has recently suggested, through an analysis of a list he compiled of nearly 80 different types of Indian cotton cloths, that the textiles that were being brought to Mozambique Island in the early 1750s originated from more geographically dispersed locales. Even allowing that this may have been the case at mid-century, the evidence I present here makes it clear that, as Vāniyā investment intensified, Jambusar-procured and -produced textiles were utterly dominant in the second half of the century. See "Indian Textiles at Mozambique Island in the Mid-Eighteenth Century", paper presented at the conference, "Textile Trades and Consumption in the Indian Ocean World, from Early Times to the Present", Indian Ocean World Centre, McGill University, 2–4 November 2012.

their purchases.[94] The level of Vāniyā investment underlines how the livelihoods of weaving households, merchant families and brokers were sustained by their interrelation with African consumers. In turn, it highlights how consumer tastes affected seemingly distant economic processes, and unmasks the importance of African consumer tastes for the vitality of one of Gujarat's centres of cloth production.

Imperial manoeuvrings and overtures

The centrality of Jambusar as the production and procurement centre for the entire African trade of the southwestern Indian Ocean had by the 1780s become a source of perennial irritation and frustration for the Portuguese authorities in India.[95] They saw its role as the predominant textile supplier for Diu and Daman Vāniyā as undermining state and private Portuguese efforts to recruit weavers and establish production in these territories, efforts that began in the early eighteenth century and would intensify from the middle of the century. Portuguese Indian officials accused the textile production of Jambusar of creating a relationship of "dependency" for Gujarati merchants, and regarded the purchase of these African textiles as a drain on capital that should have been deployed in the development of production within imperial domains. Investment capital from these territories was, as a result, "circulating in the land [the interior of Gujarat]" instead of being used to establish spinning, weaving and dying facilities.[96] Vāniyā merchants, notwithstanding occasional tensions between merchants and brokers, for example, were invested heavily in an effective procurement system that they had established over the course of the eighteenth century. It contained distinct advantages – perhaps the most important of which was the possession by weavers of knowledge of the specific tastes of African consumers – that were not as easily replicable as the Portuguese state had perhaps envisaged.

Portuguese interest in establishing textile production in India can be best understood both as a response to the aggressive procurement practices of

---

[94] MSA, Commercial Department Diary of the Bombay Government No. 27 of 1800, Petition of the Contracting Brokers, p. 510ff., quoted in Lakshmi Subramanian, "Power and the Weave: Weavers, Merchants and Rulers in Eighteenth-Century Surat", in Rudrangshu Mukherjee and Lakshmi Subramanian (eds.), *Politics and Trade in the Indian Ocean World: Essays in Honour of Ashin Das Gupta* (Delhi: Oxford University Press, 1998), 74.

[95] AHU, Moç., Cx 55 Doc. 3, Antonio Manoel de Mello e Castro to Francisco da Cunha e Menezes, 13 August 1787. See also, for example, HAG, CM 1445, Mello e Castro to da Cunha e Menezes, 14 August 1787.

[96] HAG, CDm 1061, Candido Joze Mourao Palha to Viceroy, 19 October 1801.

the English East India Company in western India in general, and in Surat in particular, especially from the middle of the century, and as part of the Portuguese imperial reforms aimed at reviving Portuguese commercial fortunes in their imperial territories in the Indian Ocean and in the process increasing their share of the European export market. In the view of officials in Goa and Lisbon, these aims could not be achieved without the establishment of a solid manufacturing base in India.[97]

European demand for South Asian textiles for intra-Asian trade in the Indian Ocean had begun to develop rapidly from the middle of the seventeenth century, as Dutch interest grew in Southeast Asian commerce and led to the establishment of Indian factories in Coromandel that from the 1680s also served European markets.[98] English capitalists established factories in the subcontinent to secure textile supplies in the seventeenth century, notably in South India and Bengal, and from the second half of the century their investments began to increase significantly.[99] The procurement of textiles, although it incorporated elements of pre-existing practices, was organized through a *dalal* (a broker employed by the company) who had extensive knowledge of local markets and identified prospective intermediary supply merchants for European companies. These intermediary merchants were responsible for arranging textile supplies from producers through the well-established contract system, which involved giving a part of the value of the contract to the weavers in advance.[100]

In the eighteenth century, however, English procurement structures underwent significant change, especially from the 1750s, as the requirement of the East India Company's textile trade expanded in India. The granting of *diwani* rights to the company in Bengal in 1765 allowed it to assume political control and increasingly exercise coercive power over weavers by switching to the *gumashta* system of procurement. Once it secured political control in South India in the last quarter of the century, the company also moved to exert greater control over the productive capacity of weavers. This was repeated by the end of the century in western India in Bombay and in Surat.[101]

---

[97] Maria de Jesus dos Mártires Lopes, *Goa Setecentista: Tradição e Modernidade (1750–1800)* (Lisbon: Universidade Católica Portuguesa, 1996), 56.

[98] Brennig, "Textile Producers", 66–89.

[99] Chaudhuri, "European Trade with India", 382–407.

[100] Prakash, *European Commercial Enterprise*, 167–168.

[101] *Ibid.*, 276–279. Details of the impact of these measures on producers in Bengal can be found in Hossain, *Company Weavers of Bengal*; for South India in Sinnappah Arasaratnam, "Trade and Political Dominion in South India, 1750–1790: Changing British-Indian Relationships", *Modern Asian Studies*, 13 (1979), 19–40; and "Weavers, Merchants and Company", 257–81; Parthasarathi, *Transition to a Colonial Economy*. For western India, see Subramanian, "Power and the Weave".

The Portuguese sought to emulate the growing prosperity from involvement in the lucrative textile trade in Coromandel and Bengal of their Dutch and English competitors from early in the eighteenth century. They thus became increasingly concerned over questions of their own textile procurement and production for African and European markets, expressing interest in following their European rivals "into the interior to have cloths manufactured" as a strategy aimed at gaining greater contact with, and possible control over, producers.[102] Although broadening their territorial reach would remain nothing more than an aspiration, the Portuguese Indian authorities focused on establishing factory production in Goa and on attracting weaving labour to Diu and Daman. The aim was to bypass the middleman of the procurement structure and assume control over production by getting merchants to negotiate directly with weavers whom they had managed to bring to Portuguese-administered territory.[103] Perhaps owing to the proximity of Diu to the cotton fields of Gujarat and to centres of textile production – and therefore its potential as a transhipment centre for both raw cotton and finished textiles – the Portuguese directed their efforts first to the island-entrepôt.

In order to succeed in their strategy, the Portuguese began appealing to Vāniyā merchants to entice weavers to Diu from the second decade of the eighteenth century, appeals they would repeat intermittently over much of the first half of the century. The imperial authorities faced significant challenges, however, the most notable of which was the combination of a mixed response from Vāniyā merchants and the difficulties in recruiting sufficient weaving labour, particularly since weavers were highly mobile and could relocate relatively easily from one locale to another. With mercantile capitalism consolidating itself in the eighteenth century, there was an expansion in the demand for textile manufactures that resulted in an increase in the need for skilled labour.[104] This was a process related to the emergence of "successor" states to the Mughal polity that promoted productive and market activity, and as a result weavers were highly sought-after in western India and Gujarat, especially from the 1750s, as South Asian and European merchants competed for

---

[102] BN, Códice 4408, Conde da Ericeira to King, 18 January 1718.
[103] BN, Códice 4408, "Livro das Cartas...", 1718.
[104] Douglas E. Haynes and Tirthankar Roy, "Conceiving Mobility: Weavers' Migrations in Pre-Colonial and Colonial India", *IESHR*, 36, 1 (1999), 47. See also David Washbrook, "Progress and Problems: South Asian Economic and Social History c. 1720–1860", *Modern Asian Studies*, 22 (1988), 57–96; Bayly, *Rulers, Townsmen and Bazaars: North Indian Society in the Age of British Expansion 1770–1870*, First Indian edn (New Delhi: Oxford University Press, 1992); *idem, Indian Society and the Making of the British Empire* (New York: Cambridge University Press, 1988); Frank Perlin, "Proto-Industrialization and Pre-Colonial South Asia", *Past & Present*, 98 (1983), 30–95.

the products of their labour. This was also a period when the East India Company, in marrying economic and political power, began to rise to dominate coastal enclaves such as Calcutta and Madras where it set about refashioning productive structures by exerting control over weavers. In western India, because company intervention came later in the first quarter of the nineteenth century, weavers maintained their autonomy and were consequently able to challenge attempts by the English to control their productive process.[105] Weavers thus maintained an advantageous position vis-à-vis buyers and could dictate the conditions under which they would work as well as the prices for which they would sell their cloths. Their mobility meant they could leave an area if they felt their interests were being threatened, migration thus serving as an effective weapon against unfair or heavy-handed treatment. Given that weavers usually had few possessions and looms could often be transported with relative ease, communities of weavers had the ability to migrate from an area at short notice.[106]

For weavers in Diu, their mobility gave them significant leverage in their dealings with the Portuguese and placed a check on imperial ambitions. While a small community of weavers and cloth dyers was to be found on the island by 1720, they were discouraged from settling by low pay and unfair treatment from Portuguese colonial officials and private merchants. Soon after they had arrived from the village of Veraval in Kathiawar, for instance, a group of dissatisfied weavers threatened to leave if conditions did not improve.[107] A renewed appeal 20 years later from the Portuguese to Gujarati merchants urging them to bring weavers to Diu suggests that it may have been difficult to create an environment that would draw and keep weavers on the island. Also, disagreements among officials as to the most propitious model to follow – continued reliance on Gujarati procurement from Jambusar or the establishment of an "independent" textile industry – undermined the establishment of a cohesive policy.[108]

---

[105] Subramanian, "Power and the Weave", 53–4, 75; *idem*, *Indigenous Capital and Imperial Expansion: Bombay, Surat and the West Coast* (Delhi: Oxford University Press, 1996); Pamela Nightingale, *Trade and Empire in Western India 1784–1806* (Cambridge University Press, 1970).

[106] Haynes and Roy, "Conceiving Mobility", 37. Parthasarathi reports weavers in the mid-1780s leaving the Pollams villages in South India within 24 hours after they had been unable to resolve differences with the East India Company. See *Transition to a Colonial Economy*, 106.

[107] BN, Códice 4408, "Livro das Cartas...", 1718; *Carta Regia* of 1721 in *PD*, 275–6.

[108] AHU, Códice 1345, Portaria, 21 October 1744; HAG, CD 1004, Antonio Leite de Souza to Francisco Antonio Veiga Cabral, Diu, 31 January 1807. It did not help that the state at times even endorsed aggressive and harassing behaviour towards weavers, as happened in 1797 in Diu according to Vāniyā merchant Thakarsi Jetha, who complained

Yet, while attracting increased numbers of weavers to Diu remained a challenge throughout the century, their numbers did increase gradually and by 1810 there were a total of 343 weavers in the central part of the island and adjoining villages.[109] However, it appears that most of their production was not destined for African markets and may instead have served local demand on the island and elsewhere in the region, and possibly also European demand. Furthermore, the weaving population fluctuated and appears to have been in decline in the 1820s.[110]

The establishment of this weaving population in Diu owed much to the involvement of Gujarati merchants. Although Vāniyās were selective in their dealings with the Portuguese colonial state, towards the end of the eighteenth century some merchants responded positively to Portuguese efforts to bring weavers to the island. In 1799, after being approached by the governor, Joze Mourão Graças Palha, a group of 67 merchants that included leading figures such as Natthu Samji and Anandji Jivan agreed both to manufacture textiles like those that "are annually acquired from Jambusar [and] sent to Mozambique and ports of East Africa" and to pay the same duties for these manufactures as if they had been brought to Diu from the Gujarati interior. In return, it was agreed that yarn imports would pay no duties. Additionally, they agreed to finance the production of "Surat" textiles for the Portuguese metropolitan market on the condition that the state would guarantee the purchase of these cloths.[111]

In Daman, where Portuguese textile manufacturing aims were similar, Vāniyā merchants agreed in the same year to finance and organize the production of textiles for the Mozambique and metropolitan markets. There was, however, one significant difference: in addition to bringing weavers to Daman, they were to import finished, undyed white cloths from Jambusar and have them dyed in pits owned by the *Fabrica Real* (Royal Factory) at a price determined annually by the cost of dyes.[112] Why

that this was disruptive behaviour aimed at benefitting Portuguese merchants; as a result it was damaging his trade. See HAG, Registos Gerais da Feitoria de Diu 7970, Complaint of Thakarsi Jetha, Panjim, 16 May 1797.

[109] Celsa Pinto, *Trade and Finance in Portuguese India: A Study of the Portuguese Country Trade, 1770–1840* (New Delhi: Concept Publishing Company, 1994), 191.

[110] Douglas E. Haynes, *Rhetoric and Ritual in Colonial India: The Shaping of a Public Culture in Surat City, 1852–1918* (Berkeley: University of California Press, 1991), 42, notes the existence of important markets for local goods in Gujarat; HAG, MR 169C, "Mapa dos Estampadores...", 31 December 1818; Pinto, *Trade and Finance*, 191.

[111] HAG, CD 1003, Joze Mourão Graças Palha to Viceroy, 15 March 1799; "Rellação dos Mercadores que hão de entrar nas novas Fabricas das fazendas de Jambuceira e do Reino...", 15 March 1799. Four Portuguese merchants were also involved but Vāniyā merhants contributed 94 per cent of the capital for these projects.

[112] HAG, CDm 1061, Caetano de Souza e Pereira to Governor, 19 March 1799; "Mercadores que contribuirão para a manufactura de fazendas", 23 February 1799.

the Portuguese chose this particular strategy is unclear but it was likely a response to the limited success of attracting greater numbers of weavers to Daman. It allowed the colonial authorities, at least, an opportunity to control one aspect of the textile production process. Vāniyā merchants followed their agreement in 1799 with a further – albeit qualified – pledge three years later to have "imitation Surat cloths manufactured ... in so far as [our] financial position would allow ... [as] Loyal Vassals of Your Majesty".[113] Their efforts thus contributed towards a steady increase in weaving households and looms in the first decade of the nineteenth century, while between 1812 and 1828 the number of textile workers expanded by almost 20 per cent. Quite how many textiles produced by this labour were exported to Lisbon is unclear but weavers never worked exclusively for the metropolitan market, weaving simultaneously for the local market. Daman also operated effectively as a conduit for Gujarati trade in Surat textiles that were exported to Lisbon, partly stimulated by an exemption of import duties on these goods in Portugal.[114]

But while the Portuguese may have continued to seek an expansion of production in Diu and Daman for African markets, increasingly their interests cohered instead around the manufacture or procurement of textiles for metropolitan and Atlantic markets. A number of state-sponsored initiatives were launched to this end from the 1750s in Goa – not surprisingly perhaps, some of these included approaches similar to the ones attempted in Diu and Daman. There were thus calls to bring weavers to Goa "from other parts of India" or, failing that, to sponsor young boys from the Portuguese Indian capital to move to Bengal and Surat to apprentice themselves to weavers in order to learn their craft. This proved unsuccessful due to the apparent reluctance of young Indian families to migrate from Goa, and while the Portuguese did manage to get weavers sent there who had been trained in Diu, the number was insufficient to sustain "independent" production.[115]

Despite these challenges, the Portuguese imperial state remained interested in the strategy of establishing factory production in Goa. The first initiative was the *Real Fabrica das Sedas e Panos* (Royal Factory of Silks

---

[113] HAG, CDm 1061, "Acordo entre mercadores Banianes e mercadores portugueses para manufacturarem roupas", n.d. [but agreement reached 14 February 1803].

[114] HAG, MR193A, "Mappa dos Estampadores...", 14 October 1814; 169C, "Mappa dos Estampadores...", 31 December 1818; and Pinto, *Trade and Finance*, appendix 15, 285–7.

[115] HAG, MR 125-B, "Carta do Vicerei para o Castelão de Diu", 5 January 1753; MR 125-B, "Carta do Marquês de Távora para o Secretário de Estado, Diogo de Mendonça Corte Real", 11 January 1753 [cited also in Martires Lopes, *Goa Setecentista*, 56]; CD 995, Tavora to Castelão, 18 September 1752.

and Cloths) founded in 1758 but its production volume was low and it could not compete with the textiles produced in Jambusar for the African market or in Surat for the metropolitan and Brazilian markets. It was abandoned within a few years after the main investor in the project withdrew his capital after financial losses from three consecutive years had deemed the company a liability.[116] There were other efforts in this vein: in the 1780s the *Fabrica Real de Cumburjua* (Royal Factory of Cambarjua) and the *Fabrica Real de Taleigão* (Royal Factory of Taleigão) were established.[117] A few private textile *fabricas* were also established with Crown encouragement and approval but they managed to manufacture only small quantities of textiles.[118]

Accompanying these developments were efforts to promote cotton cultivation in Goa which was seen not only as another step towards the possible control of textile production in the Portuguese Indian capital, but also as a potential benefit to the metropolitan industry and possibly also to Diu and Daman.[119] Although the *Fabrica de Cumbarjua* produced cotton textiles that were consumed locally and exported to Mozambique and Portugal in the first few years of its existence (even running at a small profit by the end of 1787), Portuguese ambitions were once more frustrated. Production weakened and profits were eventually slashed, leading to financial losses of around 100 per cent ten years after its establishment.[120] As a result, the *Fabrica de Cumbarjua* was suspended, and full ownership transferred into private hands but it continued to operate at a loss; it was therefore abandoned sometime in the second decade of the nineteenth century.[121] The *Fabrica de Taleigão* did not fare any better, with its textiles failing to find buyers in Lisbon because of their poor quality.[122] Attempts to sell them in Mozambique were also unsuccessful, primarily, it seems, because they had not been dyed to the satisfaction of African consumers.[123]

---

[116] The investor redirected his capital to the more profitable arenas of tax-farming and money-lending. R. J. Barendse, "Europe is Literally the Creation of the Third World", H-World Net Posting, 25 March 2002.

[117] Manoel Jose Gomes Loureiro, *Memorias dos Estabelecimentos portugueses a l'este do Cabo da Boa Esperança* (Lisbon: Typografia Filippe Nery, 1835), 398–409. See also Pinto, *Trade and Finance*, 184–93 and Martires Lopes, *Goa Setecentista*, 57–74.

[118] Martires Lopes, *Goa Setecentista*, 57–72.

[119] HAG, CD 999, Viceroy to Belchior do Amaral e Menezes, 24 November 1788. See also Bauss, "Legacy of British Free Trade Policies". A few shipments of raw cotton were sent to Diu and Daman from Goa in 1753 but this did not last.

[120] As calculated from figures in Pinto, *Trade and Finance*, 192.

[121] This is based on Gomes Loureiro, *Memorias dos Estabelecimentos portugueses*, 402–7; Pinto, *Trade and Finance*, 192–3; and BN, Códice 10801, "Reflexões...", no. 94.

[122] Martires Lopes, *Goa Setecentista*, 58, fn. 132.

[123] HAG, CM 1446, Melo e Castro to da Cunha e Menezes, 16 August 1791.

Portuguese state failures to establish full-fledged textile production in Goa were the result of lack of funds, absence of a coherent policy and especially competition from "the lands ... where the planting of cotton takes place, and where the skilled workers are raised and taught".[124] The Portuguese found it extremely difficult to attract increased numbers of weavers to their territories in order to alter fundamentally the nature of the procurement process that was held firmly in Indian hands, as it had been throughout their involvement in India.

Moreover, Portuguese state efforts were hampered by the burgeoning of private capital in imperial territories, as exemplified by merchants and families such as the Loureiros and Ribeiros who were deepening their commercial interests in Indian trade in the second half of the eighteenth century. Private investments assumed a leading role in financing textile procurement for Lisbon and the southern Atlantic slave trade from Angola controlled by Brazilian slavers in Bahia and Rio de Janeiro.[125] Private shipping and capital had been gradually supplanting Crown shipping from early in the century and constituted a cornerstone of the revival of Portuguese Euro-Asian trade from the 1760s and 1770s under favourable commercial conditions introduced by the Pombaline reforms (discussed in Chapter 1) that sought to stimulate imperial trade in order to generate greater income through taxation for the financially enfeebled Crown. The ultimate aim was to "modernize" Portugal and its empire.[126]

Asian commerce was thus opened to private metropolitan merchants in 1765 who were further encouraged to invest in imperial trade in the 1780s by the significant lowering of import and export duties at Portuguese ports as part of the related *Plano do Comercio*. However, as already noted elsewhere, these reforms undermined state efforts to regulate, control and profit from the trade because private merchants often did not declare their full cargo at customs or avoided paying duties altogether. The reforms allowed investors such as the Loureiro and Ribeiro families, together with merchants from Brazil and a few self-serving and accommodating imperial officials, to commit sizeable sums of money for the procurement of

---

[124] Gomes Loureiro, *Memorias dos Estabelecimentos portugueses*, 404. The French, by contrast, managed to establish textile factory production in Pondicherry by the middle of the nineteenth century, as described by Roberts, "Guinée Cloth".

[125] Ernestina Carreira, "O Comércio Português no Gujarat na Segunda Metade do Século XVIII: As famílias Loureiro e Ribeiro", *Mare Liberum*, 9 (1995), 83–94.

[126] Hoppe, *A África Oriental Portuguesa*, 280–315; Roquinaldo Ferreira, "A arte de furtar"; redes de comércio illegal no mercado imperial ultramarino português (c. 1690–c. 1750)", in João Fragoso and Maria de Fátima Gouvêa (eds.), *Na Trama das Redes: Política e Negócios no Império Português, séculos XVI-XVIII* (Rio de Janeiro: Civilização Brasileira, 2010), 205–41.

cloth cargoes in Gujarat. Although some of this capital was invested in Daman, much of it appears to have been channelled to Surat where the Portuguese maintained a trading factory.[127]

If these "Portuguese" merchants (the involvement of Brazil-based capitalists complicated this category) perhaps did not possess the capital resources of their English rivals, they nonetheless made significant investments in textile procurement in Surat. As a result of the customs changes in the 1780s, a dramatic increase occurred in the number of vessels taking on cargo in Goa for Lisbon between 1784 and 1788.[128] The Portuguese Indian capital was at this time (re)establishing itself as a notable transhipment centre for textiles purchased by private and state capital and organized through the Portuguese factory in Surat. With Portuguese investment growing in the final quarter of the century, the director of the factory, Jacinto Domingues, was able to place textile orders with brokers in 1787 to the value of "thousands of rupees"; a decade later these had grown to several *lakhs* (100,000s) of rupees, and by the turn of the century reached over a million rupees.[129] These sizeable investments by "Portuguese" capital alarmed servants of the English East India Company in Surat who tried doggedly to prevent the Portuguese from purchasing piece goods on which the company had advanced money. They expressed concern also that the director and merchants associated with the Portuguese factory were offering 20 per cent more for "inferior" quality goods and did so with ready cash. Portuguese competition may actually have prompted the Company to assert greater authority by 1800 for more control over textile producers in the region.[130] Such large investments, coupled with Portuguese neutrality in the European wars of the period and the Pombaline reforms, helped establish

---

[127] Further discussion of the Portuguese factory can be found in A. F. Moniz, "A Feitoria Portuguesa de Surrate: Sua importancia Politica e Comercial", *O Oriente Português*, 15, 1 and 2 (1918), 5–29; "Memorial e Informação das Feitorias Portuguezas na Costa de Malabar", in *Annaes do Concelho Ultramarino (parte não official)*, Serie I (Lisbon: Imprensa nacional, 1854–58), 525–6; "Alguns esclarecimentos dirigidos ao Ex.mo Ministro da Marinha e Ultramar...", *Annaes do Concelho Ultramarino* (parte não official), Serie II (Lisbon: Imprensa nacional, 1859–61), 1–4.

[128] A total of 24 vessels left Goa ostensibly for Lisbon (some may have sailed to Bahia or Rio) during these years. See Bauss, "Legacy of British Free Trade Policies", 93–4; Pinto, *Trade and Finance*, appendix 4, 270; *idem*, "Lisbon Investment in the Indian Textile Commerce: The Surat Feeder", *Mare Liberum*, 9 (1995)", appendix 1, 230.

[129] HAG, Copiador Indiano da Feitoria de Surrate 2533, Jacinto Domingues to João Nogueira, 8 October 1787; Nightingale, *Trade and Empire*, 154; Pinto, "Lisbon investment", appendix 5, 231.

[130] Om Prakash, "Co-operation and Conflict among European Traders in the Indian Ocean in the Late Eighteenth Century", *IESHR*, 39 (2 and 3), 2002, 134; Subramanian, "Power and the Weave", 68; *idem, Indigenous Capital and Imperial Expansion* (Delhi: Oxford University Press, 1996), 260–2.

Lisbon as a major entrepôt for the importation of Indian textiles into Europe until at least the second decade of the nineteenth century when these wars ended and British capital began to displace Portuguese merchants from both Indian Ocean and Atlantic markets.

But while these investments served ostensibly the Lisbon market, it seems that a sizeable proportion were actually directed to the procurement of cotton textiles for southern Atlantic markets. Brazilian capital from Bahia and Rio de Janeiro became increasingly involved in the procurement of Indian textiles for slave trading from Luanda and Benguela in Angola. Shipped under royal monopoly, Indian textiles were already by the mid-sixteenth century important imports in Angola, where they had been carried by vessels on the *Carreira da India* route from Goa to Lisbon. This trade grew dramatically, so that by the 1630s up to 75 per cent of Angolan commerce was funded with manufactures from the subcontinent.[131] While officially the Angola trade was to be channelled through Lisbon and financed by state capital, increasingly private merchants who were able to violate Crown regulations because of bureaucratic inefficiencies and malfeasance financed it through the acquisition of Indian cottons from the mid-seventeenth century. The contravention of state sanction on the movement of textiles – smuggling – resulted in large numbers of Indian textiles being offloaded either in Luanda or Brazilian ports instead of in Lisbon, a development that would intensify in the following century. Even the enactment of a law in the 1720s prohibiting the direct entry from India of South Asian textiles into Angola because of the competition they posed to Portuguese manufactures did not manage to arrest the influx of textiles into Portuguese West Central Africa.[132]

Brazilian merchants based in Bahia, in particular, acquired stakes in the acquisition of Indian cottons by investing in the cargoes brought from the subcontinent on *naus* that sailed from Goa to Brazil, and in some cases Angola, before returning to Lisbon. The weight of these merchants' involvement in textile purchases in India turned Bahia into a major redistribution centre for the eighteenth-century Angolan slave trade of the southern Atlantic, a process encouraged by apportionment practices for cargoes on *naus* and the liberalization of Asian commerce in the 1760s as

---

[131] Afzal Ahmad, *Portuguese Trade and Socio-Economic Changes on the Western Coast of India (1600–1663)* (Delhi: Originals, 2000); James Boyajian, *Portuguese Trade in Asia under the Habsburgs, 1580–1640* (Baltimore: Johns Hopkins University Press, 1993) quoted in Roquinaldo Ferreira, "Transforming Atlantic Slaving: Trade, Warfare and Territorial Control in Angola, 1650–1800", PhD diss., University of California, 2003, 48.

[132] Hoppe, *A África Oriental Portuguesa*, 285.

noted previously.[133] While textiles continued to arrive in Brazil on *naus* directly from India, from the 1760s and 1770s ships from Brazil began to make voyages from Bahia to the Indian Ocean in greater number, stopping at times on the Mozambique coast – together with vessels from Rio – to purchase slaves. This intensification of Brazilian commercial and financial involvement in the western Indian Ocean signalled the growing importance of private capital for the maintenance of long-distance intra-imperial trade. While little evidence appears to exist detailing the precise scale of investment by Brazilian merchants in the purchase of Surat cotton textiles, there are suggestions that it was substantial, particularly given its concentration overwhelmingly on textile procurement. Brazilian merchants benefitted also from well-placed family connections in India. The Loureiro family, for instance, whose members served at various times as directors of the Portuguese factory in Surat between the 1770s and early 1820s, had established itself a generation earlier in Brazil and maintained active business ties with Bahia and Rio de Janeiro; their imperial contacts with the southern Atlantic thus enabled the Loureiros to maintain "secret efforts" in organizing purchases of cotton cloths in Surat from the Gujarati interior.[134]

The situation for the imperial state's efforts to establish textile manufacturing in India was, however, worsened irredeemably by the possibility of Gujarati support which, despite occasional appearances to the contrary, was never truly forthcoming in Diu or Daman. The involvement of one of the most prominent Vāniyā in Daman, Jhaver Khushal, in Portuguese plans encapsulates the partial commitment of Gujarati finance. Although Jhaver contributed the third highest sum of money for the delivery of undyed cottons from Jambusar in 1799, he reneged almost immediately on these conditions by failing to include a single piece of cloth that had been produced or finished in Daman in his export cargoes for the African trade of that year. This would happen again the following year, for it appears that Jhaver had little intention of changing the procurement practices that had served him so well over the years.[135]

Vāniyā merchants were invested heavily in an efficient procurement system centred on Jambusar, which was in keeping with how regional

---

[133] Roquinaldo Ferreira, "Dinâmica do comércio intracolonial: Geribitas, panos asiáticos e guerra no tráfico angolano de escravos (século XVIII)", in J. Fragoso, M. F. Bicalho and M.F. Gouvêa (eds.), *O Antigo Regime nos Trópicos: A Dinâmica Imperial Portuguesa (Séculos XVI-XVIII)* (Rio de Janeiro: Civilização Brasileira, 2001), 341–78.

[134] HAG, MR 178A, Viceroy to Souza Coutinho, 9 April 1799; L.F. Dias Antunes, "Têxteis e metais preciosos: novos vínculos do comércio indo-brasileiro (1808–1820)", in Fragoso *et al.*, *Antigo Regime*, 379–408.

[135] HAG, CDm 1061, Caetano de Souza Pereira to Governor, 3 March 1800.

coastal exporting towns and cities were connected to the textile-producing interior of Gujarat. While it was not the case that Gujarati merchants ignored all the opportunities created by the Portuguese state, they were too firmly established within the Gujarat textile economy and marketing structure to consider patronage from it.[136] Unlike what the East India Company was able to offer Indian merchants in South India who supported it as it ascended to political power in the final quarter of the eighteenth century and introduced new forms of state power to the region that destroyed weavers' independence by bringing their labour under state control – strict adherence to contractual obligations and hence greater control over a critical aspect of the production process – Portuguese proposals to develop textile manufacturing in either Diu or Daman (or even Goa) were regarded by Vāniyās as not holding advantages which superseded those of their already existing (and independent) system of procurement.[137] The risks involved in fully supporting the actions of a financially and politically weak state were too high, and explains why, at least in their African trade, merchants continued to operate without direct access to weavers and through the intermediary function of brokers.

As a result, in the eighteenth century and throughout much of the first half of the nineteenth century, piecegoods for the African markets continued to be produced overwhelmingly in Jambusar.[138] The sustained dominance of Jambusar textiles in African markets – and the capacity of Vāniyās to supply these – is truly remarkable. Although some textiles from Surat and Bombay were exported through Diu to Africa into the mid- to late 1810s, along with manufactures from Bhavnagar (discussed below), these remained limited until the 1830s.[139] Another remarkable feature of this trade is that Vāniyā merchants continued to acquire textiles from Jambusar in a period of increasing British penetration into western India. Although the establishment of their control over Surat was a protracted affair, and the extension of British rule into other parts of Gujarat was only complete in the second decade of the nineteenth century, from the last quarter of the eighteenth century the British had

---

[136] This point draws on Raj Chandavarkar, *The Origins of Industrial Capitalism in India* (New York: Cambridge University Press, 1994), 56–7.

[137] Parthasarathi, *Transition to a Colonial Economy*. The difficulties which Indian merchants faced in compelling weavers to abide by their agreements made the authority of the company appealing because it undermined the autonomy of these producers. This resulted, according to Parthasarathi, in "an interlocking of colonial authority and dominant Indian groups [that] may explain the resilience of colonialism in India".

[138] AHU, Moç., Cx 92 Doc. 53, "Carga...", 19 January 1802; Cx 97 Doc. 25, "Carga...", 12 January 1803; Cx 148 Doc. 32, "Carga...", 3 February 1815. See also HAG, AD 4952–4956; and Registos Gerais..., Bando, 11 December 1809.

[139] See, for example, HAG, AD 4967–4969.

developed a keen interest in the Gujarati market for raw cotton, primarily for their China trade.[140] Raw cotton from Jambusar thus found its way to the coast, although this does not appear to have disrupted artisanal production in the city, and certainly not that serving the African markets of the southwestern Indian Ocean.

Slave trading and "foreign" competition

The years following the early 1790s saw exports of textiles from Diu to Mozambique drop to 150,000–250,000 pieces per year. This was due to the heightened danger of attack from French corsairs, which in turn resulted in a reduction in the number of Indian vessels arriving at the coast. This situation may have persisted into the first few years of the nineteenth century after which the number of *palas* arriving in Africa rose again to between two and four a year. The return of these vessels and their textile cargoes was – it is important to stress – also related to the growth of the African slave trade. As I argue later in the book, its growing dominance in the economy of Mozambique did not marginalize Vāniyā networks, which adapted their trade accordingly and exported a greater number of African slaves to western India for which there was a small but significant market. Their primary interest remained in ivory, which was of great cultural and social value to South Asian elites and broader populations throughout western and northern India; but their shift into slave trading reflected their responsiveness to the vagaries of changing conditions of trade.

The adaptive capacity of Vāniyā merchants rested also in Indian textiles continuing to be used in the purchase of slaves, just as they had been used for the purchase of ivory. Although imported firearms were used in exchange for slaves from the middle of the eighteenth century, and increasingly in the nineteenth century,[141] the use of cloths as exchange media was not displaced. Nor was its desirability among African consumers diminished, as suggested by a well-informed contemporary author who noted that in Quelimane, an important gateway into the Zambesi Valley and a slave-trading centre, just the opposite was true.[142] Clearly, the exchange of slaves and textiles was intimately connected, as demonstrated by the fact that many Gujarati merchants

---

[140] Nightingale, *Trade and Empire*; Subramanian, *Indigenous Capital*; Bayly, *Indian Society*, ch. 2.

[141] For details see Alpers, *Ivory and Slaves*, 14, 96–7, 110–11, 152, 195, 198.

[142] Vasconcellos e Cirne, *Memoria Sobre a Provincia de Moçambique* (ed. José Capela) (Maputo: Arquivo Histórico de Moçambique, 1990), 24.

prominently involved in the slave trade were also among the largest exporters of textiles from Diu to Africa. This helps explain why over a six-year period between 1804 and 1810, for instance, textile exports from Diu alone totalled around 1,853,000 pieces or an extraordinary seven million yards of cloth.[143] It is likely demand remained high in the following decade.

Corresponding increases in the importation of Indian cotton textiles as a result of increased slave trading was by this time not uncommon in the southwest Indian Ocean. In Madagascar, from mid-1780s, Gujarati textile exports from Surat began to arrive in greater number, and within a short time were established as the most common foreign textiles available at the weekly highland markets.[144] On the East African coast, for a slaving voyage to be successful in Kilwa, it was imperative that Gujarati cotton cloths were part of every cargo.[145] Throughout the 1820s reasonably complete records show that textile exports from Diu were fairly stable at between 160,000 and 200,000 pieces per year, although they were lower than in previous years.[146]

Although quantitative evidence does not exist for either the volume or value of textile exports from Diu after 1831, the slowdown in textile exports from Jambusar was likely caused by disruptions to the slave trade from increased British anti-slaving patrols in the western Indian Ocean. However, it was not only these pressures that undermined textile exports. Equally, if not more, significant in the decline of the Gujarati textile trade for the African markets was the increasing competition of "foreign" textiles. For instance, a knowledgeable official wrote in 1817 that he thought it "necessary that the Governors of those territories [Diu and Daman] promote improvement in manufactures through their possible means in order that the Africans lose completely their love for English trade goods [from India] ... to which they are growing

---

[143] This has been calculated from HAG, CD 995–1012; AD 4952–4969.

[144] Larson, *History and Memory*, 127–8.

[145] Monsieur Morice, "Observation on the List of Trade Goods from Another Point of View", in G. S. P. Freeman-Grenville (eds.), *The French at Kilwa Island* (Oxford: Clarendon Press, 1965), 144–5.

[146] BA, 54-XIII-3 (3), Barbosa, "Analyse Estatistica", 30 December 1821; Gonçalo de Magalhães Teixeira Pinto, *Memoria sobre as Possessões Portuguezas na Asia, escriptas no anno de 1823* (Nova Goa: Imprensa Nacional, 1859), 30–2. There was a sharp increase in textile exports in 1829 but this may have been the result of heightened demand from slavers who increased their purchases of slaves before an 1830 anti-slave trade treaty, banning imports into Brazil, came into effect. Vāniyā merhants continued to trade in cloths with the Makua in Macuana in these years, but records for 1831 show a marked decrease in Indian exports. AHU, Códice 1425, "Para o Cheque de Sancul", 22 April 1831.

accustomed, and which are a thousand times better".[147] Although small-scale textile imports by English merchants from Surat had begun to arrive at Delagoa Bay in southern Mozambique in the early nineteenth century as English trade returned to the area, implicit in this statement was the knowledge that the decision by the Portuguese Crown in 1810 to allow the "entry of English cotton goods ... made Indian manufactures disappear".[148] This resulted from the Anglo-Portuguese Treaty of Commerce and Navigation that ultimately undermined Portuguese trade in the nineteenth century. Although concern was clearly mounting over the importation of textiles from England and from English ports from the early 1810s, it does not seem that their entry into the region severely undermined Vāniyā trade until a few decades later.[149]

Rather, what Vāniyās did consider a grave danger to their textile exports and to their primacy in Mozambique from around the mid-1810s was the entry of *other* "foreign" textiles into the market. These were textiles that came from other parts of Kathiawar, especially from Bhavnagar and Mandvi in Kutch, at the time under the control of rival South Asian merchant networks. Given the focus of much of the work on South Asian textiles on production for the European markets, scholars have tended to overlook the competition that existed among different producing regions and/or exporting merchants in South Asia for markets within the Indian Ocean. This appears to have been the case with the growing competition from Bhavnagar on Jambusar, and the threat also later posed by Mandvi and its Bhātiyā merchant networks. For instance, in 1816 a vessel from Bhavnagar departed for Mozambique with textiles "suitable for the consumption of that part of Africa". Indeed, such was the threat that these textiles were seen to pose to Diu and Daman that concerned officials communicated the information directly to the exiled Portuguese Crown in Rio in 1817.[150]

It is not surprising that Bhavnagar textile exports troubled Vāniyā merchants because they were sent expressly to Mozambique for the purchase of slaves. From the 1810s, Bhavnagar seems to have become

---

[147] AHU, Moç., Cx 153 Doc. 113, Cavalcanti de Albuquerque to Marquez de Aguiar, 26 June 1817.

[148] ANTT, JC, Maço 62, Cx 202, 9 September 1815. For details of English trade in southern Mozambique, see David William Hedges, "Trade and Politics in Southern Mozambique and Zululand in the Eighteenth and Nineteenth Centuries", PhD diss., School of Oriental and African Studies, University of London, 1978.

[149] For the effects of the Anglo-Portuguese Treaty, and of British industrial production on Portugal and the Portuguese Empire in this period, see Rudy Bauss, "A Legacy of British Free Trade Policies: The End of the Trade and Commerce between India and the Portuguese Empire, 1780–1830", *Calcutta Historical Journal*, 6, 2 (1982), 81–115.

[150] HAG, CDm 1065, Castro e Almeida to Gomes Loureiro, 16 February 1817.

the second most important supplier of textiles for the Mozambique trade after Jambusar, and cases exist of Vāniyā merchants such as Gokuldas Natthu buying their textiles in Bhavnagar.[151] Notwithstanding its potential to serve as an alternative source of supply, it appears that Vāniyās were unable to exploit this source fully. They were not entrenched there as they were in Jambusar and therefore had to compete especially with Bhātiyā networks to secure textile supplies. Vāniyā merchants were too heavily invested in the procurement network centred on Jambusar to have needed to exploit other sources of supply.

There were further laments from Vāniyās in Mozambique in 1817 against the entry of "foreign textiles", which resulted in their cloths "not enjoying the trade they needed".[152] It is not entirely clear why Vāniyā merchants were unable to resist the competition of these textiles in Mozambique, a market in which they had valuable experience. Nor is it clear how these textiles came to conform to the specificities of African consumer tastes that had been so ably satisfied by Jambusar cloth. A possible explanation might be found in the famines that affected Gujarat – in particular the severe ones in 1811 and 1813.[153] These could have disrupted Vāniyā textile supplies and allowed the entry into Mozambique of textiles from Kutch and elsewhere in India. However, extant documentation does not point to a disruption in supplies from Jambusar in famine years. It is, therefore, difficult to understand why Vāniyās were unable to resist the entry of these foreign textiles into the Mozambique market.

In addition to the concerns of Vāniyās, Portuguese officials worried that textiles exported from ports outside their administration would result ultimately in a reduction in custom duties and hence state income.[154] The Portuguese authorities, always keen to blame Indian merchants for any downturn, believed that Vāniyās had brought this situation on themselves because they had "sent for the consumption of this captaincy falsified trade goods and of such poor quality that not even the Africans want them".[155] Considering Vāniyā knowledge of African consumer tastes, and their long years spent supplying these markets, it is extremely unlikely that this would have been the case. Moreover, the Portuguese accusations appear to have been overstated because of quantitative evidence showing continued demand for Jambusar textiles in Africa into the 1830s. Vāniyā concerns about the intrusion of foreign textiles into the African markets

---

[151] HAG, CD 1006, Palha to Viceroy, 18 September 1818.
[152] HAG, CM 1447, Palha to Governor, 28 July 1817.
[153] Abdul Sheriff, *Slaves, Spices & Ivory* (London: James Currey, 1987), 84–5.
[154] HAG, MR 193A, Merchants to de Azevedo, 31 December 1814.
[155] AHU, Moç., Cx 154 Doc. 105, Abreu e Menezes to Conde de Baia, 25 September 1817.

were not, though, totally misplaced. Indian merchants in Diu realized the scale of this problem in the 1820s when they wrote to the governor expressing the "inconvenience" that their trade had been caused by the "introduction of large numbers of foreign goods".[156] Daman merchants also wrote of how foreign textiles were "hurting" their trade in India and Mozambique, and they wanted them to be banned from entering Portuguese territories.[157]

A significant downturn, resulting from the arrival of textiles from Indian locales other than Diu or Daman, is clearly discernible from the 1830s. The starkest demonstration of this is found in the cargo of a Gujarati vessel which, perhaps for the first time, arrived at Mozambique Island without a single consignment of cotton piecegoods in 1832.[158] Of course, this may have been an exception, but the evidence presented above, the drop in value of piecegood exports from Jambusar to Diu and Daman,[159] and complaints about the marked fall in exports, all point to the start of a terminal decline in the textile export trade, which continued throughout the rest of the 1830s and early 1840s.[160]

The effects of the entry of foreign textiles into African markets were exacerbated by a sharp decline in the slave trade (discussed in Chapter 5), and the arrival of additional "foreign" textiles in the 1840s and 1850s. American textiles, in particular, were fast conquering the market after early forays into the African trade in the first decade of the nineteenth century.[161] As the Portuguese traveller Carlos José Caldeira wrote in the early 1850s,

Americans dominate the trade of the entire coast, they trade to the ports or at times unload easily as contraband at any place they regard as convenient the goods [which are] suitable for exchanges with Africans, such as cloths. They [Americans] introduce better and *cheaper* cotton goods than those from Diu, Daman . . . which until now were used for this commerce, and which they [American textiles] are forcing out of the market.[162]

---

[156] HAG, CD 1011, "Requerimento dos Mazanes e Negociantes. . .feitas ao Governador", 5 October 1828.

[157] HAG, CDm 1066, Indian Merchants of Daman to Castelão, 14 November 1823.

[158] *DAM*, III, 695.

[159] OIOC, P/419, Bombay Commerce, vols. 56–66. These records provide only "official" trade and therefore underestimate its real value. Indeed, the figures suggest higher values. Nonetheless, they do confirm a trend, namely the fall in the value of the trade that reflected the challenges I have been discussing.

[160] See, for example, HAG, CD 1012, "Mapa. . .", 10 February 1831; CD 997, de Macedo to Ferreira Pestana, 5 July 1845. Further details can be found in Bauss, "Legacy".

[161] AHU, Moç., Cx 107 Doc. 122, "Auto de visita do. . .Benjamin", 26 August 1804; Cx 112 Doc. 83, "Carga da Juliana", 27 August 1805.

[162] Carlos José Caldeira, *Apontamentos d'uma Viagem de Lisboa a China e da China a Lisboa, Tomo Segundo* (Lisbon: J. P. M. Lavado, 1853), 105. The emphasis is mine.

As a result, they were "establishing among the Africans a taste for finer and better patterned cloths, with grave damage to the manufactures of Diu and Daman, which were sustained by this commerce, the principal resource of those establishments".[163] This signalled the start of the challenge of machine-produced textiles for Indian handicrafts in the Indian Ocean and beyond.

English manufactures appear also at this time to have been squeezing Vāniyā textile exports out of their African markets. Although this threat had been felt in the 1810s, it was in the 1840s and 1850s that the full force of their impact became evident. A. C. P. Gamitto, a Portuguese officer who accompanied an official mission to Kazembe in interior Mozambique and produced a well-known account of the expedition, writing in 1832 remarked how the standard bale of cloths in the Zambesi Valley consisted of seven different varieties of Indian manufactured cloths; but by the time of his departure from Mozambique in 1853, he noted how cotton textiles of English and American manufacture "are preferred to the Indian weaves".[164] David Livingstone also noted this precipitous fall when he commented on how their unbleached calicoes were the only currency in use in Tete.[165] Whereas at the start of the nineteenth century piecegoods exported from Diu and Daman had constituted approximately 90 per cent of Mozambique's textile imports, by the mid-1850s they represented only about 25 per cent and declined further later in the century.[166]

At the same time as machine-produced cotton textiles were undermining Indian weaves, the position of Vāniyā merchants was being seriously challenged by Kutchi Bhātiyā merchants whose presence on the Mozambique coast became noticeable from the 1820s and 1830s. By the 1840s they were prominent in the import and export trades and appear to have displaced Vāniyā merchants of Diu and Daman.[167] It therefore appears that the Indian cloths which were being traded in the Zambesi Valley in the 1830s were imports from Kutch, rather than from Diu and Daman. These Kutchi goods were also challenged by the machine-produced American and English cotton textiles but appear to have been successful in meeting this challenge for a short time for reasons which remain unclear.

---

[163] Caldeira, *Apontamentos*.   [164] Gamitto, *King Kazembe*, II, 197
[165] David Livingstone, *Missionary Travels and Researches in South Africa* (New York: Harper, 1858), 680, quoted in Alpers, *Ivory and Slaves*, 233.
[166] HAG, AD, 4952–4953; Caldeira, *Apontamentos*, 105–6; Liesegang, "First Look", 457. Quite how this reversal took place and how it might affect our understanding of consumer dynamics in African markets and of South Asian competition in the Indian Ocean awaits further enquiry.
[167] Caldeira, *Apontamentos*, 106–7.

Conclusion

Indian weavers and weaving households, brokers in Gujarat, African middlemen and long-distance traders, African consumers of cloths along the coast and interior of Mozambique and Vāniyā merchant networks stretching from Diu and Daman to the southwestern Indian Ocean were bound together in an intimate cross-oceanic material and cultural embrace based on the exchange of cotton textiles. The importance of African consumer tastes, which affected each of these players in this inter-regional exchange, challenges the view of Africans as marginal actors in the economy of the western Indian Ocean. Vāniyā merchants were instrumental in mediating these far-flung relationships, and in their ability to coordinate the relational dynamics of production, procurement, supply and consumer demand, they were able to dominate African textile markets.

The resourcefulness, dynamism and commercial capacity of indigenous merchant networks and their capital in exploiting markets in the Indian Ocean, and the survival of Indian handicraft textile production in the face of intensified competition from factory production in the nineteenth century has been inadequately explored, yet is clear. There can be little doubt that India lost export markets in the nineteenth century but it appears to have been a gradual and differentiated process which accelerated only from the 1830s.[168] The vitality of Indian Ocean markets – particularly those in Africa – up to this period and their importance to the export production of particular areas in Gujarat has been greatly underestimated by interpretations that have emphasized instead the textile export trade to European markets.[169] While the latter may have been dominated by European capital, until the middle of the nineteenth century – and beyond, as some new work is beginning to suggest[170] – it was Vāniyā networks and capital (among others) that maintained widespread financial and commercial influence, and controlled the majority of textile exports from the subcontinent to much of the Indian Ocean.

---

[168] For the impact of Lancashire factory-produced cotton goods, for example, see B. R. Tomlinson, *The Economy of Modern India, 1860–1970* (Cambridge University Press, 1993), ch. 3.

[169] But see Pedro Machado, "Awash in a Sea of Cloth: Gujarati, Africa and the Western Indian Ocean, 1300–1800", in Giorgio Riello and Prasannan Parthasarathi (eds.), *The Spinning World* (New York: Oxford University Press, 2009), 161–79 for a change of perspective.

[170] Rajat Kanta Ray, "Asian Capital in the Age of European Domination: The Rise of the Bazaar, 1800–1914", *Modern Asian Studies*, 29, 3 (1995), 449–554; Claude Markovits, *The Global World of Indian Merchants, 1750–1947: Traders of Sind from Bukhara to Panama* (New York: Cambridge University Press, 2000); Sugata Bose, *A Hundred Horizons: The Indian Ocean in the Age of Global Empire* (Cambridge, MA: Harvard University Press, 2006).

4   White gold

Large-scale Vāniyā investment in the procurement and shipment of Gujarati cotton textiles for the African markets of Mozambique in the eighteenth and nineteenth centuries was oriented overwhelmingly towards the ivory trade. A variety of products crafted from ivory were extensively used and consumed throughout Kathiawar as it experienced a commercial efflorescence from around the 1750s, as well as in Kutch to its north and throughout parts of western India. The intensity of Indian demand for African ivory was a key factor of Vāniyā business interests in Mozambique and was critical in the expansion of ivory trading in the eighteenth century. It was behind their extensive financing of the trade in ivory tusks not only throughout the African territory's northern interior but also in its central and southern hinterlands. Vāniyā traded large volumes of ivory across the ocean, in some years exceeding 310,000 kg, accounting for between 65 and 80 per cent of the Portuguese state's import income in Diu and Daman.

Vāniyā control over the importation of trade cloths for which ivory was purchased and around which credit relations with African agents and traders were structured, along with their access to long-distance shipping capable of carrying thousands of tusks across the western Indian Ocean, ensured that they dominated the ivory trade as a mainstay of the Mozambique economy and its export market at Mozambique Island and elsewhere on the coast.

Although slave trading, the topic of the following chapter, gained ground in Mozambique from the middle of the eighteenth century as the result of burgeoning French demand in the Mascarenes for sugar plantation labour and an intensification in slaving to ports in the southern Atlantic such as Rio de Janeiro, Bahia and Montevideo – which would also involve Vāniyā merchants as financiers and directly as traders of African slaves to Kathiawar and Gujarat – the focus of Vāniyā commercial interest in Africa was ivory. Tusks in their thousands were acquired along the coast and interior of Mozambique in exchange for Gujarati cotton textiles that would also sustain the growing slave trade. In dominating imports of an indispensable cloth currency used throughout Mozambique, the Vāniyā therefore largely controlled the cloth trade in Africa and thus were able to remain committed to ivory amid the expansion in slave trading.

This chapter explores the scale and extent of Vāniyā involvement in the ivory trade of the expansive northern hinterland of Macuana directly opposite Mozambique Island where Yao long-distance traders brought their ivory; and the important role ivory came to play in the Vāniyā trans-oceanic trading nexus of textiles and slaves. It shows, furthermore, that as ivory supplies in the north were increasingly redirected to Kilwa and Zanzibar from the late eighteenth and early nineteenth centuries, Vāniyās exploited alternative ivory sources in central and southern Mozambique to extend their commercial reach into Zambesia and parts of the African territory.

Consuming ivory

Vāniyā commercial interest in the Mozambique ivory trade was integrated into a long history of South Asian demand for and acquisition of East African ivory. Already from the seventh and eighth centuries CE, South Asia had begun to emerge as a major market for East African ivory, and by the tenth century was firmly established as a leading destination of the latter's exports as attested to by Arabic sources.[1] Although ivory of Indian provenance appears to have been widely used in the subcontinent in early periods, there were certain limitations to its use.[2] Elephants in India were used extensively as beasts of burden, and were therefore too valuable to be slaughtered for their tusks in large numbers. Tusks that were large enough for carving and working were found only in male elephants, whereas both male and female African elephants were endowed with large tusks. African male elephant tusks were also generally larger than those of the Asiatic elephant. Moreover, whereas the tusks from Asian elephants were prone

---

[1] Edward A. Alpers, "The Ivory Trade in Africa", in Doran H. Ross (ed.), *Elephant: The Animal and its Ivory in African Culture* (Los Angeles: Fowler Museum of Cultural History, 1992), 352; Abdul Sheriff, "Ivory and Commercial Expansion in East Africa in the Nineteenth Century", in G. Liesegang, H. Pasch and A. Jones (eds.), *Figuring African Trade: Proceedings of the Symposium on the Quantification and Structure of the Import and Export and Long-Distance Trade in Africa 1800–1913* (Berlin: D. Reimer Verlag, 1986), 417–19; "al-Ma'sudi: The Ivory Trade", in G. S. P. Freeman-Grenville (ed.), *The East African Coast: Select Documents from the First to the Earlier Nineteenth Century* (London: Rex Collings, 1975), 14–17; Mark Horton and John Middleton, *The Swahili: The Social Landscape of a Mercantile Society* (Oxford, UK, Malden, MA: Blackwell, 2000), 76.

[2] Shereen Ratnagar, *Trading Encounters: From the Euphrates to the Indus in the Bronze Age* (New Delhi: Oxford University Press, 2004), 159–66.

to discolouring and were of a brittle nature, the African variety had a density and intensity of colour that made it greatly preferable for carving. African ivory was thus highly valued for both its quality and its longevity.[3]

Indian demand for ivory was driven by a variety of purposes since at least the Harappan period around 1300 BCE. Archaeological evidence has uncovered religious figurines, handles of various descriptions, seals, combs, hairpins, arrowheads and spindle-whorls. Ivory inlaid doors have also been identified at temple and royal sites.[4] These objects make it clear from early on that there was no single or singular use for ivory in India. Every major city in western India, and perhaps elsewhere in South Asia, had an ivory workers' quarter.[5] Nineteenth-century evidence shows that ivory carving was practised across wide regions, from western and northern India to Assam and Burma.[6] Ivory carvers were a common presence among ruling families in North India and seem to have moved between urban centres as mobile workers. In the eighteenth century, for example, an ivory carver attached to the Murshidabad court in eastern India travelled far to Jaipur located southwest of the Mughal imperial capital in Delhi. He received a generous reception, suggesting that the skills possessed by these craftsmen were well respected and highly regarded by elites in India.[7]

Ivory demand and consumption was, however, not confined to elites. Common items fashioned from ivory were bangles worn by married – and in many cases unmarried – women. Along with other items of jewellery such as gold or silver necklaces, ivory bangles were worn as part of adornment practices denoting wealth and social status. Ivory bangles demonstrating a woman's married status were worn throughout married life. In Kathiawar, where robust consumer demand underpinned the large-scale ivory imports of the Vāniyā in the eighteenth and early

---

[3] Professor Owen, "The Ivory and Teeth of Commerce", *Journal of the Society of Arts*, V, 213 (1856), 65–70.

[4] V. P. Dwivedi, *Indian Ivories: A Survey of Indian Ivory and Bone Carvings from the Earliest to the Modern Times* (Delhi: Agam Prakashan, 1976), chs. II–IX.

[5] Cecil L. Burns, "A Monograph on Ivory Carving", *Journal of Indian Art and Industry*, 9, 70–80 (1902), 53–6; Mary Kenoyer, Personal Communication (contained in Edward Alpers, Personal Communication, 22 January 2004); S. Bhattacharya, "Eastern India", in Dharma Kumar (ed.), *The Cambridge Economic History of India. Volume 2: c. 1757–c. 1970* (Cambridge University Press, 1982), 283.

[6] Burns, "Monograph on Ivory Carving"; L. M. Stubbs, "Ivory Carving in the North-West Provinces and Oudh", *Journal of Indian Art and Industry*, 9, 70–80 (1902), 41–5; T. P. Ellis, "Ivory Carving in the Punjab", *Journal of Indian Art and Industry*, 9, 70–80 (1902), 45–52; James Donald, "Ivory Carving in Assam", *Journal of Indian Art and Industry*, 9, 70–80 (1902), 57–8; H. S. Pratt, "Ivory Carving in Burma", *Journal of Indian Art and Industry*, 9, 70–80 (1902), 59–60.

[7] Dwivedi, *Indian Ivories*, 128.

nineteenth centuries, this practice seems to have once been the preserve of wealthy married women but had gradually spread down the social hierarchy. According to Emma Tarlo, "it was customary for members of all castes in the village to give at least one pair of ivory bangles to a new wife".[8] *Boloyā*, thick undecorated ivory bangles, were worn by *Kanbi*, *Koli* and low-caste women who were able to afford them as one of the symbols of marital bliss (*saubhagya*). At the time of the husband's death, a wife did not pass these on to her daughters but broke them as a sign of grief. Should she die before her husband, she was cremated along with these bridal ornaments, ensuring that there was a constant demand for ivory to produce these bangles.[9]

These factors thus ensured that Indian demand for African ivory remained consistently high. From the early to mid-eighteenth century, however, demand in specific markets for Mozambique ivory prompted an unprecedented expansion of ivory trading and Vāniyā shipments to the subcontinent. These were imports that in the 1750s were mostly coming to Mozambique Island from the northern interior, transported by Yao long-distance traders. These supplies, as I discuss later, were extremely large – in the early 1750s, for example, about 124,000 kg of ivory tusks of varying sizes were arriving each year on the island through Macuana. Ivory sourced from central Mozambique was also in the final quarter of the century being shipped from the coast. The growth in ivory trading that these exports reflected was fuelled by the equally impressive imports into Mozambique of Gujarat cotton cloths, as I examined in Chapter 3.

The extent of Indian consumer demand for Mozambique ivory is captured by the scale of Vāniyā imports into Diu and Daman, which by the 1780s were of an extraordinary volume. This was especially the case in Diu, which imported the overwhelming bulk of ivory shipped from Mozambique. In 1780, Vāniyā vessels arrived in Diu with 263,000 kg of ivory tusks, and a year later brought a little over 223,000 kg to the island-entrepôt. A highpoint was reached in 1782 when 318,400 kg entered Diu. Although of a fragmentary nature and considerably lower, imports into Daman were in the range of 25,000 to 50,000 kg in the 1780s, ensuring that combined annual imports by Vāniyā merchants into India regularly exceeded 200,000 kg. In the 1790s, despite considerable fluctuations caused by ship losses to French corsair attacks in the Mozambique Channel, shifts in the Mozambique economy (discussed below) and outbreaks of "pestilence" in Diu, Vāniyā imports to the subcontinent

---

[8] Emma Tarlo, *Clothing Matters: Dress and Identity in India* (Chicago University Press, 1996), 259.

[9] Burns, "Monograph on Ivory Carving", 56; Ellis, "Ivory Carving in the Punjab".

remained at similar levels.[10] Overall, then, around 1,700,000–2,300,000 kg of ivory entered Diu and Daman from Mozambique in the 1780s and 1790s, a striking quantitative indicator of the magnitude of India's consuming markets.[11]

In the early nineteenth century, despite a gradual drop in ivory imports that resulted in small numbers of tusks arriving at Diu and Daman by the 1830s – largely the result of a dramatic expansion in slave trading in Mozambique that affected routes along which ivory porters carried their cargoes – the amount of ivory shipped by Vāniyā merchants remained impressive and continued to reflect elevated Indian demand. Thus, even though they were low in comparison to previous decades, imports into Diu in the period from the turn of the century to 1820 amounted to over 470,000 kg; for the remainder of the decade until the early 1830s when they suffered their sharpest falls as Vāniyā ivory trading declined rapidly, total shipments at the island nonetheless reached the level of 600,000 kg. Daman imports were around 353,000 kg. Taken together, ivory imports totalled approximately 1,423,000 kg, an extremely large sum which represented 80–85 per cent of Mozambique's ivory trade.[12]

Much of this ivory was consumed in the Kathiawar peninsula, which as I noted earlier in the book, experienced a period of commercial growth from the 1750s that was underpinned by significant political changes and a highly productive artisanal sector connected to cotton production. In seeking to expand the economic foundations of their states, rulers introduced commercial policies that were aimed at increasing their regional and wider Indian Ocean trade.[13]

Located short distances from both Diu and Daman in the Gulf of Cambay, Bhavnagar in particular developed policies focused on encouraging maritime trade. The deliberate "commercial orientation" of its leader, Wakhatsinji, in consolidating the trade and economic foundation of the state as a "commercial emporium" in the final quarter of the eighteenth century distinguished it from the other two powers in the peninsula. Progressive policies, that expanded Bhavnagar's economic base through trade, generated revenue for the state and brought

---

[10] Disease outbreaks reportedly reduced Diu's trade in 1799 by 30 per cent. See HAG, CD 1004, Joze Leite de Souza to Governor (?), 2 September 1807.

[11] Calculated from HAG, CD 995–1012, CDm 1055–1068, AD 4952–4969, ADm 4836–4852.

[12] This and the preceding figures have been calculated from HAG, CD 995–1012, CDm 1055–1068, AD 4952–4969, ADm 4836–4852.

[13] Harald Tambs-Lyche, *Power, Profit and Poetry: Traditional Society in Kathiawar, Western India* (New Delhi: Manohar, 1997); Ghulam A. Nadri, "Exploring the Gulf of Kachh: Regional Economy and Trade in the Eighteenth Century", *Journal of the Economic & Social History of the Orient*, 51, 3 (2008), 460–86.

prosperity to its rulers and the many merchants who were encouraged to migrate there from surrounding areas and ports.[14] Increasingly, it was trade with Africa, specifically Mozambique and in the later nineteenth century Zanzibar, that reflected and undergirded this growth. In 1821, in stark demonstration of this commercial interest, several vessels sailed from Bhavnagar to Mozambique to trade for ivory and slaves.[15]

The growing prosperity of Bhavnagar was a powerful draw also for Vāniyā merchants from Diu and Daman, whose interests were focused on the rising demand there for ivory supplies. In 1801, for instance, it was reported by a Portuguese official that "considerable" ivory was being shipped to Bhavnagar from Diu, while a few years later Vāniyā merchants were regularly transporting large cargoes to the port.[16] That high value was placed on Mozambique ivory is evident, further, in the theft of a cargo of tusks from a shipwrecked vessel on the coast of Daman that was taken north to Bhavnagar.[17] The place of Bhavnagar as a significant ivory market for the Vāniyā had already been established by the 1780s when its ruler declared an interest in "embrac[ing] Portuguese ships". While this would have included vessels from Goa under Portuguese command, evidence suggests that only Vāniyā ships from Diu and Daman sailed north to this thriving Kathiawar port.[18] The importance of Bhavnagar as a consumer of Mozambique ivory is further apparent in the commercial relationships that the Vāniyā maintained with Bhavnagar merchants – in 1784 Khushal Khanadas, one of the "principal merchants" of Daman, sent large volumes of ivory to his "partners" in Bhavnagar in

---

[14] Tambs-Lyche, *Power, Profit and Poetry*; *Gazetteer of the Bombay Presidency, Vol. 8: Kathiawar* (Bombay: Government Central Press, 1884), 391–2; Howard Spodek, "Rulers, Merchants and Other Groups in the City-States of Saurashtra, India, around 1800", *Comparative Studies in Society and History*, 16, 4 (1974), 448–70.

[15] James Tod, *Travels in Western India* (London: WmH. Allen and Co., 1839), 263–4; John Briggs, *The Cities of Gujarashtra: Their Topography and History Illustrated, in the Journal of a Recent Tour, with Accompanying Documents* (Bombay: Times, 1849), 284–5; R. J. Barendse, "On the Arabian Seas in the Eighteenth Century", paper presented at the Workshop "Western India and the Indian Ocean", Heidelberg, 5 October 1999, 15–16. Bhavnagar would continue to attract a variety of shipping in the nineteenth century; for example, between September 1881 and June 1882 it was visited by close to 6,000 vessels. See *Gazetteer of the Bombay Presidency. Vol. 8: Kathiawar*, 228.

[16] HAG, CD 1003, Francisco Antonio da Veiga Cabral to Caetano de Souza Pereira, 27 November 1801; CD 1004, Antonio Leite de Souza to da Veiga Cabral, 8 October 1807.

[17] HAG, CDm, "Carta Testemunhavel aos Mercadores Chrisaons, gentios e Mouros e segurados desta Fortaleza", n.d. [but 1784].

[18] HAG, CD 998, de Noyers to de Souza, 26 July 1784; CDm 1056, D. Frederico Guilherme de Souza to Manoel Antonio de Faria, 26 June 1784; CDm 1060, Antonio Leite de Souza to Viceroy, 25 June 1791.

what was a well-established commercial practice by this time.[19] The town remained a central market for Mozambique ivory well into the 1820s, when the Kathiawar peninsula came under direct British rule. Indeed, in some years imports from Diu accounted for all the ivory that entered the port.[20]

Although it is not possible to determine how much ivory imported into Bhavnagar from Mozambique (or elsewhere on the East African coast) was consumed within the state or how much may have been re-exported or redistributed more broadly throughout the region, there is fragmentary evidence that at least a proportion was taken far inland from the port. Towards the turn of the nineteenth century, a Diu merchant, Bovanidas Goculdas, wrote in correspondence to the governor that the ivory he shipped to Bhavnagar was sent overland to the "far northern interior" of the Kathiawar peninsula.[21] This may have included parts of Rajasthan where women wore much ivory in the form of bracelets and armlets, and horsemen used rings made from ivory to adorn the reins of their horses.[22]

Additionally, there was high demand for Mozambique ivory in other regional markets. One of the most important of these was Kutch, and the port-city of Mandvi in particular that was its largest sea port and most populous urban centre.[23] Kutch had been one of the six *sarkars* (administrative-cum-territorial units) of the Mughal *suba* (province) of Gujarat where – despite acknowledging Mughal suzerainty – local chiefs (*zamindars* or *rajas*) exercised considerable political and administrative control. There thus existed a "cluster of chieftaincies" around the Gulf of Kutch that were practically independent of Mughal authority and who, as was the case in Bhavnagar, attracted merchants and artisans in the eighteenth century from throughout the region as far as Surat, and

---

[19] HAG, CDm 1056, "Represenatação dos mercadores gentios. . .", n.d. [but 1784]; *ibid.*, "Certificação de Manoel Antonio de Faria", 28 September 1784.

[20] HAG, CD 1006, Garcez Palha to Viceroy, 16 October 1817; OIOC, P/419, Bombay Commerce: Internal and External Reports, vols. 52–64; Tambs-Lyche, *Power, Profit & Poetry*. Political manoeuvrings between the British and Bhavnagar in the early nineteenth century can be followed in Pamela Nightingale, *Trade and Empire in Western India, 1784–1806* (Cambridge University Press, 1970). An older account, not without value, is H. Wilberforce-Bell, *The History of Kathiawad from the Earliest Times* (London: William Heinemann, 1916).

[21] HAG, CD 1003, Bovanidas Goculdas to Governor, 11 September 1799.

[22] James Macmurdo, "Remarks on the Province of Kattiwar; Its Inhabitants, Their Manners and Customs", *Transactions of the Literary Society of Bombay*, vol. *I* (London: Longman, Hurst, Rees, Orme, Brown and John Murray, 1819), 279, 283–4.

[23] J. MacMurdo, "An Account of the Province of Cutch", in *Transactions of the Literary Society of Bombay*, vol. *II* (London: Longman, Hurst, Rees, Orme, Brown and John Murray, 1820).

perhaps beyond. These had sought refuge from the military action and internal strife that had affected parts of Gujarat as rivals sought to supersede Mughal authority and claim political and fiscal control in the territory. Mandvi appears to have benefitted in this respect and emerged as a "safe haven" for weavers and other artisans, as well as merchants, and gradually established itself over the second half of the eighteenth century as a commercially dynamic regional centre.[24]

The region of Kutch had a highly productive interior from which textiles were produced in vast quantities for domestic and especially Indian Ocean markets. It also may have been connected to the vast hinterland of Sind whose system of caravan trade shifted southward as a result of particular political developments in the 1750s.[25] Textile markets in East Africa, particularly in Zanzibar and Mozambique from the 1810s and 1820s, emerged increasingly as central to the productive capacities of Mandvi. The significance of ivory from Mozambique, which drove Kutchi textile exports to the territory and competed with Vāniyā exports of Jambusar textiles (as shown in Chapter 3), was clear by the early nineteenth century when cargoes of tusks from there were preferred to all others.[26] The size of ivory imports into Kutch was large and appears to have been part of growing consumption from the middle of the eighteenth century. This reached impressive levels, with Mandvi importing twice as much ivory from East Africa in the first three decades of the nineteenth century as Bombay and Surat where English interests for the burgeoning European ivory market were beginning to have an impact. Ivory was also imported from Muscat in Oman and possibly other Gulf ports.[27] The scale of Kutchi demand for Mozambique ivory drew Vāniyā merchants to Mandvi and resulted in sizeable re-exports from Diu and Daman in the 1770s; however, the growing dominance of Kutchi Bhātiyā merchants in the ivory import trade of Mandvi from the 1790s suggests that the Vāniyā would probably have been excluded from fully exploiting this market.[28]

Significant amounts of ivory were also traded from Diu and Daman to Jambusar where demand appears to have been steady into the 1820s and

---

[24] I have based this paragraph on Nadri, "Exploring the Gulf of Kachh".   [25] *Ibid.*

[26] William Milburn, *Oriental Commerce: Containing a Geographical Description of the Principal Places in the East Indies, China, and Japan, with Their Produce, Manufactures, and Trade*, 2 vols. (London: Black, Parry & Co., 1813), I, 62.

[27] M. Reda Bhacker, *Trade and Empire in Muscat and Zanzibar: Roots of British Domination* (New York: Routledge, 1992), 160.

[28] HAG, CD 996, D. Jozé Pedro da Camara to Castellão of Diu, 12 May 1777; CD 1002, Sebastião J.ᵉ Barroco to Caetano de Souza Perreira, 21 March 1794.

early 1830s.[29] Besides being a centre of cloth production and cotton trading, Jambusar also produced "manufactures of ivory" in the eighteenth and nineteenth centuries that likely included a range of items, from ivory wedding bangles to decorative pieces.[30] Even though ivory was traded to Jambusar from Bombay and Surat, and even from Bhavnagar, the overwhelming majority of its ivory imports came from Diu and Daman. They accounted in the first quarter of the nineteenth century for 86–98 per cent of the total value of all imports into this textile producing and trading centre.[31]

There is a further aspect of the Jambusar ivory connection which is important, namely the system of exchanging tusks for cotton cloths. Middlemen who came to Diu and Daman to collect orders for textiles for the Mozambique market appear to have accepted payment directly in ivory tusks in a practice that was well established by the final quarter of the eighteenth century.[32] The ivory was likely then sold in Jambusar but would not have been exchanged with weavers who were paid in cash. No details exist of how payment in ivory for cloth bales in Diu or Daman was determined, or whether payment for cloth with ivory was a regular occurrence. The economy of Gujarat was highly monetized and characterized by the circulation of different and competing currencies. The direct exchange of trade goods between merchants, or between merchants and middlemen, may thus have been relatively uncommon. There is certainly no indication that ivory tusks at any time were utilized as currency in Gujarat or anywhere else in India.

Nevertheless, purchasing cloth with ivory may not have been too unusual, as evidence for Kutch seems to indicate. When the British military officer Lieutenant Thomas Postans visited Mandvi in the 1830s, he noted that ivory imported from East Africa had its "principal market in Marwar [a textile-weaving and cotton-growing town]", where it seems it was exchanged "in return for grain and coarse cloths".[33]

[29] See, for example, HAG, CD 1006, João Vicente Lemoza (?) to Governor, 29 November 1819; CDm 1063, Panachand Jalchand to Viceroy, 13 June 1821; HAG, Registos Gerais da Feitoria de Diu 7971, 11 December 1809.

[30] *Gazetteer of the Bombay Presidency. Vol. 2: Gujarat-Surat and Broach* (Bombay: Government Central Press, 1877), 564.

[31] OIOC, P/419, Bombay Commerce: Internal and External Reports, vols. 56–64.

[32] HAG, CDm 1067, "Representação de Panachande Galalchande...", n.d. [but 1821]; "Rellação das pessoas que tem contas...", n.d. [but 1821]; "Depoimentos de mercadores...", June 1821.

[33] T. Postans, "Some Account of the Present State of the Trade Between the Port of Mandavie in Cutch, and the Eastern Coast of Africa", *Transactions of the Bombay Geographical Society, June 1839–February 1840*, vol. III (Bombay: American Mission Press, 1840), 173.

Although it is not specified, he was likely referring to middlemen and not weavers who, as elsewhere in India, were generally paid in cash and not in kind. The examples of Diu, Daman and Kutch strongly suggest at least the possibility that an ivory-exchange economy existed in northwestern India, where tusks were used in direct payment for textiles.

Demand for Mozambique ivory was high throughout Gujarat in the eighteenth and first quarter of the nineteenth centuries, and its ivory markets and consumers influenced the scale of Vāniyā imports into Diu and Daman. Among these markets, Surat was important because it maintained its role as a notable regional financial centre, and Vāniyā merchants maintained relationships with its bankers. Despite challenges associated with Maratha military action and changes to its political structure as a result of the establishment of English jurisdictional control in 1759, Surat functioned as an ivory market with connections to the hinterland of western India and the north Indian plains.

Vāniyā merchants were active in the city by the 1770s and continued to ship ivory there well into the nineteenth century.[34] Demand was particularly strong for Mozambique ivory because its quality and durability were superior and therefore highly prized. It was so intensely sought that in 1802 merchants in Surat sailed to Daman to buy tusks directly from Vāniyā merchants in what was described as a "new trade".[35] But the robust ivory market at Surat also attracted Daman merchants regularly and wealthy merchants such as Laxmichand Motichand, whom we met in the book's introduction, shipped substantial cargoes there in the 1780s and 1790s.[36] This high level of demand also attracted English merchants to the port-city with commercial connections to southern Mozambique and its ivory trade. Surat may have been the most important importer of East African – and especially Mozambique – ivory in western India, with Portuguese reports claiming – if in non-specific terms – that "a great deal of ivory is traded [there]".[37] Some considered it the best ivory market in the region where "the largest cargoes are sold".[38] In the first decade of the nineteenth century, the value of annual Mozambique

---

[34] James Forbes, *Oriental Memoirs: A Narrative of Seventeen Years Residence in India*, vol. I, 2nd edn (London: Richard Bentley, 1834), 147.

[35] Milburn, *Oriental Commerce*, I, 62; HAG, CDm 1061, "Requerimento", 20 August 1802.

[36] HAG, CDm 1056, "Carta Testemunhavel...", n.d. [but 1784]; CDm 1060, Christivão Pereira de Castro to Governor, 25 October 1793.

[37] A. F. Moniz, "A Feitoria Portuguesa de Surrate: Sua importancia Politica e Comercial", *O Oriente Português*, 15,' 1 and 2 (1918), 13.

[38] HAG, Feitoria de Surrate 2603, 11 February 1790.

ivory imports regularly exceeded Rs 200,000 and remained high in the 1820s.[39]

As a reflection of its long-standing position as a noted market for ivory, an ivory-carving industry had been in existence in Surat since the sixteenth century and artisans continued to produce high volumes of decorative pieces, as well as jewellery, for royal households in the eighteenth century. As in Kathiawar and elsewhere in Gujarat, however, ivory consumption was not confined to wealthy elites; rather, ivory was in demand across social groups. Purchasing power among villagers and rural farmers depended on a good harvest, which, according to K. N. Chaudhuri, in turn "stimulated the sale of ivory". Thus, a report in 1740 from the East India Company's Surat factory noted that "ivory was likely to sell at a high price ... because of a plentiful crop which would allow the 'lower sort of people' to purchase ornaments made from ivory"; the report went on to state that "a good harvest always had the effect of increasing the demand for it".[40]

Although far from definitive, there are indications that Mozambique ivory imported at Surat in the eighteenth and early nineteenth centuries was traded to Maratha households. While the Maratha polity dissolved into a set of states in the final quarter of the eighteenth century, Maratha aristocracy were a consuming class and luxury markets for the consumption of ornamental ivory existed among the elites of the emergent polities. This consumption was stimulated by a vibrant commercial economy that saw trade grow between the 1740s and 1820s under state encouragement. According to Sumit Guha, Maratha potentates "were aware of the potential value of commerce for their regimes, and [were] eager to realise that potential". They were thus influential in the establishment of new market towns and in the expansion of existing

---

[39] OIOC, P/419, Bombay Commerce: Internal and External Reports, vols. 40–56. In these English trade reports concerning Surat and Bombay, the importance of Mozambique ivory was recognized also in the use of a separate eponymous category that distinguished it from the generic category of "East Africa". It is worth noting, further, that as Abdul Sheriff has argued, the extent to which Surat was "dependent" on Mozambique for its ivory by the early nineteenth century was reflected in a rise in prices for tusks in response to price increases in Mozambique. From Rs 80 per Surat *maund* (an ivory weight corresponding to 17 kg), ivory increased in price gradually until it reached a high of Rs 159 in 1808–9. Although it decreased to a low of Rs 55 in 1816–17, it levelled off at Rs 70 where it remained for much of the 1820s. See *Slaves, Spices & Ivory in Zanzibar: Integration of an East African Commercial Empire into the World Economy, 1770–1873* (London: James Currey, 1987), 81; and OIOC, P/419, Bombay Commerce: Internal and External Reports, vols. 45–63.

[40] K. N. Chaudhuri, *The Trading World of Asia and the English East India Company 1660–1760* (Cambridge University Press, 1978), 221–2.

ones.[41] The courts of Maratha kingdoms appear to have been significant consumers of textiles, among other goods, with the Peshwa's regime in Pune purchasing substantial amounts of cloth for its retainers from widespread locations.[42] What the scale of Maratha demand for ivory may have been is difficult to estimate but it was certainly another significant market for the extraordinarily large cargoes of tusks that Vāniyā merchants were shipping to India from Mozambique. I discuss these volumes later in the chapter.

From the mid-1810s, Vāniyā merchants began shipping ivory to yet another market on the west coast of India: Bombay. In 1813, Karamchand Harchand (the "principal merchant of Daman") sent *palas* loaded with ivory to this rapidly emergent commercial centre. Two years later another prominent Vāniyā, Jhaver Khushal, moved into its ivory market as Bombay increasingly became a notable ivory importer.[43] Indeed, by the 1830s, the Mozambique ivory trade in Surat appears to have been almost entirely transferred south to Bombay.[44] So while commercial interest in Mozambique ivory remained sufficiently buoyant that nine vessels under English colours sailed there in the trading season of 1820–1, by the end of the decade less than Rs 1,000 of ivory was entering Surat.[45] However, though tusks from Mozambique were entering the Bombay market at this time, increasingly its rise as a notable ivory-importing centre on the west coast of India from the 1830s and 1840s was related to the exploitation of alternative ivory sources in East Africa north of Mozambique that were traded through Zanzibar by English, American and particularly Kutchi Bhātiyā and other South Asian merchants.

This reflected, in turn, the growing demands of a burgeoning consuming class in Europe and America that from mid-century would use ivory in a variety of ornamental objects and in particular styles of adornment, as well as to manufacture items such as billiard balls and piano keys that were used in the pursuits of particular leisure activities. An expanding middle

---

[41] Sumit Guha, "Potentates, Traders and Peasants: Western India, c. 1700–1870", in Burton Stein and Sanjay Subrahmanyam (eds.), *Institutions and Economic Change in South Asia* (Oxford University Press, 1996), 84. Burton Stein, *A History of India* (Oxford: Blackwell Publishers, 1998), 189–97; C. A. Bayly, *Rulers, Townsmen and Bazaars: North Indian Society in the Age of British Expansion 1770–1870*, First Indian edn (New Delhi: Oxford University Press, 1992), 146–7.

[42] Douglas E. Haynes, *Small Town Capitalism in Western India: Artisans, Merchants and the Making of the Informal Economy, 1870–1960* (New York: Cambridge University Press, 2012), 27.

[43] HAG, CDm 1063, Rencoza to Viceroy, 7 May 1815.

[44] OIOC, P/419, Bombay Commerce: Internal and External Reports, vols. 46–63; Sheriff, *Slaves, Spices & Ivory*, 85–6.

[45] OIOC, P/419, Bombay Commerce: Internal and External Reports, vols. 57, 64.

class, in particular, raised demand for ivory dramatically. Thus, whereas in the first decade of the nineteenth century an average value close to Rs 56,000 was being imported into Bombay from East Africa, by the 1830s this had nearly quadrupled to Rs 211,300.[46] This ivory was being re-exported to London in growing quantities, to the extent that by 1850 around 70 per cent of all the ivory imported into Bombay was shipped on to the imperial capital. This expansion of the ivory trade was a feature of the second half of the century and stimulated increased elephant hunting throughout much of the interior of East Africa, pushing the ivory frontier into the far interior.[47]

By contrast, Portuguese demand in India for Mozambique ivory appears to have been modest. In Diu, ivory carving had existed since the sixteenth century, and in the 1820s ivory tusks were "still carved well, particularly in images".[48] Artisanal production was small scale, though, and served the Gujarati population on the island or the small number of Portuguese residents. While these artisans may have been producing Christian iconography for use especially in Portuguese churches, it is more likely that the bulk of this "Indo-Portuguese" production was done in Goa where trained carvers produced a variety of religious objects.[49] The extent of Portuguese demand in India – or for the markets of metropolitan Portugal – is difficult to establish but what is clear is that it would have accounted for a limited proportion of the ivory brought to India by Vāniyā merchants, and was in no way comparable to what English merchants shipped from India to London from the second quarter of the nineteenth century. Ivory demand and consumption in Bhavnagar, Kutch, throughout Kathiawar and elsewhere in the region of western India, as I have been describing, was of such a scale that it provided Vāniyā merchants with their primary markets.

There were a few other, peripheral, markets in the Indian Ocean to which Vāniyā merchants sold Mozambique ivory. Within India, Bengal appears to have emerged in the early nineteenth century as a market for Mozambique ivory. There is evidence that Vāniyā vessels sailed there, though infrequently, but we do not know how much ivory they

---

[46] OIOC, P/419, Bombay Commerce: Internal and External Reports, vols. 39–65. These figures differ significantly from those in Sheriff, *Slaves, Spices & Ivory*, appendix A, 249–50, and may be due to the inclusion in his calculations of ivory imports at Bombay from the Red Sea and Persian Gulf.

[47] This is detailed by, among others, Sheriff, *Slaves, Spices & Ivory*.

[48] José Accursio das Neves, *Considerações Politicas, e Comerciaes dos Portugueses na Africa, e na Asia* (Lisbon: Imprensa Regia, 1830), 327.

[49] John Correia Afonso, "Indo-Portuguese Ivories in the Heras Collection", *Indica*, 3, 2 (1994), 101–12.

may have transported. It is possible, nonetheless, to get a sense of this trade from a report of ivory exports from Mozambique in 1817 that indicates that 12 per cent or roughly 7,100 kg of that year's total was shipped to Bengal.[50] It is unclear whether Vāniyā merchants were responsible for this shipment but it is surely no coincidence that in the same year Shobhachand Sowchand, the prominent Vāniyā with significant investments in Mozambique, undertook a voyage to Bengal directly from Mozambique Island on a vessel carrying ivory tusks.[51] The small amount of ivory exported to Bengal, however, is probably indicative of its minor status as an importer of Mozambique ivory.[52] So, despite their large consumer base, Vāniyās did not develop these markets because of their financial commitments and commercial interests in their established Indian markets in Kathiawar and Gujarat.

Beyond India, Vāniyā vessels made occasional stops at Persian Gulf ports on their return journeys to India from Mozambique. In 1817, for instance, Chaturbhuj Kunwarji sailed with an ivory cargo worth approximately Rs 100,000 to Mukalla but the vessel was forced to put in at "Suhar" (Suhâr), a port in Oman, after strong winds blew the vessel well off course. Shortly after its arrival, however, the ruler of Suhar seized the vessel's entire shipment of tusks, to the unsurprising dismay of the owner and consigning merchants.[53] If this seizure reflected the value placed on ivory at the port, Oman's ivory trade was actually concentrated in Muscat where it was dominated by Omani Arabs and increasingly by Kutchi Bhātiyā, whose shipments from the Swahili coast (especially Zanzibar) provided regular supplies to the region. Muscat operated as a redistributive centre for the region, including for Mandvi to which Bhātiyā vessels re-exported tusks. Thus, the prominence of Bhātiyā merchants in the commercial and financial economy of this Omani port appears to have kept the Vāniyā from exploiting its ivory market.[54]

---

[50] Calculated from Edward A. Alpers, *Ivory and Slaves in East Central Africa: Changing Patterns of Trade to the Later Nineteenth Century* (London: Heinemann, 1975), 263, fn. 2.

[51] HAG, CM 1447, Jose Francisco de Paula Cavalcante de Albuquerque to Conde de Rio Pardo, 28 July 1818. The length and difficulty of the voyage would undoubtedly have meant that Shobhachand would have made stops enroute to Bengal, likely in Diu and Daman before completing his voyage.

[52] Mabel V. Jackson-Haight argues that trade between Bengal and "Portuguese East African ports" was "so small as to be included with that of other places on that coast". *European Powers and South-East Africa: A Study of International Relations on the South-East Coast of Africa* (London: Routledge, 1967), 138.

[53] HAG, CD 1006, Joaquim Garcez Palha to Viceroy, 27 April 1817.

[54] We should recall that Vāniyā merchants also called occasionally at Mocha until the 1780s and it would be surprising if they did not trade in Mozambique ivory. Details are not available, however, for how much ivory they may have shipped there in the eighteenth century, though it is unlikely to have been of any significance.

A final market to which Vāniyā shipped ivory was Macau, which throughout the eighteenth century continued to function as a Portuguese emporium in China. Some among the Portuguese officials in Diu in the 1780s actually believed that in addition to the island's commercial orientation to Mozambique, its merchants should also redirect their investments to Macau.[55] This view does not appear to have been shared by the Vāniyā themselves, due possibly to the poor returns it brought merchants. When a Vāniyā vessel carrying ivory undertook a voyage to Macau between 1816 and 1818, it suffered a punishing loss of 20 per cent.[56] At first glance, this appears surprising because the Chinese ivory market was historically robust and was indeed expanding in the nineteenth century.[57] Portuguese merchants certainly shipped Mozambique ivory to Macau through Goa and Daman between the 1770s and the late 1810s and early 1820s[58] but the growth of interest in its East Asian commerce was related mostly to the export of Malwa opium.[59] It was cultivated in a region of west-central north India that today includes parts of western Madhya Pradesh and southeastern Rajasthan, and dominated Macau imports from the 1810s and throughout its heyday in the 1820s and early 1830s, as Portuguese and other merchants sought to exploit Daman as a port falling beyond British attempts to control the subcontinent's opium trade with China.[60]

The vibrancy of Indian consumer markets, however, meant that ivory remained at the centre of Vāniyā trade and was sustained in the eighteenth and nineteenth centuries. While ivory could be sold in many areas of the western Indian Ocean, high levels of demand in Kathiawar, Gujarat and Kutch underpinned and sustained their Mozambique commerce. Ships could carry large volumes of tusks because consumers in Bhavnagar, Surat and Mandvi – and the interior markets they supplied – sought the

---

[55] HAG, CD 999, Francisco da Cunha e Menezes to Castelão, 28 November 1787.

[56] HAG, CD 997, Macedo e Couto to Ferreira Pestana, 24 November 1845.

[57] Sheriff, *Slaves, Spices & Ivory*, 44, 85.

[58] Celsa Pinto, *Trade and Finance in Portuguese India: A Study of the Portuguese Country Trade 1770–1840* (New Delhi: Concept Publishing Company, 1994), 173.

[59] See, for example, A. F. Moniz, *Noticias e Documentos para a Historia de Damão – Antiga provincia do Norte*, 4 vols. (Bastorá: Tipografia Rangel, 1904–23), II, 174; "Comercio de Opio em Damão no Governo do Prefeito Bernardo Peresda [*sic*] Silva (1833)", in *idem*, IV, 81. Although never on a large or significant scale, opium exports from Daman also involved Vāniyā merchants.

[60] W. G. Clarence-Smith, *The Third Portuguese Empire 1825–1975: A Study in Economic Imperialism* (Manchester University Press, 1985), 25–9; Pinto, *Trade and Finance*, ch. 5; José Vicente Serrão, "Macau", in Valentim Alexandre and Jill Dias (eds.), *O Império Africano 1825–1890* (Lisbon: Editorial Estampa, 1998), 744–8.

high-quality ivory that hunters and traders across the ocean in Africa were able to provide through the crucial involvement of Vāniyā merchants and financiers. That such large amounts of ivory could be supplied to these merchants depended, in turn, on access to sources and regular supplies, and it is to this that we now turn.

Procuring ivory

The success of Vāniyā merchants in satisfying large-scale Indian demand for Mozambique ivory relied on the acquisition and regular supply of tusks from African traders who brought them to the coast and points along the Zambesi River in central Mozambique. As I have already established, securing ivory (and all other) purchases along the coast and interior of Mozambique depended on Gujarati cotton textiles that Vāniyā merchants secured through access to well-organized procurement networks in India. This system operated well because the Vāniyā were able consistently to provide investment capital for intermediaries that was critical to the production of textiles, and hence ultimately central to the supply of African markets. The vast imports into Mozambique of Gujarati cotton textiles financed, in turn, the purchase of equally remarkable volumes of ivory tusks. Procurement networks on both sides of the Indian Ocean, in other words, required that Vāniyā merchants finance them adequately with credit advances.

From early in the eighteenth century, Vāniyā merchants had begun focusing their commercial operations on Mozambique Island as a business centre from which they organized and managed their credit arrangements and their trade on Macuana and elsewhere along the northern coast. These arrangements were from the earliest involvement of the Vāniyā in East Africa and Mozambique directed towards acquiring ivory for Indian consumer markets. Thus, already in the late fourteenth and early fifteenth centuries, Vāniyā merchants purchased ivory at Malindi and Pate on the Swahili coast, and together with Kilwa these functioned as important trading centres where visiting merchants could either acquire ivory from their hinterlands, arrange trading voyages to the southern ports of the Mozambique coast or more commonly trade for tusks with local merchants who sailed the route through the Mozambique Channel to Sofala and other ivory-exporting ports.[61] The latter had been connected since at least the thirteenth and fourteenth centuries with

---

[61] Malyn Newitt, *A History of Mozambique* (Bloomington: Indiana University Press, 1995).

the far interior through long-distance trade routes related also to the gold trade from the Zimbabwe plateau.[62]

The potential of the ivory trade was clear already by the early sixteenth century. In 1520, for instance, exports from both Sofala, a busy port and settlement controlled by a Muslim ruler that was situated to the south of Quelimane, and Mozambique Island where the Portuguese Crown had established an imperial presence, totalled around 23,000 kg. At mid-century it was possible to ship as much as 121,000 kg from these trading areas in a commercial environment where ivory, increasingly since the eleventh and twelfth centuries, had become firmly established as one of the principal commodities of a vigorous and large-scale western Indian Ocean trading arena.[63]

Most of these cargoes were shipped to India, and though they were carried by Portuguese vessels in this early period, were handled predominantly by Vāniyā merchants from Diu, and to some extent Daman.[64] Later, these merchants traded ivory along the coast and carried it on their own vessels to India but only established a regular commercial presence on the African coast in the seventeenth century. Their investments, as Chapter 1 of this work has shown, were focused at this time in southern Arabia and the Red Sea from which they acquired large shipments of silver specie in exchange for textiles and other Indian goods. They were also able, though, to trade for ivory in Mocha that had entered the market through Massawa and could thus draw on an alternative source of ivory.[65]

This began to change quite rapidly from the late seventeenth and early eighteenth centuries. In realizing the potential of ivory in Mozambique to

[62] *Ibid.*, 8; Sheriff, *Slaves, Spices & Ivory*, 78–9.

[63] M. N. Pearson, *Port Cities and Intruders: The Swahili Coast, India, and Portugal in the Early Modern Era* (Baltimore: Johns Hopkins University Press, 1998), 48. Details of the place of East Africa in the Indian Ocean trading world can be found in M. D. D. Newitt, "East Africa and Indian Ocean Trade: 1500–1800", in Ashin Das Gupta and M. N. Pearson (eds.), *India and the Indian Ocean, 1500–1800* (New Delhi: Oxford University Press, 1999), 201–3; M. N. Pearson, *Port Cities and Intruders: The Swahili Coast, India, and Portugal in the Early Modern Era* (Baltimore: Johns Hopkins University Press, 1998), 81–7; Manuel Lobato, "Relações comerciaes entre a Índia e a Costa Africana nos Séculos XVI e XVII. O Papel do Guzerate no Comércio de Moçambique", *Mare Liberum*, 9 (1995), 157–73; Ronald W. Dickinson, "Sofala and the Rivers of Cuama: Crusade and Commerce in S. E. Africa, 1505–1595", MA thesis, University of Cape Town, 1971; Eric Axelson, *Portuguese in South-East Africa 1488–1600* (Johannesburg: C. Struik Ltd, 1973); Fr. João dos Santos, *Etiópia Oriental e Vária História de Cousas Notáveis do Oriente* (Lisbon: Comissão Nacional para as Comemorações dos Descobrimentos Portugueses, 1999), 281–8.

[64] M. N. Pearson, *Merchants and Rulers in Gujarat: The Response to the Portuguese in the Sixteenth Century* (Berkeley: University of California Press, 1976), ch. 4.

[65] Nancy Um, *The Merchant Houses of Mocha: Trade and Architecture in an Indian Ocean Port* (Seattle: University of Washington Press, 2009), 32.

generate income for the imperial state as a taxable commerce, Portuguese authorities began to establish trading stations along the coast to the south of Kilwa all the way to Delagoa Bay "where ivory from the interior, as far south as Zululand, could be tapped".[66] Portuguese efforts to redirect the ivory trade to their settlements in Mozambique – particularly once they were expelled from Mombasa and the northern coast by Omani defeat in 1698 – coupled with a gradual diminishment of supplies to Kilwa as Yao traders redirected their trade resulted in a shift increasingly away from the northern coast. Mozambique Island in particular began to emerge early in the eighteenth century as an important entrepôt for an expanding ivory trade that in the 1730s and 1740s was falling ever more into the hands of Vāniyā merchants as a corollary to their growing textile imports. From the 1750s and 1760s the ivory trade had become controlled and dominated by them as it began to reach unprecedented heights.[67]

Ivory tusks were brought to the coast by Yao long-distance traders from east of Lake Nyasa, who had established themselves as the pre-eminent African ivory traders of northern Mozambique. By the early 1750s, around 124,000 kg of ivory was reaching Mozambique Island through the area of Macuana that was connected along trading circuits with the African interior to its west. It was carried almost entirely by the Yao who were consistently transporting approximately 95 per cent of the ivory that arrived at Mozambique Island through Macuana. Some ivory was brought to the coast by Makua traders but only in relatively small quantities. Yao ivory cargoes accounted, furthermore, for a significant proportion of Mozambique's overall ivory exports, perhaps as much as 75 per cent. This amounted to a substantial quantity of ivory – between 1759 and 1762, for example, over 500,000 kg of ivory tusks were shipped from Mozambique, with as much as 173,000 kg exported in a single year.[68]

---

[66] Newitt, "East Africa and Indian Ocean Trade", 209.

[67] Newitt, *History of Mozambique*, 175–6; Alpers, *Ivory and Slaves*, chs. 2 and 3; Sheriff, *Slaves, Spices & Ivory*, ch. 1; A. I. Salim, "East Africa: The Coast", in B. A. Ogot (ed.), *General History of Africa. Volume V: Africa from the Sixteenth to Eighteenth Centuries* (Paris: Unesco, 1992), 750–5; C. S. Nicholls, *The Swahili Coast: Politics, Diplomacy and Trade on the East African Littoral 1798–1856* (London: George Allen & Unwin, 1971), ch. 1.

[68] AHU, Moç., Cx 8 Doc. 41, Francisco de Mello e Castro to King, 20 November 1753; Anonymous, "Memorias da Costa d'Africa Oriental..." in *RMS*, 215; Alpers, *Ivory and Slaves*, 104–5; Sheriff, *Slaves, Spices & Ivory*; Newitt, *History of Mozambique*, 180, 80; Gerhard Liesegang, "A First Look at the Import and Export Trade of Mozambique, 1800–1914", in Liesegang, Pasch and Jones (eds.), *Figuring African Trade*, 502; Fritz Hoppe, *A África Oriental Portuguesa no Tempo do Marquês de Pombal (1750–1777)* (Lisbon: Agência-Geral do Ultramar, 1970), 220.

Ivory traded by the Yao thus fuelled the territory's exports and helped both to consolidate the place of Mozambique Island as a commercial hub in the region and to establish Vāniyā merchants as its primary buyers and shippers. The Vāniyā organized ivory purchases from Yao traders through *patamares* who arranged the purchase of ivory tusks on the mainland of Macuana. Once purchased, tusks were brought to Vāniyā-owned *palmares* on the coast before being transported the short distance by small coastal crafts to the island for warehousing and eventual shipment across the western Indian Ocean to India aboard Vāniyā vessels.

This structure of ivory procurement remained in place for much for the eighteenth century. From the final quarter of the century, however, there was a striking and important change to this picture. Sources for Vāniyā exports became increasingly drawn from areas other than the traditional market of Macuana. Although Yao traders continued to transport ivory tusks to the coastal hinterland in exchange for Gujarati cotton cloths until the 1810s, there was a gradual reduction in their cargoes. This reflected a growing shift by these long-distance traders away from Mossuril and other sites in Macuana and towards the growing markets of the Swahili coast that were located to the north of Mozambique Island, especially Kilwa and Zanzibar, where the presence of a greater number of Swahili, Omani and Kutchi Bhātiyā merchants were able to offer better prices for ivory. Yao trade in Macuana appears also to have been disturbed by unsettled conditions between the Portuguese and Makua in the late 1770s, and subsequent hostilities between them in the early 1780s.[69] The latter may have been fuelled in part by the attempts of the Portuguese to depress the price of ivory at Mozambique Island out of inflationary concerns, which likely affected the trade of the Yao as well.

Of perhaps greater importance in explaining this shift, however, was the growth of the slave trade, which had a significant impact on the economy of Mozambique, a theme that is taken up in Chapter 5. Indeed, although Makua traders in Macuana still traded some ivory to the coast, their main trade by the third quarter of the century was slaves. Raiding for captives would have caused further disruptions to the ivory trade of the region. The cumulative effect of this and the above factors was that by the 1780s the Yao brought no more than about 24,786–32,222 kg of ivory to Macuana, a dramatic reduction from the 1750s and 1760s.[70]

---

[69] Alpers, *Ivory and Slaves*, 154, 161, 172–85. See also Nancy Jane Hafkin, "Trade, Society and Politics in Northern Mozambique, c. 1753–1913", PhD diss., Boston University (1973).

[70] Alpers, *Ivory and Slaves*, 158.

At the time that the ivory trade of northern Mozambique was shifting towards the Swahili coast, Vāniyā merchants began to source ivory from ports and market towns to the south of Mozambique Island in a shift that has not been adequately appreciated. Beginning in the 1770s, Vāniyās moved their focus to Quelimane and other southern ports, and established trading stores in Sena in the Zambesi Valley, whose commercial structure was dominated by *prazeros* and their Chikunda traders, porters, canoe men and – importantly – elephant hunters.[71] Vāniyā merchants also established themselves in Inhambane, Sofala and the Querimba Islands.[72]

It was Quelimane, however, that particularly from the 1780s became the most regular and enduring port of call for vessels trading in ivory along the coast to the south of Mozambique Island, and it was thus likely the supplier of most of the ivory exported to India in the later eighteenth and first quarter of the nineteenth century. Although Vāniyā vessels had sailed to Quelimane earlier in the century, there was a marked and systematic increase in voyages to the port in the 1780s and 1790s.[73] These can be traced through shipping passes that, though they did not always do so, merchants were required to acquire for coastal voyages.[74] Thus, while nine passes were issued for travel to Quelimane between 1781 and 1785, in the period from 1793 to 1800 merchants made a total of 32 voyages there (Table 4.1).

A pattern of regular contact was thus established with Quelimane that would last well into the 1830s, a development that occurred at a time when the port was emerging as a notable supplier of slaves to the Indian Ocean and Atlantic trades. Indeed, by the 1820s its economy was dominated by slave exports. However, while Vāniyā merchants benefitted from commercial and financial involvement in the slave trade, it was not Quelimane's growing potential as a source of slaves that drew the merchants but rather its role as an outlet for the ivory of Zambesia and its interior. Still, the growing slave trade from Quelimane meant that Vāniyā

---

[71] AHU, Moç., Cx. 33 Doc. 71, Bando signed by Antonio Manuel de Melo e Castro, 25 April 1780. The emergence and place of the Chikunda in the Zambesi Valley has been examined recently by Allen F. Isaacman and Barbara S. Isaacman in an excellent study, *Slavery and Beyond: The Making of Men and Chikunda Ethnic Identities in the Unstable World of South-Central Africa, 1750–1920* (Portsmouth, NH: Heinemann, 2004).

[72] AHU, Códice 1332, Antonio Correa Monteiro de Mattos et al. to Governor (?), 17 August 1772.

[73] See, for example, AHU, Códice 1329, Passports Velji Amba(vi)das, 9 November 1766; Passport for Odouji Ramji, November 1766.

[74] AHU, Moç., Cx 38 Doc. 29, Jose Bras dos Campos to Governor of Mozambique, 7 March 1782.

Table 4.1 *Voyages by Vāniyā merchants to Quelimane, 1781–1828*

Date	Name	Vessel
13 December 1781	Laxmichand Nemidas	Sumaca N.Snra das Necessidades
18 December 1781	Govandgi Kanakdas	Sumaca Lanceta Santo Antonio e Almas Santas
18 December 1781	Velgi Amba[v]idas	Curveta N.Snra de Penha de Franca
29 April 1782	Velji Vada (?)	Sumaca Lanceta S: Antonio e Almas Santas
7 May 1782	Velji Vada (?)	Sumaca Lanceta S. Antonio e Almas Santas
10 May 1782	Kunwarji Narsinh	Curveta N.Snra da Conceicao e Santo Antonio
23 October 1784	Velgi Amba[v]idas	Curveta N.Snra de Penha de Franca Santo Antonio e Almas Santas (?)
6 June 1785	Laxmichand Motichand	Gurabo Santo Antonio e Almas Santas
28 September 1785	Laxmichand Motichand	Gurabo Santo Antonio e Almas Santas
25 April 1793	Laxmichand Motichand	Pala Minerva
11 May 1793	Naranji Danji	Pala N.Snra dos Remedios
15 May 1793	Purshottam Madhavjii	Bergantim N.Snra da Guia
4 November 1793	Naranji Danji	Nossa Snra dos Remedios
12 March 1794	Laxmichand Motichand	Pala Minerva
25 May 1794	Purshottam Madhavji	Bergantim N.Snra da Guia
23 August 1794	Naranji Danji	Pala N.Snra dos Remedios
24 December 1794	Laxmichand Motichand	Pala Minvera
4 May 1795	Naranji Danji	Pala N.Snra dos Remedios
28 May 1795	Laxmichand Motichand	Pala Minerva
22 September 1795	Jiv Sangaji	Bergantim Chupanga Feliz Ligeiro
8 October 1795	Morarji Amba[v]idas	Pala Aurora Feliz
16 December 1795	Jiv Sangaji	Bergantim Africano Ligeiro
25 May 1796	Morarji Amba[v]idas	Pala Aurora Feliz
19 November 1796	Naranji Danji	Pala N.Snra dos Remedios
20 December 1796	Jiv Sangaji	Bergantim Africano Ligeiro
5 January 1797	Morarji Amba[v]idas	Pala Aurora Feliz
17 October 1797	Ramji Premji	Pala Aurora Feliz
4 November 1797	Jiv Sangaji	Bergantim Africano Ligeiro
23 April 1798	Ramji Premji	Batel Santo Antonio
18 May 1798	Velji Tairsi	Bergantim Deligente
19 May 1798	Morarji Jivan	Pala Moduzia
13 June 1798	Jiv Sangaji	Bergantim Africano Ligeiro
21 June 1798	Shobhachand Sowchand	Pala Aurora Feliz
13 September 1798	Jiv Sangaji	Bergantim Africano Ligeiro
22 February 1799	Velji Tairsi	Bergantim Deligente
29 April 1799	Velji Tairsi	Bergantim Deligente

Table 4.1 (*cont.*)

Date	Name	Vessel
22 May 1799	Musaji Jivan	Pala Meduza
5 November 1799	Velji Tairsi	Bergantim Deligente
29 May 1800	Velji Tairsi	Bergantim Deligente
21 June 1800	Narsinh Ranchhod	Bergantim Bom Sucesso
7 November 1800	Velji Tairsi	Bergantim Deligente
2 June 1801	Velji Tairsi	Bergantim Deligente
21 April 1802	Laxmichand Motichand	Pala Bom Sucesso
20 May 1802	Jiv Sangaji	Bergantim Deligente
7 May 1803	Ramji Premji	Pala Aurora Feliz
10 March 1805	Jagannath Kunwarjii	Bergantiim Bom Sucesso
22 March 1805	Rafibhai Rasulbhai	Bergantim Boa Esperança
5 June 1805	Shobhachand Sowchand	(?)
14 June 1805	Narsinh Trikam	(?)
9 July 1805	Jagannath Kunwarji	Pala Bom Jardim
22 November 1805	Rafibhai Rasulbhai	Bergantim Boa Esperança
21 March 1806	Premji Karsanji	(?)
30 May 1806	Pitambar Punjia	(?)
17 June 1806	Rafibhai Rasulbhai	Bergantim Boa Esperança
8 May 1807	Jagannath Kunwarjii	Pala Bom Jardim
26 September 1807	Jagannath Kunwarji	Pala Bom Jardim
1 October 1807	Rafibhai Rasulbhai	Bergantim Boa Esperança
31 October 1808	Shobhachand Sowchand	Espadarte
27 February 1809	Devchand Ramji	(?)
17 April 1809	Devchand Ramji	(?)
25 April 1809	Saraji Valeji (?)	Pala N. Senhora de Penha de França
26 May 1810	Saraji Valeji (?)	Pala N. Senhora de Penha de França
30 October 1810	Jetha Karsanji	Gergantim Boa Fortuna
9 November 1810	Velji Natthu	Pala Santa Ana Feliz
14 November 1810	Devchand Ramji	Escuna N. Snra. do Livramento
23 November 1810	Jagannath Kunwarjii	Pala Bom Jardim
11 June 1811	Shobhachand Sowchand	Brigue Santa Paulla
18 June 1811	Devchand Ramji	Escuna N. Senhora do Livramento
26 June 1811	Jetha Karsanji	Bergantim Boa Fortuna
1 July 1811	Laca (?) Ratanji	(?)
2 January 1812	Jetha Karsanji	Bergantim Boa Fortuna
7 January 1812	Devchande Ramji	Escuna N.Snra do Livramento
18 June 1812	Karsanji Keshavji	Bergantim Vingança
7 July 1812	Jetha Karsanji	Bergantim Boa Fortuna
7 July 1812	Virchand Harichand	Escuna N. Snra. do Livramento
6 October 1812	Karsanji Keshavji	Bergantim Vingança
23 March 1813	Karsanji Keshavji	Bergantim Vingança

Table 4.1 (*cont.*)

Date	Name	Vessel
4 June 1813	Karsanji Keshavji	Bergantim Vingança
10 June 1813	Thakarsi Jetha	Escuna N.Snra do Livramento
22 November 1813	Karsanji Jetha	Bergantim Vingança
23 November 1813	Mupaji (?) Kasam/Qasim (?)	(?)
23 November 1813	Velji Natthu	(?)
7 May 1814	Shobhachand Sowchand	Palla Santa Ana Feliz
15 June 1814	Jetha Karsanji	Bergantim Boa Fortuna
16 June 1815	Jetha Karsanji	Bergantim Boa Fortuna
18 May 1816	Thakarsi Jetha	Escuna N.Snra do Livramento
5 June 1816	Jetha Karsanji	Bergantim Boa Esperanca
20 June 1816	Shobhachand Sowchand	Bergantim Generozo Abreo
11 July 1816	Thakarsi Jetha	Escuna N.Snra do Livramento
27 July 1816	Shobhachand Sowchand	
12 December 1816	Jetha Karsanji	Bergantim Boa Esperanca
16 June 1818	Shobhachand Sowchand	Bergantim S.Luis
20 June 1821	Mulchand Sam[o]ji (?)	Bergantim Boas Novas
24 November 1821	Mulchand Sam[o]ji	
27 June 1822	Mulchand Sam[o]ji	
3 October 1822	Velgi Jivan	
10 November 1823	Raghunath Sam[o]ji (?)	
9 May 1825	Jetha Nana (?)	Barquinha
3 November 1825	Amirchand Rupji (?)	Bergantim Feliz Dia
20 February 1827	Musaji Velgi	
9 July 1827	Musaji Velgi	
27 August 1827	Musaji Velgi	
1 December 1828	Daud Musaji	

Source: AHU, Códices 1345, 1355, 1365, 1376

voyages there were seldom undertaken for the acquisition only of ivory tusks.[75] Rather, vessels – both Vāniyā and Portuguese – sailed from Quelimane with mixed cargoes of ivory and slaves. As one example among many, the *curveta* that returned to Mozambique Island in 1796 with approximately 10,000 kg of ivory and 150 slaves was fairly typical.[76]

[75] In the 1790s, for example, only one voyage returned to Mozambique Island with a single cargo, slaves. See AHU, Moç., Cx 80 Doc. 101, Cargo list of *pala* Aurora Feliz, 25 April 1798.

[76] The vessel also returned with gold and provisions. AHU, Moç., Cx 74 Doc. 104, Cargo list of curveta d'viagem, 26 August 1796. Almost without exception, trading vessels that sailed south to Zambesia returned to Mozambique Island with rice and other foodstuffs

Surviving cargo lists highlight the volume of ivory that was available at Quelimane for export. The *Minerva*, for instance, a *pala* owned by Laxmichand Motichand, shipped 9,400 kg of ivory in 1794 while a year later the same vessel transported a cargo more than three times this size, reflecting the fluctuating nature of the trade.[77] Another two vessels were able to ship ivory cargoes of up to 12,300 kg in 1795 and 1796, at a time when ivory was in plentiful supply. A Portuguese official noted in 1797 that so much ivory was available that "the vessel of the voyage, because of its [limited] capacity, did not know [how] to carry [the ivory tusks]".[78] Shipments from Quelimane, as happened in 1798 because of a severe winter that destroyed crops, could be affected by food shortages among ivory traders but exports appear mostly to have been consistent at least until the slave trade became dominant in the nineteenth century.[79]

Ivory exported from Quelimane by Vāniyā merchants was drawn from trading networks that stretched over long distances and that operated in areas with large elephant herds. In particular, the savannahs, marshlands and forests of the hinterland bounded by the Luangwa and Shire Valleys were elephant-rich zones exploited by ivory hunters.[80] For example, ivory was brought to Quelimane by Bisa traders who acquired supplies from the state of the eastern Lunda, and they were also suppliers of ivory to the Yao.[81]

Critically important, however, were the relationships that Vāniyā merchants maintained with *vashambadzi* who were responsible for fulfilling economic (and other, especially tax-collecting and military) activities associated with trade in the Zambesi Valley. They were drawn from among the Chikunda, associated with the *prazo* system of the valley that lay at the heart of Afro-Portuguese society in Zambesia, and were the

---

because of the perennial shortages that the latter faced. See, for example, AHU, Moç., Cx 14 Doc. 31, "Copia da Inquisição...", 31 June 1758. I should also note that Swahili merchants from the Comoros and Omani merchants from Zanzibar and elsewhere along the northern coast were known to provision Mozambique Island but supply appears to have been sporadic. This formed part of a vibrant regional foodstuffs market, for which see Edward A. Alpers, *East Africa and the Indian Ocean* (Princeton: Markus Wiener, 2007), 23–38.

[77] The vessel carried 30,551 kg of ivory. AHU, Moç., Cx 70 Doc. 69, Passenger and cargo list of pala Minerva, 27 April 1795.

[78] AHU, Moç., Cx 77 Doc. 72, Luiz Moreira d'Ignacio (?) to D. Diogo de Souza, 9 May 1797.

[79] AHU, Moç., Cx 81 Doc. 68, (?) to Francisco Guedes de Carvalho e Menezes, 26 July 1798.

[80] Isaacman and Isaacman, *Slavery and Beyond*, 85.

[81] Alpers, *Ivory and Slaves*, 178; Andrew Roberts, *A History of Zambia* (New York: Africana Publishing Company, 1976), 110–11.

region's leading traders, porters, soldiers and canoe men of the Zambesi and neighbouring rivers.[82]

Caravans led by *vashambadzi* travelled great distances into the far interior in the eighteenth century to exchange Gujarati textiles, on which their trade depended, primarily for ivory and slaves. These expeditions could last for up to eighteen months. Apart from being in charge of caravans, *vashambadzi* also "selected the sites and negotiated the transactions" involved in exchanging imported Indian cloth for African ivory. Upon returning to the *prazos* with their cargoes of tusks, Chikunda canoe men transported the trade goods by river to Quelimane; they then helped transfer these onto Vāniyā vessels which shipped them to Mozambique Island before they were, finally, transported across the ocean to India.[83] Chikunda caravans and their *vashambadzi* leaders thus helped, as noted recently by Isaacman and Isaacman, "to forge ... [a] crucial link between diverse peoples in the South-Central African interior and the Indian Ocean commercial network".[84]

Vashambadzi played an equally central role in Vāniyā ivory acquisition when the latter began establishing trading stores in Sena from the final quarter of the eighteenth century. This commercial entrepôt on the Zambesi River was located close to neighbouring *prazos* and had served as a notable regional trading centre since the seventeenth century. From there *vashambadzi* embarked on trading expeditions for ivory upriver and to surrounding areas. Chikunda men, it should be noted, were also skilled elephant hunters of the herds that could be found in the forest adjacent to the Zambesi River, but while the ivory that this activity produced was likely traded to Vāniyā stores, much of the ivory coming to Sena was being acquired either in areas to the south of the Zambesi River or in the far northern and western interior.[85]

Ivory was thus traded from Zumbo, established by the Portuguese in the early eighteenth century as a trading fair and redistributive centre for river-borne traffic from the interior of South-Central Africa that attracted traders from some distance in the western hinterland, and Tete located hundreds of miles upriver and an old trading town and departure point whose fortunes in the century became increasingly

---

[82] Detailed histories of the *prazo* system can be found in Malyn Newitt, *Portuguese Settlement on the Zambesi: Exploration, Land Tenure and Colonial Rule in East Africa* (New York: Africana Publishing Company, 1973); and Allen F. Isaacman, *Mozambique. The Africanization of a European Institution: The Zambesi Prazos, 1750–1902* (Madison: University of Wisconsin Press, 1972).

[83] Isaacman and Isaacman, *Slavery and Beyond*, 56.

[84] Both of the quotes are from *ibid.*; the paragraph is also mostly based on the book.

[85] *Ibid.*, 57.

bound up with those of Zumbo.[86] Bisa traders from the state of the eastern Lunda brought ivory periodically to Zumbo and Tete but supplies may have been modest.[87] Ivory reached Zumbo from other areas too, in particular Urenje in the 1780s where trade grew rapidly and continued possibly until the end of the century.[88] Problems affected the Zumbo *feira* (trade fair) from the mid-1790s, however, the most significant of which was the first of a number of droughts that had an adverse effect on commercial stability.[89]

Ivory supplies were taken to Tete in the early 1790s also from the southern Lunda with whom *prazo*-holders, through *vashambadzi* and Chikunda caravans, maintained commercial relations until the 1820s. Southern Lunda trade may have accounted for a significant proportion of local Zambesi trade. Tete *prazo*-holders, however, possibly did not attract the bulk of this trade, some of which went to Sena and was handled by *vashambadzi* in the service of Vāniyā merchants. While Yao traders brought some ivory to Tete in the 1780s and 1790s, supplies mainly originated from a number of sources, including among the Gwembe Tonga, Tawara and Barue, and Shona-speaking groups in Manica. Additionally, Chikunda caravans traded with the Nsenga and southern Chewa chieftaincies of central Malawi.[90]

It was the Sena–Manica trade axis, south of the Zambesi River, though, that was likely the most important commercial zone at least until the nineteenth century (Map 4.1). *Vashambadzi* engaged by Vāniyā merchants were involved in the ivory trade with the Shona-speaking kingdom of Manica, and Masekesa – an important trading *feira* that had been re-established most likely in 1719 and was under the influence of Manica chiefs – operated as a focal point for this trade and that of the Portuguese in the eighteenth century.[91]

Ivory was also brought to Sena from the Mutapa state where elephant hunting had assumed great importance both for the tusks it produced

[86] Newitt, *History of Mozambique.*
[87] Nicola Sutherland-Harris, "Zambian Trade with Zumbo in the Eighteenth Century", in Richard Gray and David Birmingham (eds.), *Pre-Colonial African Trade: Essays on Trade in Central and Eastern Africa before 1900* (London: Oxford University Press, 1970), 231–42; Roberts, *History of Zambia*, 107; Isaacman, *Mozambique*, 80.
[88] Sutherland-Harris, "Zambian Trade", 233–7.
[89] Newitt, *History of Mozambique*, 206; *idem, Portuguese Settlement*, 75–8; Gerhard Liesegang, "Technology, Space, Climate and Biology: The Incidence and Impact of Drought, Famines, Pests, Epidemics, and Wars in the History of Mozambique, c. 1515–1990", unpublished manuscript, Maputo, 1979–1993.
[90] Isaacman, *Mozambique*, 80–1; Isaacman and Isaacman, *Beyond Slavery*, 56.
[91] Isaacman, *Mozambique*, 78; Newitt, *History of Mozambique*, 211.

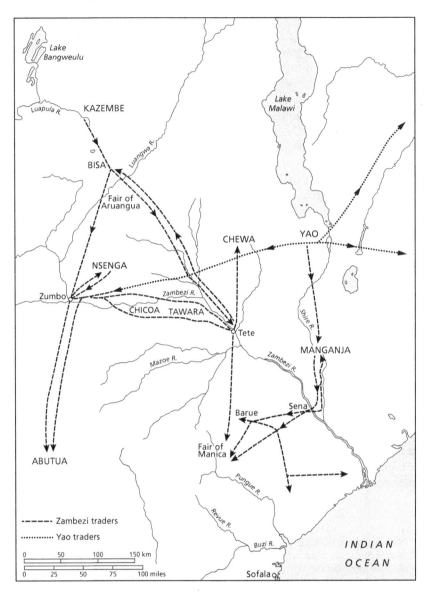

Map 4.1 Zambesi principal trade routes

and for the protein-rich meat yielded by kills.[92] The tusks were transported, as in other areas, by river canoes to Sena where cargoes were
taken by Chikunda to an assembly point on the borders of the Sena
prazos. In the eighteenth century, this was usually Sungue on the border
of Barue territory through which trading caravans had to pass to reach
Masekesa. *Vashambadzi* trading for the Vāniyā, or for the *prazo*-holders
with whom Vāniyās also maintained commercial relations, would then
bring the tusks to the trading stores that Gujarati merchants had established at Sena, before arrangements to carry the ivory to Quelimane would
be made. Despite difficulties in trading to the Masekesa fair, which
included the dangers of raids from bandits in the passage through Barue
territory, along with Portuguese bans on Chikunda or any other traders
going secretly from Sena to the fair, trade at Masekesa survived. Indeed,
by the 1790s, it appears that attempts by the Portuguese in Zambesia
to improve trade with Manica had resulted in an upswing in activity,
with Afro-Portuguese and African merchants travelling from the
Masekesa *feira* to Uteve.[93]

A period of political instability from the mid-1790s, resulting in
succession disputes, bred disorder, however, and affected the trade of
the area. Furthermore, by this time overhunting in Manica may have
begun to depopulate elephant herds. Nonetheless, this did not necessarily
end the supply of ivory from other areas in Manica beyond Masekesa
but the lack of stability made the trade challenging.[94]

These wide-ranging ivory sources in Zambesia supplied Vāniyā
merchants with significant cargoes – perhaps as much as 50–60 per cent
of all ivory exports that were carried by Vāniyā vessels to India.[95] As
significant as these were in satisfying Indian consumer demand, however,
they were not the only sources beyond northern Mozambique on which
the Vāniyā relied. Vāniyā vessels and Vāniyā-financed sailing voyages
also journeyed to Inhambane and Lourenço Marques in Delagoa Bay to
acquire ivory. The African ivory trade of the southern Mozambique
interior had intensified in the second half of the eighteenth century, with
ivory being supplied to the two ports from vast areas that by late in
the century extended to the South African high *veld* and eastern Cape

---

[92] S. I. Mudenge, *A Political History of Munhumutapa* (Harare: Zimbabwe Publishing Co.,
1986), 179.

[93] Newitt, *History of Mozambique*, 212–13; H. H. K. Bhila, *Trade and Politics in a Shona
Kingdom: The Manyika and their Portuguese and African Neighbours, 1575–1902* (Harlow:
Longman, 1982), 127, 131.

[94] Bhila, *Trade and Politics*, 34, 124–38; 165; Newitt, *History of Mozambique*, 216.

[95] Pedro Machado, "Gujarati Indian Merchant Networks in Mozambique, 1777–c. 1830",
PhD diss., University of London, 2005, 192–3.

frontier. It involved groups such as the Tonga who traded into the western interior from the coast.[96]

Vāniyā merchants had established contact with Inhambane prior to the 1770s but voyages seem to have been sporadic.[97] Inhambane had become the most important trading site south of the Zambesi Valley by the second half of the century and surpassed even Sofala. In the 1750s, possibly a high point, its ivory exports were around 49,500 kg, and though Portuguese officials complained in the 1780s that ivory was scarce, "a great deal of trade goods" continued to enter the port; and in 1791 there were reportedly "large amounts" of ivory available. It was their search for alternative sources of ivory that prompted the Vāniyā to increase their voyages to Inhambane in the 1780s. By the end of the decade, these were accounting for perhaps as much as 70 per cent of all ivory being shipped from the port, with merchants such as Harichand Laxmichand able to sail his *pala* from Inhambane with a little over 17,000 kg of ivory.[98] Despite the decline in ivory exports in the 1790s, Vāniyā merchants continued to call at Inhambane, which may have been supplying them with about 22,000 kg of ivory annually in the early nineteenth century.[99]

The success of Vāniyā merchants in securing a significant proportion of the available ivory exports from Inhambane was likely due to the relationships they had forged with Muslim traders who operated as intermediaries in organizing delivery of cargoes from the interior to the coast.[100] Its importance as an ivory export port was never firmly established in the final quarter of the eighteenth century, however, as it was eclipsed by the developing slave trade that became its dominant commercial activity by the 1820s.

Further south, though more modestly, Vāniyā voyages to Lourenço Marques and Delagoa Bay grew also in number in the final quarter of the century. Their potential as an ivory source appears to have been first exploited by European and especially English merchants who traded

---

[96] Alan [K.] Smith, "Delagoa Bay and the Trade of South-Eastern Africa", in Gray and Birmingham (eds.), *Pre-Colonial African Trade*, 282–9; Smith, "The Trade of Delagoa Bay as a Factor in Nguni Politics, 1750–1835", in Leonard Thompson (ed.), *African Societies in Southern Africa* (London: Heinemann, 1969), 171–89.

[97] For trade with Inhambane before the 1770s, see, AHU, Códices 1324 and 1329.

[98] AHU, Moç., Cx 58 Doc. 48, Cargo of 'pala de viagem' contained in "Termo de José Joaquim Ferreira...", 23 July 1789.

[99] A. Rita-Ferreira, *Presença Luso-Asiática e Mutações Culturais no Sul de Moçambique (Até c. 1900)* (Lisbon: Instituto de Investigação Científico Tropical, 1982), 115.

[100] AHU, Moç., Cx 40 Doc. 70, Monteiro José Morães Durão to Governor, 15 January 1783. Whether these were local Muslims or Swahili merchants from the northern coast of Mozambique is unclear.

there from the 1750s and 1760s.[101] Competition for the African trade of Lourenço Marques may have caused a redirection of the ivory trade away from Inhambane, especially in the 1780s. Over 50,000 kg of ivory was estimated to have been available for export already in the 1760s. This level was maintained for much of the remainder of the century as – apart from English interest and the establishment of a Portuguese trading station as part of efforts to regain some control over the Bay – Dutch and French vessels also traded at Delagoa Bay.[102] Increased commercial activity at Delagoa Bay in the 1780s and 1790s reflected the high volume of ivory that was available for export, which was possibly over 50 per cent higher than at Inhambane and may even have surpassed what was being shipped from the Zambesi Valley at this time.[103]

Although we have only fragmentary evidence, it appears that Vāniyā merchants were able to ship relatively large cargoes from Lourenço Marques. In the 1790s, in particular, Vāniyā ships managed to leave the port with over 18,500 kg of tusks.[104] Given the length of the journey from Mozambique Island and the associated risks and costs of maintaining a vessel at sea for an extended period of sailing in the Mozambique Channel, only merchants whose first voyages to the port had been successful could afford to return. In 1790, a *pala* owned jointly by Morarji Amba[v]idas and Ramji Premji voyaged south from Mozambique Island, returning in 1793. Laxmichand Motichand financed four voyages between 1795 and 1799, at times in partnership with Portuguese merchants.[105]

---

[101] David William Hedges, "Trade and Politics in Southern Mozambique and Zululand in the Eighteenth and Early Nineteenth Centuries", PhD diss., University of London, 1978, ch. V. English merchants trading at the Bay employed Indian agents from Surat and Bombay in the 1750s and 1760s. It is possible that their success had become known to some of the Vāniyā who had interests in these Indian ports, and as a result would have stimulated their interest in southern Mozambique. See Hedges, "Trade and Politics", 127–8.

[102] AHU, Códice 1366, Luis Pinto de Souza to D. Diogo de Souza, 23 September 1796; Lobato, *História do Presídio*, 408–12; "Instrucção que o Ill.mo e Ex.mo Sr. Governador...", in *RMS*, 319; Jeronimo Jose Nogueira de Andrade, "Descripção Do Estado em que ficavão os Negocios da Capitania de Mossambique nos fins de Novembro do Anno de 1789...", *Arquivo das Colonias*, I (1917), 79; Smith, "Struggle for Control"; Hedges, "Trade and Politics".

[103] Smith, "Struggle for Control", 192–3; *idem*, "The Indian Ocean Zone", in David Birmingham and Phyllis M. Martin (eds.), *History of Central Africa, Vol. 1* (Harlow: Longman, 1983), 227. Whaling was also in the final quarter of the eighteenth century beginning to draw vessels in greater number, some of whose crews traded for ivory with members of the Portuguese garrison in Lourenço Marques. See Hedges, "Trade and Politics", 148–54.

[104] AHU, Moç., Cx 72 Doc. 3 Cargo list of pala Minerva, 20 September 1795.

[105] Lobato, *História do Presídio*, 409–10.

The distance from Mozambique Island and threats of attack from French corsairs and Malagasy vessels meant that sailing south could be difficult and dangerous, resulting in vessels seldom making a direct passage to Lourenço Marques. Rather, they sailed via Inhambane so that merchants could tap an additional source of ivory and, as it grew from the late eighteenth century, trade for slaves. The itinerary of the *Minerva*, a *pala* owned by Laxmichand Motichand, is illustrative. It sailed from Mozambique Island on 14 December 1795, put in at Inhambane on 23 January 1796 for approximately three weeks, and arrived at Lourenço Marques on 20 February. It left there on 29 March, sailing directly to Mozambique Island in a journey that was completed within a month. On a second voyage, the *Minerva* left Mozambique Island towards the end of the same year on 22 December and arrived in Inhambane on 9 February 1797. After a stay of almost two months, it departed for Lourenço Marques where it arrived on 5 April. It remained in the port for another eight weeks before embarking on its return voyage, stopping once more at Inhambane between 21 June and 27 July. It arrived back at Mozambique Island on 9 August after seven and a half months.[106]

These voyages and the time spent at Inhambane allowed Vāniyā merchants to manage the complex symbiosis which the ivory and slave trades had assumed in their commerce by the final quarter of the eighteenth century. As explained previously, vessels rarely returned to Mozambique Island from voyages to southern ports with a single cargo because, as slave trading grew from the mid- to late eighteenth century in many parts of Mozambique and Vāniyā merchants participated in its expansion (detailed in Chapter 5), they married the twin commercial pursuits of purchasing and transporting ivory and slaves. *Palas* thus returned to Mozambique Island with ivory most often acquired in Lourenço Marques and slaves purchased in Inhambane.[107]

Coastal voyaging also allowed Vāniyā vessels to acquire ivory at other, lesser, sites, notably Ibo Island in the archipelago of the Querimba Islands located a short distance to the north of Mozambique Island, and at Sancul and Sangage to its south. Although Ibo became a centre of clandestine slave trafficking involving Swahili, Arab and French traders from the Mascarenes in the late 1790s, its ivory exports to Mozambique Island

---

[106] AHU, Moç., Cx 72 Doc. 3 Cargo list of pala Minerva, 20 September 1795; AHU, Moç., Cx 79 Doc. 53, "Mapa geral da escala q. fez a pala ... Minerva...", n.d. [but 1797]; Lobato, *História do Presídio*, 409–10.

[107] For example, AHU, Moç., Cx 62 Doc. 52, Governor of Inhambane to Governor of Mozambique, 1 July 1791. Lourenço Marques was not in these years a supplier of slaves, unlike other southern ports. See José Capela, *O Tráfico de Escravos nos Portos de Moçambique 1733–1904* (Porto: Edições Afrontamento, 2002), 228–9.

were not insignificant and could reach up to 10,000 kg.[108] Vāniyā such as Natthu Vissaram traded for ivory brought to Ibo from the mainland, and supplied Arab merchants with cotton cloths for their trade.[109] It is not possible to estimate how much of the ivory coming to Ibo was acquired by the Vāniyā but it appears that only a small proportion was being taken to Mozambique Island for export to India. The reason for this was that in the 1780s merchants from neighbouring Anjouan in the Comoro Islands, Kilwa, Zanzibar and as far north as Pate were sailing regularly to Ibo where they traded "all the slaves, ivory and other goods available on the island".[110] Its integration into commercial networks connected to the northern coast and its establishment by the end of the eighteenth century as a centre of illicit slave trading may have kept Ibo Island at the margins of Vāniyā activity and only contributed small amounts of ivory to their exports across the western Indian Ocean.

Sancul and Sangage added to the diversity of sources from which Vāniyā merchants acquired their ivory. They were independent sheikhdoms with which the merchants seem to have traded regularly in the second half of the eighteenth century. Portuguese settlers and the authorities at Mozambique Island had established reciprocal commercial relationships with the sheikhdom's long-standing Muslim communities based on self-interest in maintaining safe passage to the coast for the ivory caravans of the interior.[111] The proximity of these polities to Mozambique Island made sailing to them relatively easy and while details of how much ivory Vāniyā merchants acquired from them are unavailable, the sheikhs encouraged Vāniyā trade because it provided them with ready access to Gujarati textiles. But the volume of ivory that would have been available, some acquired in connection with the continued – if reduced – Yao ivory trade in the final quarter of the century, was likely to have been of a much lesser scale than was coming to Mozambique Island from Sena, Quelimane and even Inhambane and Lourenço Marques.[112]

---

[108] AHU, Códice 1324 and 1329; Anon, "Memorias da Costa d'Africa...1762", in *RMS*, 220. This may have represented only about 7 or 8 per cent of all the ivory that left the island.

[109] AHU, Moç., Cx 49 Doc. 22, Witness statements, 4 March 1785; Cx 56 Doc. 40, Antonio...(?) to de Morães, 24 December 1788.

[110] AHU, Moç., Cx 45 Doc. 22, Antonio José de Menezes to Governor, 8 March 1784; Cx 51 Doc. 43, Antonio de Mello e Castro to Joaquim da Costa Portugal, 20 June 1786; Cx 57 Doc. 31, Manoel Felipe de Menezes to Tigre, 3 April 1789; Cx 57 Doc. 34, Antonio José Tigre to Governor, 18 April 1789.

[111] Newitt, *History of Mozambique*, 186–7.

[112] Of course, we must allow that some proportion of the ivory that was acquired at the coast went undeclared by Vāniyā merchants to avoid customs payments. This "illegal" trade, however, does not appear to have been of such magnitude as to trouble the Portuguese authorities on Mozambique Island.

Vāniyā merchants exploited ivory sources beyond northern Mozambique as a response to the changing nature of the ivory trade of the Yao. Their procurement of cargoes in central and southern Mozambique brought them closer to large-scale elephant stocks and particularly in Zambesia allowed them to consolidate relationships with *vashambadzi* and their caravans of highly skilled Chikunda elephant hunters. These alternative and rich sources of ivory enabled the Vāniyā to respond to the intensification of Indian consumer demand among the populations of Kathiawar and beyond as the region underwent a significant commercial efflorescence from the middle of the eighteenth century. The large volumes of tusks transported across the ocean from Mozambique supplied vibrant markets in which ivory was utilized in a variety of ways by elites and non-elites. Clearly, ivory trading was central to Vāniyā business interests in Mozambique, made possible by their control over cloth procurement, its shipment and sale, and remained the focus throughout their commercial involvement in the territory.

Changing realities

While the second half of the eighteenth century had seen Vāniyā ivory exports reach unprecedented heights, increasingly from the first decade or so of the nineteenth century the growth of slave trading in Mozambique began to encroach upon the ivory trade and disrupted its functioning, creating difficulties for both the Vāniyā and the elephant hunters. Although they were able to respond to changing economic circumstances by continuing to ship cotton cloths from Gujarat in exchange for Spanish silver dollars brought to Mozambique by French, Brazilian and *Rioplatense* slavers – examined in the next chapter – the traditional branch of the commercial economy of Vāniyā merchants served by the ivory trade was undermined by this development.

Thus shipments of Vāniyā ivory cargoes from Mozambique began to drop markedly. For instance, in some years, Vāniyā merchant vessels arrived in Diu with no more than 23,000 kg of tusks.[113] The gradual decline in the Vāniyā ivory trade is reflected, further, in the reduction of the number of voyages (compared to the late eighteenth century) that merchants undertook to the ports of central and southern Mozambique. Those to Quelimane, for example, dropped by around 22 per cent in the first decade of the nineteenth century. This was due largely to the dangers posed by French privateers to Vāniyā and other shipping in the

---

[113] HAG, CD 995–1012; AD 4952–4969.

Mozambique Channel. Their destruction of the Portuguese Factory at Lourenço Marques and capture of vessels served as timely reminders of the realities of this danger.

There were other challenges to acquiring ivory at ports to the south of Mozambique Island, namely the increases introduced by the Portuguese authorities to customs duties on re-exports from Mozambique Island. In the years between 1787 and 1801, re-export duties to Zambesia had been reduced from 40 to 30 per cent, and in 1793 were brought down further to 10 per cent. However, in a decision lamented by Vāniyā and Portuguese merchants alike because it added considerably to the cost of commerce with Quelimane and other southern ports, they were raised once again to 30 per cent in 1801 as the state sought greater income from coastal trade.[114] This decision must be seen within a larger context where the Portuguese imperial state had used customs duties from the second half of the eighteenth century as a fiscal strategy to stimulate trade, and thus raise revenue, between and among the ports of Mozambique and territories in India, a development discussed in Chapter 1.[115] This meant that, even as slave trading was on the rise, ivory commerce continued to generate significant customs income for the Portuguese state – in 1806 and again in 1812 income from slave and ivory exports were roughly the same. Customs payments from ivory remained consistent over these years, suggesting that the trade continued to be vital for the commercial economy of Mozambique.[116]

But the level of customs duties increased the cost of trade from the island and contributed towards raising the official price of ivory. While the price of large ivory (*marfim grosso*) rose in 1787 from 60 *cruzados* to 80 *cruzados* per *arroba* (a standard Portuguese measure of weight), in 1809 African traders were demanding 104–128 *cruzados* for the best-quality tusks. In response, the official Portuguese valuation was raised to 100 *cruzados* per *arroba* in 1810. If the implication was that Mozambique was gradually pricing itself out of the Indian ivory market, unchanged duties from the 1790s on trade between Mozambique and Diu and Daman, and the likely existence of contraband exports from southern ports that

[114] AHU, Moç., Cx. 90 Doc. 47, Izidro d'Almeida Souza e Sa to D. Rodrigo de Souza Coutinho, 25 November 1801.
[115] Lobato, *História do Presídio*, 291–8, 308–13, 397–402; Alpers, *Ivory and Slaves*, 173–4.
[116] AHU, Moç., Cx. 116 Doc. 31, "Mappa do Rendimento d'Alfandega da Capital de Moçambique de 1805 e de Janeiro-Outubro de 1806, 8 November 1806"; Cx 140 Doc. 8, "Rendimento da Alfandega de Monsambique...", 10 January 1812; Mabel V. Jackson Haight, *European Powers and South-East Africa: A Study of International Relations on the South-East Coast of Africa, 1796–1856* (London: Routledge, 1967), 156–7.

were not declared at Mozambique Island, contributed towards Vāniyā merchants being able to sustain their trade into the 1820s and 1830s.[117]

Yet, we should be careful not to overstate the impact of the threat of French privateers and customs duties on ivory trading. Vāniyā merchants continued to sail to Quelimane, which remained the most important supplier of ivory in Mozambique even as it began to develop into a notable slave trading port.[118] While noting that increasing slaving was proving disruptive to the ivory trade and other commerce – anticipating its destructive force in writing that "[T]his commerce in slaves in the Rivers of Sena is, in my opinion, one of the causes of the decadence of this colony" – the governor of Tete, Villas Boas Truão, produced a report on the economy of Zambesia in 1806 in which he commented favourably nonetheless on the availability of ivory "which is the main branch of commerce because of the great value it has in the north of Asia [India]". Boas Truão estimated exports at a little over 64,000 kg and valued them at twice the export value of slaves.[119] Vāniyā vessels were thus able to sail from Quelimane to Mozambique Island in the first five years of the century with a total of more than 70,000 kg of ivory.[120] But that none of the vessels left Quelimane without slaves was both an unmistakable indication of the changing nature of the trade and of how merchants responded by integrating their traditional trade with a burgeoning one in human cargoes.

Shipping lists for other southern ports reveal also, amid the flux of the changing commercial environment, the continued focus of Vāniyā investment in ivory procurement. In Inhambane, for example, emerging by the early nineteenth century as another important slaving port, vessels were able to export between 16,000 and 25,000 kg of ivory, and in 1803 a total of almost 50,000 kg of tusks was shipped north to Mozambique Island.[121] In Lourenço Marques, up to 10,000 kg was traded in 1804

[117] The different types of ivory and how they were weighed and evaluated in Mozambique is discussed in Alpers, *Ivory and Slaves*, 118–19; 175. Sheriff, *Slaves, Spice & Ivory*, 81; AHU, Códice 1366, de Souza to Monteiro, 27 August 1796; HAG, CD 998, de Souza to Rebelo do Amaral, 25 November 1784.

[118] José Capela, *O Escravismo Colonial Em Moçambique* (Porto: Edições Afrontamento, 1993), 148.

[119] "Extracto do Plano para um regimento ou nova constituição economica e politica da Capitania de Rios de Senna...", *Annaes do Conselho Ultramarino* (parte não official), Serie I (1854–8), 407–8; Antonio Norberto de Barbosa de Villas Boas Truão, *Estatistica da Capitania dos Rios de Senna do Anno de 1806* (Lisbon: Imprensa Nacional, 1889), 14, 16.

[120] AHU, Moç., Cx 94 Doc. 3, Cargo list of pala Feliz Costa, 9 August 1802; Cx 97 Doc. 25, Cargo list of pala Feliz Costa, 4 August 1803; Cx 108 Doc. 81, Cargo list of Brig Maria, 3 September 1804.

[121] AHU, Moç., Cx 96 Doc. 59, Cargo list of Goleta Maria, 11 April 1802; Cx 97 Doc. 25, Cargo list of Brig d'viagem S. Antonio Deligente, 28 February 1803; Cargo list of Brig

and 1805. Supplies of ivory appear to have been able to meet demand in Delagoa Bay but only if merchants were willing to pay the prices demanded for cargoes by African traders.[122]

The continued activity of Vāniyā vessels at smaller ports located close to Mozambique Island in these years, either on or near Macuana such as Quitangonha, Mossuril, Mojincual, Motomonho and Mokambo, continued to supply them with additional sources of ivory. Like Sancul and Sangage discussed previously, these were under only nominal Portuguese control, being run effectively by independent Muslim rulers. Vāniyās had traded to these ports throughout the eighteenth century, in part because they could make commercial arrangements away from the glare of the Portuguese administration on Mozambique Island. They were also places to obtain foodstuffs for their own consumption or to sell on the island-capital. The relationships that Vāniyā merchants maintained with these coastal polities remained useful for the supply of ivory and for the trade in Gujarati cloths. In 1801, for example, over 12,000 kg of ivory was brought to Mozambique Island from Mokambo alone.[123]

Yet, despite a brief revival of the ivory trade in Macuana in the 1820s,[124] overwhelmingly it continued to be the case that shipments of tusks from central and southern ports, especially Quelimane but also Inhambane and Lourenço Marques, sustained Vāniyā trade up to the 1830s.[125] These supplies were declining steadily but vessels were able nonetheless to sail from Quelimane with cargoes of around 15,000–23,000 kg in the late 1810s and early 1820s, while in some years Inhambane could export up to 12,500 kg of ivory. For most years, however, these did not rise above 10,000 kg, a situation likely to have been similar in Lourenço Marques.[126]

Maria (12,889 kg), 26 February 1803; Cargo list of Goleta Maria (14,872 kg), 26 February 1803; Cx 100 Doc. 87, Joze Joaquim Felipe Carminho to Izidro de Almeida Souza e Sa, 19 July 1803 in which information is provided that the *bergantim* belonging to Velji Tairsi carried 21,068 kg. The combined total of these shipments thus amounted to 48,829 kg.

[122] AHU, Moç., Cx 107 Doc. 116, Cargo list..., 23 August 1804; Cx 112 Doc. 8, Cargo of barco de viagem, 17 June 1805; Smith, "Struggle for Control", 236.

[123] AHU, Moç., Cx 94 Doc. 50, Passport request of Manakchand Premji, ant. 24 September 1802; Cx. 56 Doc. 40, Devji Karsanji et al. to Governor, 6 October 1788.

[124] Alpers, *Ivory and Slaves*, 210.

[125] The number of Vāniyā voyages to Quelimane were consistent at around 25 to 26 in number between 1801 and 1820, while those to Inhambane almost doubled over the same period. See Machado, "Gujarati Indian Merchant Networks in Mozambique, 1777-c. 1830", Table 7.

[126] AHU, Moç., Cx 153 Doc. 9, "Relação da carga...", 13 April 1817; Cx 154 Doc. 62, "Relação de marfim...", 22 August 1817; Cx 158 Doc. 2, "Carga do Brigue...", 10 June 1818; Cx 169 Doc. 122, "Manifesto da Escuna São João Baptista", 23 June 1820; Doc. 18, "Manifesto da Escuna S. João Baptista", 11 August 1820; Cx 187 Doc. 23, Cargo list of N. Senhora do Monte, 3 August 1822; Doc. 109, Souza e Sa to Baptista Monteiro, 9

If these nineteenth-century volumes were modest compared to what was shipped to India in the late eighteenth century, the total amount of ivory taken across the ocean was nonetheless impressive – as I indicated earlier in the chapter, between the turn of the century and the early 1830s, by which time the trade had declined precipitously, Diu and Daman merchants still managed to import tusks from Mozambique totaling over 1,400,000 kg – a striking figure.

That this was possible in increasingly challenging circumstances may have been due also to occasional Vāniyā voyages to the Swahili coast. The growing importance of the ivory trade there was attracting greater numbers of merchants to East Africa, particularly from Mandvi and Muscat whose economic orientation was turning towards Zanzibar.[127] The redirection of the Yao ivory trade to Kilwa had begun taking place in the late eighteenth century, and from the 1810s an ascendant Zanzibar was establishing a prominent position as a coastal entrepôt. Vāniyā vessels had made stops at Zanzibar from as early as 1784 en route to Mozambique Island, with the vagaries of the monsoon winds at times making a stop necessary to avoid being blown off course or, worse yet, shipwrecked. Some merchants, such as Jhaver Khushal who in 1786 sent a vessel to Zanzibar, demonstrated an interest in exploring the possibilities offered by the northern coast. For the following two decades, Zanzibar was an occasional port of call for Vāniyās on their voyages to or from India.[128]

Once Zanzibar had begun to cement its place as a coastal commercial centre from the 1820s, however, Vāniyā made more regular voyages there.[129] Although there is no evidence of how much ivory they may have been able to purchase, it is reasonable to assume that some of the cargoes that arrived in Diu and Daman, especially in the 1820s, contained

September 1822; Cx 132 Doc. 31, Joze Joaquim Felipe Caminha to Governor, 17 April 1810; Cx 133 Doc. 28, same to same, 27 July 1810; Cx 137 Doc. 77, Caetano J.ᵉ Serejo de Carvalho to Governor, 25 August 1811; Cx 140 Doc. 33, Cargo list of brig S. Antonio Triunfo d'Africa, 2 April 1812; Cx 151 Doc. 13, Cargo list of brig Aliança, 12 July 1816; Cx 158 Doc. 104, Cargo list of brig Bom Dezejo, 10 July 1818; Doc. 115, Cargo list of sumaca Challassa, 14 July 1818; Doc. 133, "Manifesto da carga da escuna Flor d'Mossambique", 19 July 1818.

[127] For further details see Sheriff, *Slaves, Spices & Ivory*; Rheda Bhacker, *Trade and Empire*.

[128] HAG, CDm 1056, da Costa to Viceroy, 12 June 1784; CDm 1057, D. Christovão Perreira de Castro to Viceroy, 12 February 1786; CD 1002, Luis Caetano de Calvoz (?) Coelho e França to Governor, 22 October 1792; CD 1003, Felix José Tin.ca (?) da Gouveia (?) to Governor, 8 February 1805; CDm 1065, Castro e Almeida to Viceroy, 13 August 1817; CDm 1061, Mourão Palha to Governor, 20 August 1802; AHU, Códice 1376, Passport for Pala N. Senhora da Penha de França, 31 March 1813.

[129] Between 1821 and 1830, they made 13 voyages to Zanzibar. See AHU, Códices 1345, 1355, 1365, 1376; Alexandre Lobato, *História do Presídio de Lourenço Marques, 1787–1799*, 2 vols. (Lisbon: Tipografia Minerva, 1960), II, 409–10.

tusks that had been acquired in Zanzibar and possibly elsewhere along the coast. Intensifying competition from Kutchi Bhātiyā merchants with connections to Mandvi and Muscat for African ivory and textile markets, however, likely made it difficult for Vāniyā merchants to establish themselves in the coastal commerce of the northern Swahili coast.

Unmistakably, though, the growth and establishment of slave trading in Mozambique as a significant component of its commercial economy was by the 1820s having a profound effect on the ivory trade. At the end of the decade, vessels returning to Mozambique Island from Quelimane carried slaves and no ivory.[130] The disparity that had developed in the nineteenth century between Quelimane's two main exports is perhaps most starkly captured when comparing their relative volume and value in 1806 and 1821. In the report produced by Boas Truão discussed earlier, ivory exports were valued at 525,000 *cruzados*, while slave exports were given as 192,920 *cruzados*. By contrast, a report by Francisco Alves Barbosa in 1821 put ivory exports at 35 per cent less than those in 1806 and valued them at approximately 184,500 *cruzados*; significantly, he estimated exports of slaves at over 5,000 and valued at 655,000 *cruzados*.[131]

Similarly, in Inhambane, by the end of 1818 Portuguese officials complained about the "unsettled" state of the ivory trade, with "little ivory" available for export.[132] Ivory exports from Lourenço Marques were almost non-existent by the end of the 1820s and early 1830s, as slaving had become endemic in the area.[133] It disrupted ivory routes and the rise in widespread raiding for slaves caused growing social and economic dislocation. This was especially devastating after the mid-1820s for much of southern Mozambique. Additionally, severe drought – a recurring environmental problem from the 1790s – affected much of the Mozambique interior and contributed to the unsettled conditions.[134] Slaving both exacerbated these conditions and took advantage of them

---

[130] *DAM*, II, 808.

[131] Boas Truão, *Estatistica*, 14–16; BA, 54-XIII-3 (3), Francisco Alves Barbosa, "Analyse Estatistica", 30 December 1821.

[132] AHU, Moç., Cx 158 Doc. 100, Luis Correa Monteiro de Mattos to Joze Francisco de Paula Cavalcanti de Albuquerque, 9 July 1818.

[133] For example, the *escuna Vitoria* shipped a desultory 114 tusks to Mozambique Island in 1830. See *DAM*, II, 808.

[134] Liesegang, "Technology, Space, Climate and Biology"; Smith, "Struggle for Control"; *idem*, "Indian Ocean Zone"; Hedges, "Trade and Politics"; M. D. D. Newitt, "Drought in Mozambique 1823–1831", *Journal of Southern African Studies*, 15 (1988), 15–35; *idem*, *History of Mozambique*, 253–64; Elizabeth A. Eldredge, "Delagoa Bay and the Hinterland in the Early Nineteenth Century: Politics, Trade, Slaves, and Slave Raiding", in Eldredge and Fred Morton (eds.), *Slavery in South Africa: Captive Labor on the Dutch Frontier* (Boulder: Westview Press, 1994), 127–65.

as populations may have allowed themselves to become enslaved as an alternative to dying of hunger.[135]

In this dramatically changing environment, Vāniyā merchants expressed concern that "less ivory" was being supplied to the coast, and in the 1820s lamented the "losses" they were suffering as a result of the expansion of the slave trade. This expansion, as I show in the next chapter, had drawn Vāniyā merchants into the trade in human cargoes from the 1770s and 1780s as a response to changing economic realities. They shipped an increased – if modest – number of African slaves to Diu and Daman and became financiers of a commerce from which they benefitted, particularly through the acquisition of Spanish silver currency that slavers brought to the coast for their purchases of human cargoes. In other words, Vāniyā merchants were able to adapt successfully to the growing slave trade of Mozambique as it became, by the 1820s and 1830s, central to the Mozambique economy. Indeed, they facilitated its growth by maintaining their role as the pre-eminent suppliers of cotton textiles for which slaves were purchased in the African interior. Yet, despite their involvement in the slave trade, Vāniyā never redirected their commercial investments away from ivory but may not have anticipated the effects that raiding and trading in slaves would have on supply areas and on the routes along which tusks were transported to the coast.

The desultory state of the Vāniyā ivory trade by the early 1830s was reflected clearly in imports at Diu. In 1833, the volume of ivory arriving at the island had dropped by 62 per cent and a year later was down a further 15 per cent. They were much reduced by the end of the decade. While we lack evidence for Daman, it is unlikely that the picture would have been any different. After almost a century dominating the procurement and shipment of thousands of ivory tusks, Vāniyā merchants were facing the end of one of eighteenth- and nineteenth-century Mozambique's premier trades and a cornerstone of their African and Indian commerce.

Conclusion

In responding to robust Indian consumer demand in the eighteenth and nineteenth centuries, Vāniyā merchants financed the procurement of very

---

[135] The acute changes wrought by the slave trade on Mozambique in the nineteenth century are examined in Newitt, *Portuguese Settlement*, ch. 13; *idem*, *History of Mozambique*, ch. 11; Isaacman, *Mozambique*, ch. 8; Isaacman and Isaacman, *Slavery and Beyond*; Capela, *Tráfico de Escravos*, 273–84; Leroy Vail and Landeg White, *Capitalism and Colonialism in Mozambique: A Study of Quelimane District* (Minneapolis: University of Minnesota Press, 1980), ch. 1

large ivory cargoes. Although generally associated with East Africa and the far interiors of the Swahili coast of modern Tanzania and Kenya in the second half of the nineteenth century, this trade reveals that large-scale and intense exploitation of elephant herds was already a feature of African commerce from the 1750s and 1760s. This may have resulted in the killing of as many as 26,000–31,000 elephants in areas east of Lake Nyasa, hunting grounds north and south of the Zambesi River and the far southern interior of Inhambane and Lourenço Marques.[136]

But if the dramatic reduction in Vāniyā ivory cargoes in the 1830s reflected a waning ivory trade and signalled effectively the end of Vāniyā involvement in it, it did not represent an end to the trade in Mozambique. Along with other areas in nineteenth-century East Africa, ivory trading returned to dominate Mozambique's regional economy from the 1850s as slave trading there faced suppresionist and abolitionist pressures in the second half of the nineteenth century. The ivory "frontier" would then be pushed further inland increasingly once herds became exhausted and far interior sources were exploited to meet rising demand. This time, however, in addition to traditional markets, the ivory trade was driven by a different consumer demand emanating from an industrializing Europe and America, and their newly developing markets. Rather than involving Vāniyā merchants as key players in its procurement and shipment, though, it was Kutchi Bhātiyā along with other Kathiawar merchants such as Muslim Daudi Bohras who emerged as the renewed ivory trade's primary financiers in Africa. Their control over cloth brought to the African coast from Mandvi continued a familiar pattern of commercial exchange but undermined Vāniyā imports from Jambusar, as I discussed in the previous chapter. This did not mean the end of Vāniyā participation in the Indian Ocean, for they shifted their trade and commercial interests to another area of this aquatic inter-regional arena that they had left in the early eighteenth century, the Red Sea, where they would once again become prominent traders in ivory.

---

[136] This calculation can only be regarded as a rough estimate, derived from the overall volumes of ivory traded from Mozambique that were presented throughout the chapter. As a guide to arriving at this estimate of the number of elephants killed between the 1750s and the 1830s, I have taken the average weight of a tusk as 60 kg, as suggested by the University of Michigan's Museum of Zoology (animaldiversity.ummz.edu/accounts/Loxodonta_africana/). It is worth noting here that elephant herds in the interior of Mozambique would not be exhausted until much later in the nineteenth century.

5 Africa in India

In late 1805 or early in 1806, Shobhachand Sowchand took possession of a brig, the *General Izidro*. Already an owner of two large vessels by this time, the 350 tonne *Conquistado* and a *pala* of 200 tonnes, this prominent Gujarati merchant purchased the *General Izidro* from Joaquim do Rosario Monteiro, a notable Portuguese slave merchant with whom he had maintained a business relationship since the mid-1790s. The transaction both reflected their shared commercial involvement and made clear Shobhachand's commitment to the expanding trade in African slaves.

The development of a significant slave trade in Mozambique from the middle of the eighteenth century, into which Shobhachand entered, owed its initial growth to French sugar planters who sought to satisfy rising demands for servile labour in the Mascarene islands of Mauritius and Réunion. Mozambique slaves were also traded to Madagascar to work in the highlands of the Merina empire or – together with Malagasy slaves – were resold in places along the coast to slavers with interests in the Mascarene trade or to Swahili merchants for the markets of the Arabian Peninsula and Persian Gulf. Furthermore, slaves were shipped to Cape Town for use by the Dutch and English charter companies and their colonists, and taken to South and Southeast Asia to be employed in various domestic capacities and throughout coastal trading factories. Reaching into the Atlantic in the nineteenth century, Brazilian merchants from Bahia and especially Rio de Janeiro, who also maintained trading relationships with slavers from Montevideo and the Río de la Plata, sent slaving ships to the Southeast African coast of Mozambique in search of alternative labour supplies as their long-standing sources in West Central Africa were subjected to increasing British anti-slave trade surveillance.

Slave trading from Mozambique, for which Shobhachand had purchased the *General Izidro*, had thus become by the end of the eighteenth century not only part of a regional western Indian Ocean slaving economy but also connected to a broader trans-oceanic and global exchange of chattel labour.[1] Such was the expansion in African slave trading that by the second decade of the nineteenth century slaves were a mainstay of the export economy of northern Mozambique. This growth in human trafficking had an impact on the trade in ivory, disrupting routes along which tusks were transported to the coast but it did not entirely displace ivory as an export, largely because alternative source areas were developed in the central and southern regions of Mozambique. Gujarati merchants remained invested throughout this period, therefore, in acquiring ivory supplies to satisfy the robust South Asian demand that continued to exist for much of the nineteenth century, as we saw in Chapter 4. Still, as the trade in African slaves expanded, Vāniyā merchants increasingly participated in it in a variety of ways, with Shobhachand epitomizing the scale of Gujarati involvement as a shipper of slaves and supplier of some of the vessels used by Portuguese, French and Brazilian slavers along the coast of Mozambique and throughout the Mozambique Channel.

Vāniyā merchants had owned slaves on Mozambique Island and on the Macuana mainland from the first quarter of the eighteenth century, where they laboured as sailors and ship hands and were used to load and unload ship cargoes. Once they were allowed to own and openly trade in slaves in 1746 – in a context of growing regional slave trading – no Vāniyā ship sailed from the Mozambique coast for Diu or Daman from mid-century without a cargo of slaves for the markets of western India.

Most importantly, however, Shobhachand and other Vāniyā extended credit to slave merchants in the form of cotton cloths. The central place of Gujarati textiles in the logics of material exchange in Mozambique – they remained the "currency that is accepted in ports" – meant that, as the procurers and suppliers of these cottons, most Gujarati merchants became indirectly involved in underwriting the expansion of slaving. Any merchant who arrived on the coast of Mozambique to trade for slaves either bought trade cloths from Vāniyā merchants or from Portuguese officials and merchants invested in the trade who had themselves at some point purchased textiles from Gujarati merchants. Sustained African demand for Indian cottons thus likely underpinned the slave extraction process in the region and fuelled the advantage that Gujarati merchant networks enjoyed over European and African competitors.[2]

---

[1] Richard B. Allen, "Satisfying the 'Want for Labouring People': European Slave Trading in the Indian Ocean, 1500–1850", *Journal of World History*, 21, 1 (2010), 45–73.

[2] I draw here on an insight gained from Richard Eaton's discussion of the fifteenth- and sixteenth-century slave trade from Ethiopia to western India, in "The Rise and Fall of Military Slavery in the Deccan, 1450–1650", in Indrani Chatterjee and Eaton (eds.), *Slavery & South Asian History* (Bloomington: Indiana University Press, 2006), 118–19.

Vāniyā also invested actively in the shipment of slave cargoes for regional destinations such as the Mascarenes and the Cape, the southern Atlantic from the late eighteenth century, and particularly the markets of Kathiawar, Kutch and western India. They became firmly entrenched, therefore, in the logics of slave demand that were tied to discrete but interrelated markets: the Mascarenes, Madagascar, the Cape, Brazil and the Río de la Plata, and western India.

Slave merchants financed their purchases of Gujarati textiles with imports of Spanish silver dollars, either *piastres* or *patacas*.[3] These first began arriving on the African coast in large quantities from Atlantic sources in the 1760s and 1770s, primarily aboard French slave vessels and later also on Brazilian slavers from Bahia and Rio de Janeiro. The exchange of cloth for silver specie was an attractive proposition for Vāniyā merchants because of the existence of a robust silver market in Gujarat in which the bankers from whom merchants received credit for their local and trans-oceanic trade were active participants. Silver could be utilized by merchants to secure credit arrangements and guarantee favourable terms for *hundis*, which were critical to the organization of Gujarati commerce (discussed earlier in the book). Silver imports were thus important in financing the mechanisms that undergirded the commercial economy of Gujarati merchants both in the subcontinent and in the wider Indian Ocean. Their success in acquiring large quantities of silver coin was a function of their success in the cloth trade.

India had long been an importer of precious metals and from the seventeenth century European companies exchanged sizeable quantities of "bullion for goods".[4] In this way, the exchange of cottons along the Mozambique coast for silver *piastres* conformed to an older pattern of exchange in South Asia and the Indian Ocean. What was different, however, was that this silver was shipped to the subcontinent from Africa. The place of Africa as a notable source of silver for South Asia has been largely overlooked because scholars have concentrated on imports from the Levant, Europe or the Middle East, or focused on the Chinese silver market.[5] The imperatives of commercial exchange in Mozambique and

---

[3] *Piastres* and *patacas* were the French and Portuguese names respectively for the Spanish dollar that served as a basic trading currency in the western Indian Ocean. Its purpose was thus similar to that of the Maria Theresa dollar that would become prominent from the 1830s and 1840s.

[4] Om Prakash, "Bullion for Goods: International Trade and the Economy of Early Eighteenth-Century Bengal", *Indian Economic and Social History Review*, 13 (1976), 159–87.

[5] See, for example, Richard von Glahn, *Fountain of Fortune: Money and Monetary Policy in China, 1000–1700* (Berkeley: University of California Press, 1996); Dennis O. Flynn and Arturo Giráldez, "Born with a 'Silver Spoon': The Origin of World Trade", *Journal of World History*, 6, 2 (1995), 201–21.

the dynamics of the slave trade together propelled the arrival on the African coast of significant cargoes of silver *piastres* in the eighteenth and nineteenth centuries.

Vāniyā participation in the extensive and far-reaching African slave trade, as I have already suggested, resulted also in their shipping slaves to Kathiawar and the markets of Gujarat and northwestern India. As the economy of Mozambique became increasingly focused on slave trading from the middle of the eighteenth century, the existence of African slave markets in India offered Gujarati merchants further possibilities for broadening the scale of their involvement in slave trading in Africa and in the transport of slaves across the western Indian Ocean. The arrival of African slaves in India co-existed, and overlapped, with internal networks of exchange in unfree South Asian labour tied to agricultural production, family and kinship reproduction and military service, and with a broader Indian Ocean trade in Indian and other "Asian" slaves.[6] This reflected the complex and multidirectional nature of slave trading in the ocean.[7] If scholarly neglect within African diaspora studies of the Asian dimension of this dispersal of African peoples is no longer quite as pronounced as it once was, our knowledge of various aspects of the dynamics of trafficking in chattel labour in this part of the world remains far from complete.[8] In examining the involvement of Gujarati merchants both in providing

---

[6] Sanjay Subrahmanyam, "Notas sobre a mão-de-obra na India pre-colonial (seculos XVI a XVIII)", in Eduardo França Paiva and Carla Maria Junho Anastasia (eds.), *O Trabalho Mestiço: Maneiras de Pensar e Formas de Viver-Seculos XVI a XIX* (São Paulo: Annablume, 2002), 463–79; Indrani Chatterjee, *Gender, Slavery and Law in Colonial India* (New Delhi: Oxford University Press, 1999); *idem*, "Colouring Subalternity: Slaves, Concubines and Social Orphans in Early Colonial India", in Gautam Bhadra, Gyan Prakash and Susie Tharu (eds.), *Subaltern Studies X* (New Delhi: Oxford University Press, 1999), 49–97; Chatterjee and Eaton, *Slavery & South Asian History*.

[7] The precise nature of the relationship between these trades of "unfreedom" is still poorly understood and articulated but see, for example, Richard B. Allen, "'Carrying Away the Unfortunate': The Exportation of Slaves from India during the Late Eighteenth Century", in Jacques Weber (ed.), *Le Monde créole: Peuplement, sociétés et condition humaine XVIIᵉ-Xxᵉ siècles* (Paris: Les Indes Savantes, 2005), 285–98; Marina Carter, "Slavery and Unfree Labour in the Indian Ocean", *History Compass*, 4, 5 (2006), 800–13; Gwyn Campbell, "Slavery and the Trans-Indian Ocean World Slave Trade: A Historical Outline", in Himanshu Prabha Ray and Edward A. Alpers (eds.), *Cross Currents and Community Networks: The History of the Indian Ocean World* (New Delhi: Oxford University Press, 2007), 286–305; and *idem*, "Slave Trades and the Indian Ocean World", in John C. Hawley (ed.), *India in Africa/Africa in India: Indian Ocean Cosmopolitanisms* (Bloomington: Indiana University Press, 2008), 17–51 for suggestive ways forward.

[8] But see, for example, the following works for useful discussions of the challenges and possibilities for studying African slavery and diaspora in the Indian Ocean: Helene Basu, "The Siddi and the Cult of Bava Gor in Gujarat", *Journal of the Indian Anthropological Society*, 28 (1993), 289–300; R. R. S. Chauhan, *Africans in India: From Slavery to Royalty* (New Delhi: Asian Publication Services 1995); Shanti Sadiq Ali, *African Dispersal in the*

finance and credit in an expanding trade in African slaves and in supplying slaves to Indian markets, this chapter broadens our understanding of one small but important branch of this larger history.

The East African and Mozambique slave trade and the western Indian Ocean

The trade in slaves from Mozambique and East Africa, in which Vāniyā participated, extended back centuries and into the trading economies of numerous groups throughout the Indian Ocean. Africans – both enslaved and free – could be found in many parts of the ocean, and by the fourteenth and fifteenth centuries CE were increasingly working and living in the major ports of the Indian Ocean's western reaches. Some laboured as sailors on merchant vessels while other slaves settled permanently in littoral communities to work in a range of occupations, including in states' military-administrative structures and in domestic servitude.[9]

Deccan (New Delhi: Orient Longman, 1996); Emmanuel Akyeampong, "Africans in the Diaspora: The Diaspora and Africa", *African Affairs, Centenary Issue: A Hundred Years of Africa*, 99 (2000), 183–215; Edward A. Alpers, "The African Diaspora in the Northwest Indian Ocean: Reconsideration of an Old Problem, New Directions for Research", *Comparative Studies of South Asia, Africa and the Middle East*, 17, 2 (1997), 62–81; *idem*, "Recollecting Africa: Diasporic Memory in the Indian Ocean World", *African Studies Review, Special Issue: Africa's Diaspora*, 43, 1 (2000), 83–99; *idem*, "The African Diaspora in the Indian Ocean: A Comparative Perspective", in Shihan de S. Jayasuriya and Richard Pankhurst (eds.), *The African Diaspora in the Indian Ocean* (Trenton, NJ: Africa World Press, 2003), 19–50; Gary Leupp, "Africans in Portuguese Asia, 1510–ca. 1800: The Black Presence in Goa, Macao, and Nagasaki", paper presented at Conference *Blacks and Asians: Encounters in Time and Space*, Boston University, 12–14 April 2002; Gwyn Campbell, (ed.), *The Structure of Slavery in Indian Ocean African and Asia* (London: Frank Cass and Routledge, 2004); Amy Catlin-Jairazbhoy and Edward A. Alpers (eds.), *Sidis and Scholars: Essays on African Indians* (Delhi: Rainbow Publishers, and Trenton, NJ: Red Sea Press, 2004); Shihan de Silva Jayasuriya and Jean-Pierre Angenot (eds.), *Uncovering the History of Africans in Asia* (Boston: Brill, 2008).

[9] For details of the widespread markets to which African slaves were sent in these early periods, see for instance, Gwyn Campbell, "African Diaspora in Asia", in Melvin Ember *et al.* (eds.), *Encyclopedia of Diasporas*, vol. 1 (New York: Springer, 2004); Joseph C. Harris, *The African Presence in Asia: Consequence of the East African Slave Trade* (Evanston: Northwestern University Press, 1971); Walter Raunig, "Yemen and Ethiopia – Ancient Cultural Links between two Neighbouring Countries on the Red Sea", in Werner Daum (ed.), *Yemen: 3000 Years of Art and Civilisation in Arabia Felix* (Frankfurt: Umschau-Verlag, 1987), 409–18; Albert Hourani, *A History of the Arab Peoples* (Cambridge, MA: Belknap Press of Harvard University Press 1991), 117; Bernard Lewis, *Race and Slavery in the Middle East: An Historical Enquiry* (New York: Oxford University Press, 1990). See also R. B. Serjeant, *Studies in Arabian History and Civilisation* (London: Variorum, 1981); *idem*, "Some Observations on African Slaves in Arabia", paper presented at the *Workshop on the Long-Distance Trade in Slaves across the Indian Ocean and the Red Sea in the 19th Century*, School of Oriental and African Studies, University of London, 17–19 December 1987; *idem*, *Society and Trade in South Arabia* (Aldershot: Variorum, 1996). Ehud R. Toledano, *Slavery and Abolition in the Ottoman Middle East* (Seattle: University of Washington Press, 1998), 7.

South Asian merchants – from Sind in northwestern India who were active in East African commerce – may by this time have become involved in the coastal slave trade but the extent of their participation is unclear.[10]

What is clear is that African slaves were used extensively in India. In the first half of the fourteenth century, "Abyssinian" slaves from the highlands of Ethiopia were present from North India to Ceylon, and there is evidence of African slaves – "Habshīs" – being used in Bengal in military service in the third quarter of the fifteenth century and as eunuchs.[11] We encounter African captives also on the Deccan plateau in central India and in Gujarat where they served prominently in the armies of domestic rulers and in Indian navies.[12]

When the Portuguese arrived on the East African coast in the late fifteenth and early sixteenth centuries, they therefore encountered a commercial environment in which slavery and trading in African slaves was widespread throughout the western Indian Ocean. Islamic trading networks extended in the 1580s and 1590s as far south as Sofala and possibly Inhambane on the southern coast of Mozambique, and involved the resident Swahili community of Madagascar (the *Antalaotra*), Swahili merchants primarily from Lamu and Pate, and Muslim merchants from the Comoros as well as Hadrami and Yemeni Arabs. Slaves from Madagascar were shipped to the East African coast and from there were sent on to destinations in the Middle East and possibly also to South Asia. This trade may have resulted in over 150,000 slaves being exported from Madagascar in the seventeenth century.[13] It is likely that South Asian merchants –from Gujarat and elsewhere in western India – were involved in this trafficking because by the 1630s and 1640s they were purchasing African slaves for markets in western India at Red Sea ports such as

---

[10] Randall L. Pouwels, "Eastern Africa and the Indian Ocean to 1800: Reviewing Relations in Historical Perspective", *International Journal of African Historical Studies*, 35, 2–3 (2002), 396.

[11] H. A. R. Gibb, *The Travels of Ibn Baṭṭūṭa, A.D. 1325–1354*, 2 vols. (Cambridge University Press, 1958–62), II, 414–16. A few of these slaves rose to positions of power and military influence.

[12] Eaton, "Rise and Fall"; Ann Pescatello, "The African Presence in Portuguese India", *Journal of Asian History*, 11, 1 (1977), 27–8; Harris, *African Presence*, ch. 7; Richard Pankhurst, "The Ethiopian Diaspora to India: The Role of Habshis and Sidis from Medieval Times to the End of the Eighteenth Century", in Jayasuriya and Pankhurst, *African Diaspora*, 189–221; Rudolph T. Ware III, "Slavery in Islamic Africa, 1400–1800," in David Eltis and Stanley Engerman (eds.), *The Cambridge World History of Slavery. Vol. 3: AD 1420 – AD 1804* (New York: Cambridge University Press, 2011), 47–80.

[13] Thomas Vernet, "Slave Trade and Slavery on the Swahili Coast, 1500–1750", in Paul Lovejoy, Behnaz A. Mirzai and Ismael M. Montana (eds.), *Slavery, Islam and Diaspora* (Trenton, NJ: Africa World Press, 2009), 37–76. This is an expanded version of the author's original article, "Le commerce des ésclaves sur la côte Swahili, 1500–1750", *Azania*, 38 (2009), 69–97. See also Ware, "Slavery in Islamic Africa".

Mocha and Jidda. They do not appear to have been trading directly for slaves along the African coast at this time, however, nor did their vessels carry human cargoes exclusively.[14]

By contrast, Portuguese merchants inserted themselves quickly into local slave trading networks and began to transport slaves from the East African coast, northern Mozambique and Madagascar across the western Indian Ocean to their possessions in South Asia and the rest of the *Estado da Índia*, as they came to rely on captive labour (including South Asian and other "Asian" slaves) to meet a variety of labour and military needs.[15] Indeed, by the end of the sixteenth century, it was noted that "great numbers" of slaves were being shipped from Mozambique to India.[16] But after reaching a high point when a thriving market supplied African captives not only locally but also to the outposts of the *Estado da Índia*, Portuguese slave imports into Goa appear to have declined significantly. Although the reasons for this change are unclear, they may have been related to rising Portuguese involvement from the early seventeenth century in trafficking "Asian" slaves, primarily from southeastern Bengal and Burma, often via Melaka to Manila. Slaves were then re-exported to Spanish imperial destinations such as Mexico.[17] Trade in Africans to and from Goa never ceased, however, and as we shall see was revived from the late eighteenth century through French demand from the Mascarene islands of Mauritius and Réunion.[18]

The use of African slave crews persisted into later centuries, when they were utilized along the coasts of East Africa and Mozambique on both

---

[14] Sinnappah Arasaratnam, *Maritime India in the Seventeenth Century* (Delhi: Oxford University Press, 1994), 263.

[15] For a recent survey of this imperial slave trade, see Leupp, "Africans in Portuguese Asia".

[16] Arthur Coke Burnell, ed. *The Voyage of John Huyghen van Linschoten*, 2 vols. (London: Hakluyt Series 1, 1885), I, 275 quoted in Pescatello, "African Presence", 30.

[17] Tatiana Seijas, "The Portuguese Slave Trade to Spanish Manila, 1580–1640", *Itinerario*, 32, 1 (2008), 19–29; David Wheat, "The Afro-Portuguese Maritime World and the Foundations of Spanish Caribbean Society, 1570–1640", PhD diss., Vanderbilt University, 2009; Sanjay Subrahmanyam, "Slaves and Tyrants. Dutch Tribulations in Seventeenth-Century Mrauk-U", *Journal of Early Modern History*, 1, 3 (1997), 201–53; *idem*, "Notas sobre a mão-de-obra", 475; Rila Mukherjee, "Mobility in the Bay of Bengal World: Medieval Raiders, Traders, States and the Slaves", *Indian Historical Review*, 36, 1 (2009), 109–29; Sinnappah Arasaratnam, "Slave Trade in the Indian Ocean in the Seventeenth Century", in K. S. Mathew (ed.), *Mariners, Merchants and Oceans: Studies in Maritime History* (New Delhi: Manohar, 1995), 197; Eaton, "Rise and Fall". Chinese slaves traded through Macau were also taken to Manila for sale.

[18] Teotonio de Souza, "Mhamai House Records: Indigenous Sources for Indo-Portuguese Historiography", *The Indian Archives*, 31, 1 (1982), 33–41; *idem*, "French Slave-trading in Portuguese Goa (1773–1791)", in de Souza (ed.), *Essays in Goan History* (New Delhi: Concept Publishing House, 1989), 119–31.

Portuguese and Indian vessels, and in crossings from the African coast to western India. Moreover, African slaves appear to have been used by private Portuguese traders or *casados* from Goa and elsewhere in the empire on slaving voyages to the Bay of Bengal and other parts of the eastern Indian Ocean, to which I made reference earlier. Besides being used in Portuguese garrisons in the sixteenth and seventeenth centuries, slaves seem to have served largely in domestic capacities. Europeans prized them also for their prestige value as embodiments of African exotica.[19]

Although the Portuguese became involved in the African trade almost immediately upon arriving on the East African coast, with no plantation agriculture in the Portuguese territories of the *Estado da Índia* requiring large-scale importation of labour, there "simply was no great Portuguese demand for slaves from East Africa within the context of the western Indian Ocean System".[20] Therefore, the Portuguese slave trade to India was modest at perhaps 125–250 captives annually who were shipped for various purposes from as far south as Sofala and as far north as Zanzibar and perhaps even Mombasa, where the Portuguese maintained an active presence. Yet, overall, Portuguese coastal exports to the empire "rarely reached as many as one thousand individuals in any one year".[21] It was nonetheless steady and quickly became an integral part of their commercial involvement in the western Indian Ocean in the sixteenth and seventeenth centuries.

Over the course of the next century and a half, this involvement grew in the context of rising European – particularly French – and Brazilian demand for slave labour that would transform the economy of Mozambique. It was focused increasingly (but not exclusively) from the beginning of the eighteenth century on the Mozambique coast south of Cape Delgado because of the expansion of Omani political authority and interests in the Swahili city-states that from the middle of the seventeenth century challenged Portugal's African presence. This resulted, significantly, in the expulsion of the Portuguese from Mombasa in 1698 and the concentration of slave trading interests from Muscat in Pate, Kilwa, the Querimba archipelago and elsewhere that gradually supplanted the Malagasy slave trade routes discussed earlier. Despite the conflicts that

---

[19] Pescatello, "African Presence", 41–3; *DSPM*, IX, 116–17. See also Leupp, "Africans in Portuguese Asia"; Jeanette Pinto, *Slavery in Portuguese India 1510–1842* (Bombay: Himalaya Publishing House, 1992), 27–8.

[20] Edward A. Alpers, "The French Slave Trade in East Africa (1721–1810)", *Cahiers d'Etudes Africaines*, 37 (1970), 82.

[21] Edward A. Alpers, *The East African Slave Trade* [Historical Association of Tanzania Paper No. 3] (Nairobi: East African Publishing House, 1967), 5; Allen, "Satisfying the 'Want'," 62–3 (table 1).

arose during the first half of the eighteenth century between Omani forces and some Swahili city-states, and between rival Omani factions in Swahili towns that were the result of several civil wars in Oman, the growth of Omani participation in the slave trade reoriented coastal trading routes and networks to the north of Cape Delgado. Slave exports eventually became centred on Zanzibar from the final third of the century, as Swahili traders became ever more dependent on Muscat.[22]

While Omani demands stimulated the expansion of slave trading to the north of Cape Delgado – some traffic did continue nonetheless in Kilwa and the Querimbas – it was developing French interest in establishing coffee and sugar plantation agriculture in the Mascarenes that provided a fillip to its growth in Mozambique. While labour demands from the French Atlantic were also a factor, albeit of a more limited nature, the scale of French interest helped establish slave trading as a factor of major economic significance for the East African and Mozambique coast and interior.[23] Their interests in the trade were prompted by the labour-intensive requirements of coffee production in Réunion in the 1720s but of far greater significance was the development of sugar production in Mauritius from the late 1790s and early 1800s.[24] Following the passing of a royal decree in 1769 liberalizing trade in the Mascarenes and, in 1796, the opening of Madagascar's trade to French citizens, slave trading increased dramatically both with long-standing sources of chattel labour such as Madagascar and with others along the Eastern African coast, particularly Mozambique. African slaves also provided critical labour services at port facilities and grew foodstuffs needed by naval squadrons and other vessels sailing in the region.[25]

Sources of slaves fluctuated, and while distinguishing slave imports from the Swahili coast from those that were coming from Mozambique is often difficult, the overwhelming number of Africans shipped to the Mascarenes appear to have come from the latter's ports by the final quarter of the century. Thus, whereas in 1735 and 1765 Malagasy slaves dominated imports at Réunion, in 1806–08 slaves from Mozambique comprised the bulk of chattel labour on Mauritius and Réunion; they

---

[22] For details, see Vernet, "Slavery on Swahili Coast".

[23] Alpers, "French Slave Trade", 82.

[24] Gwyn Campbell, "The Origins and Development of Coffee Production in Réunion and Madagascar, 1711–1972", in William Gervase Clarence-Smith and Steven Topik (eds.), *The Global Coffee Economy in Africa, Asia, and Latin America, 1500–1989* (New York: Cambridge University Press, 2003), 67–99.

[25] Richard B. Allen, *Slaves, Freedmen and Indentured Laborers in Colonial Mauritius* (New York: Cambridge University Press, 1999); *idem*, "Suppressing a Nefarious Traffic: Britain and the Abolition of Slave Trading in India and the Western Indian Ocean, 1770–1830", *William and Mary Quarterly*, 66, 4 (2009), 888.

remained a clear majority on both islands in the late 1820s. According to the estimates of Richard B. Allen, slave exports from "Eastern Africa" (a category that included Mozambique and the Swahili coast but in which slaves from the former predominated) totalled approximately 99,600–115,200 in the years between 1770 and 1810; and from 1811 when the trade became illegal until 1848 when slavery was abolished in Réunion, the number of African captives sent to the islands from ports such as Ibo in the Querimba Islands and Inhambane was roughly 75,800–88,800.[26] Slavery thus came to define social and economic life on the islands that stimulated (together with Saint Domingue in the French Atlantic) an unprecedented demand for Mozambique slave labour. It was the development of this trade in the second half of the century that first drew Gujarati Vāniyā merchants into greater involvement in regional slave trading.

Of equal importance in fuelling the expansion of the slave trade from Mozambique at this time was merchant interest from Brazil. Atlantic merchants first sought to trade for slaves in Mozambique in the early 1640s after Dutch forces had occupied Angola and used it as the primary source of slaves for the markets of Bahia and Rio de Janeiro. This interest was short-lived for a variety of reasons, not least of which was Portugal's regaining of the Angolan territory from the Dutch in 1648. This did not entirely end Brazilian interest in acquiring slaves in Mozambique but dampened direct slave trading from the southwestern Indian Ocean to the southern Atlantic. Thus, while a few merchants undertook voyages around the Cape to Mozambique, they became involved mostly in regional or intra-Asian trade.[27]

---

[26] Richard B. Allen, "The Mascarene Slave Trade and Labour Migration in the Indian Ocean during the Eighteenth and Nineteenth Centuries", in Campbell, *Structure of Slavery*, 33–50; *idem*, "Licentious and Unbridled Proceedings: The Illegal Slave Trade to Mauritius and the Seychelles during the Early Nineteenth Century", *Journal of African History*, 42, 1 (2001), 91–116. The range in these estimates is due to the application of either a 1.74 or 2.54 percent average net slave mortality rate. See also Hubert Gerbeau, "L'Océan Indien n'est pas l'Atlantique: la traite illegal à Bourbon au XIXe siècle", *Revue Outre-mers, Revue d'histoire*, 89, 2 (2002), 79–108; Alpers, "French Slave Trade"; *idem, Ivory and Slaves in East Central Africa: Changing Pattern of International Trade to the Later Nineteenth Century* (London: Heinemann 1975); M. D. D. Newitt, *A History of Mozambique* (Bloomington: Indiana University Press, 1995); Gill Shepherd, "The Comorians and the East African Slave Trade", in James L. Watson (ed.), *Asian and African Systems of Slavery* (Berkeley: University of California Press, 1980), 73–99. For an attempt to provide a "global" picture of Mozambique's slave trades in the eighteenth and nineteenth centuries, see Edward A. Alpers, "Mozambique and 'Mozambiques': Slave Trade on a Global Scale", in Benigna Zimba, Allen Isaacman and Alpers (eds.), *Slave Routes and Oral Tradition in Southeastern Africa* (Maputo: Filsom Entertainment, 2005), 39–61.

[27] José Capela, *O Tráfico de Escravos nos Portos de Moçambique, 1733–1905* (Porto: Edições Afrontamento, 2002), 30–1.

This changed from the late eighteenth and early nineteenth centuries, largely as a result of an intensification of British anti-slaving measures in the Atlantic that would by 1819 result in the establishment of a permanent anti-slave trade squadron in West African waters. Mixed commissions were also established to try smugglers. The abolition of the slave trade by Britain in 1807 resulted in a great deal of pressure being brought to bear on Portugal by its "oldest ally" to similarly abolish the trade in slaves.[28] Hoping to open up Brazilian ports to British commerce, Britain was, however, unable to force the Portuguese into full compliance with its policies. Therefore, it conceded that Portuguese nationals were allowed to trade in slaves between Portuguese territories, enshrined by treaty in 1810 and modified in 1815 and 1817 to restrict the slave trade to Portuguese possessions in Africa south of the equator.[29] Merchants from Bahia manifest their interest in trading for slaves in Mozambique already in the 1750s but it was the involvement of Rio merchants from the end of the century that became significant. From relatively modest beginnings between 1797 and 1811 when approximately 13,000 slaves arrived in Rio de Janeiro from Mozambique, the following years witnessed a dramatic increase in the trade as Brazil's rapidly re-emerging position as a major supplier of sugar – and later also coffee – to world markets necessitated the continued importation of large supplies of slave labour.[30] The following two decades thus saw close to 146,000–147,000 slaves leave the shores of Mozambique for Rio, a figure that represented around 20–25 per cent of all imports at the Brazilian port. When added to the much smaller exports to Bahia and Recife in the years 1812–19 and 1819–31 respectively, as many as 164,300–180,500 slaves may have been shipped to Brazil overall from Mozambique in these 20 years.[31] Together with French exports, then, the

---

[28] Mabel V. Jackson Haight, *European Powers and South-East Africa: A Study of International Relations on the South-East Coast of Africa 1796–1856* (London: Routledge, 1967), 63; Alpers, *Ivory and Slaves* 210–211; Leroy Vail and Landeg White, *Capitalism and Colonialism in Mozambique: A Study of Quelimane District* (Minneapolis: University of Minnesota Press, 1980), 17.

[29] Vail and White, *Capitalism and Colonialism*, 17.

[30] *Voyages: The Trans-Atlantic Slave Trade Database* (hereafter *Voyages*), http://slavevoyages. org/tast/assessment/estimates.faces?yearFrom=1795&yearTo=1811&embarkation=8& disembarkation=804 (accessed 29 October 2013).

[31] Herbert S. Klein, "The Trade in African Slaves from Rio de Janeiro, 1795–1811", in Klein, *The Middle Passage: Comparative Studies in the Atlantic Slave Trade* (Princeton University Press, 1978), 56; Alpers, "Mozambique and 'Mozambiques'", 53–5; Manolo Florentino, "Slave Trade between Mozambique and the Port of Rio de Janeiro, *c.* 1790–*c.* 1850, Demographic, Social and Economic Aspects", in Alpers *et al.*, *Slave Routes and Oral Tradition*, 63–90; *idem*, *Em Costas Negras: Uma História do Tráfico Atlântico de Escravos entre a África e o Rio de Janeiro (Séculos XVIII e XIX)* (Rio de Janeiro: Arquivo Nacional, 1995). The higher estimates are from *Voyages*, http://slavevoyages.org/tast/assessment/ estimates.faces?yearFrom=1812&yearTo=1831&embarkation=8&disembarkation=804

southern Atlantic Brazilian trade in "Moçambiques" contributed significantly to the expansion of slaving in Mozambique.[32]

One other important slave market promoted the growth of the
Mozambique slave trade: Madagascar. The sixteenth- and seventeenth-
century trade in Malagasy slaves discussed earlier was eclipsed in the
nineteenth century by trade in "East African" slaves, among whom captives from Mozambique were the overwhelming majority. Slaves were
exported from the 1820s across the Mozambique Channel to the west
coast of Madagascar and then either transported to the interior highland
markets or, in many cases, re-exported to the Mascarenes. Labour
demands as a result of Merina imperial expansion pushed annual imports
to 2,000–3,000 slaves by 1824, while a decade later around twice as many
slaves from Mozambique may have been entering Madagascar in certain
years.[33] Madagascar remained a market for (and source of) slaves for
much of the remainder of the century, as it played a central role in the
expansion of the southern slave networks of the Indian Ocean.

Gujarati networks, slavery and slave trading in Mozambique

Vāniyā merchants were integral to the expansion of these African slave
trades in the eighteenth and nineteenth centuries. They became intimately involved in the burgeoning trade from Mozambique as financiers, suppliers of trade goods to visiting merchants and slavers in their
own right to the markets of western India. As the major importers
especially of Indian trade cloths, Vāniyās became unavoidably and inex-
tricably bound up with the growth of these trades, particularly those of
European and Brazilian slavers. But this involvement had been predated
by their own extensive experiences of slavery, with Gujarati merchants
making use of African slaves in various capacities from their earliest
involvement in Mozambique Island, Macuana and elsewhere along
the coast. Slaves worked as sailors in voyages on Gujarati vessels in the
Mozambique Channel as far south as Delagoa Bay, and were utilized as

---

and http://slavevoyages.org/tast/assessment/estimates.faces?yearFrom=1812&yearTo=
1831&embarkation=8&disembarkation=804.805.801.802.803) (both accessed 29
October 2013). I thank David Eltis for his help.

[32] For those interested in understanding the Indian Ocean dimensions of the Trans-
Atlantic slave trade, the recent essay by Jane Hooper and David Eltis is useful: "The
Indian Ocean in Transatlantic Slavery", *Slavery & Abolition* (2012), DOI: 10.1080/
0144039X.2012.734112.

[33] Gwyn Campbell, *An Economic History of Imperial Madagascar, 1750–1895* (Cambridge
University Press, 2005), ch. 9.

quayside labour to unload vessels and carry textile and other cargoes to merchant warehouses.

The extent to which Gujarati merchants used slaves in Mozambique emerges in correspondence from the first quarter of the eighteenth century in which Portuguese authorities expressed mounting concern over the use (and "conversion") of African slaves by Muslims on Mozambique Island. Indeed, "Arab" and Swahili merchants were regarded as owning and trading slaves by the 1720s to a degree that the Portuguese considered alarming. Islam was perceived as a menacing threat to the European presence on the coast because of the belief that any growth in the number of slaves in Muslim hands would enlarge the general population of Muslims in East Africa. Official rhetoric stressing the "nefarious" influence of Islam on the African population actually disguised fear of Muslim commercial competition that led to Portuguese attempts over the course of the century to curb these merchants' ownership of, and trade in, African slaves.[34]

It was in this environment of general and innate distrust of non-Christians that the Portuguese published a Proclamation in the early 1740s extending prohibitions against Muslim ownership of slaves to "Hindu" merchants. In protest, and reflecting the extent to which slaves had become integral to their labour requirements in the territory in the first half of the eighteenth century, Vāniyās drafted a petition which demanded that they be allowed to trade and own slaves "as they have until the present, to make use of them while they [Vāniyās] are on [Mozambique] island".[35] They argued that, as "Hinduism" was not a proselytizing religion and their "inviolable laws" did not allow them to convert Africans, the prohibitions should not apply to them. They added, moreover, that they allowed their slaves to be baptized and encouraged them to attend Catholic church services on the island regularly.[36]

In attempting to mollify the Portuguese authorities further, Vāniyā merchants stressed that they had not in fact actively sought to own slaves.

---

[34] *APO*, VI, 286–7 and 302; *RSEA*, V, 144–5; Nancy Jane Hafkin, "Trade, Society and Politics in Northern Mozambique, c. 1753–1913". PhD diss., Boston University (1973), ch. II mentions sanctions against Muslims; AHU, Moç., Cx 5 Doc. 27, Jorge Barbosa Leal to Governor, 17 November 1734; Cx 6 Doc. 6, Bishop Gov D. Luis Caetano de Almeyda to King, 13 May 1741; Cx 15 Doc. 59, Bando, 30 December 1758; Cx 18 Doc. 60, "Copia do Bando...", 12 August 1760; Edward A. Alpers, "East Central Africa", in Nehemia Levtzion and Randall L. Pouwells (eds.), *The History of Islam in Africa* (Athens, OH: Ohio University Press, 2000), 305–6.

[35] *APO*, VI, 467–9. See AHU, Moç., Cx 5 Doc. 27, Jorge Barbosa Leal to Juiz Ordinario, 17 November 1734, for the undesirability of selling slaves to Hindu Indians, and Muslims.

[36] *APO*, VI, 468.

They had come to possess some of their slaves at this time as a result of accepting captives as "payment" for purchases of Gujarati textiles or in the settlement of an owner's debts. According to the merchants, this happened often when "other goods that were sufficiently satisfactory" for these purchases or for the extension of credit were unavailable on Mozambique Island.[37] Apart from revealing some of the transactional practices by which Gujarati merchants acquired slaves on the coast (slaves were also purchased, especially from the middle of the century), the petition suggests that there was widespread slave ownership among Vāniyās by this time. Furthermore, it not only confirms that a well-developed commercial slave economy was in place on the island by the 1740s and 1750s where slaves were accepted in payment for trade goods and for settling debts, but also reflects perhaps the existence of a more entrenched practice in the western Indian Ocean. In Maharashtra in western India, for example, among the ways in which slaves were transacted in the eighteenth century was by being sold to cover an owner's debts.[38]

Vāniyā merchants took a further step in trying to convince the Portuguese authorities of their non-complicity with Muslims by declaring that whenever a (Hindu) Indian left Mozambique his slaves would never be sold to them, only to "Christians". In making their case, the merchants emphasized the extent to which they had come to rely on captives to satisfy their labour needs on the island-capital and elsewhere in Mozambique in their "houses and vessels". Such was their reliance on African slaves that they threatened to relocate to another part of East Africa should the Portuguese insist in their prohibition.

Perhaps not surprisingly, given how critical Gujarati merchants were to the economic and financial life of the colony, the viceroy responded by granting them permission in 1746 to continue to own and trade openly in slaves.[39] This decision was tempered, however, with a recommendation issued specifically to the governors of Diu and Daman that they "note precisely the number of slaves that are *usually* taken from Mozambique Island in the vessels of those ports". As an added reflection of the continued Portuguese paranoia surrounding non-Christian influence, the recommendation stated that the governors in India should "take care to prevent [African slaves] from passing from these destinations to ones that are not Catholic".[40] This response to the growing number of African slaves in Indian hands in Diu and Daman possibly reflected the overall

---

[37] *APO*, VI, 468–9.
[38] Sumit Guha, "Slavery, Society and the State in Western India, 1700–1800", in Chatterjee and Eaton, *Slavery & South Asian History*, 171.
[39] *APO*, VI, 467–8.   [40] *APO*, VI, 468–9. Emphasis added.

extent to which the Portuguese were becoming concerned with Indian slave ownership by this time.[41]

It appears, therefore, that Vāniyā involvement in slave trading in Mozambique was sufficiently pronounced by the 1740s that it allowed them to ship slaves regularly to western India. It is unclear when this trade began or how many slaves were transported annually across the ocean to the subcontinent. The number would likely not have been very large because the slave trade from Mozambique to the Mascarenes and beyond had not yet developed, and therefore slaves were not as readily available on the market as they would be increasingly from the middle of the century. Moreover, large-scale military demand for African slaves in India was much diminished by the eighteenth century.

There do not appear to have been any further restrictions placed on Indian ownership of slaves in Mozambique from the 1740s. Slaves continued to be used extensively throughout the 1750s and 1760s on Mozambique Island and elsewhere to meet the labour needs of loading and offloading goods shipped from India. Once trade goods had been declared at the customs house, slaves were also used to carry them to the storage warehouses, generally located a short distance from the harbour.[42] There is evidence of slaves serving in domestic labour as palanquin bearers but slave retinues do not appear to have characterized Vāniyā households.[43] Few merchants owned more than half a dozen slaves,[44] and although some did own ten or more slaves, the majority residing on Mozambique Island had no more than two or three in their households.[45]

Vāniyā-owned slaves were also employed as agricultural labour to cultivate *machambas*, or garden plots, on *palmares* (tracts of land) attached to properties on the mainland opposite Mozambique Island. Gujarati merchants were acquiring plots of land in increasing number in the final quarter of the eighteenth century from their debtors defaulting on loan payments.[46] Slaves primarily grew vegetables on these plots, which were

---

[41] For example, in 1749 it was reported that Daman had 270 slaves, mostly females. See António Bocarro, 'Livro da Plantas de todas as Fortalezas ... do Estado da India,' in A. B. de Bragança Pereira (ed.), *Arquivo Português Oriental*, 11 vols. (Bastorá: Tipografia Rangel, 1936–1940), IV, 2 (Part III), 94. No figure is available for Diu.

[42] AHU, Moç., Cx 74 Doc. 84, Bando, 5 August 1796.

[43] A palanquin was a box-litter that was used as a means of leisurely transport and reflected status within the social hierarchies of the island.

[44] AHU, Moç., Cx 18 Doc. 60, "Copia do Bando...", 12 August 1760; Cx 23 Doc. 57, Silva Barba to Crown, 31 January 1763.

[45] AHU, Moç., Cx 30 Doc. 13, "Relação...", 10 September 1770.

[46] AHU, Moç., Cx 34 Doc. 38, Vicente Caetano Maria Vasconcellos to Governor, 10 March 1780; Cx 35 Doc. 94, Representação of João Nogueira da Cruz to Secretary of State, 17 March 1781; Cx 40 Doc. 4, "Representação...", ant. 9 October 1782; Cx 30 Doc. 68, "Oficio de Pereira do Lago", 10 August 1772.

used predominantly for the household subsistence of their owners and as food for the slaves themselves.[47] As happened on Mozambique Island, slaves in Macuana were responsible for carrying the bales of Gujarati cloth and other trade goods that were stored at these properties before being sent into the interior. Although the details are vague, it appears that these Vāniyā slaves – including also those sent directly from Mozambique Island – traded cloth with inland long-distance traders such as the Yao on behalf of their masters in Macuana and Mossuril, a mainland settlement close to Mozambique Island.[48]

Use of slave labour by Vāniyā merchants in these areas was thus widespread and entrenched by the 1770s. Details are fragmentary but Vāniyā slaves appear to have been predominantly Makua, who would be sold increasingly into slavery from late in the century and over the course of the nineteenth as the power of Makua chiefs was ended in northern Mozambique and regional slave trading expanded.[49] Vāniyās also owned a few Yao slaves, as well as captives that were drawn from Zambesia and southern Mozambique to which Gujarati merchants were trading regularly by the final quarter of the century.[50] Further, they maintained commercial relationships with slave caravan leaders in the Zambesi Valley, the *vashambadzi*, discussed in the book's first chapter, but did not "own" these slaves.

Other African slaves were heavily employed in maritime labour as crew on Vāniyā-owned vessels, on voyages both across the Indian Ocean and along the coast of Mozambique. The crew of Natthu Vissaram's *batel*, which was transporting goods to the Querimba Islands in 1795, was entirely made up of slaves.[51] In 1810, Lalchand Jivan sailed along the coast of Mozambique with "slave sailors" manning his *batel*, and young slave boys serving as onboard cooks.[52] As the result of having spent years at the coast, in some cases from a young age, these slaves would have acquired maritime skills that enabled them to navigate often-dangerous waters.

---

[47] Jeronimo José Nogueira de Andrade, "Descripção do Estado...", *Arquivo das Colonias*, I (1917), 278 states that *moradores*, who lost their *palmares*, were forced to purchase fruits and provisions from Indians as owners of the *palmares*.

[48] AHU, Moç., Cx 40 Doc. 4, Representação of Vassals of King at Moçambique to Members of Senate of the Camara, ant. 9 October 1782; Cx 59 Doc. 80, de Souza to Francisco Gomes, 23 November 1789.

[49] Hafkin, "Trade, Society and Politics in Northern Mozambique".

[50] AHU, Moç., Cx 96 Doc. 61, "Relação da gente que faleceo...", 31 January 1803; Cx 93 Doc. 17, Purchase of Makua slave..., July 1802.

[51] AHU, Moç., Cx 72 Doc. 107, Crew List of Batel..., 29 April 1795.

[52] AHU, Moç., Cx 131 Doc. 20, Passport for Lalchand Jivan for Terras Firmes, n.d. [but 1810].

Owners also rented out skilled slaves, many of whom were allowed to keep a portion of their payment as a wage. For instance, Devchand Vachara owned the vessel *Bons Amigos* on whom a caulker, the slave of an unnamed individual who had rented him out, worked for a monthly wage of 30 *cruzados*.[53] Other forms of payment included a share in the cargo of the vessel, or permitting slaves to trade their own goods independently at the ports at which vessels made stops along the Mozambique coast. In making use of African slaves for maritime trade, Vāniyās were tapping into a labour resource that was widely used throughout the northwestern Indian Ocean in the eighteenth and nineteenth centuries.[54]

The entrenched ownership and use of slaves by Vāniyā merchants is reflected in census information. A 1782 inventory recorded that 49 Indian merchants in Mozambique Island, Mossuril and the Cabaceiras (all settlements on Macuana) owned 1,245 slaves, a considerable number.[55] This high figure may have included slaves for export to India or slaves that were being held temporarily in Indian hands as the result of commercial relationships with Portuguese or other slavers.

A census from 1802 recorded Vāniyā slave ownership on Mozambique Island alone as totalling 650 individuals, while almost three decades later the number had increased to just under 900 on the island-capital and the *Terras Firmes*, the mainland directly opposite Mozambique Island.[56] Many Vāniyā merchants owned less than ten slaves, on average two or three, because of the costs of maintaining a large retinue of slaves; but slaves were often cheap enough that even "poor" Indians could purchase and maintain one or two.[57] It was only the wealthiest, however, who could afford to own large numbers of slaves – for instance, besides the number owned by the Shobhachand Sowchand family firm mentioned earlier, Fatehchand Jetha owned 76 slaves on Mozambique Island and Macuana in 1830.[58]

---

[53] The caulker laboured for three years in this position on voyages to Lourenço Marques. AHU, Moç. Cx 91 Doc. 6, Licence request, n.d. [but 1801].

[54] Janet J. Ewald, "Crossers of the Sea: Slaves, Freedmen, and Other Migrants in the Northwestern Indian Ocean, c. 1750–1914", *American Historical Review*, 105, 1 (2000), 69–91; *idem*, "Slaves and Seedies in British Ports and Vessels, 1840–1900", paper presented at the conference "Slave Systems in Asia and the Indian Ocean: Their Structure and Change in the 19th and 20th Centuries", Avignon, 18–20 May 2000.

[55] Fritz Hoppe, *A África Oriental Portuguesa no Tempo do Marquês de Pombal (1750–1777)* (Lisbon: Agência-Geral do Ultramar, 1970), 182; AHU, Códice 1345, 1 June 1781.

[56] AHU, Moç., Cx 96 Doc. 62, "Mapa das Propriedades de cazas...", 10 November 1802; *DAM*, II, 114–15.

[57] AHU, Moç., Cx 93 Doc. 17, "Representação...", 19 March 1802.

[58] *DAM*, II, 114–15.

Extensive experiences of slave ownership by Gujarati merchants in the eighteenth and nineteenth centuries were matched by their broader involvement in the Mozambique slave trade as it grew from the 1770s and 1780s. This was reflected, partly, in changes to their coastal shipping routes. Vāniyā merchants began to sail south from Mozambique Island more regularly from this time, and the port that drew them most often and with which they maintained enduring contact was Quelimane.[59] It is no coincidence that this development closely paralleled the latter's emergence as one of the leading suppliers of slaves for the Indian and Atlantic Ocean slave trades. That it became at the same time an important alternative outlet for the region's ivory trade only elevated its status in Gujarati commerce. With the establishment of a liberalized trade regime in Mozambique in the last quarter of the eighteenth century as a result of shifts in official Portuguese imperial policy (discussed in Chapter 1), Quelimane – along with other southerly Mozambique coastal settlements such as Inhambane – attracted increased coastal shipping as they developed into important African slaving entrepôts. But it was Quelimane in particular that rose to prominence from the 1790s as the territory's largest provider of slaves. Unsettled conditions in the Zambesi Valley in the final quarter of the eighteenth century, such as drought and famine, made possible the large supply of slaves, as did the encouragement of Portuguese officials who actively participated in the trade or gained financially from it by appropriating customs payments.[60]

The extension of Vāniyā shipping to Quelimane allowed merchants to expand their markets for Indian textiles, while shipping slaves to Mozambique Island. Of the 19 vessels that sailed from the island to this port in 1794 and 1795, half were owned and sailed by Gujarati merchants and crew; in the final years of the decade, they made an average of four voyages per year. They were all loaded with large cargoes of textiles of varying texture and colour that were sold to visiting slavers. These years began a pattern of sustained contact that lasted until the late 1820s and 1830s.[61]

However, as Chapter 4 made clear, Gujarati voyages were undertaken not solely to acquire slaves, as Quelimane flourished until the early 1820s

---

[59] This is based on shipping passport information contained in AHU, Códices 1345, 1355, 1366 and 1376.

[60] For details see Newitt, *History of Mozambique*, 252; Gerhard Liesegang, "'Technology, Space, Climate and Biology': The Incidence and Impact of Drought, Famines, Pests, Epidemics, and Wars in the History of Mozambique, c. 1515–1990", unpublished manuscript, Maputo, 1979–1993; José Capela, *O Escravismo Colonial em Mozambique* (Porto: Edições Afrontamento, 1993), 135.

[61] Capela, *Escravismo Colonial*, 138; AHU, Códice 1355.

also as an ivory-exporting port, with gold and especially silver in the form of *piastres* and *patacas*, and foodstuffs such as rice and wheat, sent regularly north to Mozambique Island. It was only once Brazilian slaving interest intensified from around 1825 that slave trading at the port began to dominate exports.[62] In most instances, therefore, Vāniyā merchants transported slaves (some of whom were received in payment for Gujarati textiles) together with ivory, silver coins and other trade cargoes on their vessels. This allowed merchants, importantly, to spread their risk on coastal voyages that were at times treacherous because of the vagaries of the weather or because of the threat of attack from "pirates" or corsairs in the Mozambique Channel. The latter was a particular concern in the first decade of the nineteenth century when French corsairs attacked shipping in the channel. This dire possibility was never sufficient to dissuade Gujarati (or other) merchants entirely from sailing to Quelimane, however, and in 1808 Motichand Laxmichand returned to Mozambique Island from there with 82 slaves on board his vessel. Others also returned to the *ilha* in the same year with slave cargoes ranging from 27 to 54 slaves.[63] Once the threat of French attacks lessened in the 1810s as a result of the takeover of the Mascarenes by British forces, Gujarati voyages returned to their 1790s levels. They may actually have been higher because shipping passports contained a generic category called "south" that, though it likely referred in many instances to ports located short distances from Mozambique Island such as Quinga, may have included more distant southerly destinations such as Quelimane (Table 5.1).

Quelimane was at this time unmistakably ascendant as a slave exporting port. A contemporary observer estimated that 1,500 slaves were shipped from it on an annual basis in the first three years of the nineteenth century, the majority of whom were sent to Mozambique Island before they were transhipped to other destinations.[64] In 1806, a Portuguese official confirmed the scale of exports when he reported a figure of 1,484 slaves having been trafficked from there. Once again, most of the slaves were transported to Mozambique Island, while the remainder were sent to the Ile de France.[65] Exports from Quelimane over this decade amounted to around 20,800 slaves, and expanded considerably in the 1810s. Due to its being "uniquely placed to supply large numbers of slaves" – it was located

[62] Capela, *Escravismo Colonial*, 148–50.

[63] AHU, Moç., Cx 123 Doc. 56, Cargo of Brigue Joaquim, 23 March 1808; Códice 1365.

[64] Manuel Joaquim Mendes de Vasconcellos e Cirne, *Memória Sobre a Provincia de Moçambique* (ed. José Capela) (Maputo: Arquivo Histórico de Moçambique, 1990), 58.

[65] Antonio Norberto de Barbosa de Villas Boas Truão, *Estatistica da Capitania dos Rios de Senna do Anno de 1806* (Lisbon: Imprensa Nacional, 1889), 14.

Table 5.1 *Number of voyages made by Vāniyā merchants to select ports in Mozambique, 1781–1830*

PORT	1781–85	1790–1800	1801–10	1811–20	1821–30
Quelimane	9	32	25	30	11
Sofala	4	5	2^a	3^b	9
Inhambane	1^c	8	6	11	7
Lourenço Marques	–	9	2^d	3^e	–
'South'^{f}	–	3	67	62	25
Angoche	–	6	4	7^g	3^h
Quitangonha	–	1^i	11	8^j	4^k
Sangage	–	5	6	13	16
Querimba	3	11	6	–	3^l
Mojincual	2^m	5	11	8	4^n
Mossuril	–	–	23^o	–	5^p
Motomonho	–	5	26	54	13
Mokambo	–	4	13	13	–
'North'^{q}	–	–	44	43	12
Zanzibar	–	–	1^r	1^s	13

Notes:

[a] 1802–5

[b] 1811–16

[c] 1785

[d] 1801–2

[e] 1812–14

[f] This general category referred to voyages south of Mozambique Island and may therefore have included voyages to Quelimane and Inhambane.

[g] 1811–15

[h] 1823–26

[i] 1794

[j] 1811–13

[k] 1821–3

[l] 1823–4

[m] 1784

[n] 1821–2

[o] 1803–5

[p] 1825–8

[q] 'North' referred to voyages to the north of Mozambique Island that likely included Ibo in the Querimbas, an important slave trading port in the 1820s and 1830s.

[r] 1808

[s] 1820

Source: AHU, Códices 1345, 1355, 1365, 1376; Alexandre Lobato, *História do Presídio de Lourenço Marques: 1787–1799*, 2 vols. (Lisbon: Tipografia Minerva, 1960), II, 409–10.

in the vicinity of the *prazos* that offered potential suppliers well-established routes extending deep into the interior, as I discuss below – Quelimane thus saw its exports double between 1811 and 1816.[66] By 1820 annual exports were consistently around 5,000 and for the following two decades when the Mozambique slave trade reached its zenith and established Quelimane as one of the most vibrant marts for slaves on the east coast at this time, in certain years as many as 10,000 slaves were being taken from this southerly port.[67]

This growth in slave trading was reflected on Mozambique Island which served as an export and transhipment centre for the entire coast (Map 5.1). In the second decade of the nineteenth century, a total of 53,000 slaves left from its shores and neighbouring sites; in the 1820s this figure increased dramatically to approximately 116,000 slaves. When taken together, the rise in slave shipments from Mozambique Island and Quelimane accounted for as much as 85 per cent of all slaves exported east of the Cape after 1800.[68]

The expansion of slave trading was made possible by the existence of a vast supply area from which slaves were brought to the coast. They were transported along two main trading nexus. The first involved the Yao and Makua homelands that were linked to Mozambique Island, and extended as far inland as the southern Lunda and southern Tanzania. In the second, Quelimane was connected to its hinterland that stretched at times also as far south as the southern Lunda kingdom of Kazembe and the Rozvi kingdom of Changamira in present-day Zimbabwe. Slaves were drawn mainly from Nsenga, Manganja and particularly the southern Chewa chieftaincies in the highlands north of the Zambesi.[69]

---

[66] Vail and White, *Capitalism and Colonialism*, 16–17; Capela, *Escravismo Colonial*, 190.

[67] Gerhard Liesegang, "A First Look at the Import and Export Trades of Mozambique", in G. Liesegang, H. Pasch and A. Jones (eds.), *Figuring African Trade: Proceedings of the Symposium on the Quantification and Structure of the Import and Export and Long Distance Trade in Africa, 1800–1913* (Berlin: D. Reimer Verlag), 463. These figures revise those in Allen F. Isaacman, *Mozambique. The Africanization of a European Institution: The Zambesi Prazos, 1750–1902* (Madison: University of Wisconsin Press, 1972); Vail and White, *Capitalism and Colonialism*. For contemporary descriptions in the 1830s of Quelimane as the most important slave trading port on the east coast of Africa, see Lt. Wolf, "Narrative of Voyages to Explore the Shores of Africa, Arabia and Madagascar", *The Journal of the Royal Geographical Society*, III (1833), 206; and Thomas Boteler, *Narrative of a Voyage of Discovery to Africa and Arabia, performed in His Majesty's Ships Leven and Barracouta, from 1821 to 1826* (London: Richard Bentley, 1835), 248–53.

[68] Alpers, "Mozambique and 'Mozambiques'"; Liesegang, "First Look", 463; Campbell, *Economic History*. See also Eduardo Medeiros, *As Etapas da Escravatura no Norte de Moçambique* (Maputo: Arquivo Histórico de Moçambique, 1988), ch. 4.

[69] Isaacman, *Mozambique*; Campbell, *Economic History*.

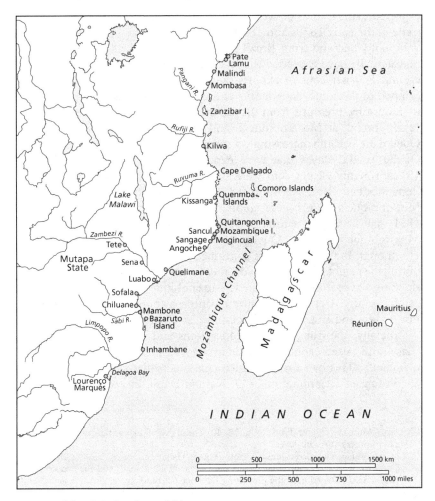

Map 5.1 Southeast African coast

French slave demand from the Mascarenes, as noted earlier, stimulated slaving in the Mozambique interior and increased exports from the coast. This traffic, which had begun in the final quarter of the eighteenth century, continued during the early nineteenth century, including after 1811 when the importation of slaves into the Mascarenes became illegal. Slave census and other data suggest that the number of slaves imported into Mauritius and Réunion from Mozambican ports may have accounted for 50–60 per cent of the overall estimated 123,000–145,000 African slaves exported to the islands between 1811 and the end of the illegal Mascarene trade in the early 1830s and 1840s.[70]

Equally, demand from Brazil drove up slave exports at this time and may actually have exceeded the level of the Mascarenes trade. By 1820, around 8–9 per cent of exports from Mozambique Island were being shipped to the southern Atlantic, and once Portugal succumbed in 1811 to mounting pressure from Brazilian slavers to remove the need for vessels to call at Mozambique Island before sailing to southerly ports, Quelimane became increasingly a supplier of note and direct feeder port. Of the 16,400 slaves that were exported from Quelimane in the late 1810s, roughly 92 per cent were shipped to Rio de Janeiro, Bahia and Pernambuco.[71] But, as I indicated earlier, the majority of slaves who left Mozambique's shores were shipped to Rio, which between 1811 and 1831 may have seen a total of 127,000–128,700 slaves primarily from Mozambique Island and Quelimane arrive at its shores.[72]

Although Indian merchants continued to trade primarily in ivory even during the height of the slave trade, there were those whose involvement in shipping slaves from Quelimane to Mozambique Island in the late eighteenth century deepened by entering into partnerships with established Portuguese and Brazilian, and possibly also French, slavers.

Crucially, Vāniyās provided trade cloths and shipping for slave purchases and raised capital for slaving voyages by extending credit to slave merchants. This has not been adequately recognized. Let us consider a few instances. Beginning in 1793, Naranji Danji directed his *pala Nossa*

---

[70] Allen, "Mascarene Slave Trade", 36, 38, 40. These overall export figures included very small numbers of Asian slaves.

[71] This percentage has been calculated from Jackson Haight, *European Powers*, 228 for slave exports to these three ports; and from Liesegang, "First Look", 463 for exports from Quelimane. Information in the preceding sentence is from Capela, *Escravismo Colonial*, 134–46; Alpers, *Ivory and Slaves*, 216–17; Alpers, "Mozambique and 'Mozambiques'".

[72] The first figure is calculated from *Voyages*, http://slavevoyages.org/tast/assessment/estimates.faces?yearFrom=1811&yearTo=1831&embarkation=8&disembarkation=804 (accessed 19 October 2013), where I have assumed its regional designations of "Southeast Africa and Indian Ocean islands" as embarkation points and "Southeast Brazil" as disembarkation points refer predominantly to Mozambique and Rio. The slightly higher figure comes from Alpers, *Ivory and Slaves*, 213, 216–17; Vail and White, *Capitalism and Colonialism*, 17; Capela, *Escravismo Colonial*, 134–46; Jackson Haight, *European Powers*, 228; Liesegang, "First Look", 463; Alpers, "Mozambique and 'Mozambiques'". A significant portion of these slaves were exported in the last few years of the 1820s as merchants reacted to the agreement reached between Brazil and Britain – outlawing imports to Brazil after 1830 – by intensifying their trading before the treaty came into effect. Clandestine trading continued nevertheless to supply slavers with captives after this date. Details are available in Newitt, *History of Mozambique*, 251; Capela, *Tráfico de Escravos*, 27–133; Leslie Bethell, *The Abolition of the Brazilian Slave Trade: Britain, Brazil and the Slave Question, 1807–1869* (Cambridge University Press, 1970).

Senhora dos Remedios to undertake regular voyages to Quelimane, some of which appear to have been exploratory in nature. Seemingly convinced of the viability of the port as an exporter of slaves, in 1795 the vessel sailed south from Mozambique Island in May and returned some months later with a sizeable cargo of almost 200 slaves. It carried no ivory or any other goods on board, reflecting the exclusive purpose of the voyage. The vessel continued to make these southern voyages in the 1790s that, although details are missing, were ostensibly for slave trading.[73] Jiv Sangaji sent his *brigue, Africano Ligeiro*, to Quelimane in 1798 from which it returned to the island-capital in April of that year with 218 slaves. This particular slave cargo had been organized with one of the most prominent Portuguese slavers at the time, Joaquim do Rosario Monteiro, with whom Gujarati merchants appear to have entered into business on a regular basis. Jiv Sangaji and Rosario Monteiro took personal ownership of 38 and 79 slaves respectively. A "large number" of bales of Gujarati cotton cloths represented the credit supplied to Rosario Monteiro by Jiv Sangaji, who as part of the credit agreement financed the costs of the provisions associated with the Portuguese merchant's slaves.[74]

As co-owner with Ramji Premji of the *pala Aurora Feliz*, Morarji Ambavidas was also invested towards the end of the century in the transport of slaves from Quelimane to Mozambique Island. The *Aurora Feliz* made its first slaving voyage in 1796 and carried close to 200 slaves from the south. Its captain was none other than the well-known Portuguese slaver José Henriques da Cruz Freitas, who had an interest in the cargo and maintained commercial relationships with a number of Vāniyā on Mozambique Island. The ship made further voyages in 1797 and 1798, carrying away a total of 451 slaves from Quelimane, and it continued its activity into the early nineteenth century. In this case, we know only that Ramji Premji and Morarji Ambavidas sold Gujarati cottons for slave purchases to da Cruz Freitas.[75]

Other Gujarati merchants took advantage of and participated in the Brazilian market by organizing the sale of slaves in ports in the southern Atlantic. When this trade was becoming significant, Premchand Virji consigned 42 slaves for sale in Bahia in 1818 on the brig *Paquete Real*, which carried a total of 228 slaves. A few years later, Narsin Kunwarji financed the sale of 35 slaves in Rio de Janeiro through the slaver Manuel

[73] AHU, Códice 1365; Cx 64 Doc. 8, Cargo list of Pala N. Senhora dos Remedios, 27 November 1793; Códice 1355; Moç., Cx 71 Doc. 25, 31 July 1795.
[74] AHU, Moç., Cx 80 Doc. 102, Cargo of Brigue Africano Ligeiro, 15 April 1798.
[75] AHU, Moç., Cx 74 Doc. 81, Cargo of Pala Aurora Feliz, 6 August 1796; Cx 77 Doc. 76, Cargo of Pala Aurora Feliz, 10 May 1797; Cx 79 Doc. 40, de Souza to Alfandega, n.d. [but 1797].

Francisco de Souza.[76] However, the small numbers involved and the absence of detailed information may suggest that Vāniyā merchants did not become more widely involved in the shipment of slaves to Brazilian ports. Still, it is clear that at least some merchants explored the possibility of establishing themselves more directly as slavers to these markets. Lack of greater Gujarati involvement in this trade is likely attributed to its financial underpinnings and organization being Brazilian and European, thus making it difficult for Vāniyās to penetrate fully.

Gujarati merchants may also have financed slave voyages to Madagascar in the nineteenth century. They sailed to its west coast from the mid-1810s to the mid-1820s but do not appear to have become extensively involved in this trafficking either as shippers or as financiers. This is likely explained by the increasing presence in coastal Madagascar of Khoja and Bohora Shi'a Muslim merchants from Kutch who, together with Bhātiyā merchants, established a significant presence there as financiers of the slave trade from the second decade of the nineteenth century. By the 1830s these so-called *karany* in particular provided intense competition for the Gujarati merchants operating from Mozambique, while Bhātiyā merchant networks from Mandvi in Kutch would ultimately undermine the dominant place of Gujarati merchants in the cloth and other trades of Mozambique from the 1840s and 1850s.[77]

To understand fully the extent of Gujarati merchant participation in the Mozambique slave trade requires discussion of two of its most prominent and active members: Laxmichand Motichand and Shobhachand Sowchand. By the late eighteenth century, Laxmichand Motichand was a firmly established figure in the commercial milieu of Mozambique Island, regularly sending vessels either owned or financed by him to destinations along the coast, such as Sofala and Quelimane, in the 1780s. The itinerary of one of these voyages illustrates the nature of Laxmichand's involvement in the shipping of slaves. Sailing with a large crew of 22 "lascars" to Quelimane in March 1794, the *pala Minerva* returned to Mozambique

---

[76] AHU, Moç., Cx 156 Doc. 42, "Escravos embarcados no Brigue Paquete Real", 31 January 1818. Another Vāniyā, Chaturbhuj Kunwarji, consigned three slaves on the same vessel.

[77] Gwyn Campbell, "Madagascar and Mozambique in the Slave Trade of the Western Indian Ocean 1800–1861", in W. G. Clarence-Smith (ed.), *The Economics of the Indian Ocean Slave Trade in the Nineteenth Century* (London: Frank Cass, 1989), 169; *idem*, "The East African Slave Trade, 1861–1895: The 'Southern' Complex", *International Journal of African Historical Studies*, 22, 1 (1989), 1–26; *idem*, "Madagascar and the Slave Trade, 1810–1895", *Journal of African History*, 22, 3 (1981), 203–227; NA, "Correspondence respecting Sir Bartle Frere's mission to the East Coast of Africa, 1872–1873" (Parliamentary Papers. 1873. LXI).

Island with 96 African slaves.[78] On board the vessel was José Henriques da Cruz Freitas, the majority owner of the slave cargo, and "one of the first great slavers of Mozambique".[79] Da Cruz Freitas had consolidated his relationship and partnership with Laxmichand in the early 1790s, serving as captain and first pilot of the *Minerva* in 1793 and as its "commander" in 1794.[80] He sailed again on the *pala* when it made a return voyage to Quelimane in 1795, arriving at Mozambique Island with 154 slaves.[81] The large slave cargo reflected the ascendency of Quelimane as a slave trading entrepôt and the involvement of another Portuguese slaver of note, Joaquim do Rosario Monteiro, with whom Laxmichand had also established and maintained a partnership.

It was Shobhachand Sowchand, however, who became most widely involved in the slave trade from Mozambique. While other Vāniyā shipped slaves from Quelimane to Mozambique Island, and across the western Indian Ocean to India, Shobhachand broadened his participation in the trade to emerge as a slaver in his own right through extensive financial commitments to the purchase and shipping of African slaves. This entailed regular visits to Quelimane and other southerly ports such as Inhambane and, for a few years in the early nineteenth century, included trafficking slaves to the Cape in partnership with do Rosario Monteiro. After a first voyage to Quelimane in 1798, Shobhachand and his vessels called regularly at ports to the south of Mozambique Island to purchase slaves in the first two decades of the nineteenth century.[82] This was a period of increased Indian shipping along the coast of Mozambique but it was only merchants such as Shobhachand who could afford to ship slaves in any significant number.

The extent of Shobhachand's involvement in regional slave trading is illustrated perhaps most clearly in 1806 and 1807. Already a merchant shipowner of two large vessels at the end of the eighteenth century, the 350 tonne *Conquistado* and the *pala Feliz Aurora* of 200 tonnes, Shobhachand added a third 200 tonne ship to his fleet some time in late 1805 or early 1806 when he took possession of the brig the *General Izidro*. The vessel, originally from Brest, had by this time been used widely in the French slave trade of the southwest Indian Ocean where its ownership had changed hands several times, possibly as the result of business partnerships or close commercial relations between merchants on the Mozambique

[78] AHU, Códice 1365.
[79] Capela, *Escravismo Colonial*, 138. For a useful biographical sketch of da Cruz Freitas, see 172–3.
[80] AHU, Codice 1365; Cx 68 Doc. 76, Cargo list of Pala Minerva, August 1794.
[81] AHU, Moç., Cx 70 Doc. 69, Passenger and Cargo List of Pala Minerva, 27 April 1795.
[82] AHU, Códices 1345, 1355, 1365, 1376.

coast and in the Mascarenes. In 1803 it was purchased from an unnamed French slaver by Sebastião José Rodrigues who may have been working for Joaquim do Rosario Monteiro or in partnership with him. A year later the *General Izidro* appeared on shipping passports as owned by Rosario Monteiro, from whom Shobhachand would purchase the vessel and consolidate a growing relationship based on trafficking slaves from the Mozambique coast to Mozambique Island. Their establishment of a partnership in the early nineteenth century to ship slaves to the Cape colony was a further manifestation of their intimate business relationship and revealed the importance of credit arrangements secured by Shobhachand for the ship's voyages.[83]

Shobhachand was drawn into the largely ignored Mozambique–Cape slave trade during the early years of the First British Occupation of the Cape that lasted between 1795 and 1803. Despite the colonial government being officially opposed to slave importation, the extent of colonist demand was such that it acceded to limited numbers being brought to the colony. The regulation of the traffic in slaves, however, was often circumvented by clandestine arrangements and activity. Indeed, two years after the British took possession of the Cape from Dutch rule in 1795, the enterprising Rosario Monteiro made his first voyage to the Cape on board the *Joaquim* where he sold 95 per cent of the ship's cargo, and appears to have been the first Portuguese merchant to sell slaves there after the British take-over.[84] The voyage was likely prompted by the continued robust demand for slaves at the colony and may therefore have served to gauge the size and demand of the slave market. With the success of this first voyage, a second followed in 1799 from which 422 of a full cargo of 450 slaves were sold; Rosario Monteiro was evidently convinced of the viability of the Cape slave market thereafter.[85]

It appears that Shobhachand's involvement in this southern trade allowed Rosario Monteiro to expand his slaving business. They had established a firm trading relationship in Mozambique from the late eighteenth century based primarily on slave exports from Quelimane to Mozambique Island, and both probably viewed favourably the opportunity to enter the Cape slave trade nexus. Their partnership provided the necessary combination of market knowledge on the part of Rosario Monteiro with the financial resources of Shobhachand; where the former

---

[83] Capela, *Trafico de Escravos*; *The Naval Chronicle*, 16 (July–December 1806), 80.

[84] Michael Charles Reidy, "The Admission of Slaves and 'Prize Slaves' into the Cape Colony, 1797–1818", MA thesis, University of Cape Town (1997), 37. The total number of slaves sold was 354 from a cargo of 370.

[85] AHU, Códice 1362; 113; Códice 1365.

acted as an intermediary for the sale of slaves at the Cape, the latter provided the capital that enabled the voyages to take place. Shobhachand's purchase of the *General Izidro* from Rosario Monteiro in 1806, after which it had made two voyages to the Cape in 1804 and 1805 during the short period of Dutch Batavian rule when "[M]ore slaves were imported to the Cape … than during the First British Occupation … on a proportional scale", both reflected the Gujarati merchant's financial standing and confirmed his commitment to the slave trade.[86] In January of 1806, Shobhachand was granted a passport to sail the vessel to the Cape "laden with slaves" and from there "onto any Portuguese port in South America".[87] A month later, the vessel made landfall at the Cape to take on water and provisions, purportedly en route to Rio de Janeiro, but Shobhachand seemingly had not intended for the vessel to complete its journey; its entire cargo of 242 slaves was sold at the Cape. Gaining entry into the port under the pretext of acquiring water and provisions by presenting false logbooks was a commonly used strategy that Rosario Monteiro and others had employed effectively when dropping anchor there ostensibly on the way to Rio de Janeiro or Montevideo and the Río de la Plata.[88]

For a merchant involved in the slave trade from Mozambique to the Cape, the attraction of selling slaves there lay in the considerably shorter, and therefore safer, voyage of three weeks as opposed to the lengthy crossings to the Atlantic that could take up to 90 days. There was, additionally, the possibility of acquiring "Spanish coin" as payment for slaves from British colonial slave merchants. The Cape was part of the south-western Indian Ocean's silver nexus where, as I show later, *piastres* circulated between the Mascarenes, Madagascar, Mozambique and the East African coast in large quantities, while *patacas* in significant volume were also brought to the coast from Brazil. Slave prices at the Cape in the early nineteenth century were especially high as part of a general inflationary trend in goods, and while slaves were often bought with paper money in the colony, "Spanish coin" was also readily available and highly sought by Mozambique slave traders. It is unclear how much silver specie Rosario Monteiro and Shobhachand were able to acquire at the Cape, however, in part because smuggling often took place to evade the British regulation of silver exports. Indeed, in March 1807, when the *General Izidro* was preparing to return to Mozambique from the Cape, the ship's supercargo and brother of Rosario Monteiro, Antonio Salvador Monteiro, was caught attempting to smuggle Spanish coin out of the colony.[89]

---

[86] Reidy, "Admission of Slaves", 67.   [87] AHU, Código 1355.
[88] Reidy, "Admission of Slaves", 93–4.   [89] *Ibid.*

The growing threat posed by shipping embargoes and patrols, which the British were beginning to enforce at the colony to regulate slave importation after it was recaptured from the Dutch in 1806 in anticipation of the legal abolition of slavery in the colony, meant that these voyages became increasingly risky. The risk appears to have become a reality in March of that year when the *General Izidro* was captured by a Royal Naval squadron off the Cape coast. While few details of its capture exist, the vessel appears to have been released because in June and December of that year it was carrying slaves from Mozambique to Mauritius.[90] The unusual release of a vessel may have been made possible by concerns that alienating Portugal as an ally in the nascent British efforts to end slave trading in the Atlantic and Indian Oceans would have outweighed the limited effects of condemning a single vessel. Shobhachand and Rosario Monteiro thus organized another voyage for the *General Izidro* to the Cape in October 1807, where it arrived with a slave cargo in late November. The voyage was undertaken partly to settle the debt that Rosario Monteiro's brother had accrued with a local agent, and in order to pay his fine for attempting to smuggle silver specie from the colony. Although this may have been the vessel's final voyage to the Cape as the *General Izidro*, there is evidence suggesting that it was renamed the *Restaurador* shortly before its arrival at the colony in 1807, no doubt as an obfuscation tactic given the vessel's well-established slave trading reputation under its previous moniker. As the *Restaurador*, the ship continued to transport slaves to Rio de Janeiro and the Cape between 1807 and 1811.[91]

An intensification of British anti-slaving patrols from 1808, a year after the Slave Trade Act outlawing slave trading at the colony came into effect, made slave trafficking to the Cape a highly fraught affair. Vessels that were apprehended along the southern African coast and found to be carrying slaves were condemned and their cargoes, the so-called "prize slaves", were taken to the Cape.[92] This increased surveillance, and the concern

---

[90] *Naval Chronicle*, 80; Richard B. Allen, personal communication, 5 April 2012; Capela, *Tráfico de Escravos*, 326.

[91] Reidy, "Admission of Slaves", 72. Details of how many slaves the *General Izidro/Restaurador* sold at the Cape on this voyage do not appear to exist. Capela, *Tráfico de Escravos*, 326–8. The vessel appears as the *Restauradora* in the *Voyages* database, which records two voyages for the vessel from Mozambique to Rio in 1808 and 1809.

[92] These slaves were "emancipated" and indentured as "apprentices" to serve in various capacities among the colony's free residents. Some, though, were resold by the British Navy. For details see, for example, Christopher Saunders, "'Free, Yet Slaves', Prize Negroes at the Cape Revisited", in Clifton Crais and Nigel Worden (eds.), *Breaking the Chains: Slavery and Its Legacy in the Nineteenth-Century Cape Colony* (Johannesburg: University of the Witwatersrand Press, 1994), 99–116; Robert Shell, *Children of Bondage: A Social History of the Slave Society at the Cape of Good Hope, 1652–1838* (Johannesburg: Wits University Press, 1997).

that the capture of the *General Izidro* would have aroused (despite its release), likely dissuaded Shobhachand and Rosario Monteiro from sending further slave vessels to the colony. Their partnership may have continued, nevertheless, because both remained active in slave trafficking from the coast of Mozambique. For Rosario Monteiro, his focus shifted largely to exporting slaves to Brazil, specifically to Rio de Janeiro, to which he relocated in 1807 or 1808 until his death a few years later. According to some slave merchants in Mozambique, Rosario Monteiro and Shobhachand nonetheless continued to arrange to "trade for slaves" from Mozambique Island, Quelimane and elsewhere along the coast to Mauritius and the southern Atlantic.[93]

Shobhachand concentrated on the trade to the Ile de France, to which one of his vessels, the *Viriato*, was making voyages in 1807.[94] He also purchased additional vessels for this trade, involving partnerships with other Portuguese merchants in a competitive commercial environment. Shobhachand formed one such partnership with Ricardo de Souza, to whom he entrusted the task of sailing to Port Louis to purchase a 500–600 tonne, two–three mast, vessel in 1806. He also provided de Souza with credit to purchase slaves in Mozambique. In the following year, Shobhachand financed another slave merchant with whom he had reached an agreement, Manuel José Gomes, to go to the same port to purchase a second ship of similar dimensions for use also in slave trafficking.[95] Shobhachand remained intensively involved in the slave trade for the rest of the decade and throughout the 1810s, as confirmed by his ownership – among others – of the slaver *Santo António Triunfo d'Africa* in 1817 and 1818 that shipped slaves from Quelimane and Mozambique Island to India.[96]

Shobhachand's participation in the slave trade was thus as both financier and shipper. He was directly involved in the purchase and trafficking of slaves, and likely owned a significant number of the 650 slaves that were in Gujarati hands on Mozambique Island in 1802.[97] As the wealth and commercial success of his family grew over the first quarter of the nineteenth century, Shobhachand maintained the most sizeable slave retinue

[93] Capela, *Tráfico de Escravos*, 325–8 lists the voyages undertaken by Rosario Monteiro; AHU, Moç., Cx 131 Doc. 129, Antonio da Cruz e Almeida to Antonio Manoel de Mello Castro e Mendonça, 30 March 1810.

[94] Capela, *Tráfic de Escravoso*, 326.

[95] AHU, Códice 1365. I have found no additional biographical information about Ricardo de Souza or Manuel José Gomes.

[96] AHU, Códice 1376; Capela, *Tráfico de Escravos*, 155, 330.

[97] AHU, Moç., Cx 96 Doc. 62, List of properties and slaves on Mozambique Island, 10 November 1802.

of all Gujarati merchants on the island-capital; a census taken in 1820 listed 41 slaves in his possession, some of whom may have been rented out as manual and maritime labour.[98]

Shobhachand's purchases and ownership of vessels such as the *General Izidro*, the *Viriato* and others at the Ile de France and Mozambique Island were investments in the slave trade, whose costs were recouped through the sale of slaves and the payment of freight charges by merchants for the use of these vessels. He leased a vessel to the East India Company for their trade at Bengal, for example.[99] Purchasing vessels which had been in service in the Indian Ocean likely provided a safeguard against crippling financial loss in the event of capture or shipwreck.[100] Also, Shobhachand leased larger vessels from the Portuguese for use in the slave trade.[101] Whereas his involvement overall in the Mozambique slave trade may have been less as an "active" participant in the shipping of slaves, and more as a supplier of ships for voyages along the coast, this was not the case for the majority of Vāniyās who exported slaves to Kathiawar in the eighteenth and nineteenth centuries.

Vāniyā involvement in the slave trade, as both financiers and shippers of captives, conformed closely with the practices of *karany* merchants, who from the 1830s and 1840s were involved in the sizeable Madagascar slave trade in the Mozambique Channel. The *karany* had ties with Zanzibar and the Arabian Peninsula, and by the latter half of the nineteenth century were active also in the clandestine slave trade in Mozambique.[102] In contrast to Vāniyā merchants, however, it seems that the *karany* "rarely took an active role in the actual shipment of slaves".[103]

The broad contours of nineteenth-century financial involvement of Indian merchants in the East African slave trade is relatively well known but evidence relating specifically to Gujarati Vāniyā networks discussed

---

[98] AHU, Moç., Cx 166 Doc. 83, "Mapa Geral dos Banianes...", 15 December 1819; ANTT, MR, Maço 499, Cx. 622, "Mapa Geral dos Banianes...", 5 December 1820.

[99] ANTT, Ministerio do Reino, Maço 499, "Relação das Embarcaçoens de Gavia...", 21 August 1801. Details of the terms of the lease of the 350 tonne *Conquistado* do not exist.

[100] NA, "Correspondence respecting Sir Bartle Frere's mission to the East Coast of Africa, 1872–1873".

[101] AHU, Moç., Cx 107 Doc. 112, "Fretamento", 12 May 1804.

[102] OIOC, Political & Secret Memorials c. 1840–1947, L/P&S/18, Memorandum B 12, cited in Claude Markovits, "Indian Merchant Networks Outside India in the Nineteenth and Twentieth Centuries: A Preliminary Survey", *Modern Asian Studies*, 33, 4 (1999), 899. The *karany* may have been involved in slave trafficking in Mozambique already in the 1820s.

[103] Campbell, "Madagascar and Mozambique", 172. See also *idem*, "East African Slave Trade"; *idem*, "Madagascar and the Slave Trade". For details on the Indian community in Madagascar, see Sophie Blanchy, *Karana et Banians: Les Communautés Commerçantes d'origine indienne à Madagascar* (Paris: L'Harmattan, 1992).

here strongly suggests not only that merchants were not averse to shipping slaves but also that many were actually actively involved in the trade already from the eighteenth century. There does not appear to have been any Hindu opposition to, or prescription against, the shipping of African slaves. Indeed, in the nineteenth century Indian merchants shipped slaves from Zanzibar and elsewhere to Kutch, Kathiawar and further afield, and continued to do so even once slave trafficking became more difficult because of British anti-slaving patrols from the 1840s. They also became active at that time in the shipment of *engagé* labour to French Indian Ocean islands. But the involvement of both Vāniyā merchants in the coastal and trans-western Indian Ocean African slave trades has been largely overlooked, and as a consequence has been greatly under-appreciated.

Silver and the wider world of slave trading

If growth of regional slave trading in the southwest Indian Ocean from the middle of the eighteenth century allowed merchants such as Shobhachand Sowchand and Laxmichand Motichand to derive financial gains from direct involvement in the shipment of slaves from coastal Mozambique to the Mascarenes, Madagascar and the Cape, most Vāniyā played a crucial role by being involved indirectly in the trade through the sale of cotton textiles to Portuguese, French and Brazilian slavers. These slavers depended on Gujarati cottons to be able to participate in the trade and could not have sustained their business without the participation of Vāniyā merchants. In order to purchase slaves, merchants first had to acquire Gujarati cotton textiles that functioned as the essential exchange media for commercial transactions throughout the coast and interior of the territory of Mozambique. The dual value of imported cloth as currency and its socio-cultural and political uses among the Makua, Makonde and other African groups from whom slaves were drawn gave it a unique value and central role in the commercial world of the southwestern Indian Ocean. With their understanding of the contours of African consumer demand, and their control over the procurement and shipment of textiles from India that I discussed in Chapter 3, Vāniyā merchants effectively monopolized the sale of cloth to African and European merchants alike, and thus were as deeply embedded in the slave trade as any French or Brazilian slaver.

But if African merchants could purchase cottons in the eighteenth and nineteenth centuries with ivory cargoes that were in high demand in Indian markets, Europeans financed their purchases of cloth with New World silver. They utilized gold in various forms as well but in vastly inferior quantities. Although specie in the form of silver coins had been brought to the coast of Mozambique in the early eighteenth century, it was from the 1750s and 1760s, and increasingly from the 1780s as the slave trade grew, that large quantities of Spanish silver dollars in the form of *piastres* and *patacas* began arriving on the Mozambique coast on board French, Portuguese and later Brazilian slave vessels, and for a period between the late eighteenth and early nineteenth centuries *Rioplatense* ships from Montevideo and Buenos Aires. Even if merchants purchased slaves directly with cash on Mozambique Island or elsewhere along the coast, those slaves would have been bought in the interior with cloth; in other words, cash had to be converted ultimately into cloth currency to purchase slaves.

Both French and English traders may have used *piastres* as early as 1700 to purchase goods in the Comoros;[104] however, it was not until the French began to use the coin as a medium of exchange in the Mascarenes in the 1740s, due to the restrictions placed on the circulation of French minted currencies outside of the metropole by French authorities, that it began to appear regularly in the southwestern Indian Ocean. Increasingly from the middle of the century, the *piastre* emerged as a currency of exchange that gained in importance for the purchase of slaves in Madagascar. With the liberalization of trade at the Mascarenes in 1769 and the opening of Madagascar trade to French citizens in 1796, the number of private traders on the great island grew markedly.

Equally, the demand for silver from Malagasy merchants at the coast and in the highland interior grew dramatically, so that any trader interested in purchasing slaves had to do so with *piastres* or face rejection in a highly competitive market. By the first years of the nineteenth century, as argued by Pier Larson, "the entire commercial system was predicated upon a delicate balance of competing strategies among the various strata of French and Malagasy merchants for obtaining and retaining as much silver as possible".[105] Contemporary French estimates for the number of coins flowing into the slave trade with Madagascar in the late eighteenth and early nineteenth centuries ranged from 120,000 to 140,000, alarming French authorities in the Mascarenes concerned about the haemorrhaging of silver to Madagascar and the impact it was having on the cost of slaves. Due to its place as a "necessity" of the slave trade by the end of the eighteenth century, connected to its status as a key tool in new Malagasy strategies of elite dominance and influence in mediating economic and

---

[104] Jane Hooper, "An Empire in the Indian Ocean: The Sakalava Empire of Madagascar", PhD diss., Emory University (2010), 166.
[105] Pier M. Larson, *History and Memory in the Age of Enslavement: Becoming Merina in Highland Madagascar, 1770–1822* (Portsmouth, NH: Heinemann, 2000), 79.

social transactions, they were unable to stem the flow of *piastres* from the Mascarenes to Madagascar.[106]

They appear also to have been unable to prevent large quantities of the coin from entering Mozambique. The first clear indication of a significant increase in the number of *piastres* being brought to its shores was in 1788 when over 100,000 entered Mozambique Island; a year later the number had nearly doubled. Vessels arrived with cargoes ranging from 4,000 and 5,000 to as many as 16,000–18,000 *piastres*. As a result of the purchase of an annual average of 7,000 slaves in the 1790s for markets in Madagascar and the Mascarenes, French slavers imported 150,000–180,000 of these silver coins into the island-capital, figures consistent with the estimates of French contemporaries as to the volume of silver coins entering Madagascar. By the end of the decade, as many as 1.5 million *piastres* had been brought to Mozambique.[107]

Although details are fragmentary, we can also get a sense of the value of these shipments by considering the voyages of the *Le Général Moreau*, a French slave ship of the early nineteenth century. In 1803, for example, the vessel left Saint-Malo in Brittany with $7,810 *piastres* on board for slave purchases at Kilwa, while on a second voyage it carried cargo valued at $8,000 that likely consisted almost entirely of *piastres*. When it made a further voyage to Mozambique Island, the vessel carried *piastres* and goods worth $10,751, while a fourth voyage to Madagascar saw the captain spend $8,000 in *piastres* and merchandize to acquire a cargo of rice.[108] As the regular currency of Mauritius and Bourbon in the eighteenth and nineteenth centuries, *piastres* were readily available as French slaving activity brought substantial and steady streams of specie into the Mascarenes. Over the 20-year period of the illegal slave trade from 1811 to 1831 perhaps as much as $2,900,000 in *piastres* circulated in the region. Indeed, for a leading scholar of French slaving in the Indian Ocean, even French vessels sailing to the Indian Ocean that were not involved in the slave trade likely carried *piastres* and thus contributed to a significant flow of specie into the region.[109]

---

[106] Much of this paragraph is based on Larson, *History and Memory*, 74–81. The profound effects of silver on the social, economic and political lives of highland Malagasy are discussed on 131–47.

[107] These figures are based on a large number of documents contained in AHU, Moç., Cxs 57–68, and Códice 1366.

[108] Richard B. Allen, "The Constant Demand of the French: The Mascarene Slave Trade and the Worlds of the Indian Ocean and Atlantic during the Eighteenth and Nineteenth Centuries", *Journal of African History*, 49 (2008), 61; Allen, personal communication, 30 January 2009.

[109] Allen, personal communication, 30 January 2009.

Brazilian slavers also arrived in the waters of the western Indian Ocean from the mid- to late eighteenth century with cargoes comprised overwhelmingly of silver specie. Although vessels carried gold in addition to silver, *patacas* were of critical importance – as *piastres* were for French slavers – for their participation in the slave trade along the Mozambique coast and islands. A small number of merchant vessels had already sailed from Bahia to Mozambique with silver coins in the early eighteenth century but their involvement grew only from mid-century. It was Brazilian merchants from Rio de Janeiro, however, who from the 1780s and 1790s, and especially in the first half of the nineteenth century, made the greatest number of slaving voyages to the Indian Ocean as part of a strategy to avoid capture by British anti-slavery squadrons in the Atlantic, and to take advantage of cheaper slave prices.[110] While relatively few details exist of the quantities of silver carried by Brazilian vessels into the Indian Ocean, it is possible to get a sense of the magnitude of this trade if we consider the information that exists for Goan imports from the southern Atlantic. Between 1808 and 1820, for instance, a combined annual total of as much as $4,000,000–7,500,000 in silver specie was sent to Goa, Calcutta and Bombay primarily from Brazil; the cargoes of vessels were consistently comprised primarily of *patacas*, most of which was used in India to purchase textiles for the slave trade.[111]

The provenance of this silver is difficult to identify precisely but a likely source were the mines of Alto Perú (Upper Peru) in the viceroyalty of the Río de la Plata. According to John TePaske, although little or no silver was mined in Brazil, it was nevertheless abundant enough for it to be coined at Brazilian mints, suggesting that silver was almost entirely smuggled into the Portuguese colony from Spanish America.[112] Furthermore, in the late 1790s, merchants from Buenos Aires and Montevideo established commercial relationships with Rio de Janeiro and Bahia to which they shipped local products such as hides and dried and salted beef, and bought African slaves with silver specie (Map 5.2). Such was the extent of the export of silver from the Brazilian trade that these Luso-Spanish networks generated, together with the involvement of *Rioplatense* merchants in slaving in

---

[110]   For details, see Florentino, *Em Costas Negras*; *idem*, "Slave Trade".

[111]   Ernestina Carreira, "Navegação comercial entre o Brasil e a Asia portuguesa durante a estadia da corte no brasil, 1808–1821", *Actas do Congresso Internacional: Espaço Atlântico de Antigo Regime – Poderes e Sociedades* (Lisbon: FCSH/UNL, 2005), n.p.; Rudy Bauss, "A Legacy of British Free Trade Policies: The End of the Trade and Commerce between India and the Portuguese Empire, 1780–1830", *Calcutta Historical Journal*, 6, 2 (1982), 104.

[112]   John J. TePaske, *A New World Gold and Silver*, ed. Kendall W. Brown (Boston: Brill, 2010), 283–5. I thank Alex Borucki for this reference.

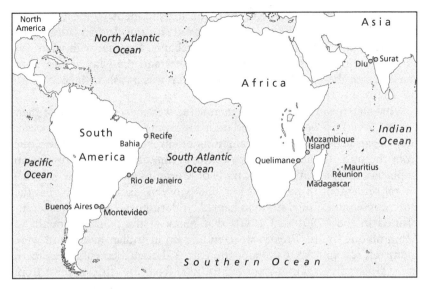

Map 5.2 Atlantic and Indian Ocean

the Atlantic and Indian Oceans, that Spanish colonial officials had serious concerns about the drain of money from the viceroyalty.

For a brief period between 1796 and 1812, *Rioplatense* slave merchants also financed voyages to Mozambique and the Mascarenes to which foodstuffs such as salted beef, bacon and preserved tongues – together with hides – were traded. In the recent estimates of Alex Borucki, at least 12,600 slaves were shipped from Mozambique Island to Montevideo and Buenos Aires, while around 3,400 Africans were sent from ports such as Quelimane and Kilwa. Slaves wère purchased with these foodstuffs and especially with large volumes of silver *pesos* that were carried by every visiting merchant vessel. As a result of the trade with the Río de la Plata, perhaps as many as 130,000 pieces of Spanish silver were brought to Mozambique in this period.[113] The trade was centred on Mauritius and Port Louis that operated as an "excellent center in which platine [*sic*] captains and merchants engaged other slaving ships to acquire human

---

[113] Alex Borucki, "The Slave Trade to the Río de la Plata, 1777–1812: Trans-Imperial Networks and Atlantic Warfare", *Colonial Latin American Review*, 20, 1 (2011), 81–107. See also Ernestina Carreira, "De la Piastre a l'Opium: Connexions commerciales entre les espaces periphériques des empires portugais et espagnol à la fin du XVIIIe siècle", in Maria Graciete Besse (ed.), *Cultures Lusophones et Hispanophones: Penser la Relation* (Paris: Indigo, 2010), 166–80.

cargo on their account in Mozambique for shipment to the Río de la Plata".[114] The amount of silver carried to the Indian Ocean by *Rioplatense* and particularly Brazilian merchants, together with what was carried by French slavers from French ports and the Mascarenes, thus ensured that the southwestern Indian Ocean was awash with specie into the 1840s and 1850s.

What this meant for Gujarati merchants was that, as a result of their control over the procurement and trade in cotton textiles across the ocean, they began acquiring sizeable amounts of silver specie in Mozambique from the mid- to late eighteenth century. Imports of silver brought an important diversification to the trade of Mozambique and made a multilateral settlement of payments possible between visiting merchants, the Portuguese and Gujarati merchants.[115] Portuguese authorities complained in the 1780s and 1790s that many of the *piastres* brought to Mozambique by the French were ending up in Indian hands and were ultimately re-exported to the subcontinent. Although their volumes varied, every Gujarati vessel that returned to India from the African coast from this time carried silver, and in some years they carried no other cargo.[116] If we assume that a sizeable proportion of the 150,000–180,000 *piastres* carried by the French annually to Mozambique in the 1790s was being acquired by Vāniyā merchants, in addition to the *patacas* shipped by Brazilian merchants in the nineteenth century, and consider further customs evidence for Diu detailing imports of silver specie from 1804 to 1831, these merchants appear to have transported between 1,000,000 and 1,500,000 silver coins to India between the late eighteenth and first half of the nineteenth centuries. Although silver had been brought to Diu from other sources in the western Indian Ocean, such as Mocha and Mukalla in the 1780s, none could match or were as important as the supplies that came from Mozambique.[117]

---

[114] Jerry W. Cooney, "Silver, Slaves and Food: The Rio de la Plata and the Indian Ocean, 1796–1806", *Tijdschrift voor Zeegeschiedenis*, 5, 1 (1986), 41. See also *idem*, "Oceanic Commerce and Platine Merchants, 1796–1806: The Challenge of War", *The Americas*, 45, 4 (1989), 509–52; A. J. R. Russell-Wood, "A dinâmica da presença brasileira no Indico e no Oriente. Séculos CVI-XIX", *Topoi*, 3 (2001), 9–40.

[115] As noted also by Newitt, *History of Mozambique*, 246.

[116] AHU, Moç., Cx 57 Doc. 3, Antonio Manoel de Mello e Castro to Martinho de Mello e Castro, 24 August 1790; Gonçalo de Magalhaes Teixeira Pinto, *Memorias Sobre as Possessoes Portuguezas na Asia...* (Nova Goa: Imprensa Nacional, 1859), 41–3; de Andrade, "Descripção do Estado", 234–77. In 1786 and 1789, for example, vessels arrived in Diu from Mozambique with only *patacas* onboard. See HAG, CD 999, "Mappa...", 8 October 1786; CD 1001, "Mappa...", 20 October 1789.

[117] HAG, AD 4952–4969; HAG, CD 999, Francisco da Cunha e Menezes to Gustavo Adolfo Hercules de Charmont, 28 March 1787; CD 1001, Belchior do Amaral de Menezes to Governor, 28 January 1789.

While some of this silver remained in Diu or Daman (it is difficult to determine how much), according to Portuguese officials "a great deal" was re-distributed to other parts of Kathiawar and Gujarat where it may have been minted for internal circulation as money. Portuguese authorities in Diu did attempt to get Vāniyās to mint imports of *piastres* and *patacas* into rupees for use within the island or elsewhere in Portuguese India in an effort to control the supply of money in territories under their administration. However, they were decidedly unable to prevent the outflow of specie into regional markets, prompting regular complaints of a shortage of specie on Diu in the 1780s, while officials reported the departure of large shipments of coinage in the 1820s to coastal western India.[118] Where these shipments were destined is difficult to identify precisely but there are indications that a number were taken to Bhavnagar and Porbandar on the coast of Kathiawar, perhaps in exchange for provisions and occasional cloth purchases.

The bulk of the silver sent to India, however, appears to have been shipped to Surat to settle debts and to finance the discounting of *hundis* with the city's powerful *shroffs* that was crucial for commercial exchange throughout Gujarat, western India and the wider Indian Ocean. In 1808, customs officials in Diu lamented the "drain" of silver to the port as a result of the "credit arrangements" of Gujarati merchants, and were uncertain of how to reverse the situation.[119] *Hundis* were financed by silver imports and circulated widely in the region, and the ability of *shroffs* to discount them – and thereby raise money – depended on the inflow of silver specie from sources in the ocean.[120] It is thus no exaggeration to claim that the edifice of the banking system on which Vāniyā in Diu and

---

[118] HAG, CD 999, Kurji Narsi, Mulji Raghunath et al. to Governor, 23 December 1786; CD 1009, Velji Darsi, Natthu Sowji et al. to Provisional Government, n.d. [but 1826].

[119] HAG, CD Joze Leite de Souza to Conde de Sarzedes, 6 January 1808.

[120] M. Torri, "Trapped Inside the Colonial Order: The Hindu Bankers of Surat and Their Business World during the Second Half of the Eighteenth Century", *Modern Asian Studies*, 25, 2 (1991), 53. Historically, of course, silver has played an important role in India's trade with the regions of the Indian Ocean and beyond, particularly from the establishment of the Mughal empire in the sixteenth century. Its significance has been noted recently by Najaf Haider, who writes that "the volume of metallic money defined the scope and size of credit [and] the continuous flow and absorption of precious metals, particularly silver, provided the monetary basis upon which the credit structure rested". See "The Networks of Monetary Exchange in the Indian Ocean Trade, 1200–1700", in Himanshu Prabha Ray and Edward A. Alpers (eds.), *Cross Currents and Community Networks: The History of the Indian Ocean World* (New Delhi: Oxford University Press, 2007), 200. For two useful overviews of the history of precious metal flows into India, see M. N. Pearson, "Asia and World Precious Metal Flows in the Early Modern Period", in John McGuire, Patrick Bertola and Peter Reeves (eds.), *Evolution of the World Economy, Precious Metals and India* (New Delhi: Oxford University Press, 2001), 21–57; and Om Prakash, "Global Precious Metal Flows and India, 1500–1750", in *ibid.*, 59–76.

Daman depended for participation in the commercial world of the south-western Indian Ocean was undergirded by silver imports coming from their Africa trade. They were both a function of Gujarati success in the cloth trade and, because of their need to exchange specie for cottons, reflected the competitive inefficiencies of European and Brazilian merchants alike that were not shared by Vāniyā merchants.[121]

The scale of these Indian silver imports from Africa as a result of the slave trade challenges further the notion that most of the world's output of the precious metal was taken to China. A view has persisted among scholars that in the seventeenth and eighteenth centuries, due to the "premium value accorded silver" there, the bulk of New World production "wound up in China".[122] But as Prasannan Parthasarathi has recently argued, "[T]hese writers have misconstrued India's place in the global trading system and the place of bullion in the commercial world of the Indian subcontinent." Evidence for the two centuries between 1600 and 1800 show that around 28,000 tons of silver (in bullion and silver equivalents), which represented about 20 per cent of the world's production of 142,000 tons, entered the Indian subcontinent from the Persian Gulf and the Red Sea, Central and Southeast Asia and Europe via the Cape route. Other routes included the Manila to India trade, by which silver from the Pacific flowed primarily into South India. Large quantities of these imports were coined and circulated as money; for instance, throughout the Mughal empire and in the eighteenth century at decentralized mints throughout western India. Therefore, although there is no denying that China maintained a "voracious appetite" for silver, equally India was a major importer of silver bullion and specie in these centuries.[123] The *piastres* and *patacas* carried from Africa to India by Gujarati merchants were part of an additional, and underappreciated, route by which silver reached the subcontinent, and further underscored India's place in the silver nexus of the early modern world. But while Vāniyā acquisition of silver was closely tied to the rise of slaving in the southwestern Indian Ocean, it reflected unmistakably their control over the trade in cotton textiles. The intersection between silver and slaves was therefore undergirded by Indian cloth.

---

[121] I am indebted to William Gervase Clarence-Smith for this insight. Personal communication, 3 November 2008.

[122] Richard von Glahn, *Fountain of Fortune: Money and Monetary Policy in China, 1000–1700* (Berkeley: University of California Press, 1996), 231–2, quoted in Prasannan Parthasarathi, *Why Europe Grew Rich and Asia Did Not: Global Economic Divergence, 1600–1850* (New York: Cambridge University Press, 2011), 46.

[123] Parthasarathi, *Why Europe Grew Rich*, 46.

South Asian slave imports

The growth in silver imports in Diu and Daman from the middle of the eighteenth century reflected both the changing nature of the Mozambique economy and the increased participation of Gujarati merchants in the slave-trading complex of the southwestern Indian Ocean. As a result of their greater involvement in regional African slave trading, Vāniyā also shipped slaves to western India. While it was rare for Vāniyā vessels to sail from Mozambique Island with cargoes consisting entirely of slaves, from the 1750s onwards every Indian vessel that left the African coast for the subcontinent transported slaves. The sustained demand for African slaves in Kathiawar, Kutch and western India made shipping slaves viable and served to complement their primary commercial interest in ivory trading.

Over the past two or three decades, studies have detailed various aspects of the African slave trade in the western Indian Ocean. Focused primarily on the eighteenth and especially the nineteenth century when demand for African slave labour intensified with the development of plantation agriculture in the Mascarenes and along the Swahili coast, this literature (as I have already partly indicated) has provided much information on the volume and movements of Africans from Mozambique to Madagascar and the Mascarenes; from Madagascar to the Mascarenes, Swahili coast and Arabian Peninsula; from the interiors of East and East Central Africa to the Swahili coast; and from the Swahili coast to Arabia, the Red Sea and Persian Gulf.[124]

By contrast, the South Asian dimensions of the traffic in African slaves have been almost entirely overlooked. Thus, while there is scholarship exploring, for example, the "Habshi" and "Sidi" contribution to the early modern political history of India, the plight of African-descended communities in the subcontinent who have been marginalized from

---

[124] Frederick Cooper, *Plantation Slavery on the East Coast of Africa* (New Haven: Yale University Press, 1977); Abdul Sheriff, *Slaves, Spices & Ivory in Zanzibar: Integration of an East African Commercial Empire into the World Economy, 1770–1873* (London: James Currey, 1987); Allen, "Mascarene Slave Trade"; *idem*, "Constant Demand of the French"; *idem*, "Licentious and Unbridled Proceedings"; *idem*, "Satisfying 'Want for Labouring People'"; *idem*, *Slaves, Freedmen and Indentured Laborers*; Jonathon Glassman, *Feasts and Riot: Revelry, Rebellion and Popular Consciousness on the Swahili Coast, 1856–1888* (London: James Curry, 1995) Campbell, *Economic History*; Rakoto Ignace (ed.), *La Route des Esclaves: Système servile et traite dans l'est malgache* (Paris: L'Harmattan, 2000); Larson, *History and Memory*; Vernet, "Slave Trade and Slavery"; Capela, *Tráfico de Escravos*; W. G. Clarence-Smith, *Economics of Indian Ocean Slave Trade* (London: Frank Cass, 1989); Ralph Austen, *African Economic History* (London: James Currey, 1987), ch. 3; Patrick Manning, *Slavery and African Life. Occidental, Oriental and African Slave Trades* (Cambridge University Press, 1990); Paul E. Lovejoy, *Transformations in Slavery: A History of Slavery in Africa*, 2nd edn (Cambridge University Press, 2000).

mainstream Indian society in the twentieth century and the histories of their religious syncretism, how they were traded and brought to India has been greatly overlooked. This has meant that the fundamental issues about the structure and organizational dynamics of the trade in African slaves, its quantitative dimensions and intersection with pre-existing South Asian slave trades have remained inadequately addressed, resulting in a generalized and less than complete understanding of its contours.[125]

Fragmentary evidence suggests that South Asian merchants – particularly Sindhis – may have been shipping African slaves from the Swahili coast to western India by the fifteenth century in a trade that was widespread and important in providing soldiers to the vast military markets of the subcontinent.[126] Although few details exist, Gujarati merchants were also likely early participants in this trade, given their presence along the African coast by this time. The extent to which they were involved in the purchase and transport of slaves to India is thus unclear but likely did not match that of Swahili, Hadrami and other groups whose far-reaching networks brought large numbers of slaves to western and northern India either directly from the coasts of East Africa, the Horn of Africa and the southern Red Sea or indirectly through the ports of the Arabian peninsula.

This began to change from the late sixteenth and seventeenth centuries, as Gujarati merchants expanded their trade in the western Indian Ocean on the strength of rising demand for cotton textiles throughout coastal East Africa.[127] This expansion was related, primarily, to ivory trading (as I discuss in Chapter 4) but as a feature of coastal and regional commerce, merchants would have encountered slaves and slave trading on a regular and daily basis. Slave trafficking had, in other words, become part of

---

[125] For Habshi and Sidi histories, see, for example, Chauhan, *Africans in India*; Catlin-Jairazbhoy and Alpers, *Sidis and Scholars*; Kenneth X. Robbins and John McLeod (eds.), *African Elites in India: Habshi Amarat* (Ahmedabad: Mapin Publishing, 2006). For the marginality of African-descended communities, see, for example, James Micklem, *Sidis in Gujarat* (Occasional Papers, 88) (Edinburgh University, Centre for African Studies, 2001) and Anirudha Gupta (ed.), *Minorities on India's West Coast: History and Society* (Delhi: Kalinga, 1991). For religious practices, particularly surrounding Bava Gor, see the pioneering works of Helene Basu, for example "Siddi and Cult of Bava Gor" and "Slave, Soldier, Trader, Fakir: Fragments of African Histories in Gujarat", in Jayasuriya and Pankhurst, *African Diaspora*, 223–50. Useful summaries of recent work on the African diaspora in the Indian Ocean can be found in Vijayalakshmi Teelock and Edward A. Alpers, *History, Memory and Identity* (Port Louis: Nelson Mandela Centre for African Culture and University of Mauritius, 2001); Jayasuriya and Pankhurst, *African Diaspora*; and Shihan de Silva Jayasuriya and Jean-Pierre Angenot, *Uncovering the History of Africans in Asia* (Boston: Brill, 2008). It is worth noting a recent exception to the neglect of African and South Asian forms of slavery in the subcontinent: Chatterjee and Eaton, *Slavery & South Asian History*.
[126] Pouwels, "Eastern Africa and Indian Ocean to 1800", 396.
[127] See, for example, *DPSM*, II, 296; V, 596.

the fabric of coastal exchange and was therefore unavoidable as a reality for those conducting business along the coast. Vāniyā merchants would therefore likely have become implicated, even if only at first indirectly as cloth suppliers to slave merchants, in the trade in African slaves in the seventeenth century. Some may even have trafficked slaves to India but a lack of details makes it difficult to get a sense of its organization or of the numbers involved.

As Gujarati commercial interest along the southern Swahili and Mozambique coast grew and intensified from early in the eighteenth century, however, so too did their involvement in the developing European slave trade from Mozambique Island and elsewhere on the coast. This deepening involvement, exemplified by merchants such as Laxmichand Motichand and Shobhachand Sowchand from the 1750 and 1760s, reflected the centrality of Gujarati textiles, financial capital and credit to trade in the southwestern Indian Ocean. With the rise of slave trading, Gujarati merchants began for the first time to ship slaves regularly to the subcontinent as a way of adjusting to this emergent shift in African commerce that was bringing ever-greater numbers of captives to the coast. It complemented but never replaced their focus on ivory trading.

Slave cargoes, carried on vessels equipped mostly to ship ivory tusks, were generally not very large. For the 1770s, Rudy Bauss has estimated that approximately 25 slaves were entering Diu and Daman annually – a plausible figure. His estimates of slave imports for subsequent years, however, have greatly underestimated the total numbers of slaves who arrived from Mozambique because they relied on incomplete sources and only partial secondary evidence.[128] When analysed in detail, the extant sources for Diu suggest that in the first half of the 1780s average annual imports were around 54 slaves, and when combined with available figures and estimates for Daman, suggests that the numbers of African slaves arriving at these Gujarati ports were as much as 50–60 per cent higher than Bauss estimated, reaching over 100 in some years (Table 5.2). By the end of the decade, Vāniyā imports were increasing as the slave trade grew

---

[128] Rudy Bauss, "The Portuguese Slave Trade from Mozambique to Portuguese India and Macau and Comments on Timor, 1750–1850: New Evidence from the Archives", *Camões Center Quarterly*, 6, 1/ 2 (1997), 22. Bauss relied on Jeannette Pinto's cursory and largely anecdotal examination of available slave trade materials in *Slavery in Portuguese India*. See also Bauss, "A Demographic Study of Portuguese India and Macau, 1750–1850", *Indian Economic and Social History Review*, 34, 2 (1997), 199–216. Other works have also provided equally incorrect figures: Celsa Pinto, *Trade and Finance in Portuguese India: A Study of the Portuguese Country Trade, 1770–1840* (New Delhi: Concept Publishing House, 1994); P. P. Shirodkar, "Slavery in Coastal India", *Purabhilka-Puratatva*, 3, 1 (1985), 27–44; *idem*, "Slavery on [sic] Western Coast", in Shirodkar, *Researches in Indo-Portuguese History*, vol. I (Jaipur: Publication Scheme, 1998).

Table 5.2[a] *Slave imports into Diu, Daman and Goa[b] from Mozambique, 1770–1834*

Year	Diu	Daman	Total imports	Mortality rate[c]	Total exports from Mozambique
1770–9[d]	25 (250 over the ten years)	25 (250 over the ten years)	500	18%	590
1780	67	25[e]	92	18%	109
1781	49	25	74	18%	87
1782	72	25	97	18%	114
1783	32	25	57	18%	67
1784	50	25	75	18%	89
1785	25[f]	25	50	18%	59
1786	25	25	50	18%	59
1787	71	25	96	18%	113
1788	25	25	50	18%	59
1789	25	25	50	18%	59
1790	77	25	102	18%	120
1791	47[g]	19	66	18%	78
1792	43[h]		43	18%	51
1793	35	55	90	18%	106
1794	61		61	18%	72
1795	44[i]		44	18%	52
1796	41		41	18%	48
1797	37[j]		37	18%	44
1798	33		33	18%	38
1799	14		14	18%	16
1800	42	177	219	18%	258
1801	40	287[k]	327	18%	386
1802	9		9	18%	10
1803	31[l]	72[m]	103	18%	121
1804	10	97	107	18%	114
1805	3		3	18%	4
1806	23		23	18%	27
1807	23		23	18%	27
1808	23		23	18%	27
1809	33		33	18%	39
1810	91		91	18%	107
1811	31		31	18%	36
1812	44[n]		44	18%	52
1813	44		44	18%	44
1814	44		44	18%	44
1815	37[o]	78	115	18%	136
1816	44		44	18%	52
1817	68		68	18%	80
1818	32		32	18%	37
1819	52	132[p]	184	18%	217
1820	37[q]	80	117	18%	138
1821	26		26	18%	30
1822	22		22	18%	25
1823	10		10	18%	11
1824	28		28	18%	33
1825	50	23[r]	73	18%	86
1826	50		50	18%	60
1827	41[s]	21	62	18%	73
1828	63	65	128	18%	151
1829	75	34	109	18%	129
1830	3	51	54	18%	64
1831	14	43	57	18%	67

Table 5.2 (cont.)

Year	Diu	Daman	Total imports	Mortality rate[c]	Total exports from Mozambique
1832	23[t]	40	63	18%	74
1833	50	69	119	18%	140
1834	25		25	18%	29
Goa 1770–1830			3,000	18%	3,540
Total	2,364	1,868	4,232 plus Goa total: 7,232		4,994 plus Goa total: 8,534

Notes:

[a.] These figures revise those in Pedro Machado, "A Forgotten Corner of the Indian Ocean: Gujarati Merchants, Portuguese India and the Mozambique Slave Trade, c. 1730–1830", Slavery & Abolition, 24, 2 (2003), 17–32.

[b.] The tentative figure for Goa is based on personal communication with Rudy Bauss, who posits that an annual average of at least 50 African slaves entered Goa over the period 1770–1830. It is possible, given the relatively high number of slaves present in Goa at the beginning of the nineteenth century, that this estimate is conservative. Extensive research is clearly necessary in the records before we can arrive at more satisfactory data for slave imports over this period.

[c.] This rate has been calculated from the following: Esmond B. Martin and T. C. I. Ryan, "A Quantitative Assessment of the Arab Slave Trade of East Africa, 1770–1896", Kenya Historical Review 5, 1 (1977), 77 which, by using Alpers' ("French Slave Trade") estimate of a 20 per cent death rate on a 40-day journey from East Africa, and the logic that "transit mortality is an increasing function of travel time", calculated mortality on crossings from East Africa to the Gulf at 9 per cent for voyages lasting 17–20 days; Allen, "Mascarene Slave Trade", suggests an average mortality rate of 20–25 per cent for crossings from India to the Mascarenes; HAG, CDm 1067, 24 October 1820 which indicates that of the 96 slaves embarked at Moçambique, only 80 survived the voyage to India for a mortality rate of around 17 per cent. Voyages from Mozambique to India lasted, on average, about 30–5 days. We should note that it was not uncommon for slave deaths to be high on vessels such as Gujarati palas that were not specialized for the slave trade because they failed to provide adequate onboard provisions or living conditions when slaves were not necessarily considered the most valuable "cargo". Professor W. G. Clarence-Smith, private communication, 3 September 2001.

[d.] These figures are drawn from Bauss "A Demographic Study of Portuguese India and Macau, 1750–1850" and represent low-end averages.

[e.] Figures for the decade of 1780 are based on estimates from Bauss 1997a.

[f.] Although they are likely low, I have used Bauss' "A Demographic Study of Portuguese India and Macau, 1750–1850" annual estimates from the 1770s (25) for the years 1785, 1786, 1788 and 1789.

[g.] This figure represents an annual average for the decade of the 1780s.

[h.] This figure is based on five-year averages on either side of the gap.

[i.] This figure is based on five-year averages on either side of the gap.

[j.] This figure is based on five-year averages on either side of the gap.

[k.] Vāniyā merchants imported 118 of these slaves, with the rest imported by Portuguese and American merchants.

[l.] This figure is based on five-year averages on either side of the gap.

[m.] Indian merchants imported less than half (23) of this total.

[n.] Figures for 1812, 1813, 1814 and 1816 are estimated averages based on available figures for the decade.

[o.] This figure is based on five-year averages on either side of the gap.

[p.] Calculated from D. Frei Bartolomeu dos Mártires, Memoria Chorographica da Provincia ou Capitania de Moçambique edited by Virginia Rau, "Aspectos étnicos-culturais da ilha de Moçambique em 1822", Studia, 11 (1963), 123–163; Bauss, "A Demographic Study of Portuguese India and Macau, 1750–1850", 22; and the import figure for Diu.

[q.] This figure is based on five-year averages on either side of the gap.

[r.] This figure is taken from Bauss "A Demographic Study of Portuguese India and Macau, 1750–1850", 23.

[s.] This figure represents an annual average for the decade of the 1820s.

[t.] This figure represents an annual average for the available figures for the decade of the 1830s.

Source: HAG, CD 999–1013; AD 4952–4969; CDm 1055–1070; ADm 4836–4849.

in scope along the Mozambique coast. Writing in 1789, Jeronimo José Nogueira de Andrade, a prominent slave trader and military official who held a number of public posts and thereby gained intimate knowledge of the dynamics of the territory's slave trade, noted this development in Mozambique.[129] In a wide-ranging account of commercial conditions in the colony, Nogueira de Andrade estimated that between 40 and 60 slaves were shipped annually to Diu from Mozambique Island by Gujarati merchants; in Daman, the number was approximately half. He also provided estimates of exports to Goa of 100–150 slaves per year, "the greatest number of which are for the Captain and officials of the vessel, and the remainder belong to the settlers of Mozambique Island who offer them as presents to their family and friends". Taken together, then, his estimates suggest that annual exports from Mozambique Island to Portuguese India were around 160–240 in the late 1780s, of which around 38 per cent were transported by Vāniyā merchants.[130] Nogueira de Andrade's estimates were consistent with those of a contemporary official who recorded annual slave exports to "Asia" as between 400 and 500 slaves.[131]

These estimates provide a sense of the scale of the trade to India towards the end of the eighteenth century, and are a further reflection of how Gujarati merchants were becoming increasingly bound up with the slave trafficking from Mozambique. Indeed, the pervasive nature of slavery on Mozambique Island and in nearby coastal areas, as well as in Quelimane and on much of the coast between the island and Inhambane, made it an indelible part of commercial life. Although seemingly small, these estimates must be added to the numbers owned by Vāniyā merchants in Mozambique and understood as supplementary to Vāniyā involvement in the slave trade that was fundamentally financial.

Slave imports into the subcontinent fluctuated considerably from year to year – for instance, in 1790 close to 80 slaves arrived at Diu, while in 1793 a total of 55 slaves entered Daman. This was reflected also in overall imports, where peaks were reached in 1800 and 1801 (219 and 327). Of the 177 slaves landed at Daman in 1800, the majority (107) were transported on Vāniyā vessels while the remainder were imported by Joaquim do Rosario Monteiro, the prolific Portuguese slaver we encountered earlier and with whom certain Vāniyā merchants maintained commercial slaving relationships.

Higher slave imports into Daman in certain years were likely due to its integration into a European slave trade nexus that also connected it

---

[129] Capela, *Tráfico de Escravos*: 161.
[130] Nogueira de Andrade, "Descripçâo do Estado", 34.
[131] AHU, Moç., Cx 57 Doc. 3, Martinho de Mello e Castro to King, 14 January 1789.

to slavers and slave trading in Goa. Portuguese slave merchants such as Rosario Monteiro sent slave cargoes regularly on Gujarati vessels to Daman and traded them from there to Goa, Macau and Brazil. American slavers were also known to call at Daman, as were English vessels that carried slaves to Ceylon for possible transhipment to other destinations.[132] French slave merchants were perhaps the most regular European visitors at Daman where, unhindered by the Portuguese authorities who profited from the trade, they purchased slaves for the Mascarenes. Slaves were also occasionally transhipped to Pondicherry and the Ile de France primarily, it would seem, through Goa. In 1787, a Portuguese priest sought to sell a slave to French slavers who were in Daman "buying slaves".[133] There were instances in the early nineteenth century of slaves being sold to the French "who were resident in Daman for that purpose".[134] Moreover, French merchants called at Goa, where they maintained contacts with Portuguese slave merchants and Saraswat Brahmins who may have supplied them with African slaves.[135] By contrast, systematic European slave trafficking was not known to occur at Diu, which was part of the northwestern Indian trading complex. The focus of Gujarati merchants, as I will elaborate below, was Kathiawar and Kutch, though slaves in some instances were traded further afield to Maharashtra and coastal western India.

In the nineteenth century, Gujarati slave imports showed fluctuations similar to those of the eighteenth century. They dipped in Diu in the first decade of the century to approximately 237, possibly due to a reduced number of voyages to Quelimane. Particularly low imports were recorded in 1802, and from 1804 to 1805 when only 13 slaves arrived, although numbers increased thereafter to reach almost 100 in 1810. In the following two decades, annual imports returned to an average of 40–60 slaves. At Daman, although the evidence is fragmentary, imports appear to have been high from the start of the nineteenth century, reflecting their different commercial structures. They numbered 287 in 1801 and 97 in 1804, and of the slaves shipped in 1801, 118 were carried on Gujarati vessels, 99 on a Portuguese vessel and 70 on an American vessel. This trend of larger imports continued in the 1810s and 1820s, and even into the 1830s, but began to suffer in the 1840s as a result of British anti-slave trading

[132] HAG, CDm 1063, D. Joze M.a de Castro e Almeida to Viceroy, 7 January 1812.
[133] A. F. Moniz, *Noticias e Documentos para a Historia de Damão – Antiga provincia do Norte*, 4 vols. (Bastorá: Tipografia Rangel, 1904–23), IV, 107–8.
[134] Pescatello, "African Presence", 46.
[135] de Souza, "Mhamai House Records", and "French Slave Trading".

pressures that also affected imports into Diu. I discuss the impact of these measures later.

While relatively small when compared with slave exports to the Mascarenes, Brazil or the southern Arabian Peninsula, the African slave trade to Diu and Daman suggests that broader assessments of the numbers of Africans shipped to South Asia more generally are in need of revision. Efforts to quantify the greater East African slave trade have proved difficult, not least slave exports to the subcontinent. Abdul Sheriff's estimate of 3,000 slaves shipped annually to markets in Arabia, the Persian Gulf and India during the first half of the nineteenth century is close to those of Esmond Martin and T. C. I. Ryan (2,500 for 1770–1829) and Ralph Austen (roughly 2,300 from 1770–1815).[136] Sheriff's rejection of these authors' argument that slave exports to these regions expanded after the Napoleonic Wars likely underestimates the demand for maritime, urban, domestic and military slave labour, notably in South Asia where demand for slaves in agriculture was small.[137] The slave traffic to Arabia and the Persian Gulf was far greater than to India but Austen's estimate, that from 1800 to 1850 some 500 slaves were imported annually into South Asia, is overly conservative given the evidence presented here of Gujarati (and Portuguese) imports which indicates that sometimes close to half this number alone, and in some years possibly 350 to 500 slaves, were entering just into Portuguese Indian ports from Mozambique.[138] Furthermore, if estimates are correct that by the 1830s annual slave imports

[136] Sheriff, *Slaves, Spices & Ivory*; Esmond B. Martin and T. C. I. Ryan, "A Quantitative Assessment of the Arab Slave Trade of East Africa, 1770–1896", *Kenya Historical Review*, 5, 1 (1977), 71–91; Ralph Austen, "The Islamic Slave Trade out of Africa (Red Sea and Indian Ocean): An Effort at Quantification", paper presented at the conference "Islamic Africa: Slavery and Related Institutions", Princeton University, 1977.

[137] Sheriff, *Slaves, Spices & Ivory*, 40; Cooper, *Plantation Slavery*, 43; Austen, "The 19th Century Islamic Slave Trade from East Africa (Swahili and Red Sea Coasts): A Tentative Census", in W. G. Clarence-Smith (ed.), *The Economics of the Indian Ocean Slave Trade in the Nineteenth Century* (London: Frank Cass, 1989), 21–44. Despite Austen having lowered his estimates for East African slave exports in the nineteenth century to the Middle East and South Asia to a little over 300,000 in response to Sheriff, and a little under 500,000 across the Red Sea and Gulf of Aden, recent scholarship has suggested that there were expanding markets for African slaves in the Middle East because of labour demands in date farming and pearl diving: see Mathew Hopper, "The African Presence in Arabia: Slavery, the World Economy and African Diaspora in Eastern Arabia, 1840–1940", PhD diss., University of California, 2006; Behnaz Mirzai, "Slavery, the Abolition of the Slave Trade and the Emancipation of Slaves, 1828–1929", PhD diss., York University, 2004.

[138] Austen, "19th Century Islamic Slave Trade", 23; Alpers, *Ivory and Slaves*, 192; Martin and Ryan, "Quantitative Assessment", 78; see also Henry Salt, *A Voyage to Abyssinia ... in the Years 1809 and 1810; in which are included, An Account of the Portuguese Settlements on the East Coast of Africa...* (London: F.C. and J. Rivington, 1814), 32–3; Rau, "Aspectos étnico-culturais".

into Karachi reached 150, and into Mandvi were 400 to 500, total imports into South Asia were possibly double the figure proposed by Austen.[139] Further research in receiving areas is therefore necessary before definitive pronouncements are possible but my evidence strongly suggests that an upward revision in imports is likely.[140]

Slave markets and demand in South Asia

For the majority of African slaves shipped across the western Indian Ocean by Gujarati merchants, Diu and Daman was not their final destination. As in the Red Sea region, southern Arabia and the Persian Gulf, slaves were often transhipped or moved overland several times as they changed hands before reaching their final destination.[141] Slaves who arrived in Diu remained on the island only as long as it took to arrange for their sale or transhipment. Although difficult to estimate, it appears that a small number were brought to the island on "consignment" for Portuguese merchants and officials, or were sold privately to them on the island itself once the slaves had been disembarked.[142] No formal slave "market" appears to have existed on Diu because the sale of slaves was a private transaction between individuals and the numbers involved seldom exceeded two or three slaves. These small-scale sales accounted for the gradual but modest increase in the slave population from the late eighteenth century to the late 1830s. Census figures are fragmentary and must be used cautiously but indicate that slaves represented 2.5–4 per cent of Diu's population over this 40-year period.[143] It is difficult to estimate

---

[139] Assistant Resident in Charge to Secretary to Indian Government, Bhuj Residency, 29 Dec. 1835 enclosed in OIOC, Residency Records, 18/A/71; Leech, "Memoir on the Trade ... of the Port of Mandavi in Kutch (submitted 1837)", OIOC, Selections of the Records, V/23/212; "Extract from Lt. Carless' Memoir on Kurrachee dated 1st February 1838", enclosed in OIOC, European MSS, Euro E293/125, "Memorandum and summary regarding slave trade in Kathiawar and Kutch and its subsequent suppression".

[140] Pier Larson has recently provided overall estimates of the slave trades of Africa and Madagascar into the Indian Ocean over the period 1501–1900 (but that do not include South Asia) in *Ocean Of Letters: Language and Creolization in an Indian Ocean Diaspora* (New York: Cambridge University Press, 2009), table 1.2. This has been elaborated to include slaves traded to the Americas over the same four centuries in Hooper and Eltis, "Indian Ocean in Transatlantic Slavery", table 1.

[141] Thomas Ricks, "Slaves and Slave Trades in the Persian Gulf, 18th and 19th Centuries: An Assessment", in Clarence-Smith *Economics of the Indian Ocean Slave Trade*, 64.

[142] HAG, AD 4952–4969.

[143] In 1792, the African population was recorded at just over 100 individuals in a census of the parishes of the island. Its omission of the slaves owned by Gujarati merchants likely meant that a more accurate figure would have been 150–180. The slave population increased to 272 in 1819 and to about 310 a decade later. In 1831, it was up to 350 or about 4 per cent of the total Diu population of 8,959. See HAG, MR 173, 262, cited in

the slave population of Daman but also with no slave market, small privately arranged sales and regular purchases there by French slavers, it is likely that its population was no larger than that in Diu.[144] Those slaves who remained on the island worked for their Portuguese owners (predominantly in domestic work, such as personal attendants and palanquin bearers), though some laboured in garrisons in a practice that was of long-standing duration in the *Estado da Índia*.[145] They do not appear to have been used for agricultural work in either Diu or Daman, as was common in other parts of the western Indian Ocean.[146] Those retained in Diu were also employed as deck hands on ships involved in the coastal and larger oceanic trade, and as dock labour.

However, rather than remain on Diu, slaves brought to the island by Vāniyās were overwhelmingly absorbed by demand in Kathiawar and Kutch. The merchants visited nearby coastal destinations on a regular basis and even made occasional voyages to Karachi to deliver slaves.[147] In remarking that Indian merchants used African slaves from Mozambique "for their service", a Portuguese official also noted in 1818 that they took slaves with them to surrounding ports to sell or deliver according to pre-arranged agreements. Details of these agreements are not available but they suggest that merchants brought slaves to the subcontinent with their sale already guaranteed.[148] Vāniyā vessels took slaves to Porbandar, experiencing a lively traffic within a context of commercial prosperity in the late eighteenth and early nineteenth centuries, and sailed "bound for other ports" to deliver slaves throughout the region.[149] Merchants also trafficked slaves to Bhavnagar, located northeast of Diu at the entrance to the Gulf of Cambay, whose rulers were sending ships to East Africa and Mozambique in the first decade of the nineteenth century expressly to purchase slaves. In 1821, the Rana of Bhavnagar "hired [one of his larger

Pinto, *Slavery in Portuguese India*, 31; Bauss, "Portuguese Slave Trade", 23; and *idem*, "Demographic study", 211; HAG, CD 1011, Mapa pelo qual se mostra o rezumo..., 15 November 1829; HAG, Diu 2314, Mapa da População de Diu 1838. I should note that my estimates of the African slave population are lower than those of Ernestina Carreira, who calculated the African population and its "descendants" as representing 6 per cent of the Diu population in 1838. See Carreira, "India", in Valentim Alexandre and Jill Dias (eds.), *O Império Africano 1825–1890* (Lisbon: Editorial Estampa, 1998), 686.

[144] This is suggested by the limited demographic information provided by Bauss, "Demographic Study", 211.

[145] For a summary, see Timothy Walker, "Slaves or Soldiers? African Conscripts in Portuguese India, 1857–1860", in Chatterjee and Eaton, *Slavery & South Asian History*, 237–41.

[146] Ricks, "Slaves and Slave Trades", 64.

[147] See, for example, HAG, AD 4955, 4960, 4964.

[148] HAG, CD 1006, Joaquim Mourão Garcez Palha to Viceroy, 14 December 1818.

[149] OIOC, European MSS Eur E 293/125 (Willoughby Collection), "Memo and Summary regarding Slave Trade in Kathiawar and Kutch and its subsequent suppression (1835)".

vessels] to a merchant" to ship slaves from Mozambique in a trade that seemed already established by this time and that reflected further its upturn in economic fortunes.[150]

These were not, however, the only markets for Mozambique slaves. Gujarati merchants in Diu sold slaves through pre-arranged agreements to merchants who called at the island from Surat and possibly from elsewhere along the west coast of India. Whether these were dedicated slave traders is unclear but they certainly purchased cargoes of slaves. In one case, a visiting merchant purchased 19 slaves in 1794 "for his partners in Surat" while others sailed from Diu regularly with ten or more slaves.[151] Surat may not have been, for reasons explained previously, the final destination for African slaves. Although we lack details of the organization of this trade and of the networks that facilitated its operation, if the merchants trafficking the slaves from Diu were indeed slave traders or at least made sustained investments in trafficking African slaves in India, it is likely that slaves were moved on from Surat. They might have been sold again either to merchants who visited the port from places such as Muscat and Hadramawt, or transported from Surat into the interior of western India where slave transactions were commonplace. At least one Portuguese official in Diu claimed that this is what happened with some Vāniyā slaves.[152] In another example from around the middle of the eighteenth century, a young "East African" girl was sold in Pune, and in the 1760s up to 30 African slave women were working in auxiliary military services in the Konkan. In the early nineteenth century, the *nawabs* of Karnataka also owned African slaves.[153] As in Kathiawar, African slaves were transacted and exchanged throughout western India.

---

[150] OIOC, L/MAR/C, Marine Records 586, "Steam Communication with East Coast of Africa, 1811", in which Captain T. Smee observed a vessel from Bhavnagar at Zanzibar; James Tod, *Travels in Western India* (London: WmH. Allen and Co., 1839), 263–4. See also John Briggs, *The Cities of Gujarashtra: Their Topography and History Illustrated, in the Journal of a Recent Tour, with Accompanying Documents* (Bombay: Times, 1849), 284–5.

[151] HAG, CD Sebastião Joze Ferreira Barroco to Caetano de Souza Pereira, 21 March 1794; "reprezentação de Rupchande Vada, Hamirchand Kurji etc", n.d. [but 1794].

[152] HAG, CD 1003, Caetano de Lisboa Pereira to Governor, 5 October 1802.

[153] Sumit Guha, "Slavery, Society and the State in Western India, 1700–1800", in Chatterjee and Eaton, *Slavery & South Asian History*, 170, 172. It is possible, also, that in a cash-flush eighteenth century, rising competitive displays of wealth in the form of dowries among Rajput chiefdoms saw African female slaves presented as part of dowry payments (that included Indian slaves) to secure interstate marriages and bolster the prestige of chiefly households. See Ramya Sreenivasan, "Drudges, Dancing Girls, Concubines: Female Slaves in Rajput Polity, 1500–1850", in Eaton and Chatterjee, *Slavery & South Asian History*, 136–61.

This trade in African slaves existed within the context of a widespread trade in South Asian slaves within western India.[154] A loosely united confederacy of Maratha rulers had emerged in the region in the early eighteenth century in the wake of rapidly waning Mughal imperial power, and extended its reach into northern and southern India until it was arrested by British colonialism in 1818. Indian slaves were trafficked throughout the region in transactions that could be both straightforward and often complex, particularly those involving women and children where disputes often erupted over title. Slaves were offered as gifts between ruling families and "circulated from household to household". Ruling families also gifted slaves to loyal and favoured servants, though slaves were also acquired through outright purchase. Subordinate chiefs, in their turn, sent female slaves to the *peshva* as a form of tribute. This traffic in Indian slaves was, as Sumit Guha has noted, "only part of a larger series of sales" involving East African slaves.[155] In other words, owners in eighteenth-century western India were purchasing Indian and African slaves at the same time, whenever the opportunity arose to do so. It does not appear, therefore, that separate markets existed for these slaves but rather that the trafficking in Indian and African slaves co-existed as complementary and overlapping trades. It would be reasonable to speculate, then, that for some of the African slaves brought from Mozambique to the subcontinent by Vāniyā merchants and taken to the west coast of India, they moved along some of the same internal networks that in western India organized the traffic in Indian slaves.

For much of the eighteenth- and early nineteenth-century African slave trade, adult male slaves were in highest demand in India. At Diu, the average male to female import ratio for adult African slaves was traditionally 3:1, but in the mid- to late 1820s this changed in favour of boys and women for reasons that are unclear. Female slaves and young boys had been shipped to India throughout the eighteenth century, of course, but their arrival in larger numbers probably reflected shifts in Indian demand, rather than any changes to slave supply in Mozambique. Demand for

---

[154] Slavery and slave trading in India took a variety of forms, and were connected to a complex array of relationships shaped by kin, caste, rank, status and gender. For a discussion of these relationships in the making of Indian slavery, and its importance to the history of the subcontinent, see Indrani Chatterjee, "Renewed and Connected Histories: Slavery and the Historiography of South Asia", in Chatterjee and Eaton, *Slavery & South Asian History*, 17–43.

[155] I have based this paragraph, and taken both quotes, from Guha, "Slavery, Society and the State", 170. Guha cites the example of Ramaji Mahadev who purchased two Indian slave-women and an East African man and young girl. See also Sylvia Vatuk, "Bharattee's Death: Domestic Slave Women in Nineteenth-Century Madras", in Chatterjee and Eaton, *Slavery & South Asian History*, 215.

African boys, who were less likely to flee than adult males, was particularly strong in Kutch where they were utilized primarily as deck hands.[156] Imports of African boys continued well into the middle of the nineteenth century despite British efforts at sea through patrols and pressures on Indian states to end slave trading across their borders.[157] As an indication of this demand, in the 1830s "a great number of African boys" were present in Diu, and in Rajkot served "in attendance upon the Chiefs of Kathiawar".[158] Greater numbers of female than male slaves were also entering Diu by this time. Whereas in the late eighteenth century the average male to female import ratio for adult African slaves was 3:1, in the 1820s and 1830s this changed to 3:2.[159] Women and young girls were in demand in Kathiawar and Kutch as domestic workers and concubines, and there are cases of Kutchi women being sent to East Africa to acquire young girls. Some were imported to become the wives of African slaves, as in Mandvi where they were to be "married to the Seedhis now in Kutch".[160]

---

[156] OIOC, European MSS Eur E 293/125 (Willoughby Collection), "Memo and Summary Regarding Slave Trade in Kathiawar and Kutch and its subsequent suppression (1835)"; MSA, Political Department, Kutch, Slave Trade, vol. no. 106/990, "Memorandum of 20 slaves brought to Mandvi from East Africa, 1838".

[157] MSA, Political Department, Slave Trade, vol. 169 (1852), Political Agent, Kathiawar, to Chief Secretary of Bombay Government, 8 April 1852. For details of British concerns and efforts in western India, see Andrea Major, "Enslaving Spaces: Domestic Slavery and the Spatial, Ideological and Practical Limits of Colonial Control in the Nineteenth-Century Rajput and Maratha States", *Indian Economic and Social History Review*, 46, 3 (2009), 315–42. Major also provides a useful discussion of the political, economic and discursive dynamics of the anti-slavery campaign in India in "'The Slavery of East and West': Abolitionists and 'Unfree' Labour in India, 1820–1833", *Slavery & Abolition*, 31, 4 (2010), 501–525. See also Allen, "Suppressing a Nefarious Traffic".

[158] OIOC, European MSS Eur E 293/125 (Willoughby Collection), "Memo and Summary". The shipment of significant numbers of children across the waters of the western Indian Ocean has been largely overlooked, if not ignored, by historians, due partly at least to their "invisibility" in the archival record. This is beginning to be remedied as scholars come to appreciate that – along with women – children comprised a large part of the slave cargoes of the ocean. See Richard B. Allen, "Children and European Slave Trading in the Indian Ocean during the Eighteenth and early Nineteenth Centuries", in Gwyn Campbell, Suzanne Miers and Joseph C. Miller (eds.), *Children in Slavery through the Ages* (Athens, OH: Ohio University Press, 2009), 35–54; Fred Morton, "Small Change: Children in the Nineteenth-Century East African Slave Trade", in *ibid.*, 55–70; and Gwyn Campbell, "Children and Bondage in Imperial Madagascar, c. 1790–1895", in Campbell, Suzanne Miers and Joseph C. Miller (eds.), *Child Slaves in the Modern World* (Athens, OH: Ohio University Press, 2011), 37–63.

[159] These ratios have been calculated from HAG, CD 995–1012 and AD 4952–69.

[160] OIOC, Residency Records, 18/A/71, Political Secretary to Government of India, Bhuj Residency, 18 November 1836; and Letter from Assistant Resident to Secretary to Government of India, Bhuj Residency, 29 December 1835; MSA, Political Department, Kutch, Slave Trade, vol. no. 106/990, "Memorandum of 20 slaves".

Both male and female African slaves worked in a variety of occupations. Men brought to the thriving port of Mandvi in Kutch satisfied demand for maritime labour in a region that was sparsely populated and affected by high rates of male out-migration.[161] African slaves, often women but also men, served in domestic spheres in the households of rulers, including in kitchens as suggested by a report in 1819 that "Seedee" cooks were serving the "Iharejah chieftains" of Kathiawar.[162] Apart from being employed in domestic labour, in Kathiawar and surrounding areas they laboured for the armies of the chiefs of the area, among whom it was said they found a "ready sale".[163] The "uneasy balance of force" that prevailed in Kathiawar in the eighteenth and nineteenth centuries saw a number of city-states competing with one another for positions of power, thus increasing the demand for military personnel.[164] Although the days when Africans had played a prominent role as military slaves and even commanders in Indian armies had passed – the "Habshis" (Africans from present-day Ethiopia) in the sixteenth- and seventeenth-century Deccan come readily to mind – they continued to serve in different occupational and other capacities in the armies of the peninsula.[165] Elsewhere, African female slaves performed ancillary military tasks – for example, in Maharashtra, East African slave women prepared gunpowder in the arsenals of forts.[166]

Slaves may have served other, symbolic purposes by increasing the prestige of a ruler or individual. The gifting of slaves by the Marathas described previously, for example, enhanced the respectability of households that was measured by the number of their dependents, thereby making ownership of African – as well as Indian – slaves a marker

[161] T. Postans, "Some Account of the Present State of the Trade Between the Port of Mandvie in Cutch, and the Eastern Coast of Africa", *Transactions of the Bombay Geographical Society, June 1839–February 1840*, vol. III (Bombay: American Mission Press, 1840), 174

[162] James Macmurdo, "Remarks on the Province of Kattiwar; its Inhabitants, their Manners and Customs", *Transactions of the Literary Society of Bombay, vol. I* (London: Longman, Hurst, Rees, Orme, Brown and John Murray, 1819), 279.

[163] OIOC, European MSS, Eur E 293/125 (Willoughby Collection), "Memo and Summary".

[164] Howard Spodek, "Rulers, Merchants and Other Groups in the City-States of Saurashtra, India, around 1800", *Comparative Studies in Society and History*, 16, 4 (1974), 448–70 See also Harald Tambs-Lyche, *Power, Profit and Poetry: Traditional Society in Kathiawar, Western India* (New Delhi: Manohar, 1997).

[165] For a useful overview of military slavery in the Deccan, see Eaton, "Rise and Fall of Military Slavery".

[166] Guha, "Slavery, Society and the State". The Maratha regime, which had sizeable infantry and cavalry units in western India, does not seem to have used African male slaves for military purposes to any great degree, drawing instead on freelance local and foreign soldiers.

of status.[167] African slaves may actually have been more desirable, in certain respects, than Indian slaves because of concerns on the part of higher-caste owners over the threat of being degraded by the touch of often lower-caste slaves, in particular women. Thus, we find that two female slaves of a Brahman *peshva* were described in 1746 as being of "good caste", supposedly reassuring their owner that their proximity to him would be non-polluting.[168] Falling outside of caste prescriptions, African slaves may have presented little or no danger of such a threat, particularly in the intimate spaces of the domestic sphere where slaves often laboured.

An "end" to African slave trading

Indian demand for African slaves among political elites in Kathiawar, Kutch and western India, while modest compared to other markets in the western Indian Ocean such as the Red Sea and Arabian Peninsula, remained steady into the 1820s and 1830s. By this time, however, British officials had become concerned over the imports of African slaves into western India as part of efforts to curtail and end slave trafficking in East India Company territories and, more broadly, to abolish slave trading in the western Indian Ocean. Even before the British abolition of the trans-atlantic slave trade in 1807, the company had formally prohibited the importation and exportation of slaves, both African and Indian, from its territories, and prosecuted European slave traders in British India from the late eighteenth century.

Yet, because of political expediencies that compelled the company to maintain stability and reduce its expenditure by ruling through indigenous structures, it was cautious in dealing with indigenous slave systems. Once company officials determined that slavery was allowed by both Hindu and Muslim "laws", and in a colonial context where it was constructed as relatively "benign" when compared to Atlantic plantation slavery, they followed a non-interventionist approach that maintained the domestic and agricultural labour arrangements of Indian elites. Even after slavery was "delegalized" in India in 1843, and criminalized in 1860, the British were ambivalent in their implementation of the supposed abolition and were often supportive of slaveholders' property rights.[169]

---

[167] Lionel Caplan, "Power and Status in South Asian Slavery", in Watson, *Asian and African Systems*, 186–7.

[168] Guha, "Slavery, Society and the State", 173.

[169] This discussion is based on Major, "Enslaving Spaces", 318 and *idem*, *Slavery, Abolitionism and Empire in India, 1772–1843* (Liverpool University Press, 2012), 8–9.

British reluctance to interfere in "domestic slavery" in India meant that both Indian and African slaves continued to be traded in, and brought to, the subcontinent for much of the nineteenth century. In Kathiawar, to which most of the slaves shipped by Gujarati merchants from Mozambique were traded, British efforts were further hampered by the "variation of arrangements according to territorial specificities" that the colonial state maintained with local rulers who countenanced and in many cases actively encouraged slave trafficking. The region was characterized by a number of principalities and polities (ranging from states such as Bhavnagar and Jamnagar to single-village chiefdoms), and despite the creation of the residency system in the states of Kathiawar (and elsewhere) that sought to control the diplomatic relations of these states, the company – and later even the government of India – exercised "precious little control" over its populations.[170] So, despite pressuring certain rulers, British authorities were unable, effectively, to put a stop to the imports of African slaves in Kathiawar and Kutch. That British relations with states fluctuated widely, depending on their respective strength and on the role it was hoped they would play politically, reflected pragmatic considerations that often ran counter to metropolitan abolitionist ideas. Furthermore, as Indrani Chatterjee has noted, "the general willingness to look the other way when Africans entered the domains of the Indian rulers as personal servants, or as 'wives'" was quite widespread.[171] Thus, while anti-slavery language often condemned slavery and slave trafficking in India, particularly that involving the kidnapping or violent seizure of individuals, the socially sanctioned use of slave labour in South Asian and colonial homes alike was regarded as acceptable.[172]

British efforts to end slave trading extended also, of course, to the trafficking of slaves along the many waterways of the Indian Ocean. Of particular interest was the trade in African slaves from East Africa and

---

See also Indrani Chatterjee, "Abolition by Denial: The South Asian Example", in Gwyn Campbell (ed.), *Abolition and its Aftermath in Indian Ocean Africa and Asia* (New York: Routledge, 2005), 150–68. There were exceptions to British reticence to intervene in the holding and trading of slaves in India and these related often to cases when colonial stability or the rule of law were threatened.

[170] This quote is from an earlier, conference paper version, of Chatterjee, "Abolition by Denial", 7, paper presented at the Conference "Slavery, Unfree Labour and Revolt in the Indian Ocean Region", Avignon, 4–6 October, 2001. For discussion of political structures in Kathiawar, see Harald Tambs-Lyche, "Reflections on Caste in Gujarat", in Edward Simpson and Aparna Kapadia (eds.), *The Idea of Gujarat: History, Ethnography and Text* (New Delhi: Orient Black Swan, 2010), 106.

[171] Chatterjee, "Abolition by Denial", 158.

[172] This suggested, as argued by Major, "tension between exported metropolitan ideas and the specific social and political context of colonial India". See *Slavery, Abolitionism and Empire*, 91.

Mozambique, for which the British government signed agreements with the Portuguese state. These included treaties in 1815 and 1817 that limited the slave trade to the region south of the equator, and perhaps most importantly the Anglo-Portuguese Treaty of 1842 whose purpose was to end definitively the slave trade from Portuguese Africa to destinations in the Indian Ocean. Significantly, it guaranteed rights of mutual search after which the British Navy's Anti-Slave Trade Patrol began regularly to cruise along the East African coast and Mozambique Channel. Earlier, Brazil had officially banned the imports of slaves in 1830.[173]

Demand for African slaves, though, remained robust, particularly in newly independent Brazil where the trade prospered throughout the 1830s. World sugar prices were high at this time and, despite a dip in the early 1840s, continued to rise while coffee production boomed and revived the plantation sector of the Brazilian economy. The clandestine trade thus maintained its volume in the 1850s, even once Brazilian markets were closed in 1851, as Cuba and the United States continued to import large numbers of slaves until the early 1860s when they closed their slave markets. Closer to Mozambique, markets opened up in the new sugar-growing islands of Nossi Bé and Mayotte (which the French had acquired in the 1840s), as well as in Réunion, where the French introduced the *engagé* labour system in 1854 to conceal their trade in African slaves.[174] Slaving centres also developed along the Mozambique coast, notably in Angoche, which in the 1840s established itself as the most important port conducting clandestine trade involving Muslim traders and rulers. With such buoyant slave demand, it is therefore not surprising that, with rare exception, Portuguese officials in Mozambique (as also in India) were complicit in contravening the anti-slave trade legislation.[175]

These evasions of anti-slave trading agreements notwithstanding, British pressures were not entirely without success. From the 1830s and

---

[173] I base this discussion on Newitt, *History of Mozambique*, 248, 268 and 324; and Walker, "Slaves or Soldiers".

[174] Slaves entered into contracts which technically – but not in practice – turned them into "free" labour, thereby allowing the French in the face of diplomatic pressure to claim that they were adhering to anti-slaving agreements. *Engagé* labour was used until 1864, when the French finally discontinued it.

[175] I have drawn here extensively from Newitt, *History of Mozambique*, 268–70. For details about the resistance of Portuguese officials to ending slave trading in Goa, see Timothy Walker, "Abolishing the Slave Trade in Portuguese India: Documentary Evidence of Popular and Official Resistance to Crown Policy, 1842–1860", in Edward A. Alpers, Gwyn Campbell and Michael Salman (eds.), *Slavery and Resistance in Africa and Asia* (New York: Routledge, 2005), 82–98. The most recent analysis of abolitionist debates in Portugal is João Pedro Marques, *The Sounds of Silence: Nineteenth-Century Portugal and the Abolition of the Slave Trade* (New York: Bergahn Books, 2006).

1840s, as naval patrols intensified, slaving vessels were seized and condemned, their crews prosecuted in vice-admiralty courts and their slaves "emancipated".[176] The presence of naval squadrons concerned slavers and had a considerable impact on how the trade was conducted by pushing it into small clandestine centres along the coast. Along with others, Gujarati merchants were uneasy about how British efforts were affecting the commerce of Mozambique. The position of the slave trade as a principal determinant of the Mozambique economy by the 1820s meant that Vāniyā commercial engagement with the territory had become increasingly reliant on it.

Merchants therefore reacted unfavourably in 1830 to the impact that the slowing slave trade was having on their commerce. Vāniyā disquiet eventually developed into vocal complaints that year about how "business did not go well, and most of the trade goods in Mozambique have been delayed".[177] Their prominent position as the providers of the trade cloths that were an essential currency for the acquisition of slaves from the interior of Mozambique made Vāniyās acutely aware of the extent to which their own survival had by this time become contingent on the continuation of the slave trade, even as they remained focused on ivory. Portuguese officials in Diu, in particular, were equally alarmed about the threat that the end of the slave trade would pose for the future of Vāniyā trade and by extension the trade of the island:

The trade with the capital of Mozambique is the only way open to make this island [Diu] prosper but the news of the ending of the slave trade has meant that most of the goods exported last year have not been successfully traded; as a result the return has been very small, and has discouraged the merchants from continuing their trade in the land.

In light of the success of the trade through one Portuguese port (Daman), the author suggested as an alternative to the slave trade that merchants invest in the export of opium from western India to Macau.[178]

---

[176] In many cases, slaves were not returned "home" but were, instead, delivered into apprenticeships whose terms and conditions could be oppressive. For details of the capture by British Royal Navy squadrons of slaving vessels in the southwestern Indian Ocean and their prosecution in vice-admiralty courts (e.g. Cape Town), see Allen, "Suppressing a Nefarious Traffic".

[177] HAG, CD 1011, da Gama Araujo to Portugal e Castro, 14 November 1829; HAG, CD 1010, Oficio, 7 January 1830.

[178] HAG, CD 1011, Joaquim Piedade Mascarenhas to Viceroy, 11 November 1829. Malwa opium, traded primarily through Daman so as to circumvent British controls, was by the 1820s an important feature of the colony's export economy. For details, see Gervase Clarence-Smith, *The Third Portuguese Empire, 1825–1975: A Study in Economic Imperialism* (Manchester University Press, 1985), 25–9.

By the 1830s, Vāniyā merchants were also facing further challenges to their position in Mozambique and the southwestern Indian Ocean. The continued demand for African slaves brought an increase in slave raiding throughout much of the interior of Mozambique, causing social dislocation, warfare and disruption to trade routes along which ivory, in particular, was brought to the coast.[179] The effects on Gujarati merchants were pronounced, leading the governor-general of Mozambique, Xavier Botelho to note the growing "absence" of Vāniyā merchants in Quelimane and Mozambique.[180] In 1831 Vāniyā vessels appear to have delayed their arrival in Mozambique, and were also undertaking significantly fewer voyages to Quelimane from Mozambique Island.[181] The growth in the use of firearms as exchange commodities for the purchase of slaves may also by this time have begun to affect the Gujarati cotton textile trade. Although there is evidence that Vāniyā merchants were trading in firearms in Mozambique in the 1820s, their lack of direct access to firearm production may have undermined their impact on this growing trade.[182] This is not to say that Gujarati cloths did not remain important; indeed, as I have shown in Chapter 3, they remained of paramount importance in the economy of Mozambique until possibly the middle of the nineteenth century. Nonetheless, the growth of firearm imports into the economy of Mozambique, a trade controlled by European merchants, may have further contributed towards undermining the position of Vāniyā merchants in a commercial context in which the sale of weapons connected to the slave trade assumed an importance hitherto unknown in the economy of Mozambique.

A second, familiar, challenge to the place of Gujarati merchants in the economy of Mozambique in the 1830s and 1840s was the heightened competition of Kutchi Bhātiyā merchants and their cloth imports from Mandvi. Textiles such as the richly indigo-dyed *taujiri* came into fashion and increasingly displaced Vāniyā textiles among African consumers.[183] Kutchi investments in the region propelled Bhātiyā merchants into important financial and commercial positions, particularly in Zanzibar

---

[179] For the most recent assessment of the impact of the slave trade on Mozambique, see Capela, *Tráfico de Escravos*, 273–303.

[180] *DAM*, III, 344.   [181] *DAM*, III, 94–5.

[182] Numerous examples exist of Gujarati merchants' involvement in this trade; see, for example, *DAM*, I: 400, 732, 733, 1011, 1015, 1018, 1019, 1093, 1098, 1106, 1107, 1108, 1114, 1115, 1120.

[183] Jeremy Prestholdt, "Africa and the Global Lives of Things", in Frank Trentmann (ed.), *The Oxford Handbook of the History of Consumption* (New York: Oxford University Press, 2012), 85–103.

as it established itself under Omani influence as a major entrepôt in the western Indian Ocean by the 1830s.

These challenges for Gujarati merchants were reflected in the decreasing numbers of slaves imported in Diu. Although slaves continued to be brought to the island throughout the 1830s, they arrived only sporadically and in small numbers. British reports of slaving activity noted this and indeed, raiding of Vāniyā vessels by Royal squadrons off India's west coast may have contributed further to the drop in slave imports.[184] By the late 1840s and early 1850s, the traffic was at a standstill and after this date it was rare for slaves to be imported at all from Mozambique or the East African coast.

Conclusion

Gujarati involvement in the Mozambique slave trade during the eighteenth and nineteenth centuries was essential to its broader contours, and was shaped by a number of contingencies. Rising French demand for African slaves in the Mascarenes, together with rapidly growing Brazilian interest in Mozambique from the early nineteenth century, created a commercial environment that by the 1810s was increasingly dominated by large-scale trafficking that was reliant on the currency of Gujarati cotton textiles. The involvement of Gujarati networks in the burgeoning trade in slaves over this period, as well as supplying a steady demand for African slaves in western India within a context of established slave commercial systems in the subcontinent, did not displace Vāniyā interest in ivory. Rather, it represented a response to changing economic circumstances that – while relying on their textiles as a critical unit of currency for slave trading – were not entirely of their own making. However, the active participation of men such as Shobhachand Sowchand in the trade reflected the availability of significant capital resources among Gujarati networks, and suggests that these merchants played a much more prominent role in the underwriting of slave exports from Mozambique to the western Indian Ocean and southern Atlantic than has hitherto been recognized. Gujarati merchant networks were thus firmly and crucially embedded in the complex regional and global slave systems because of their role in the supply of textiles and their ability to

---

[184] MSA, Political Department (Kutch), Slave Trade, vol. no. 106/990 (1838), 28 September 1838. For the capture in 1840 of a Vāniyā vessel suspected of slave trading from Mozambique, the brig *Dom Pedro Duque do Porto* partly owned by Jiv Kunwarji, see HAG, CD 997, 25 November 1844.

finance slave exchange. The scale and extent of their activities under-scores the need to reconsider our conceptualization of both the Atlantic and Indian Oceans as discrete historical spaces and the critical importance of seemingly marginal actors to the overall operation of the oceanic slave economy.[185]

---

[185] Discussions with Richard Allen over the years has reinforced this point for me. See also concluding remarks in Allen, "Constant Demand of the French".

Conclusion

In 1873, Sir Bartle Frere, former governor of Bombay, was sent by the British Foreign Office to East Africa on a mission to collect information regarding the slave trade. A long-serving colonial official in India who would later be appointed as consul to Zanzibar, Frere was taken aback at the extent of Indian involvement in the economy of the Swahili coast, and reported to London with evident surprise that

> throughout the Zanzibar coast-line, extending along 14° of latitude . . . all banking and mercantile business passes through Indian hands. Hardly a loan can be negotiated, a mortgage effected, or a bill cashed without Indian agency; not an import cargo can be distributed, nor an export cargo collected, of which almost every bale goes through Indian hands. The European or American, the Arab or Swahili may trade and profit but only as an occasional link in the chain between producer and consumer, of which the Indian trader is the one invariable and most important link of all.[1]

Indian business interests "occupy every place where there is trade", which had resulted in a "silent occupation of this coast".[2] The merchants observed by Frere, however, were not Vāniyās from Diu or Daman; they were predominantly Kutchi Bhātiyā from Mandvi who had begun expanding their involvement in the economy and trade of the East African coast from the late eighteenth century.[3] Intensifying in the 1820s and 1830s, their expansion was related to the creation of an Omani commercial empire that in 1840 resulted in the relocation of the Muscat sultanate to Zanzibar. As exponents of Kutch's economic potential and growing importance in the trade of the Arabian Sea, Bhātiyā merchants – together with Kutchi

---

[1] NA, "Correspondence respecting Sir Bartle Frere's mission to the East Coast of Africa, 1872–1873" (Parliamentary Papers. 1873. LXI), "Inclosure 1 in No. 51", 102.

[2] NA, FO881/2270, Frere to Granville, 27 February 1873, and "Memorandum Regarding Banians or Natives of India in East Africa" of 31 March 1873, enclosure in Frere to Granville, 7 May 1873, quoted in Thomas R. Metcalf, *Imperial Connections: India in the Indian Ocean Arena, 1860–1920* (Berkeley: University of California Press, 2007), 165.

[3] Omani and Hadrami Arab merchants were also prominent in the developing nineteenth-century East African and western Indian Ocean commercial arenas.

Memon and Khoja merchants, Ismaili Muslim followers of the Aga Khan – had become integral to the commercial aspirations of Omani leadership in Muscat and both encouraged and benefitted from the extension of Busaidi imperial rule to the Swahili coast. As I have noted throughout this book, Kutchi Bhātiyā capital gradually encroached upon Vāniyā trade, primarily through its investments in Kutchi textiles that super-seded Mozambique imports from Jambusar, and by the 1840s they had largely displaced Vāniyā merchants from Diu and Daman in the com-mercial economy of Mozambique.

Vāniyā merchants belonged to separate and distinct commercial net-works that had competed for the Indian Ocean commerce of Mozambique and its Southeast African coast and interior in the eighteenth and first half of the nineteenth centuries. Their success in dominating the com-mercial economy and financial sector of Mozambique, and their centrality to trade in Diu and Daman, was the result of no single cause but rather due to a number of interrelated factors. Most important was Vāniyā access to an efficient cotton textile procurement and supply network in Gujarat that, together with the specialized productive capacities of weavers who made cloth expressly for the African markets of Mozambique, supplied merchants with regular shipments of manufactures. As the "currency of the land", exchange relations in Mozambique, and indeed throughout much of the East African coast, were dependent on Gujarati textiles that were at the heart of the trading nexus bringing ivory and slaves from the Mozambique interior to the coast. These closely connected trades were driven by high demand on both sides of the western Indian Ocean, as African consumers of cotton cloths and Indian consumers of ivory sus-tained exchange markets of remarkable size and durability.

Critically, the ability of Vāniyā merchants to mediate the relations between these markets owed much to their access to their own long-distance shipping and the availability of skilled navigators and sailing crews. Daman's shipyards in particular provided merchants with expertly constructed vessels that could withstand the rigours of cross-oceanic voyaging and were equipped to carry large volumes of trade goods. The availability of building materials, most significantly teakwood, enhanced the capacity of Daman's shipbuilders to construct durable ships and allowed Vāniyās to withstand the encroachment of British shipping in the western Indian Ocean.

Equally important, the capacity of Vāniyā merchants such as Laxmichand Motichand, with whom we began our story, and Shobhachand Sowchand to mobilize capital through credit relations with bankers in Diu, Daman and especially in Surat provided them with the financing required for long-distance oceanic trade. The financial structure underpinning

Vāniyā trade, organized primarily through the issuing and circulation of *hundis*, in turn enabled Vāniyās to provide credit and make loans to private Portuguese merchants, officials and the state in Mozambique, a capital-poor economy lacking formal banking institutions. These "services" were crucial for the functioning of commerce, underwriting the extensive trades in ivory and slaves, and were vital to the movement of capital between ports in Mozambique, and between Africa and India.

Vāniyā business organization, based around family firms and their associated kin structure, provided elements of cohesiveness and hierarchical ordering that contributed significantly to the success of Vāniyā trade across the Indian Ocean. Informational flows about market conditions and the commercial needs of individual firms, communicated through a regular exchange of correspondence, kept principals in Diu and Daman informed about the activities of agents in Mozambique. This correspondence contributed decisively to generating trust among members of family firms, both between kin and non-kin members, due to the importance of maintaining a reputation for trustworthiness that was critical to a merchant or agent's commercial interactions, given that past behaviour defined future commercial opportunities and possibilities. Vāniyā merchants were not, however, above attempting to impugn the reputation of fellow merchants and call their credit- and trustworthiness into question. That this was increasingly done before Portuguese imperial judges with limited capacity to enforce judicial authority, and not among members of the Vāniyā *mahajan*, was significant. Perhaps precisely because of the importance of reputation, merchants sought in a competitive environment to level accusations of dishonest and untrustworthy behaviour publicly at rivals in an attempt to undermine their position in the market. By contrast, when their collective interests were threatened, especially in Mozambique by officials of the imperial state, Vāniyā merchants were able jointly to oppose such action and protect their trade.

The relationship between Vāniyā merchants and the Portuguese imperial state in Mozambique, Diu and Daman was informed by the stark reality that their vital contributions – both in terms of their role in facilitating commerce and their financial contributions through customs payments to state income – were fundamental to the imperial presence in the western Indian Ocean. While it would perhaps be overstating the case to claim that without the involvement of Vāniyā merchants in its commercial and economic structure the *Estado da Índia* would not have been able to exist in these Indian territories, the imperial presence would have been much diminished and of a wholly different character without them. The extent of Vāniyā influence in the Portuguese imperial economy raises broader questions about the role of indigenous capital in sustaining and undergirding European imperial edifices in South Asia, Africa and elsewhere in the eighteenth- and nineteenth-century worlds of the Indian Ocean.

Vāniyā channels of trade and exchange had been formed along routes that defined particular arenas of the ocean's inter-regional commercial sphere between the 1750s and 1840s. They were successful in shaping these arenas, linking coastal Kathiawar, its consumers and the textile-producing regions of Gujarat with the elephant highlands and cloth markets of Mozambique. These arenas were not, however, discrete and immune from the intrusions of such groups as the Bhātiyā merchants of Mandvi. Competition from the 1750s for the consumer and production markets of the ocean is often generally assumed, though, to have been dominated by the contest between the growing capitalist interests of East India Company traders and British merchants, and South Asian merchants. Often overlooked in the narrative of expanding company trade and the rising Pax Britannica in India and across the Indian Ocean is the competition that existed between South Asian merchant networks *themselves* for the commercial markets of the ocean. The successful penetration of Kutchi Bhātiyā merchants into the Mozambique economy and their displacement of Vāniyā merchants from Diu and Daman represented the substitution of one South Asian network by another.

Bhātiyā involvement in Mozambique did not result in the retreat of Vāniyās from the western Indian Ocean, however. Instead, through a process of redeployment and reorientation, merchants of Diu in particular shifted their trade to the southern Red Sea. Reports of Vāniyā vessels sailing to Mukalla already in 1817 "to benefit from the advantages of that port" and of merchants trading to "Arabia" in the 1830s presaged their developing involvement in these alternative commercial spheres.[4] Ports such as Aden and especially Massawa drew Vāniyā capital that was invested in the trades in gold, ivory, musk and increasingly the marine product economy, especially pearls and mother-of-pearl. They also became prominent in banking and provided credit to local and visiting merchants, as well as providing money-lending services.[5] While evidence from the late nineteenth century suggests that some Vāniyās from Diu and Daman returned to Mozambique where they participated in the retail trade and in the growing agricultural cash-crop economy, the majority of

---

[4] HAG, CD 1006, Joaquim Mourão Garcez to Viceroy, 27 April 1817; CD 1010, Registo de Officios de D. Manoel Portugal e Castro to Castelão of Diu, 20, 16 November 1829.

[5] Jonathan Miran, *Red Sea Citizens: Cosmopolitan Society and Cultural Change in Massawa* (Bloomington: Indiana University Press, 2009).

South Asian merchants were either from Kutch, other parts of Kathiawar such as Porbandar or in many cases from Bombay.[6]

Burgeoning company interests in India and increasing British – and to a more limited extent American – involvement in the region of the western Indian Ocean cannot of course be dismissed as inconsequential for South Asian merchant networks and capital. American traders from New England, for instance, brought ever-larger volumes of machine-made, unbleached cotton cloths known as *merekani* to Mozambique and Zanzibar from the 1830s that challenged the dominance of Kutchi imports as the popularity of these textiles grew among African consumers. However, the US Civil War dealt a devastating blow to the dominance of American cottons in the textile import trade of East Africa, resulting in their replacement by Indian cloth exports from Kutch and Bombay that were financed largely by South Asian merchants.[7]

But the rising tide of British capital in India and the extension and formalization of imperial rule in the second half of the nineteenth century introduced a more serious challenge to the place of South Asian merchant networks in the waterways and economies of the Indian Ocean. Although the establishment of political authority and commercial control in western India in the late eighteenth and early nineteenth centuries had been a more gradual and fractured process than elsewhere on the subcontinent, shielding the princely states in Kathiawar with whom Vāniyā merchants traded extensively from the full encroachment of empire, from the 1850s and 1860s British supremacy in the western Indian Ocean threatened the position and role of South Asian merchant networks in oceanic commerce. Notably, the growth of steamships in the long-distance carrying trades of the ocean exposed Indian (and other local) shipping to economies of scale they could not match, and lessened the reliance of seafarers on the winds of the monsoon system, while railway investments secured access to the markets of the subcontinent and imperialists sought to remake agrarian relations and establish new labour regimes.

An enduring teleology of the triumph of empire has seen the consolidation of British rule in India and the large-scale financial commitments of British and European capital in oceanic trade as signalling a break with the past and its replacement by a new era marked by the logics of industrial capitalism, in which South Asian merchant networks were subverted and displaced from their arenas of commerce and exchange and made

---

[6] Maria Luisa Norton Pinto Teixeira, "Trade and Commerce in Mozambique: Indian Enterprise in Zambezia, ca. 1870–1900", PhD diss., Queen's University, 2001.

[7] Jeremy Prestholdt, *Domesticating the World: African Consumerism and the Genealogies of Globalization* (Berkeley: University of California Press, 2008).

subservient to the demands of colonial masters.[8] However, as evidence of the continued vitality of Diu Vāniyā merchants in the Red Sea during a period of imperial contestation for control of the region between Egyptian, Ottoman, Italian and British authorities and capital, and of the prominent involvement of Kutchi Bhātiyā merchants along the East African coast suggests, this view has obscured the commercial and financial realities on the ground not only in the western Indian Ocean but also throughout the ocean's vast waterways that included a variety of Asian merchant networks. Rather than representing a transformative moment in the history of the ocean's inter-regional exchange and commerce, the imposition of colonial rule and the demands of industrial capitalism did not fatally undermine these networks and their exchange economies.

According to Rajat Kanta Ray, South Asian merchant networks became part of an oceanic, pan-Asian "bazaar" economy that existed within the European-dominated global economy from the 1850s.[9] The bazaar nexus – encompassing a wide range of commercial and financial transactions – was organized around Asian interests that, though they may have intersected with those of Europeans, were guided and governed by largely independent indigenous concerns. In the nineteenth century, it was seen to exist as a parallel economic reality to the colonial European-dominated commercial system, and stretched from the southwestern Indian Ocean to Singapore, comprising peasants, peddlers and, most importantly, mobile Indian and Chinese merchants groups that maintained "a distinct international system that never lost its identity in the larger dominant world system of the West".[10] These merchant groups are viewed as critical in occupying an intermediary position between European capital and localized groups in nineteenth- and early twentieth-century exchange, and in certain sectors such as currency arbitrage were pre-eminent economic actors, enabling linkages between local markets and both small-scale and long-distance global trade.

Thus, although some merchant groups resisted the attempts of colonial rule to structure and control indigenous networks of exchange, many adapted to changing realities by taking advantage of the commercial opportunities offered by the "colonial expansion of the international

---

[8] This was exemplified in the works of K. N. Chaudhuri, *Trade and Civilization in the Indian Ocean: An Economic History from the Rise of Islam to 1750* (New York: Cambridge University Press, 1985); and *Asia Before Europe: Economy and Civilization in the Indian Ocean from the Rise of Islam to 1750* (Cambridge University Press, 1990).

[9] R. K. Ray, "Asian Capital in the Age of European Domination", *Modern Asian Studies*, 29, 3 (1995), 449–554. See also Sugata Bose, *A Hundred Horizons: The Indian Ocean in the Age of Global Empire* (Cambridge, MA: Harvard University Press, 2006).

[10] Ray, "Asian Capital", 553–4.

capitalist economy of Europe" to establish themselves in new ports and trades.[11] A number of Vāniyā merchants moved their base of operations south from Diu and Daman to Bombay as it emerged in the first half of the nineteenth century as an important imperial commercial and shipping centre on the west coast of India.[12] Nattukottai Chettiar merchants of Tamil Nadu in South India responded to the growing limitations for financial investment and the constricting credit markets in India in the late nineteenth century by servicing the credit needs of indigenous Southeast Asians and migrant Indians in the context of rapidly developing rubber and tin industries in Malaya and an emergent rice market in Burma. Utilizing ties to British banks and firms for an additional source of investment capital, along with their own financial and organizational resources, Chettiar merchants managed to dislodge their Chinese competitors and establish themselves as the dominant bankers in mainland and coastal Southeast Asia.[13]

But the interpretive model of the bazaar economy tends perhaps to exaggerate the extent to which Asian merchant networks were subordinated to the global capitalist economy and therefore operated primarily in a dependent capacity within it. In confronting the realities of growing European commercial and financial investments in this global economy, South Asian merchant participation was crucial to elements of its regional structure and dynamics. It also, as we have seen throughout this book, enabled European colonial markets – such as the Portuguese – to establish early foundations upon which they later came to rely. In other words, South Asian networks did not simply "adapt" to changing landscapes but shaped them in fundamental ways.

This was clearly illustrated in the later period by Marwari merchants who expanded their operations throughout India from the 1860s, while Sindhi merchants from northwestern India, in particular "Sindworkies" from Hyderabad, thrived during the colonial period by specializing in two branches of international trade – the silk and curio trades – that stretched to most of the major ports of the world. Using financial as much as marketing skills, Sindworkies profited from currency speculation and maintained business relationships with exchange banks to finance their

---

[11] *Ibid.*, 554.

[12] This may have begun quite early, as evidenced by two prominent Daman merchants, Karamchand Arca and Jhaver Khushal, moving to Bombay in the early to mid-1810s – HAG, CDm 1063, João Vicente Remcoza to Viceroy, 7 May 1815. See also Christine Dobbin, *Urban Leadership in Western India: Politics and Communities in Bombay City, 1840–1885* (London: Oxford University Press, 1972), ch. 1.

[13] David West Rudner, *Caste and Capitalism in Colonial India: The Nattukottai Chettiars* (Berkeley: University of California Press, 1994).

trade and commercial operations. They moved in the 1920s and 1930s into global textile markets by supplying West Africa and Southeast Asia with Japanese-manufactured cloth.[14] In functioning in the entrails of a complex global economy, Marwari and Sindhi networks moulded its contours and influenced its configurations in particular ways.

The relationships maintained by South Asian merchants to the global economy at the apogee of colonial rule in the Indian Ocean between the late nineteenth century and the 1930s and 1940s was of course quite different to those maintained by the Vāniyā merchants of Diu and Daman between the 1750s and 1850s. Yet, without claiming continuity between the precolonial and colonial periods, careful consideration of the histories of such networks exposes their varied and long-standing place in the structure and functioning of the global economy of the Indian Ocean.

---

[14] For Marwaris, see T. A. Timberg, *The Marwaris: From Traders to Industrialists* (New Delhi: Vikas Publishing House, 1978); and the useful discussion in Claude Markovits, "Merchant Circulation in South Asia (Eighteenth to Twentieth Centuries): The Rise of Pan-Indian Merchant Networks", in Markovits, Jacques Pouchepadass and Sanjay Subrahmanyam (eds.), *Society and Circulation: Mobile People and Itinerant Cultures in South Asia, 1750–1950* (Delhi: Permanent Black, 2003), 131–62. On Sindhis, the work of Markovits is also indispensible: *The Global World of Indian Merchants, 1750–1947: Traders of Sind from Bukhara to Panama* (New York: Cambridge University Press, 2000).

Bibliography

ARCHIVES

UNITED KINGDOM

National Archives – Kew, London
Parliamentary Papers. 1873. LXI, Correspondence Respecting Sir Bartle Frere's Mission to the East Coast of Africa, 1872–1873

Oriental and India Office Collection – British Library, London
L/MAR/C, Marine Records, 586, Steam Communication with East Coast of Africa, 1811
R/2, Residency Records, 18/A/71
V/23, Selections from the Records, 212
P/419, Bombay Commerce: Internal and External Reports, vols. 39–66
L/P+S/18, Political and Secret Department, Memoranda, B. 82–90
F/4/905, Board's Collection, 25,644
V/23, Selections from the Records, 212/16
Eur E 293/125, European MSS
Eur E 293/66, European MSS

PORTUGAL

Arquivo Histórico Ultramarino – Lisbon
Documentação Avulsa Moçambicana:
Caixas – 30–243
Códices – 1310; 1324; 1329; 1332; 1345; 1347; 1355; 1362; 1365; 1366; 1370; 1374; 1376; 1377; 1381; 1383; 1425; 1468

Arquivo Nacional da Torre do Tombo – Lisbon
Ministério do Reino, Maços 499, 602, 603, 604
Junta do Comércio, Maço 62

Biblioteca da Ajuda – Lisbon
BA, 54-XIII-3(3)

Biblioteca Nacional – Lisbon
Fundo Geral, Códices 866, 2319, 2320, 3205, 4180, 4406, 4408, 8105, 8470, 8554, 8841, 9452, 10648, 10801
Arquivo da Casa da Tarouca, Coleção Tarouca, no. 53

INDIA

Historical Archives of Goa – Panjim, Goa
Correspondencia de Diu 995–1013
Correspondencia de Damão 1055–1068
Correspondencia de Moçambique 1443–1448
Alfandegas de Diu 4952–4970
Alfandegas de Damão 4836–4852
Copiador Indiano da Feitoria de Surrate 2533
Feitoria de Surrate 2603
Registos Gerais da Feitoria de Dio 7970–7971
Diu 2314
Escravos 2981
Correspondecia Para o Reino, 2784
Livros da Fianças, II
Monções do Reino, 125B, 147A, 152A, 162A, 169C, 173, 178A, 191D, 192B, 193A

Maharashtra State Archives – Mumbai
Political Department, Kutch, Slave Trade, vol. no. 106/990
Political Department, Slave Trade, vol. 169

MOZAMBIQUE

Arquivo Histórico de Moçambique, Maputo
Fundo do Século XIX:
Códices – 11–5; 11–1173; 11–1226; 11–1227; 11–1655; 11–1715; 11–1716; 11–1719; 11–1725; 11–1726; 11–1727; 11–1748; 11–1830; 11–2486; 11–4474; 11–4476; 11–4480; 11–4482; 11–4486; 11–4488; 11–4544; 11–4552; 11–4638; 11–4722; 11–4779; 11–4783; 11–4792; 11–4793; 11–4783; 11–4806; 11–4840; 11–4848; 11–4849; 11–4953; 11–5830
Governo-General – 8–1; 8–9; 8–21; 8–37; 8–48; 8–138; 8–147; 8–162; 8–182; 8–215; 8–227; 8–234

PUBLISHED RECORDS

"Alguns esclarecimentos dirigidos ao Ex.mo Ministro da Marinha e Ultramar...". In *Annaes Do Conselho Ultramarino (Parte Não Officia)*, Serie II. Lisbon: Imprensa Nacional, 1859–61.
"al-Ma'sudi: The Ivory Trade". In *The East African Coast: Select Documents from the First to the Earlier Nineteenth Century*, edited by G. S. P. Freeman-Grenville, London: Rex Collings, 1975.
Andrade, António Alberto de. *Relações de Moçambique Setecentista*. Lisbon: Agência Geral do Ultramar, 1955.

Andrade, Jeronimo Jose Nogueira de. "Descripção Do Estado em que ficavão os Negocios da Capitania de Mossambique nos fins de Novembro do Anno de 1789...". *Arquivo Das Colonias*, I, (1917): 75–96, 115–34, 166–84, 213–35, 275–88; II (1918): 32–49.

Bocarro, António. 'Livro da Plantas de todas as Fortalezas ... do Estado da India'. In *Arquivo Português Oriental*, edited by A. B. de Bragança Pereira, 11 vols. Bastorá: Tipografia Rangel, 1936–1940.

Boteler, Thomas. *Narrative of a Voyage of Discovery to Africa and Arabia, Performed in His Majesty's Ships Leven and Barracouta, from 1821 to 1826*. London: Richard Bentley, 1835.

Bragança Pereira, A. B. de, ed. *Arquivo Português Oriental*, 11 vols. Bastorá: Tipografia Rangel, 1936–40.

Os Portugueses em Diu. Bastorá: Tipografia Rangel, 1938.

Briggs, Henry George. *The Cities of Gujarashtra: Their Topography and History Illustrated, in the Journal of a Recent Tour, with Accompanying Documents*. Bombay: Times, 1849.

Burnell, Arthur Coke, ed. *The Voyage of John Huyghen van Linschoten to the East Indies*. 2 vols. London: Hakluyt Series, 1885.

Burnes, Alexander. "On the Maritime Communications of India, As Carried on by the Natives, Particularly from Kutch, at the Mouth of the Indus". *Journal of the Royal Geographical Society*, 6 (1836): 23–9.

Burns, Cecil L. "A Monograph on Ivory Carving". *Journal of Indian Art and Industry* 9, 70–80 (1902): 53–6.

Burton, Richard F. *The Lake Regions of Central Africa*. 2 vols. London: Longman, Green, Longman, and Roberts, 1860.

Caldeira, Carlos José. *Apontamentos d'uma viagem de Lisboa a China e da China a Lisboa*. Lisbon: J. P. M. Lavado, 1852–3.

Cattelani, G. *L'avvenire coloniale d'Italia nel Benadir*. Naples: F. Giannini e Figli, 1897.

Dalgado, Sebastião Rodolfo. *Glossário Luso-Asiático*. Coimbra: Imprensa da Universidade, 1919–21.

Descripçao dos Rios de Sena por Francisco de Mello e Castro, anno de 1750. Nova Goa: Imprensa Nacional, 1861.

Dias, Luís Fernando de Carvalho. *Fontes Para a História, Geográfia e Comércio De Moçambique, Séc. XVIII*. Lisbon: Junta de Investigações do Ultramar, 1954.

Donald, James. "Ivory Carving in Assam". *Journal of Indian Art and Industry* 9, 70–80 (1902): 57–8.

Ellis, T. P. "Ivory Carving in the Punjab". *Journal of Indian Art and Industry* 9, 70–80 (1902): 45–52.

"Extracto do Plano para um regimento ou nova constituição economica e politica da Capitania de Rios de Senna, com todas as observações e informações necessarias para o referido fim: organisado pelo Governador da mesma colonia Antonio Norberto de Barbosa de Villas-Boas Truão, no anno de 1806 (datada de 20 de maio em Tete)", *Annaes do Conselho Ultramarino* (parte não official), Serie I (1854–8).

Feliciano, José Fialho and Victor Hugo Nicolau, eds. *Memórias De Sofala*. Lisbon: Comissão Nacional para as Comemorações dos Descobrimentos Portugueses, 1998.

Figueiredo, Luis Antonio de. "Noticia do Continente de Mossambique, e abriviada relação do seo comercio..." In *Fontes para a Historia, Geografia e Comercio de Moçambique (sec. XVIII)*, edited by Luis Fernando de Carvalho Dias. Lisbon: Junta de Investigações do Ultramar, 1954.

Forbes, James. *Oriental Memoirs: A Narrative of Seventeen Years Residence in India*. 2 vols. 2nd edn. London: Richard Bentley, 1834.

Freeman-Grenville, G.S.P., ed. *The East African Coast: Select Documents from the First to the Earlier Nineteenth Century*. London: Rex Collings, 1975.

The French at Kilwa Island: An Episode in Eighteenth Century East African History. Oxford: Clarendon Press, 1965.

Frere, Bartle. *Correspondence Respecting Sir Bartle Frere's Mission to the East Coast of Africa, 1872–73*. London: Harrison and Sons, 1873.

Gamitto, A. C. P. *King Kazembe and the Marave, Cheva, Bisa, Bemba, Lunda, and Other Peoples of Southern Africa, Being the Diary of the Portuguese Expedition to That Potentate in the Years 1831 and 1832*. 2 vols. Lisbon: Junta de Investigações do Ultramar, 1960.

Gazetteer of the Bombay Presidency. Vol. 2: Gujarat: Surat and Broach. Bombay: Government Central Press, 1877.

Gazetteer of the Bombay Presidency. Vol. 8: Kathiawar. Bombay: Government Central Press, 1884.

Gibb, H. A. R. *The Travels of Ibn Battūta, A. D. 1325–1354*. 2 vols. Cambridge University Press, 1958–62.

Hove, A. P. *Tours for Scientific and Economical Research made in Guzerat, Kattiawar, and the Conkuns in 1787–88*. Bombay: Government Central Press, 1855.

Lacerda, José Maria Almeida e Araújo de Portugal Corréa de. *Diccionario Encyclopedia ou Novo Diccionario da Lingua Portuguesa para uso dos Portugueses e Brazileiros, Correcto e augmentado, n'esta nova ediçã. Vol. II*, 5th edn. Lisbon: Imprensa Nacional, 1879.

Leitão, H. and Lopes, J. Vicente. *Dicionario da Linguagem de Marinha antiga e actual*, 2nd edn. Lisbon: Centro de Estudos Historicos Ultramarinos da Junta de Investigacoes Cientificas do Ultramar, 1974.

Liesegang, G. ed. *Resposta Das Questoens Sobre Os Cafres' Ou Notícias Etnográficas Sobre Sofala Do Fim Do Século XVIII*. Lisbon: Junta de Investigações do Ultramar, 1966.

Livingstone, David. *Missionary Travels and Researches in South Africa*. New York: Harper, 1858.

Lorimer, John Gordon. *Gazetteer of the Persian Gulf, Omān, and Central Arabia*. 2 vols. Calcutta: Superintendent Government Printing, 1908–15.

Loureiro, Manoel Jose Gomes. *Memorias Dos Estabelecimentos Portugueses a L'este Do Cabo Da Boa Esperança*. Lisbon: Typografia Filippe Nery, 1835.

Macmurdo, James. "Remarks on the Province of Kattiwar; Its Inhabitants, Their Manners and Customs". In *Transactions of the Literary Society of Bombay, vol. I*. London: Longman, Hurst, Rees, Orme, Brown, and John Murray, 1819.

"An Account of the Province of Cutch". In *Transactions of the Literary Society of Bombay*, vol. II. London: Longman, Hurst, Rees, Orme, Brown, and John Murray, 1820.

Marinho, J. Pereira de. *Treze meses de administração geral da Provincia de Moçambique.* Lisbon: Oficina de Manoel de Jesus Coelho, 1847.

Memoria E Documentos Acerca Dos Direitos De Portugal Aos Territorios De Machona E Nyassa. Lisbon: Imprensa Nacional, 1890.

"Memorial e Informação das Feitorias Portuguezas na Costa de Malabar". In *Annaes Do Conselho Ultramarino (Parte Não Officia)*. Nova Goa: Imprensa Nacional, 1854–8.

Milburn, William. *Oriental Commerce; Containing a Geographical Description of the Principal Places in the East Indies, China, and Japan, with Their Produce, Manufactures, and Trade*. 2 vols. London: Black, Parry & Co., 1813.

Moniz, A. F. "A Feitoria Portuguesa De Surrate: Sua Importancia Politica E Comercial". *O Oriente Português* 15, 1 and 2 (1918): 5–29.

Noticias e Documentos para a Historia de Damão – Antiga provincia do Norte. 4 vols. Bastorá: Tipografia Rangel, 1904–23.

Montaury, João Baptista. "Moçambique, Ilhas Querimbas . . . *c*. 1788". In *Relações de Moçambique Setecentista*, edited by António Alberto Andrade. Lisbon: Agência Geral do Ultramar, 1955.

Montez, Caetano. *Descobrimento e Fundação De Lourenço Marques, 1500–1800*. Lourenço Marques: Minerva Central Editora, 1948.

Arquivo Histórico de Moçambique. Inventário do Fundo do Século XVIII. Lourenço Marques: Imprensa Nacional de Moçambique, 1958.

Morice, Monsieur. "Observation on the List of Trade Goods from Another Point of View". In *The French at Kilwa Island*, edited by G. S. P. Freeman-Grenville. Oxford: Clarendon Press, 1965.

The Naval Chronicle, 16 (July–December 1806), 80.

Neves, José Accursio das. *Considerações Politicas, e Comerciaes dos Portugueses na Africa, e na Asia*. Lisbon: Imprensa Regia, 1830.

Owen, Professor. "The Ivory and Teeth of Commerce". *Journal of the Society of Arts*, V, 213 (1856): 65–70

Owen, W. F. W. *Narrative of Voyages to Explore the Shores of Africa, Arabia, and Madagascar; performed in H. M. Ships Leven and Barracouta, under the direction of Capt. W. F. W. Owen*. 2 vols. London: Richard Bentley, 1833.

Postans, T. "Some Account of the Present State of the Trade between the Port of Mandavie in Cutch, and the Eastern Coast of Africa". In *Transactions of the Bombay Geographical Society, June 1839-February 1840*, vol. III. Bombay: American Mission Press, 1840.

Pratt, H. S. "Ivory Carving in Burma". *Journal of Indian Art and Industry*, 9, 70–80 (1902): 59–60.

Prior, James. *Voyage Along the Eastern Coast of Africa, to Mosambique, Johanna, and Quiloa; to St. Helena; to Rio de Janeiro, Bahia, and Pernambuco in Brazil in the Nisus Frigate*. London, 1819.

Rau, Virginia. "Aspectos étnico-culturais da ilha de Moçambique em 1822", *Studia*, 11 (1963): 123–63.

Rivara, J. H. da Cunha Rivara ed., *Archivo Portuguêz Oriental*, 9 vols. Nova Goa: Imprensa Nacional, 1857–77.

Salt, Henry. *A Voyage to Abyssinia ... in the Years 1809 and 1810; in Which Are Included, an Account of the Portuguese Settlements on the East Coast of Africa...* London: F. C. and J. Rivington, 1814.

Santana, Francisco ed. *Documentação Avulsa Moçambicana do Arquivo Histórico Ultramarino*. 3 vols. Lisbon: Centro de Estudos Históricos Ultramarinos, 1964–74.

Santos, Fr. João dos. *Etiópia Oriental e Vária História de Cousas Notáveis do Oriente.* Lisbon: Comissão Nacional para as Comemorações dos Descobrimentos Portugueses, 1999.

Silva, João Julião da. "Memoria...". In *Memórias De Sofala*, edited by José Fialho and Victor Hugo Nicolau Feliciano. Lisbon: Comissão Nacional para as Comemorações dos Descobrimentos Portugueses, 1998.

Stubbs, L. M. "Ivory Carving in the North-West Provinces and Oudh". *Journal of Indian Art and Industry*, 9 70–80 (1902): 41–5.

Teixeira Pinto, Gonçalo de Magalhães. *Memorias Sobre as Possessões Portuguezas Na Asia, escriptas No Ano De 1823....* Nova Goa: Imprensa Nacional, 1859.

Theal, George McCall. *Records of South-Eastern Africa: Collected in Various Libraries and Archive Departments in Europe*, 9 vols. Cape Town: Printed for the Government of the Cape Colony, 1898–1903.

Tod, James. *Travels in Western India*. London: Wm H. Allen and Co, 1839.

Truão, Antonio Norberto de Barbosa de Villas Boas. *Estatistica da Capitania dos Rios de Senna do Anno de 1806*. Lisbon: Imprensa Nacional, 1889.

Ultramarino, Conselho. "Extracto do Plano para um regimento ou nova constituição economica e politica da Capitania de Rios de Senna...". In *Annaes Do Conselho Ultramarino (Parte Não Official). Volume I: 1854–1858*, edited by Conselho Ultramarino. Lisbon: Imprensa Nacional, 1854–8.

Vasconcelos e Cirne, Manuel Joaquim Mendes de. *Memoria Sobre a Provincia De Moçambique*. Edited by José Capela. Maputo: Arquivo Histórico de Moçambique, 1990.

Wolf, Lt. "Narrative of Voyages to Explore the Shores of Africa, Arabia and Madagascar". *Journal of the Royal Geographical Society*, Vol. III. London: John Murray, 1833.

BOOKS, ARTICLES AND PAPERS

Abdulaziz, Mohamed H. *Muyaka, 19th Century Swahili Popular Poetry*. Nairobi: Kenya Literature Bureau, 1979.

Adas, Michael. "Immigrant Asians and the Economic Impact of European Imperialism: The Role of the South Indian Chettiars in British Burma". *Journal of Asian Studies*, 33, 3 (1974): 385–401.

Adenaike, Carolyn. "West African Textiles, 1500–1800". In *Textiles: Production, Trade and Demand*, edited by Maureen Fennell Mazzaoui. Aldershot: Varorium, 1998.

Ahmed, Afzal. *Portuguese Trade and Socio-Economic Changes on the Western Coast of India, 1600–1663*. Delhi: Originals, 2000.

"AHR Forum: Oceans of History". *American Historical Review* 111, 3 (2006): 717–80.

Akyeampong, Emmanuel. "Africans in the Diaspora: The Diaspora and Africa". *African Affairs, Centenary Issue: A Hundred Years of Africa*, 99 (2000): 183–215.

Allen, Calvin H., Jr. "The Indian Merchant Community of Masqaṭ". *Bulletin of the School of Oriental and African Studies, University of London*, 44, 1 (1981): 39–53.

Allen, Richard B. *Slaves, Freedmen and Indentured Laborers in Colonial Mauritius*. New York: Cambridge University Press, 1999.

"Licentious and Unbridled Proceedings: The Illegal Slave Trade to Mauritius and the Seychelles during the Early Nineteenth Century". *Journal of African History*, 42, 1 (2001): 91–116.

"The Mascarene Slave Trade and Labour Migration in the Indian Ocean During the Eighteenth and Nineteenth Centuries". In *The Structure of Slavery in Indian Ocean Africa and Asia*, edited by Gwyn Campbell. London: Frank Cass/Routledge, 2004.

"'Carrying Away the Unfortunate:' The Exportation of Slaves from India During the Late Eighteenth Century". In *Le Monde créole: Peuplement, sociétés et condition Humaine Xviie-Xxe siècles*, edited by Jacques Weber. Paris: Les Indes Savantes, 2005.

"The Constant Demand of the French: The Mascarene Slave Trade and the Worlds of the Indian Ocean and Atlantic During the Eighteenth and Nineteenth Centuries". *Journal of African History*, 49, 1 (2008): 43–72.

"Children and European Slave Trading in the Indian Ocean During the Eighteenth and Early Nineteenth Centuries". In *Children in Slavery through the Ages*, edited by Suzanne Miers, Joseph C. Miller and Gwyn Campbell. Athens, OH: Ohio University Press, 2009.

"Suppressing a Nefarious Traffic: Britain and the Abolition of Slave Trading in India and the Western Indian Ocean, 1770–1830". *The William and Mary Quarterly*, 66, 4 (2009): 873–94.

"Satisfying the 'Want for Labouring People': European Slave Trading in the Indian Ocean, 1500–1850". *Journal of World History*, 1 (2010): 45–73.

European Slave Trading in the Indian Ocean, 1500–1850. Athens, OH: Ohio University Press, forthcoming.

Alpers, Edward A. *The East African Slave Trade*. Nairobi: East African Pub. House, 1967.

"The French Slave Trade in East Africa (1721–1810)". *Cahiers d'Études Africaines*, 37 (1970): 80–124.

Ivory and Slaves in East Central Africa: Changing Pattern of International Trade in East Central Africa to the Later Nineteenth Century. London: Heinemann, 1975.

"Gujarat and the Trade of East Africa, c. 1500–1800". *International Journal of African Historical Studies*, 9, 1 (1976): 22–44.

"Madagascar and Mozambique in the Nineteenth Century: The Era of the Sakalava Raids (1800–1820)". *Omaly sy Anio*, 5–6 (1977): 37–53.

"Futa Benaadir; Continuity and Change in the Traditional Cotton Textile Industry of Southern Somalia, C. 1840–1980". In *Entreprises Et Entrepreneurs En Afrique, Xixe Et Xxe Siècles*, edited by A. Forest and C. Coquery-Vidrovitch. Paris: L'Harmattan, 1983.

"The Ivory Trade in Africa" In *Elephant: The Animal and Its Ivory in African Culture*, edited by Doran H. Ross. Los Angeles: Fowler Museum of Cultural History, 1992.

"The African Diaspora in the Northwest Indian Ocean: Reconsideration of an Old Problem, New Directions for Research". *Comparative Studies of South Asia, Africa and the Middle East*, 17, 2 (1997): 62–81.

"East Central Africa". In *The History of Islam in Africa*, edited by Nehemia Levtzion and Randall L. Pouwels. Athens: Ohio University Press, 2000.

"Recollecting Africa: Diasporic Memory in the Indian Ocean World". *African Studies Review, Special Issue: Africa's Diaspora*, 42, 1 (2000): 83–99.

"The African Diaspora in the Indian Ocean: A Comparative Perspective". In *The African Diaspora in the Indian Ocean*, edited by Shihan de S. Jayasuriya and Richard Pankhurst. Trenton, NJ: Africa World Press, 2003.

"Mozambique and 'Mozambiques': Slave Trade on a Global Scale". In *Slave Routes and Oral Tradition in Southeastern Africa*, edited by Benigna Zimba, Allen Isaacman and Edward A. Alpers. Maputo: Filsom Entertainment, 2005.

East Africa and the Indian Ocean. Princeton: Markus Wiener, 2007.

"Indian Textiles at Mozambique Island in the Mid-Eighteenth Century". Paper presented at the conference "Textile Trades and Consumption in the Indian Ocean World, from Early Times to the Present", Indian Ocean World Centre, McGill University, 2–4 November 2012.

"On Becoming a British Lake: Piracy, Slaving, and British Imperialism in the Indian Ocean during the First Half of the Nineteenth Century". In *Indian Ocean Slavery in the Age of Abolition*, edited by Robert Harms, Bernard K. Freamon and David W. Blight. New Haven and London: Yale University Press, 2013.

Antunes, Luis Frederico Dias. "The Trade Activities of the Banyans in Mozambique: Private Indian Dynamics in the Panel of the Portuguese State Economy (1686–1777)". In *Mariners, Merchants and Oceans: Studies in Maritime History*, edited by K. S. Mathew. New Delhi: Manohar, 1995.

"Têxteis E Metais Preciosos: Novos Vínculos Do Comércio Indo-Brasileiro (1808–1820)". In *O Antigo Regime Nos Trópicos: A Dinâmica Imperial Portuguesa (Séculos XVI-XVIII)*, edited by M. F. Bicalho, M. F. Gouvêa and J. Fragoso. Rio de Janeiro: Civilização Brasileira, 2001.

Appadurai, Arjun. "Introduction: Commodities and the Politics of Value". In *The Social Life of Things: Commodities in Cultural Perspective*, edited by Arjun Appadurai. Cambridge University Press, 1985.

Arasaratnam, Sinnappah. "Trade and Political Dominion in South India, 1750–1790: Changing British-Indian Relationships". *Modern Asian Studies*, 13 (1979): 19–40.

"Weavers, Merchants and Company: The Handloom Industry in Southeastern India, 1750–1790". *Indian Economic and Social History Review*, 17, 3 (1980): 257–82.

Maritime India in the Seventeenth Century. Delhi: Oxford University Press, 1994.

"Slave Trade in the Indian Ocean in the Seventeenth Century" In *Mariners, Merchants and Oceans: Studies in Maritime History*, edited by K. S. Mathew. New Delhi: Manohar, 1995.

Aslanian, Sebouh David. *From the Indian Ocean to the Mediterranean: The Global Trade Networks of Armenian Merchants from New Julfa*. Berkeley: University of California Press, 2011.

Austen, Ralph. "The Islamic Slave Trade out of Africa (Red Sea and Indian Ocean): An Effort at Quantification". Paper presented at the conference "Islamic Africa: Slavery and Related Institutions", Princeton University, 1977.

African Economic History. London: James Currey, 1987.

"The 19th Century Islamic Slave Trade from East Africa (Swahili and Red Sea Coasts): A Tentative Census". In *The Economics of the Indian Ocean Slave Trade in the Nineteenth Century*, edited by W. G. Clarence-Smith. London: Frank Cass, 1989.

Austin, Gareth. *Industrial Growth in the Third World*. London School of Economics Working Paper, 44/98 (1998), 5.

Axelson, Eric. *Portuguese in South-East Africa 1488–1600*. Johannesburg: C. Struik, 1973.

Ballantyne, Tony. "Putting the Nation in its Place?: World History and C. A. Bayly's The Birth of the Modern World". In *Connected Worlds: History in Transnational Perspective*, edited by Ann Curthoys and Marilyn Lake. Canberra: ANU E-Press, 2005.

Barendse, R. J. *The Arabian Seas, 1640–1700*. Research School CNWS, Leiden University, 1998.

"On the Arabian Seas in the Eighteenth Century". Paper presented at the workshop "Western India and the Indian Ocean", Heidelberg, 5 October 1999.

"Reflections on the Arabian Seas in the Eighteenth Century". *Itinerario*, 25, 1 (2001): 25–49.

"Europe Is Literally the Creation of the Third World". H-World Net 2002.

"History, Law and Orientalism under Portuguese Colonialism in Eighteenth-Century India". *Itinerario*, 26, 1 (2002): 33–59.

Basu, H. "The Siddi and the Cult of Bava Gor in Gujarat". *Journal of the Indian Anthropological Society*, 28, 3 (1993): 289–300.

"Slave, Soldier, Trader, Fakir: Fragments of African Histories in Gujarat". In *The African Diaspora in the Indian Ocean*, edited by Shihan S. Jayasuriya and Richard Pankhurst. Trenton, NJ: Africa World Press, 2003.

Bauss, Rudy. "Indian and Chinese Control of the Portuguese Eastern Empire (1770–1850)". *Purabhilekh-Puratatva*, 10, 1 (1992): 1–19.

"A Demographic Study of Portuguese India and Macau, 1750–1850". *Indian Economic and Social History Review*, 34, 2 (1997): 199–216.

"The Portuguese Slave Trade from Mozambique to Portuguese India and Macau and Comments on Timor, 1750–1850: New Evidence from the Archives". *Camoes Center Quarterly*, 6, 1/2 (1997): 21–6.

"Textiles, Bullion and Other Trades of Goa: Commerce with Surat, Other Areas of India, Luso-Brazilian Ports, Macau and Mozambique, 1816–1819". *Indian Economic and Social History Review*, 34, 3 (1997): 275–87.

"A Legacy of British Free Trade Policies: The End of the Trade and Commerce between India and the Portuguese Empire, 1780–1830". *The Calcutta Historical Journal*, 6, 2 (1982): 81–115.

Bayly, C. A. *Indian Society and the Making of the British Empire*. New York: Cambridge University Press, 1987.

Rulers, Townsmen and Bazaars: North Indian Society in the Age of British Expansion 1770–1870. First Indian edn. New Delhi: Oxford University Press, 1992.

"Pre-Colonial Indian Merchants and Rationality". In *India's Colonial Encounter: Essays in Memory of Eric Stokes*, edited by Mushirul Hasan and Narayani Gupta. New Delhi: Manohar, 1993.

The Birth of the Modern World, 1780–1914: Global Connections and Comparisons. Malden, MA: Blackwell, 2004.

Beckert, Sven. "Reconstructing the Empire of Cotton: A Global Story". In *Contested Democracy: Freedom, Race and Power in American History*, edited by Manisha Sinha and Penny Von Eschen. New York: Columbia University Press, 2007.

Benjamin, N. "Arab Merchants of Bombay and Surat (c 1800–1840)". *Indian Economic and Social History Review*, 13, 1 (1976): 85–95.

Berg, Maxine. "In Pursuit of Luxury: Global History and British Consumer Goods in the Eighteenth Century". *Past & Present*, 182, 1 (2004): 85–142.

Luxury and Pleasure in Eighteenth-Century Britain. Oxford University Press, 2005.

Bersselaar, Dmitri van den. *The King of Drinks: Schnapps Gin from Modernity to Tradition*. Leiden and Boston: Brill, 2007.

Bethell, Leslie. *The Abolition of the Brazilian Slave Trade: Britain, Brazil and the Slave Question, 1807–1869*. Cambridge University Press, 1970.

Bhacker, M. Reda. *Trade and Empire in Muscat and Zanzibar: Roots of British Domination*. New York: Routledge, 1992.

Bhattacharya, S. "Eastern India". In *The Cambridge Economic History of India. Volume II: c. 1757-c. 1970*, edited by Dharma Kumar. Cambridge University Press, 1982.

Bhila, H. H. K. *Trade and Politics in a Shona Kingdom: The Manyika and Their Portuguese and African Neighbours, 1575–1902*. Harlow: Longman, 1982.

Blanchy, Sophie. *Karana Et Banians: Les Communautés Commerçantes D'origine Indienne À Madagascar*. Paris: L'Harmattan, 1992.

Borucki, Alex. "The Slave Trade to the Rio De La Plata, 1777–1812: Trans-Imperial Networks and Atlantic Warfare". *Colonial Latin American Review*, 20, (2011): 81–107.

Bose, Sugata. "Space and Time on the Indian Ocean Rim: Theory and History". In *Modernity and Culture: From the Mediterranean to the Indian Ocean*, edited by Leila Tarazi Fawaz, C. A. Bayly and Robert Ilbert. New York: Columbia University Press, 2002.

A Hundred Horizons: The Indian Ocean in the Age of Global Empire. Cambridge, MA: Harvard University Press, 2006.

Bowen, H. V., Elizabeth Mancke and John G. Reid, eds. *Britain's Oceanic Empire: Atlantic and Indian Ocean Worlds, c. 1550–1850*. New York: Cambridge University Press, 2012.

Boyajian, James C. *Portuguese Trade in Asia under the Habsburgs, 1580–1640*. Baltimore: Johns Hopkins University Press, 1993.

Brennig, Joseph J. "Textile Producers and Production in Late Seventeenth Century Coromandel". In *Merchants, Markets and the State in Early Modern India*, edited by Sanjay Subrahmanyam. Delhi: Oxford University Press, 1990.

"Silver in Seventeenth-Century Surat: Monetary Circulation and the Price Revolution in Mughal India". In *Precious Metals in the Late Medieval and Early Modern Worlds*, edited by J. F. Richards. Durham, NC: Carolina Academic Press, 1983.

Brewer, John and Roy Porter. *Consumption and the World of Goods*. London: Routledge, 1994.

Bulley, Anne. *The Bombay Country Ships: 1790–1833*. Richmond: Curzon Press, 2000.

Burke, Timothy. *Lifebuoy Men, Lux Women: Commodification, Consumption & Cleanliness in Zimbabwe*. Durham and London: Duke University Press, 1996.

Campbell, Gwyn. "Madagascar and the Slave Trade, 1810–1895". *Journal of African History*, 22, 3 (1981): 203–27.

"The East African Slave Trade, 1861–1895: The 'Southern' Complex". *International Journal of African Historical Studies*, 22, 1 (1989): 1–26.

"Madagascar and Mozambique in the Slave Trade of the Western Indian Ocean 1800–1861". In *The Economics of the Indian Ocean Slave Trade in the Nineteenth Century*, edited by W. G. Clarence-Smith. London: Frank Cass, 1989.

"The Origins and Development of Coffee Production in Réunion and Madagascar, 1711–1972". In *The Global Coffee Economy in Africa, Asia, and Latin America, 1500–1989*, edited by William Gervase Clarence-Smith and Steven Topik. New York: Cambridge University Press, 2003.

"African Diaspora in Asia" In *Encyclopedia of Diasporas*, edited by Melvin Ember et al. New York: Springer, 2004.

The Structure of Slavery in Indian Ocean Africa and Asia. London: Frank Cass/ Routledge, 2004.

An Economic History of Imperial Madagascar, 1750–1895. Cambridge University Press, 2005.

"Slavery and the Trans-Indian Ocean World Slave Trade: A Historical Outline". In *Cross Currents and Community Networks: The History of the Indian Ocean World*, edited by Himanshu Prabha Ray and Edward A. Alpers. New Delhi: Oxford University Press, 2007.

"Slave Trades and the Indian Ocean World". In *India in Africa/Africa in India: Indian Ocean Cosmopolitanisms*, edited by John C. Hawley. Bloomington: Indiana University Press, 2008.

"Children and Bondage in Imperial Madagascar, c. 1790–1895". In *Child Slaves in the Modern World*, edited by Suzanne Miers, Joseph C. Miller and Gwyn Campbell. Athens, OH: Ohio University Press, 2011.

Candido, Mariana P. "Different Slave Journeys: Enslaved African Seamen on Board of Portuguese Ships, *c.* 1760–1820s". *Slavery and Abolition*, 31, 3 (2010): 395–409

Capela, José. *O Escravismo Colonial Em Moçambique*. Porto: Edições Afrontamento, 1993.

O Tráfico De Escravos Nos Portos De Moçambique, 1733–1904. Porto: Edições Afrontamento, 2002.

and Eduardo Medeiros. *O tráfico de escravos de Moçambique para as ilhas do Índico, 1720–1902*. Maputo: Núcleo Editorial da Universidade Eduardo Mondlane, 1987.

Caplan, Lionel. "Power and Status in South Asian Slavery". In *Asian and African Systems of Slavery*, edited by James L. Watson. Oxford: Blackwell, 1980.

Carreira, Ernestina. "Moçambique, Goa E Macau Durante as Guerras Napoleonicas 1801–1810". In *As Rellações Entre a Índia Portuguesa, a Asia Do Sueste E O Extremo Oriente: Actas Do Vi Seminario Internacional De Historia Indo-Portuguesa*, edited by Luis F. F. Reis Thomaz and Artur Teodoro de Matos. Macau and Lisbon: Comissão Nacional para as Comemorações dos Descobrimentos Portugueses, 1993.

"O Comércio Português no Gujarat na Segunda Metade do Século XVIII: As Famílias Loureiro e Ribeiro". *Mare Liberum*, 9 (1995): 83–94.

"India". In *O Império Africano 1825–1890*, edited by Valentim Alexandre and Jill Dias. Lisbon: Editorial Estampa, 1998.

"L'Empire et ses Vaisseaux: La Construction Navale dans l'Ocean Indien Occidental aux XVIIIe et XIXe Siècles". In *Éclats d'empire, du Brésil à Macao*, edited by Ernestine Carreira and Idelette Muzart-Fonseca dos Santos. Paris: Maisonneuve et Larose, 2003.

"Navegação Comercial Entre O Brasil E a Asia Portuguesa Durante a Estadia Da Corte No Brasil, 1808–1821". In *Actas Do Congresso Internacional: Espaço Atlântico De Antigo Regime – Poderes E Sociedades*. Lisbon: FCSH/ UNL, 2005.

"From Decline to Prosperity: Shipbuilding in Daman, 18th–19th Centuries". In *Indo-Portuguese Encounters: Journeys in Science, Technology and Culture*, edited by Lotika Varadarajan. New Delhi: Aryan Books International, 2006.

"De La Piastre a L'opium: Connexions Commerciales Entre Les Espaces Periphériques Des Empires Portugais Et Espagnol À La Fin Du XVIIIe Siècle". In *Cultures Lusophones Et Hispanophones: Penser La Relation*, edited by Maria Graciete Besse. Paris: Indigo, 2010.

Carter, Marina. "Slavery and Unfree Labour in the Indian Ocean". *History Compass*, 4, 5 (2006): 800–13.

Catlin-Jairazbhoy, Amy and Edward A. Alpers. *Sidis and Scholars: Essays on African Indians*. Delhi: Rainbow Publishers and Trenton, NJ: Red Sea Press, 2004.

Chakravarti, Ranabir. "Nakhudas and Nauvittakas: Ship-Owning Merchants in the West Coast of India (c. AD 1000–1500)". *Journal of the Economic and Social History of the Orient*, 43, 1 (2000): 34–64.

Chandavarkar, Raj. *The Origins of Industrial Capitalism in India*. New York: Cambridge University Press, 1994.

Chatterjee, Indrani. "Colouring Subalternity: Slaves, Concubines and Social Orphans in Early Colonial India". In *Subaltern Studies X*, edited by Gyan Prakash and Susie Tharu Gautam Bhadra. New Delhi: Oxford University Press, 1999.

Gender, Slavery and Law in Colonial India. New Delhi: Oxford University Press, 1999.

"Abolition by Denial". Paper presented at the conference "Slavery, Unfree Labour and Revolt in the Indian Ocean Region", l'Université d'Avignon, Avignon, 4–6 October 2001.

"Abolition by Denial: The South Asian Example". In *Abolition and Its Aftermath in Indian Ocean Africa and Asia*, edited by Gwyn Campbell. New York: Routledge, 2005.

"Renewed and Connected Histories: Slavery and the Historiography of South Asia". In *Slavery and South Asian History*, edited by Indrani Chatterjee and Richard Eaton. Bloomington: Indiana University Press, 2006.

and Richard Eaton, eds. *Slavery and South Asian History*. Bloomington: Indiana University Press, 2006.

Chaudhuri, K. N. *The Trading World of Asia and the English East India Company, 1660–1760*. Cambridge University Press, 1978.

"European Trade with India". In *The Cambridge Economic History of India. Vol. I: c. 1200-c. 1750*, edited by Tapan Raychaudhuri and Irfan Habib. Cambridge University Press, 1982.

Trade and Civilization in the Indian Ocean: An Economic History from the Rise of Islam to 1750. New York: Cambridge University Press, 1985.

Asia before Europe: Economy and Civilization in the Indian Ocean from the Rise of Islam to 1750. Cambridge University Press, 1990.

"The Structure of Indian Textile Industry in the Seventeenth and Eighteenth Centuries". In *Cloth and Commerce: Textiles in Colonial India*, edited by Tirthankar Roy. New Delhi: Sage, 1996.

Chaudhury, Sushil and Morineau, Michel, eds. *Merchants, Companies and Trade: Europe and Asia in the Early Modern Era*. Cambridge University Press, 1999.

Chauhan, R. R. S. *Africans in India: From Slavery to Royalty* New Delhi: Asian Publication Services, 1995.

Clarence-Smith, W. G. *The Third Portuguese Empire 1825–1975: A Study in Economic Imperialism*. Manchester University Press, 1985.

Economics of Indian Ocean Slave Trade. London: Frank Cass, 1989.

"Indian Business Communities in the Western Indian Ocean in the Nineteenth Century". *The Indian Ocean Review*, 2, 4 (1989): 18–21.

"Indian and Arab Entrepreneurs in Eastern Africa (1800–1914)". In *Négoce Blanc En Afrique Noire*, edited by Hubert Bonin and Michel Cahen. Paris: Société Française d'Histoire d'Outre-Mer, 2001.

"The Cotton Textile Industry of Sub-Saharan Eastern Africa in the Longue Durée". Paper presented at the conference "Understanding African Poverty over the Longue Durée", Accra, Ghana, 15–17 July 2010.

"The Expansion of Cotton Textile Production in the Western Indian Ocean, c1500–c1850". In *Reinterpreting Indian Ocean Worlds: Essays in Honour of Prof.*

K. N. Chaudhuri, edited by Stefan Halikowski-Smith. Newcastle: Cambridge Scholars Publishing, 2011.

Coclanis, Peter A. "Atlantic World or Atlantic/World?" *The William and Mary Quarterly*, 63, 4 (2006): 725–42.

Cooney, Jerry W. "Silver, Slaves and Food: The Rio De La Plata and the Indian Ocean, 1796–1806". *Tijdschrift voor Zeegeschiedenis*, 5, 1 (1986): 35–45.

"Oceanic Commerce and Platine Merchants, 1796–1806: The Challenge of War". *The Americas*, 45, 4 (1989): 509–52.

Cooper, Frederick. *Plantation Slavery on the East Coast of Africa*. New Haven: Yale University Press, 1977.

Correia-Afonso, John. "Indo-Portuguese Ivories in the Heras Collection". *Indica*, 31, 2 (1994): 101–12.

Cunnison, Ian. "Kazembe and the Portuguese, 1798–1832", *Journal of African History*, 2/1 (1961): 61–76.

Curtin, Philip D. *Cross-Cultural Trade in World History*. New York: Cambridge University Press, 1984.

Dale, Stephen Frederic. *Indian Merchants and Eurasian Trade, 1600–1750*. New York: Cambridge University Press, 1994.

Das Gupta, Ashin. "Trade and Politics in 18th-Century India". In *Islam and the Trade of Asia*, edited by D. S. Richards. Philadelphia: University of Pennsylvania Press, 1970.

"Indian Merchants and the Trade in the Indian Ocean, c. 1500–1750". In *The Cambridge Economic History of India. Volume I: c. 1200–c. 1750*, edited by Tapan Raychaudhuri and Irfan Habib. Cambridge University Press, 1982.

Indian Merchants and the Decline of Surat c. 1700–1750. New Delhi: Manohar, 1994.

"The Early 17th Century Crisis in the Western Indian Ocean and the Rise of Gujarati Shipping in the Early 18th Century". In *Essays in Maritime Studies*, edited by B. Arunachalam. Mumbai: Maritime History Society, 1998.

"India and the Indian Ocean in the Eighteenth Century". In *India and the Indian Ocean 1500–1800*, edited by Das Gupta and M. N. Pearson. New Delhi: Oxford University Press, 1999.

"Gujarati Merchants and the Red Sea Trade, 1700–1725". In *The World of the Indian Ocean Merchant, 1500–1800: Collected Essays of Ashin Das Gupta*, compiled by Uma Das Gupta. New Delhi: Oxford University Press, 2001.

"The Maritime Merchant and Indian History". In *The World of the Indian Ocean Merchant, 1500–1800: Collected Essays of Ashin Das Gupta*, compiled by Uma Das Gupta. New Delhi: Oxford University Press, 2001.

The World of the Indian Ocean Merchant, 1500–1800 : Collected Essays of Ashin Das Gupta, compiled by Uma Das Gupta. New Delhi: Oxford University Press, 2001.

and M. N. Pearson. *India and the Indian Ocean, 1500–1800*. New York: Oxford University Press, 1987.

Datoo, Bashir. "Misconceptions About the Use of Monsoons by Dhows in East African Waters". *East African Geographical Review*, 8 (1970): 1–10.

Davison, Patricia and Patrick Harries. "Cotton Weaving in South-East Africa: Its History and Technology" In *Textiles of Africa*, edited by Dale Idiens and K. G. Ponting. Bath: Pasold Research Fund, 1980.

Deloche, Jean. *Transport and Communications in India Prior to Steam Locomotion. Volume II: Water Transport.* New York: Oxford University Press, 1994.

Dimmock, L."The Lateen Rig". *Mariner's Mirror,* 32 (1946), 35–41.

Divekar, V. D. "Western India". In *The Cambridge Economic History of India. Volume II: c. 1757–1979,* edited by Dharma Kumar. Cambridge University Press, 1982.

Dobbin, Christine E. *Urban Leadership in Western India: Politics and Communities in Bombay City, 1840–1885.* Oxford University Press, 1972.

Asian Entrepreneurial Minorities: Conjoint Communities in the Making of the World-Economy, 1570–1940. Richmond: Curzon, 1996.

Dwivedi, V. P. *Indian Ivories: A Survey of Indian Ivory and Bone Carvings from the Earliest to the Modern Times.* Delhi: Agam Prakashan, 1976.

Eaton, Richard. "The Rise and Fall of Military Slavery in the Deccan, 1450–1650". In *Slavery & South Asian History,* edited by Indrani Chatterjee and Richard Eaton. Bloomington: Indiana University Press, 2006.

Eldredge, Elizabeth A. "Delagoa Bay and the Hinterland in the Early Nineteenth Century: Politics, Trade, Slaves, and Slave Raiding". In *Slavery in South Africa: Captive Labor on the Dutch Frontier,* edited by Elizabeth A. Eldredge and Fred Morton. Boulder: Westview Press, 1994.

Ewald, Janet J. "Crossers of the Sea: Slaves, Freedmen, and Other Migrants in the Northwestern Indian Ocean, c. 1750–1914". *American Historical Review,* 105, 1 (2000): 69–91.

"Slaves and Seedies in British Ports and Vessels, 1840–1900". Paper presented at the conference "Slave Systems in Asia and the Indian Ocean: Their Structure and Change in the 19th and 20th Centuries", Université d'Avignon, Avignon, 18–20 May 2000.

Fawaz, Leila Tarazi, C. A. Bayly and Robert Ilbert. *Modernity and Culture: From the Mediterranean to the Indian Ocean.* New York: Columbia University Press, 2002.

Ferreira, Roquinaldo. "Dinâmica do comércio intracolonial: Geribitas, panos asiáticos e guerra no tráfico angolano de escravos (século XVIII)", in *O Antigo Regime nos Trópicos: A Dinâmica Imperial Portuguesa (Séculos XVI-XVIII),* edited by J. Fragoso, M. F. Bicalho and M. F. Gouvêa. Rio de Janeiro: Civilização Brasileira, 2001.

"'A Arte De Furtar:' Redes De Comércio Illegal No Mercado Imperial Ultramarino Português (*C.* 1690-*C.* 1750)". In *Na Trama das Redes: Política e Negócios no Império Português, séculos XVI-XVIII,* edited by João Fragoso and Maria de Fátima Gouvêa. Rio de Janeiro: Civilização Brasileira, 2010.

Florentino, Manolo. *Em Costas Negras: Uma História Do Tráfico Atlântico De Escravos Entre a África E O Rio De Janeiro (Séculos XVIII E XIX).* Rio de Janeiro: Arquivo Nacional, 1995.

"Slave Trade between Mozambique and the Port of Rio de Janeiro, c. 1790–c. 1850, Demographic, Social and Economic Aspects". In *Slave Routes and Oral Tradition in Southeastern Africa,* edited by Benigna Zimba, Allen Isaacman, and Edward A. Alpers. Maputo: Filsom Entertainment, 2005.

Flynn, Dennis O. and Arturo Giráldez. "Born with a 'Silver Spoon': The Origin of World Trade in 1571". *Journal of World History,* 6, 2 (1995): 201–21.

Gerbeau, Hubert. "L'océan Indien N'est Pas L'atlantique: La Traite Illegal À Bourbon Au Xixe Siècle". *Revue Outre-mers, Revue d'histoire*, 89, 2 (2002): 79–108.

Gilbert, Erik. *Dhows and the Colonial Economy in Zanzibar, 1860–1970*. Oxford: James Currey, 2004.

Glahn, Richard von. *Fountain of Fortune: Money and Monetary Policy in China, 1000–1700*. Berkeley: University of California Press, 1996.

Glassman, Jonathon. *Feasts and Riot: Revelry, Rebellion, and Popular Consciousness on the Swahili Coast, 1856–1888*. Portsmouth, NH: Heinemann, 1995.

Goody, Jack. *The East in the West*. New York: Cambridge University Press, 1996.

Gopal, Surendra. *Commerce and Crafts in Gujarat, 16th and 17th Centuries: A Study in the Impact of European Expansion on Precapitalist Economy*. New Delhi: People's Pub. House, 1975.

Greif, Avner. "Reputation and Coalitions in Medieval Trade: Evidence on the Maghribi Traders". *Journal of Economic History*, 49, 4 (1989): 857–82.

"The Organization of Long-Distance Trade: Reputation and Coalitions in the Geniza Documents and Genoa During the Eleventh and Twelfth Centuries". *The Journal of Economic History*, 51, 2 (1991): 459–62.

"Contract Enforceability and Economic Institutions in Early Trade: The Maghribi Traders' Coalition". *American Economic Review*, 83, 3 (1993): 525–48.

Institutions and the Path to the Modern Economy: Lessons from Medieval Trade. New York: Cambridge University Press, 2006.

Guha, Sumit. "Potentates, Traders and Peasants: Western India, c. 1700–1870". In *Institutions and Economic Change in South Asia*, edited by Burton Stein and Sanjay Subrahmanyam. Oxford University Press, 1996.

"Slavery, Society and the State in Western India, 1700–1800". In *Slavery and South Asian History*, edited by Indrani Chatterjee and Richard Eaton. Bloomington: Indiana University Press, 2006.

Gupta, Anirudha, ed. *Minorities on India's West Coast: History and Society*. Delhi: Kalinga, 1991.

Guy, John. *Woven Cargoes: Indian Textiles in the East*. London: Thames and Hudson, 2002.

Habib, Irfan. "Usury in Medieval India". *Comparative Studies in Society and History*, 4 (1964): 393–419.

"The System of Bills of Exchange (Hundis) in the Mughal Empire". In *Proceedings of the Indian History Congress*. Delhi: Indian History Congress Association, 1973.

"Merchant Communities in Precolonial India". In *The Rise of Merchant Empires: Long-Distance Trade in the Early Modern World, 1350–1750*, edited by James Tracey. Cambridge University Press, 1990.

Haider, Najaf. "The Networks of Monetary Exchange in the Indian Ocean Trade, 1200–1700". In *Cross Currents and Community Networks: The History of the Indian Ocean World*, edited by Himanshu Prabha Ray and Edward A. Alpers. New Delhi: Oxford University Press, 2007.

Hall, Bruce S. "How Slaves Used Islam: The Letters of Enslaved Muslim Commercial Agents in the Nineteenth-Century Niger Bend and Central Sahara". *The Journal of African History*, 52, 3 (2011): 279–97.

"Enslaved Paths of Circulation in the Sahara: Commercial Networks and Slave Agency between Ghadames (Libya) and Timbuktu (Mali) in the Nineteenth Century". In *Confluence of Cultures*, edited by Chouki el Hamel and Paul Lovejoy. Princeton: Marcus Wiener, forthcoming.

Hardiman, David. *Feeding the Baniya: Peasants and Usurers in Western India*. New York: Oxford University Press, 1996.

"Penetration of Merchant Capital in Pre-Colonial Gujarat". In *Capitalist Development: Critical Essays*, edited by Ghanshyam Shah. Bombay: Popular Prakashan, 1990.

Hariharan, Shantha. *Cotton Textiles and Corporate Buyers in Cottonopolis: A Study of Purchases and Prices in Gujarat, 1600–1800*. Delhi: Manak Publications, 2002.

Harris, Joseph C. *The African Presence in Asia: Consequence of the East African Slave Trade*. Evanston: Northwestern University Press, 1971.

Hawkins, Clifford W. *The Dhow: An Illustrated History of the Dhow and Its World*. Lymington: Nautical Publishing, 1977.

Haynes, Douglas E. *Rhetoric and Ritual in Colonial India: The Shaping of a Public Culture in Surat City, 1852–1928*. Berkeley: University of California Press, 1991.

Small Town Capitalism in Western India: Artisans, Merchants and the Making of the Informal Economy, 1870–1960. New York: Cambridge University Press, 2012.

"Surat City, Its Decline and the Indian Ocean, 1730–1940". In *Port Towns of Gujarat*. Delhi: Primus, forthcoming.

and Tirthankar Roy. "Conceiving Mobility: Weavers' Migrations in Pre-Colonial and Colonial India". *Indian Economic and Social History Review*, 36, 1 (1999): 35–67.

and Abigail McGowan. "Introduction". In *Towards a History of Consumption in South Asia*, edited by Abigail McGowan, Douglas E. Haynes, Tirthankar Roy, and Haruka Yanagisawa. New Delhi: Oxford University Press, 2010.

História, Departamento de (Universidade Eduardo Mondlane), *História de Moçambique*, 3 vols. Maputo: Departamento de História & Tempo, 1983–93.

Hofmeyr, Isabel. "AHR Conversation: On Transnational History". *American Historical Review*, 111, 5 (2006): 1441–64.

Hooper, Jane and David Eltis. "The Indian Ocean in Transatlantic Slavery". *Slavery & Abolition* (2012), DOI:10.1080/0144039X.2012.734112.

Hopkins, A. G. *Globalization and World History*. New York: W. W. Norton, 2002.

Global History: Between the Universal and the Local. New York: Palgrave Macmillan, 2006.

Hoppe, Fritz. *A África Oriental Portuguesa no tempo do Marquês de Pombal 1750–1777*. Lisbon: Agência-Geral do Ultramar, 1970.

Hornell, James. "The Sailing Craft of Western India". *Mariner's Mirror*, 32 (1946): 195–217.

Horton, Mark. "Early Muslim Trading Settlements on the East African Coast: New Evidence from Shanga". *Antiquaries Journal*, 67, 2 (1987): 290–323.

"Artisans, Communities, and Commodities: Medieval Exchanges between Northwestern India and East Africa". *Ars Orientalis*, 34, (2004): 62–80.

and John Middleton. *The Swahili: The Social Landscape of a Mercantile Society*. Oxford, UK, Malden, MA: Blackwell, 2000.

Hossain, Hameeda. *The Company Weavers of Bengal: The East India Company and the Organization of Textile Production in Bengal, 1750–1813.* New Dehli: Oxford University Press, 1988.

Hourani, Albert. *A History of the Arab Peoples.* Cambridge, MA: Belknap Press of Harvard University Press 1991.

Irwin, John and P. R. Schwartz. *Studies in Indo-European Textile History.* Ahmedabad: Calico Museum of Textile, 1966.

Isaacman, Allen F. *Mozambique. The Africanization of a European Institution: The Zambesi Prazos, 1750–1902.* Madison: University of Wisconsin Press, 1972.

and Barbara Isaacman. *Slavery and Beyond: The Making of Men and Chikunda Ethnic Identities in the Unstable World of South-Central Africa, 1750–1920.* Portsmouth, NH: Heinemann, 2004.

Jackson-Haight, Mabel V. *European Powers and South-East Africa: A Study of International Relations on the South-East Coast of Africa.* London: Routledge, 1967.

Jain, L. C. *Indigenous Banking in India.* London: Macmillan and Co. Limited, 1929.

Jayasuriya, Shihan de S. and Jean-Pierre Angenot. *Uncovering the History of Africans in Asia.* Boston: Brill, 2008.

and Richard Pankhurst. *The African Diaspora in the Indian Ocean.* Trenton, NJ: Africa World Press, 2003.

Keyes, Carolyn Maureen. "West African Textiles, 1500–1800". In *Textiles: Production, Trade and Demand,* edited by Fennell Mazzaoui. Aldershot: Varorium, 1998.

Klein, Herbert S. "The Trade in African Slaves from Rio De Janeiro, 1795–1811". In *The Middle Passage: Comparative Studies in the Atlantic Slave Trade,* edited by Herbert S. Klein. Princeton University Press, 1978.

Landa, Janet T. *Trust, Ethnicity, and Identity: Beyond the New Institutional Economics of Ethnic Trading Networks, Contract Law, and Gift-Exchange.* Ann Arbor: University of Michigan Press, 1994.

Larson, Pier Martin. *History and Memory in the Age of Enslavement: Becoming Merina in Highland Madagascar, 1770–1822.* Portsmouth, NH: Heinemann, 2000.

Ocean Of Letters: Language and Creolization in an Indian Ocean Diaspora. New York: Cambridge University Press, 2009.

Leupp, Gary "Africans in Portuguese Asia, 1510–Ca. 1800: The Black Presence in Goa, Macao, and Nagasaki". Paper presented at conference "Blacks and Asians: Encounters in Time and Space", Boston University, 12–14 April 2002.

Levi, Scott Cameron. *The Indian Diaspora in Central Asia and Its Trade, 1550–1900.* Boston: Brill, 2002.

"Multanis and Shikarpuris: Indian Diasporas in Historical Perspective". In *Global Indian Diasporas: Exploring Trajectories of Migration and Theory,* edited by Gijsbert Oonk. Amsterdam University Press, 2008.

Lewis, Bernard. *Race and Slavery in the Middle East: An Historical Enquiry.* New York: Oxford University Press, 1990.

Liesegang, G. "A First Look at the Import and Export Trade of Mozambique, 1800–1914". In *Figuring African Trade: Proceedings of the Symposium on the Quantification and Structure of the Import and Export and Long Distance Trade in*

Africa, 1800–1913, edited by G. Liesegang, H. Pasch and A. Jones. Berlin: D. Reimer Verlag, 1986.

"Nguni Migrations between Delagoa Bay and the Zambezi, 1821–1839". *African Historical Studies*, 3, 2 (1970): 317–37

"'Technology, Space, Climate and Biology': The Incidence and Impact of Drought, Famines, Pests, Epidemics, and Wars in the History of Mozambique, *C*. 1515–1990". Unpublished manuscript, Maputo, 1979–93.

Lobato, Alexandre. *Relações Luso-Maratas, 1658–1737*. Lisbon: Centro de Estudos Históricos Ultramarinos, 1965.

Ilha de Moçambique: Panorama Estético. Lisbon: Agência-Geral do Ultramar, 1966.

Evolução Administrativa E Económica De Moçambique, 1752–1763, 1ª Parte: Fundamentos da criação do Governo-Geral em 1752. Lisbon: Publicações Alfa, 1989.

História Do Presídio De Lourenço Marques: 1787–1799. 2 vols. Lisbon: Junta de Investigação do Ultramar, 1957.

Lobato, Manuel. "Relações Comerciais Entre a India E a Costa Africana Nos Séculos Xvi E Xvii: O Papel Do Guzerate No Comércio De Moçambique". *Mare Liberum* 9, July (1965): 157–73.

Lombard, Denys and Jean Aubin. *Asian Merchants and Businessmen in the Indian Ocean and the China Sea*. New York: Oxford University Press, 2000.

Lopes, Maria de Jesus dos Mártires. *Goa Setecentista: Tradição E Modernidade (1750–1800)*. Lisbon: Universidade Católica Portuguesa, 1996.

Lovejoy, Paul E.. *Transformations in Slavery: A History of Slavery in Africa*. 2nd edn. Cambridge University Press, 2000.

Ludden, David. "World Economy and Village India". In *South Asia and World Capitalism*, edited by Sugata Bose. Delhi: Oxford University Press, 1990.

"History Along the Coastal Zones of Southern Asia". Paper presented at the South Asia Seminar, Columbia University, New York, 18 October 1999.

"Presidential Address: Maps in the Mind and the Mobility of Asia". *Journal of Asian Studies*, 62, 4 (2003): 1057–78.

Machado, Pedro. "A Forgotten Corner of the Indian Ocean: Gujarati Merchants, Portuguese India and the Mozambique Slave Trade, c. 1730–1830". *Slavery & Abolition*, 24, 2 (2003): 17–32.

"Awash in a Sea of Cloth: Gujarat, Africa and the Western Indian Ocean, 1300–1800". In *The Spinning World: A Global History of Cotton Textiles, 1200–1850*, edited by Giorgio Riello and Prasannan Parthasarathi. New York: Oxford University Press, 2009.

"Cloths of a New Fashion: Indian Ocean Networks of Exchange and Cloth Zones of Contact in Africa and India in the Eighteenth and Nineteenth Centuries". In *How India Clothed the World: The World of South Asian Textiles, 1500–1850*, edited by Giorgio Riello and Tirthankar Roy. Leiden: Brill, 2009.

Major, Andrea. "Enslaving Spaces: Domestic Slavery and the Spatial, Ideological and Practical Limits of Colonial Control in the Nineteenth-Century Rajput and Maratha States". *Indian Economic and Social History Review*, 46, 3 (2009): 315–42.

"'The Slavery of East and West': Abolitionists and 'Unfree' Labour in India, 1820–1833". *Slavery & Abolition*, 31, 4 (2010): 501–25.

Slavery, Abolitionism and Empire in India, 1772–1843. Liverpool University Press, 2012.

Manning, Patrick. *Slavery and African Life. Occidental, Oriental and African Slave Trades*. Cambridge University Press, 1990.

Margariti, Roxani Eleni. *Aden & the Indian Ocean Trade: 150 Years in the Life of a Medieval Arabian Port*. Chapel Hill: University of North Carolina Press, 2007.

Markovits, Claude. "Indian Merchant Networks Outside India in the Nineteenth and Twentieth Centuries: A Preliminary Survey". *Modern Asian Studies*, 4 (1999): 883–911.

The Global World of Indian Merchants, 1750–1947: Traders of Sind from Bukhara to Panama. New York: Cambridge University Press, 2000.

"Merchant Circulation in South Asia (Eighteenth to Twentieth Centuries): The Rise of Pan-Indian Merchant Networks", in *Society and Circulation: Mobile People and Itinerant Cultures in South Asia, 1750–1950*, edited by Claude Markovits, Jacques Pouchepadass and Sanjay Subrahmanyam. Delhi: Permanent Black, 2003.

"Indian Merchant Networks and the British Empire". Paper presented at the XIV International Economic History Congress, Helsinki, 21–5 August 2006.

and Jacques Pouchepadass and Sanjay Subrahmanyam, eds. *Society and Circulation: Mobile People and Itinerant Cultures in South Asia, 1750–1950*. Delhi: Permanent Black, 2003.

Marques, João Pedro. *The Sounds of Silence: Nineteenth-Century Portugal and the Abolition of the Slave Trade*. New York: Bergahn Books, 2006.

Martin, Esmond B. and T. C. I. Ryan. "A Quantitative Assessment of the Arab Slave Trade of East Africa, 1770–1896". *Kenya Historical Review*, 5, 1 (1977): 71–91.

Maxwell, Kenneth. *Pombal, Paradox of the Enlightenment*. New York: Cambridge University Press, 1995.

McPherson, Kenneth. *The Indian Ocean: A History of People and The Sea*. New Delhi: Oxford University Press, 1998.

Medeiros, Eduardo. *As Etapas da Escravatura no Norte de Moçambique*. Maputo: Arquivo Historico de Moçambique, 1988.

Metcalf, George. "A Microcosm of Why Africans Sold Slaves: Akan Consumption Patterns in the 1770s". *Journal of African History*, 28, 3 (1987): 377–94.

Metcalf, Thomas R. *Imperial Connections: India in the Indian Ocean Arena, 1860–1920*. Berkeley: University of California Press, 2007.

Micklem, James. *Sidis in Gujarat* Occasional Papers, 88. Centre of African Studies, Edinburgh University, 2001.

Miller, Joseph C. "Imports at Luanda, Angola, 1785–1823". In *Figuring African Trade*, edited by G. Liesegang *et al.* Berlin: D. Reimer Verlag, 1986.

"Slave Prices in the Portuguese Southern Atlantic, 1600–1830". In *Africans in Bondage: Studies in Slavery and the Slave Trade* (Essays in Honour of Philip D. Curtin on the Occasion of the 25th *Anniversary of African Studies at the University of Wisconsin*), edited by Paul Lovejoy. Madison: University of Wisconsin Press, 1986.

Way of Death: Merchant Capitalism and the Angolan Slave Trade, 1730–1830. Madison: University of Wisconsin Press, 1988.

Mintz, Sidney. *Sweetness and Power: The Place of Sugar in Modern History.* New York: Penguin Viking, 1985.

Miran, Jonathan. *Red Sea Citizens: Cosmopolitan Society and Cultural Change in Massawa.* Bloomington: Indiana University Press, 2009.

"Space, Mobility, and Translocal Connections across the Red Sea Area since 1500". *Northeast African Studies*, 12, 1 (2012): ix–xxvi.

Morton, Fred. "Small Change: Children in the Nineteenth-Century East African Slave Trade". In *Children in Slavery through the Ages*, edited by Suzanne Miers, Joseph C. Miller and Gwyn Campbell. Athens, OH: Ohio University Press, 2009.

Mudenge, S. I. G. "Afro-Indian Relations before 1900: A Southeast Central African Perspective". In *India and the Western Indian Ocean States*, edited by Shanti Sadiq Ali and R. R. Ramchandani. Bombay: Allied Publishing, 1981.

A Political History of Munhumutapa. Harare: Zimbabwe Publishing Co, 1986.

A Political History of Munhumutapa, c1400–1902. Rev. ed. Harare: African Pub. Group, 2011.

Mukherjee, Rila. "Mobility in the Bay of Bengal World: Medieval Raiders, Traders, States and the Slaves". *Indian Historical Review*, 36, 1 (2009): 109–29.

Nadri, Ghulam A. *Eighteenth-Century Gujarat: The Dynamics of Its Political Economy, 1750–1800.* Leiden: Brill, 2008.

"Exploring the Gulf of Kachh: Regional Economy and Trade in the Eighteenth Century". *Journal of the Economic and Social History of the Orient*, 51, 3 (2008): 460–86.

Newitt, M. D. D. *Portuguese Settlement on the Zambesi: Exploration, Land Tenure and Colonial Rule in East Africa.* New York: Africana Pub. Co., 1973.

"The Comoro Islands in Indian Ocean Trade before the Nineteenth Century". *Cahiers d'Etudes Africaines*, 23 (1983): 139–65

"Drought in Mozambique 1823–1831". *Journal of Southern African Studies*, 15, 1 (1988): 15–35.

A History of Mozambique. Bloomington: Indiana University Press, 1995.

"East Africa and Indian Ocean Trade: 1500–1800". In *India and the Indian Ocean, 1500–1800*, edited by Ashin Das Gupta and M. N. Pearson. New Delhi: Oxford University Press, 1999.

Nicholls, C. S. *The Swahili Coast: Politics, Diplomacy and Trade on the East African Littoral, 1798–1856.* London: George Allen & Unwin, 1971.

Nightingale, Pamela. *Trade and Empire in Western India, 1784–1806.* Cambridge University Press, 1970.

Pankhurst, Richard. "Indian Trade with Ethiopia, the Gulf of Aden and the Horn of Africa in the Nineteenth and Early Twentieth Centuries". *Cahiers d'Études Africaines*, 14, 3 (1974): 453–97.

"The 'Banyan' or Indian Presence at Massawa, the Dahlak Islands and the Horn of Africa". *Journal of Ethiopian Studies.* 12, (1974): 185–212.

"The Ethiopian Diaspora to India: The Role of Habshis and Sidis from Medieval Times to the End of the Eighteenth Century". In *The African*

Diaspora in the Indian Ocean edited by Shihan de S. Jayasuriya and Richard Pankhurst. Trenton, NJ: Africa World Press, 2003.

Parthasarathi, Prasannan. *The Transition to a Colonial Economy: Weavers, Merchants, and Kings in South India, 1720–1800*. New York: Cambridge University Press, 2001.

"Global Trade and Textile Workers, 1650–2000". Paper presented at the conference "Globalization and Trade", International Institute of Social History, November 2004.

Why Europe Grew Rich and Asia Did Not: Global Economic Divergence, 1600–1850. New York: Cambridge University Press, 2011.

Pearson, M. N. *Merchants and Rulers in Gujarat: The Response to the Portuguese in the Sixteenth Century*. Berkeley: University of California Press, 1976.

"Banyas and Brahmins: Their Role in the Portuguese Indian Economy". In *Coastal Western India: Studies from the Portuguese Records*, edited by M. N. Pearson. New Delhi: Concept Publishers, 1981.

The Portuguese in India. New York: Cambridge University Press, 1987.

"Brokers in Western Indian Port Cities". *Modern Asian Studies*, 22, 3 (1988): 455–72.

"Goa-Based Seaborne Trade, 17th–18th Centuries". In *Goa Through the Ages: An Economic History*, edited by Teotonio de Souza. New Delhi: Concept Publishing Company, 1989.

"Indians in East Africa: The Early Modern Period". In *Politics and Trade in the Indian Ocean World: Essays in Honour of Ashin Das Gupta*, edited by Rudrangshu Mukherjee and Lakshmi Subramanian. New Delhi: Oxford University Press, 1998.

Port Cities and Intruders: The Swahili Coast, India, and Portugal in the Early Modern Era. Baltimore: Johns Hopkins University Press, 1998.

"Asia and World Precious Metal Flows in the Early Modern Period". In *Evolution of the World Economy, Precious Metals and India* edited by Patrick Bertola, Peter Reeves and John McGuire. New Delhi: Oxford University Press, 2001.

The Indian Ocean. New York: Routledge, 2003.

"Markets and Merchant Communities in the Indian Ocean: Locating the Portuguese". In *Portuguese Oceanic Expansion, 1400–1800*, edited by Francisco Bethencourt and Diogo Ramada Curto. New York: Cambridge University Press, 2007.

"History of the Indian Ocean: A Review Essay". *Wasafiri*, 26, 2 (2011): 78–99.

Perlin, Frank. "Proto-Industrialization and Pre-Colonial South Asia". *Past & Present*, 98 (1983): 30–95.

Pescatello, Ann M. "The African Presence in Portuguese India". *Journal of Asian History*, 11, 1 (1977): 26–48.

Peterson, J. E. "Britain and the Gulf: At the Periphery of Empire". In *The Persian Gulf in History*, edited by Lawrence G. Potter. New York: Palgrave Macmillan, 2009.

Pinto, Celsa. "At the Dusk of the Second Empire: Goa-Brazil Commercial Links, 1770–1825". *Purabhilekh-Puratatva*, VII, 1 (1990): 41–69.

Trade and Finance in Portuguese India: A Study of the Portuguese Country Trade 1770–1840. New Delhi: Concept Pub. Co., 1994.

"Lisbon Investment in the Indian Textile Commerce: The Surat Feeder". *Mare Liberum*, 9, July (1995): 217–33.

Situating Indo-Portuguese Trade History: A Commercial Resurgence, 1770–1830. Tellicherry: Institute for Research in Social Sciences and Humanities, 2003.

Pinto, Jeanette. *Slavery in Portuguese India 1510–1842*. Bombay: Himalaya Publishing House, 1992.

Pinto, Rochelle. "Race and Imperial Loss: Accounts of East Africa in Goa". *South African Historical Journal*, 57, 1 (2007): 82–92.

Pouwels, Randall L. "Eastern Africa and the Indian Ocean to 1800: Reviewing Relations in Historical Perspective". *International Journal of African Historical Studies*, 35, 2–3 (2002): 385–425.

Prakash, Om. "Bullion for Goods: International Trade and the Economy of Early Eighteenth Century Bengal". *Indian Economic and Social History Review*, 13, 2 (1976): 159–87.

European Commercial Enterprise in Pre-Colonial India. Cambridge University Press, 1998.

"Global Precious Metal Flows and India, 1500–1750". In *Evolution of the World Economy, Precious Metals and India*, edited by Patrick Bertola, Peter Reeves and John McGuire. New Delhi: Oxford University Press, 2001.

"Co-Operation and Conflict among European Traders in the Indian Ocean in the Late Eighteenth Century". *Indian Economic and Social History Review*, 39, 2/3 (2002): 131–48.

Prange, Sebastian. "'Trust in God, but Tie Your Camel First': The Economic Oganization of the Trans-Saharan Slave Trade between the Fourteenth and Nineteenth Centuries". *Journal of Global History*, 1, 2 (2006): 219–39.

"A Trade of No Dishonor: Piracy, Commerce, and Community in the Western Indian Ocean, Twelfth to Sixteenth Century". *American Historical Review*, 116, 5 (2011): 1269–93.

Prestholdt, Jeremy. "As Artistry Permits and Custom May Ordain: The Social Fabric of Material Consumption in the Swahili World, Circa 1450–1600". *Program of African Studies Working Papers, 3*. Evanston: Program of African Studies, Northwestern University, 1998.

"On the Global Repercussions of East African Consumerism". *American Historical Review*, 3 (2004): 755–81.

Domesticating the World: African Consumerism and the Genealogies of Globalization The California World History Library. Berkeley: University of California Press, 2008.

"Africa and the Global Lives of Things". In *The Oxford Handbook of the History of Consumption*, edited by Frank Trentmann. New York: Oxford University Press, 2012.

Prins, A. H. J. "The Persian Gulf Dhows: Two Variants in Maritime Enterprise". *Persica*, 2, (1966): 1–18.

Qaisar, A. Jan. "From Port to Port: Life on Indian Ships in the Sixteenth and Seventeenth Centuries". In *India and the Indian Ocean*, edited by Das Gupta and Pearson. New Delhi: Oxford University Press, 1999.

Raj, Kapil. *Relocating Modern Science: Circulation and the Construction of Knowledge in South Asia and Europe, 1650–1900*. Basingstoke: Palgrave Macmillan, 2007.

Rakoto, Ignace ed. *La Route des Esclaves: Système servile et traite dans l'est malgache*. Paris: L'Harmattan, 2000.

Ratnagar, Shereen. *Trading Encounters: From the Euphrates to the Indus in the Bronze Age*. New Delhi: Oxford University Press, 2004.

Raunig, Walter "Yemen and Ethiopia – Ancient Cultural Links between Two Neighbouring Countries on the Red Sea". In *Yemen: 3000 Years of Art and Civilisation in Arabia Felix*, edited by Werner Daum. Frankfurt: Umschau-Verlag, 1987.

Ray, Aniruddha. "Cambay and its Hinterland: Early Eighteenth Century", in *Ports and Their Hinterlands in India (1700–1950)*, edited by Indu Banga. New Delhi: Manohar Publications, 1992.

"Malet Collection on Cambay (Gujarat) at the End of the 18th Century". In *Sources Européennes Sur Le Gujarat*, edited by Ernestine Carreira. Paris: Société d"Histoire de l"Orient and L'Harmattan, 1998.

Ray, Rajat Kanta. "Asian Capital in the Age of European Domination: The Rise of the Bazaar, 1800–1914". *Modern Asian Studies*, 29, 3 (1995): 449–554.

"Chinese Financiers and Chetti Bankers in Southern Waters: Asian Mobile Credit During the Anglo-Dutch Competition for the Trade of the Eastern Archipelago in the Nineteenth Century". *Itinerario*, 11, 1 (1987): 209–34.

Raychaudhuri, Tapan and Irfan Habib, eds. *The Cambridge Economic History of India. Vol. I: c. 1200–c. 1750*, edited by Tapan Raychaudhuri and Irfan Habib. Cambridge University Press, 1982.

Richardson, David. "West African Consumption Patterns and Their Influence on the Eighteenth-Century English Slave Trade". In *The Uncommon Market: Essays in the Economic History of the Atlantic Slave Trade*, edited by A. Gemery and J. Hogendorn. New York: Atlantic Press, 1979.

Ricks, Thomas. "Slaves and Slave Trades in the Persian Gulf, 18th and 19th Centuries: An Assessment". In *The Economics of the Indian Ocean Slave Trade in the Nineteenth Century*, edited by W. G. Clarence-Smith. London: Frank Cass, 1989.

Rita-Ferreira, A. *Fixação Portuguesa e História Pré-colonial de Mocambique*. Lisbon: Junta de Investigações Ciêntificas do Ultramar, 1982.

Presença Luso-Asiática e Mutações Culturais no Sul de Moçambique (Até c. 1900). Lisbon: Instituto de Investigação Científic Tropical, 1982.

"Moçambique e os Naturais da Índia Portuguesa". In *II Seminário Internacional De História Indo-Portuguesa*, edited by Luís de Albuquerque and Inácio Guerreiro. Lisbon: Instituto de Investigação Científica Tropical, 1985.

African Kingdoms and Alien Settlements in Central Mozambique (c. 15th-17th Cent.). Coimbra, Portugal: Departamento de Antropologia, Universidade de Coimbra, 1999.

Robbins, Kenneth X. and John McLeod, eds. *African Elites in India: Habshi Amarat*. Ahmedabad: Mapin Publishing, 2006.

Roberts, Andrew. *A History of Zambia*. New York: Africana Publishing Company, 1976.

Roberts, Richard. "Guinée Cloth: Linked Transformations within France's Empire in the Nineteenth Century". *Cahiers d'Études Africaines*, 32, 4 (1992): 597–627.

Two Worlds of Cotton. Colonialism and the Regional Economy in the French Soudan, 1800–1946. Stanford University Press, 1996.

Rockel, Stephen J. *Carriers of Culture: Labor on the Road in Nineteenth-Century East Africa*. Portsmouth, NH: Heinemann, 2006.

Roy, Tirthankar, ed. *Cloth and Commerce: Textiles in Colonial India*. New Delhi: Sage, 1996.

"Introduction". In *Cloth and Commerce: Textiles in Colonial India*, edited by Tirthankar Roy. New Delhi: Sage, 1996.

India in the World Economy: From Antiquity to the Present. New York: Cambridge University Press, 2012.

Rudner, David. "Banker's Trust and the Culture of Banking among the Nattukottai Chettiars of Colonial South India". *Modern Asian Studies*, 23, 3 (1989): 417–58.

Caste and Capitalism in Colonial India: The Nattukottai Chettiars. Berkeley: University of California Press, 1994.

Russell-Wood, A. J. R. "A dinâmica da presença brasileira no Indico e no Oriente. Séculos CVI–XIX". *Topoi*, 3, (2001): 9–40.

Sadiq Ali, Shanti. *African Dispersal in the Deccan*. New Delhi: Longman, 1996.

Sakarai, Lawrence J. "Indian Merchants in East Africa. Part I: The Triangular Trade and the Slave Economy". *Slavery & Abolition*, 1, 3 (1980): 292–338.

"Indian Merchants in East Africa. Part II: British Imperialism and the Transformation of the Slave Economy". *Slavery & Abolition*, 1, 4 (1980): 2–30.

Salim, A. I. "East Africa: The Coast". In *General History of Africa. Volume V: Africa from the Sixteenth to Eighteenth Centuries*, edited by B. A. Ogot. Paris: Unesco, 1992.

Salvadori, Cynthia. *Through Open Doors: A View of Asian Cultures in Kenya*. Nairobi: Kenway Publications, 1981.

We Came in Dhows. Nairobi: Paperchase Kenya Ltd., 1996.

Sanchez, Samuel. "Navigation et gens de mer dans le canal du Mozambique: Les boutres dans l'activité maritime de Nosy Be et de l'Ouest de Madagascar au XIXe siècle". In *Madagascar et L'afrique: Entre Identité Et Appartenances Historiques*, edited by Didier Nativel et Faranirina V. Rajaonah. Paris: Karthala, 2003.

Saunders, Christopher. "'Free, yet Slaves': Prize Negroes at the Cape Revisited". In *Breaking the Chains: Slavery and Its Legacy in the Nineteenth-Century Cape Colony*, edited by Clifton Crais and Nigel Worden. Johannesburg: University of the Witwatersrand Press, 1994.

Schneider, Jane. "The Anthropology of Cloth". *Annual Review of Anthropology*, 16 (1987): 409–48

Seijas, Tatiana. "The Portuguese Slave Trade to Spanish Manila: 1580–1640". *Itinerario*, 32, 1 (2008): 19–38.

Sequeira Nazareth, Casimiro de. "Barcos Nativos da India". *O Oriente Portugues*, 9 (1912): 227–234.

Serjeant, R. B. *Studies in Arabian History and Civilisation*. London: Variorum, 1981.

"The Hindu, Bāniyān Merchants and Traders". In *San'a: An Arabian Islamic City*, edited by R. B. Serjeant and R. Lewcock. London: World of Islam Trust, 1983.

"Some Observations on African Slaves in Arabia". Paper presented at the "Workshop on the Long-Distance Trade in Slaves across the Indian Ocean and the Red Sea in the 19th Century", School of Oriental and African Studies, University of London, 17–19 December 1987.

Society and Trade in South Arabia. Aldershot: Variorum, 1996.

Serrão, José Vicente. "Macau". In *O Império Africano 1825–1890*, edited by Valentim Alexandre and Jill Dias. Lisbon: Editorial Estampa, 1998.

Sharma, G. D. "Urban Credit and the Market Economy in Western India, c. 1750–1850". In *Local Suppliers of Credit in the Third World, 1750–1945*, edited by G. Austin and K. Sugihara. London: Macmillan, 1993.

Sheikh, Samira. "A Gujarati Map and Pilot Book of the Indian Ocean, c. 1750". *Imago Mundi*, 61, 1 (2009): 67–83.

Shell, Robert. *Children of Bondage: A Social History of the Slave Society at the Cape of Good Hope, 1652–1838*. Johannesburg: Wits University Press, 1997.

Shepherd, Gill. "The Comorians and the East African Slave Trade". In *Asian and African Systems of Slavery*, edited by James L. Watson. Berkeley: University of California Press, 1980.

Sheriff, Abdul. "Ivory and Commercial Expansion in East Africa in the Nineteenth Century". In *Figuring African Trade: Proceedings of the Symposium on the Quantification and Structure of the Import and Export and Long-Distance Trade in Africa 1800–1913*, edited by G. Liesegang, H. Pasch and A. Jones. Berlin: D. Reimer Verlag, 1986.

Slaves, Spices & Ivory in Zanzibar: Integration of an East African Commercial Empire into the World Economy, 1770–1873. London: James Currey 1987.

Dhow Cultures of the Indian Ocean: Cosmopolitanism, Commerce, and Islam. London: Hurst, 2010.

Shirodkar, P. P. "Slavery in Coastal India". *Purabhilka-Puratatva*, 3, 1 (1985): 27–44.

"Slavery on [Sic] Western Coast". In *Researches in Indo-Portuguese History*, edited by P. P. Shirodkar. Jaipur: Publication Scheme, 1998.

Siddiqi, Asiya, ed. *Trade and Finance in Colonial India 1750–1860*. Delhi: Oxford University Press, 1995.

Simpson, Edward. *Muslim Society and the Western Indian Ocean: The Seafarers of Kachchh*. New York: Routledge, 2006.

Smith, Alan [K]. "The Trade of Delagoa Bay as a Factor in Nguni Politics, 1750–1835". In *African Societies in Southern Africa*, edited by Leonard Thompson. London: Heinemann, 1969.

"Delagoa Bay and the Trade of South-Eastern Africa". In *Pre-Colonial African Trade: Essays on Trade in Central and Eastern Africa before 1900*, edited by Richard Gray and David Birmingham. London: Oxford University Press, 1970.

"The Indian Ocean Zone". In *History of Central Africa. Vol. 1*, edited by David Birmingham and Phyllis M. Martin. Essex: Longman, 1983.

Sood, Gagan D. S. "Correspondence is Equal to Half a Meeting: The Composition and Comprehension of Letters in Eighteenth-Century Islamic Eurasia". *Journal of the Economic and Social History of the Orient*, 50, 2–3 (2007): 172–214.

"The Informational Fabric of Eighteenth-Century India and the Middle East: Couriers, Intermediaries and Postal Communication". *Modern Asian Studies*, 43, 5 (2009): 1085–116.

Souza, Teotonio R. de. "Marine Insurance and Indo-Portuguese Trade History: An Aid to Maritime Historiography", *Indian Economic and Social History Review*, 14, 3 (1977): 377–84.

"Mhamai House Records: Indigenous Sources for Indo-Portuguese Historiography". *Indian Archives*, 31, 1 (1982): 25–45.

"French Slave-Trading in Portuguese Goa (1773–1791)" In *Essays in Goan History*, edited by Teotonio R. de Souza. New Delhi: Concept Publishing House, 1989.

Spodek, Howard. "Rulers, Merchants and Other Groups in the City-States of Saurashtra, India, around 1800". *Comparative Studies in Society & History*, 16, 4 (1974): 448–70.

Sreenivasan, Ramya. "Drudges, Dancing Girls, Concubines: Female Slaves in Rajput Polity, 1500–1850". In *Slavery and South Asian History*, edited by Indrani Chatterjee and Richard Eaton. Bloomington: Indiana University Press, 2006.

Stein, Burton. *A History of India*. Oxford: Blackwell Publishers, 1998.

Studnicki-Gizbert, Daviken. *A Nation Upon the Ocean Sea: Portugal's Atlantic Diaspora and the Crisis of the Spanish Empire*. New York: Oxford University Press, 2007.

Subrahmanyam, Sanjay. *The Political Economy of Commerce: Southern India, 1500–1650*. Cambridge University Press, 1990.

The Portuguese Empire in Asia, 1500–1700: A Political and Economic History. London & New York: Longman, 1993.

"Of Imârat and Tijârat: Asian Merchants and State Power in the Western Indian Ocean, 1400 to 1750". *Comparative Studies in Society and History*, 37, 4 (1995): 750–80.

"Connected Histories: Notes Towards a Reconfiguration of Early Modern Eurasia". *Modern Asian Studies*, 31, 3 (1997): 735–62.

"Slaves and Tyrants. Dutch Tribulations in Seventeenth-Century Mrauk-U". *Journal of Early Modern History*, 1, 3 (1997): 201–53.

"Notas sobre a mão-de-obra na India pre-colonial (seculos XVI a XVIII)". In *O Trabalho Mestiço: Maneiras de Pensar e Formas de Viver-Seculos XVI a XIX*, edited by Eduardo França Paiva and Carla Maria Junho Anastasia. São Paulo: Annablume, 2002.

Explorations in Connected History: From the Tagus to the Ganges. New Delhi: Oxford University Press, 2005.

and C. A. Bayly. "Portfolio Capitalists and the Political Economy of Early Modern India". In *Merchants, Markets and the State in Early Modern*

India, edited by Sanjay Subramanyam. Delhi, Oxford University Press, 1990.

Subramanian, Lakshmi. "Imperial Negotiations: The Dynamics of British-Indian Social Networks in Early Colonial Bombay". Unpublished paper.

"Banias and the British: The Role of Indigenous Credit in the Process of Imperial Expansion in Western India in the Second Half of the Eighteenth Century". *Modern Asian Studies*, 21, 3 (1987): 473–510.

"The Eighteenth-Century Social Order in Surat: A Reply and an Excursus on the Riots of 1788 and 1795". *Modern Asian Studies*, 25, 2 (1991): 321–65.

Indigenous Capital and Imperial Expansion: Bombay, Surat, and the West Coast. Delhi: Oxford University Press, 1996.

"Power and the Weave: Weavers, Merchants and Rulers in Eighteenth-Century Surat". In *Politics and Trade in the Indian Ocean World: Essays in Honour of Ashin Das Gupta*, edited by Rudrangshu Mukherjee and Lakshmi Subramanian. Delhi: Oxford University Press, 1998.

Medieval Seafarers of India. New Delhi: Roli Books, 2005.

"Merchants in Transit: Risk-Sharing Strategies in the Indian Ocean". In *Cross Currents and Community Networks: The History of the Indian Ocean World*, edited by H. P. Ray and Edward A. Alpers. New Delhi: Oxford University Press, 2007.

"Of Pirates and Potentates: Maritime Jurisdiction and the Construction of Piracy in the Indian Ocean". In *Cultures of Trade: Indian Ocean Exchanges*, edited by Devleena Ghosh and Stephen Muecke. Newcastle: Cambridge Scholars Publishing, 2007.

"The Politics of Restitution: Shipwrecks, Insurance and Piracy in the Western Indian Ocean". Paper presented at conference "The Story of the Voyage Colloquium", University of the Witwatersrand, Johannesburg, 2–3 October 2008.

"The Political Economy of Textiles in Western India: Weavers, Merchants and the Transition to a Colonial Economy". In *How India Clothed the World: The World of South Asian Textiles, 1500–1850*, edited by Giorgio Riello and Tirthankar Roy. Leiden: Brill, 2009.

Sutherland-Harris, Nicola. "Zambian Trade with Zumbo in the Eighteenth Century". In *Pre-Colonial African Trade: Essays on Trade in Central and Eastern Africa before 1900*, edited by Richard Gray and David Birmingham. London: Oxford University Press, 1970.

Tambs-Lyche, Harald. *Power, Profit and Poetry: Traditional Society in Kathiawar, Western India*. New Delhi: Manohar, 1997.

"Reflections on Caste in Gujarat". In *The Idea of Gujarat: History, Ethnography and Text*, edited by Edward Simpson and Aparna Kapadia. New Delhi: Orient BlackSwan, 2010.

Tarlo, Emma. *Clothing Matters: Dress and Identity in India*. Chicago University Press, 1996.

Teelock, Vijayalakshmi and Edward A. Alpers. *History, Memory and Identity*. Port Louis: Nelson Mandela Centre for African Culture and University of Mauritius, 2001.

TePaske, John Jay. *A New World Gold and Silver*, edited by Kendall W. Brown. Boston: Brill, 2010.

Thomaz, Luís Filipe F. R. "Melaka and Its Merchant Communities at the Turn of the Sixteenth Century". In *Asian Merchants and Businessmen in the Indian Ocean and the China Sea*, edited by Denys Lombard and Jean Aubin. New Delhi: Oxford University Press, 2000.

Tibbetts, G. R. *Arab Navigation in the Indian Ocean before the Coming of the Portuguese*. London: Royal Asiatic Society of Great Britain and Ireland, 1971.

Timberg, T. A. *The Marwaris: From Traders to Industrialists*. New Delhi: Vikas Publishing House, 1978.

Toledano, Ehud R. *Slavery and Abolition in the Ottoman Middle East*. Seattle: University of Washington Press, 1998.

Tomlinson, B. R. *The Economy of Modern India, 1860–1970*. Cambridge University Press, 1993.

Topik, Steven, Carlos Marichal and Zephyr Frank, eds. *From Silver to Cocaine: Latin American Commodity Chains and the Building of the World Economy, 1500–2000*. Durham: Duke University Press, 2006.

Torri, Michelguglielmo. "Trapped inside the Colonial Order: The Hindu Bankers of Surat and Their Business World during the Second Half of the Eighteenth Century". *Modern Asian Studies*, 25, 2 (1991): 39–79.

Travers, Robert. "Imperial Revolutions and Global Repercussions: South Asia and the World, C. 1750–1850". In *The Age of Revolutions in Global Context, c. 1760–1840*, edited by David Armitage and Sanjay Subrahmanyam. Basingstoke: Palgrave Macmillan, 2010.

Trentmann, Frank, ed. *The Oxford Handbook of the History of Consumption*. Oxford University Press, 2012.

Tripathi, D., ed. *Business Communities of India: A Historical Perspective*. New Delhi: Manohar, 1984.

Trivellato, Francesca. "Sephardic Merchants in the Early Modern Atlantic and Beyond: Toward a Comparative Historical Approach to Business Cooperation". In *Atlantic Diasporas: Jews and Cryto-Jews in the Age of Mercantilism*, edited by Richard L. Kagan and Philip Morgan. Baltimore: Johns Hopkins University Press, 2005.

The Familiarity of Strangers: The Sephardic Diaspora, Livorno, and Cross-Cultural Trade in the Early Modern Period. New Haven: Yale University Press, 2009.

Tuchscherer, Michael. "Coffee in the Red Sea Area from the Sixteenth to the Nineteenth Century". In *The Global Coffee Economy in Africa, Asia, and Latin America, 1500–1989*, edited by William Gervase Clarence-Smith and Steven Topik. Cambridge University Press, 2003.

Um, Nancy. *The Merchant Houses of Mocha: Trade and Architecture in an Indian Ocean Port*. Seattle: University of Washington Press, 2009.

Vail, Leroy and Landeg White. *Capitalism and Colonialism in Mozambique: A Study of Quelimane District*. Minneapolis: University of Minnesota Press, 1980.

Varadarajan, Lotika. "Syncretic Symbolism and Textiles: Indo-Thai Expressions". In *Commerce and Culture in the Bay of Bengal 1500–1800*, edited by Om Prakash and Denys Lombard. New Delhi: Manohar, 1999.

Vatuk, Sylvia. "Bharattee's Death: Domestic Slave Women in Nineteenth-Century Madras". In *Slavery and South Asian History*, edited by Indrani Chatterjee and Richard Eaton. Bloomington: Indiana University Press, 2006.

Vernet, Thomas. "Le commerce des ésclaves sur la côte Swahili, 1500–1750". *Azania*, 38, (2009): 69–97.

"Slave Trade and Slavery on the Swahili Coast, 1500–1750". In *Slavery, Islam and Diaspora*, edited by Behnaz A. Mirzai, Ismael M. Montana and Paul Lovejoy. Trenton, NJ: Africa World Press, 2009.

Vink, Markus P. "Indian Ocean Studies and the 'New Thallassology'". *Journal of Global History*, 2, (2007): 41–62.

Walker, Timothy. "Abolishing the Slave Trade in Portuguese India: Documentary Evidence of Popular and Official Resistance to Crown Policy, 1842–1860". In *Slavery and Resistance in Africa and Asia* edited by Gwyn Campbell, Michael Salman and Edward A. Alpers. New York: Routledge, 2005.

"Slaves or Soldiers? African Conscripts in Portuguese India, 1857–1860". In *Slavery and South Asian History*, edited by Indrani Chatterjee and Richard Eaton. Bloomington: Indiana University Press, 2006.

Ware III, Rudolph T. "Slavery in Islamic Africa, 1400–1800". In *The Cambridge World History of Slavery. Volume 3: AD 1420–AD 1804*, edited by David Eltis and Stanley Engerman. New York: Cambridge University Press, 2011.

Washbrook, David. "Progress and Problems: South Asian Economic and Social History c. 1720–1860". *Modern Asian Studies*, 22, 1 (1988): 57–96.

"India in the Early Modern World Economy: Modes of Production, Reproduction and Exchange". *Journal of Global History*, 2, 1 (2007): 87–111.

Watson, James L., ed. *Asian and African Systems of Slavery*. Oxford: Blackwell, 1980.

Weiner, Annette B. and Jane Schneider. "Introduction". In *Cloth and Human Experience*, edited by Annette B. Weiner and Jane Schneider. Washington: Smithsonian Institution Press, 1989.

Wilberforce-Bell, H. *The History of Kathiawad from the Earliest Times*. London: William Heinemann, 1916.

Wink, André. *Al-Hind: The Making of the Indo-Islamic World. Volume I: Early Medieval India and the Expansion of Islam 7th–11th Centuries*. New Delhi: Oxford University Press, 1999.

Wong, Kwok-Chu. *The Chinese in the Philippine Economy, 1898–1941*. Quezon City: Ateneo De Manila University Press, 1999.

Xavier, Carlos. "A Cidade e o Porto de Damão nos séculos XVIII e XIX". *Studia*, 46 (1987): 287–301.

UNPUBLISHED DISSERTATIONS

Allen, Calvin H. "Sayyids, Shets and Sultans: Politics and Trade in Masqat under the Al Bu Said, 1785–1914". PhD diss., University of Washington, 1978.

Antunes, Luis Frederico Dias. "A Actividade Da Companhia De Comércio Dos Baneanes De Diu Em Moçambique (1686–1777)". MA thesis, Universidade Nova de Lisboa, 1992.

Dickinson, Ronald W. "Sofala and the Rivers of Cuama: Crusade and Commerce in S. E. Africa, 1505–1595". MA thesis, University of Cape Town, 1971.

Ferreira, Roquinaldo. "Transforming Atlantic Slaving: Trade, Warfare and Territorial Control in Angola, 1650–1800". PhD diss., University of California, 2003.

Hafkin, Nancy Jane. "Trade, Society and Politics in Northern Mozambique, c. 1753–1913". PhD diss., Boston University, 1973.

Hedges, David William. "Trade and Politics in Southern Mozambique and Zululand in the Eighteenth and Nineteenth Centuries". PhD diss., University of London, 1978.

Hooper, Jane. "An Empire in the Indian Ocean: The Sakalava Empire of Madagascar". PhD diss., Emory University, 2010.

Hopper, Mathew. "The African Presence in Arabia: Slavery, the World Economy and African Diaspora in Eastern Arabia, 1840–1940". PhD diss., University of California, 2006.

Machado, Pedro. "Gujarati Indian Merchant Networks in Mozambique, 1777-c. 1830". PhD diss., University of London, 2005.

Martins, Xavier Mariona. "Portuguese Shipping and Shipbuilding in Goa, 1510–1780". PhD diss., Goa University, 1994.

Mirzai, Behnaz. "Slavery, the Abolition of the Slave Trade and the Emancipation of Slaves, 1828–1929". PhD diss., York University, 2004.

Reidy, Michael Charles. "The Admission of Slaves and 'Prize Slaves' into the Cape Colony, 1797–1818". MA thesis, University of Cape Town, 1997.

Smith, Alan K. "The Struggle for Control of Southern Mozambique, 1720–1835". PhD diss., University of California, 1970.

Teixeira, Maria Luisa Norton Pinto. "Trade and Commerce in Mozambique: Indian Enterprise in Zambezia, Ca. 1870–1900". PhD diss., Queen's University, 2001.

Wheat, David. "The Afro-Portuguese Maritime World and the Foundations of Spanish Caribbean Society, 1570–1640". PhD diss., Vanderbilt University, 2009.

Zimba, Benigna de Jesus Lurdina Mateus Lisboa. "Overseas Trade, Regional Politics, and Gender Roles: Southern Mozambique, Ca. 1720 to Ca. 1830". PhD diss., University of Michigan, 1999.

Index